Teaching and Learning at Business Schools

Teaching and Learning at Business Schools

Transforming Business Education

EDITED BY PÄR MÅRTENSSON,
MAGNUS BILD and KRISTINA NILSSON

GOWER

Published by
Gower Publishing Limited
Gower House
Croft Road
Aldershot
Hampshire
GU11 3HR
England

Gower Publishing Company
Suite 420
101 Cherry Street
Burlington
VT 05401-4405
USA

Pär Mårtensson, Magnus Bild and Kristina Nilsson have asserted their moral right under the Copyright, Designs and Patents Act, 1988, to be identified as the authors of this work.

British Library Cataloguing in Publication Data
Teaching and learning at business schools : transforming
  business education
  1. Business schools – Cross-cultural studies
  I. Martensson, Par II. Bild, Magnus III. Nilsson, Kristina,
  1945–
  650'.0711

  ISBN-13: 9780566088209

Library of Congress Cataloging-in-Publication Data
Teaching and learning at business schools : transforming business education / edited by Par
  Martensson, Magnus Bild and Kristina Nilsson.
    p. cm.
  Includes index.
  ISBN 978-0-566-08820-9
  1. Business schools--Cross-cultural studies. I. Martensson, Par, 1963– II. Bild, Magnus. III.
  Nilsson, Kristina, 1945–

  HF1111.T43 2008
  650.071'1--dc22

                                                                                    2008003567

Printed and bound in Great Britain by TJ International Ltd, Padstow, Cornwall.

Contents

PART I   INSIDE THE CLASSROOM

Setting the Stage

Teaching Techniques and Approaches

Dealing with Different Contexts

List of Figures

List of Tables

Acknowledgements

This book would never have been completed without the valuable support from many different individuals and associations. The contributors of the chapters have generously found time in their busy lives to share their experiences and views on teaching and learning.

The idea to start this book project came from our joint experience of running the International Teachers Programme (ITP) for 2 years. Our thanks to the Board of the International Schools of Business Management (ISBM), then chaired by Pierre Batteau, for accepting us on the job. Thanks also to the present and former President of the Stockholm School of Economics, Lars Bergman and Leif Lindmark, for letting us embark on this journey.

The immense support and constructive comments from Per-Jonas Eliaeson and Claes-Robert Julander, board members of ISBM and former Presidents of Stockholm School of Economics, made our stewardship of the ITP more successful than it would have been otherwise.

Jonathan Norman, Gillian Steadman and their colleagues at Gower Publishing have shown great faith in the project and have been instrumental in improving the volume to its present standard. We did start the project without having a publisher. The risk of doing that was balanced by generous financial support from Ragnar Söderbergs Stiftelse.

Our colleagues within the MED division of the Academy of Management deserve a special thank you for keeping up the spirit for teaching and learning issues.

Last, but not least, a very warm and grateful thank you to our families for your understanding and cheerful support.

Pär Mårtensson, Magnus Bild and Kristina Nilsson
Stockholm

List of Contributors

Elena P. Antonacopoulou, University of Liverpool Management School, UK.

Magnus Bild, Bild & Runsten AB, Stockholm, Sweden.

Peter Daly, EDHEC Business School, Lille, France.

Aswath Damodaran, Stern School of Business at New York University, New York, USA.

Marie-Laure Djelic, ESSEC Business School, Paris, France.

Pierre Dussauge, HEC – School of Management, Paris, France.

Göran von Euler, POCKET, Stockholm, Sweden.

Josep Franch, ESADE, Barcelona, Spain.

H. Landis Gabel, INSEAD, Fontainbleau, France.

Seán Gaffney, Stockholm School of Economics in Riga, Riga, Latvia.

Charlotte Holgersson, Royal Institute of Technology, Stockholm, Sweden.

Christer Karlsson, Copenhagen Business School, Copenhagen, Denmark.

Kamran Kashani, IMD, Lausanne, Switzerland.

Christine Kelly, MIT Sloan School of Management, Cambridge, USA.

Thomas Lavelle, Stockholm School of Economics, Stockholm, Sweden.

Pär Mårtensson, Stockholm School of Economics, Stockholm, Sweden.

Philippa Morrison, London Business School, London, UK.

Hellicy Ngambi, University of South Africa (Unisa), Pretoria, South Africa.

Kristina Nilsson, Stockholm School of Economics, Stockholm, Sweden.

Pedro Parada, ESADE, Barcelona, Spain.

Ferdinando Pennarola, Bocconi University, Milan, Italy.

Catharina Pramhäll, Swedish National Accounting Standards Board, Stockholm, Sweden.

Tom Pugel, Stern School of Business at New York University, New York, USA.

Johan Roos, Stockholm School of Economics, Stockholm, Sweden.

Isabelle Sequeira, EDHEC Business School, Lille, France.

Jan Shubert, Babson College, Boston, USA.

Mel Silberman, Temple University, Philadelphia, USA.

Andrea Sironi, Bocconi University, Milan, Italy.

Udo Zander, Stockholm School of Economics, Stockholm, Sweden.

Preface

Pär Mårtensson, Magnus Bild and Kristina Nilsson

The book you hold in your hand, *Teaching and Learning at Business Schools – Transforming Business Education*, is a by-product of the International Teachers Programme (ITP). We, the editors, had the privilege of being program directors when this rotating faculty development program was hosted by the Stockholm School of Economics (SSE) from 2003 to 2005.[1] We felt that the immense wisdom and experience imbedded in 'our' faculty members and in 'our' participants deserved an ever wider audience. That is the reason why this book has been written.

The volume is foremost about sharing experiences to improve teaching and learning at business schools. Using a metaphor, the book is like a smorgasbord. Not all the food in the world is there, but what is there has been carefully selected to be enriching. We invite you to taste the dishes (that is, the chapters); if there is one you enjoy please try more of it, if there is another you dislike, leave it for someone else. See what happens when you try the dishes in a different order.

We believe that the group of chefs (that is, the authors) is truly unique. There are award-winners, deans, editors and many more from various parts of the world, united in their passion for teaching and their deep interest in developing the conditions for the learner as well as the learning facilitator: the teacher.

There are numerous books on different teaching techniques and approaches used at business schools: case-teaching, problem-based learning, and so on. There are also many books on teaching and learning in general in higher education. We found, however, that there were fewer books focused on the broader aspects of teaching and learning in the specific setting of business schools. Business schools and their faculty are today facing challenges such as:

- an increased international competition;
- tougher assessment and evaluation criteria;
- higher mobility of the faculty;
- tighter financial restrictions;
- increased diversity in the student cohort;
- less tolerance for poor teaching.

In this dynamic environment, we have opted to write primarily for three target groups:

- *Individual faculty members* at business schools who want to improve their teaching and their course management activities.
- *People involved in faculty development activities* at business schools who search for a platform for discussions in different forms of faculty development initiatives.
- Last, but certainly not least, for *people in management positions at business schools*. We hope that the book can give valuable ideas about what measures one can take to improve teaching and learning at business schools.

---

1   Learn more about the ITP in Chapter 20 by Ferdinando Pennarola in this volume.

Given the metaphor of a smorgasbord, it might seem contradictory that we have grouped the chapters in a specific order. But it isn't; even at a smorgasbord there is some structure. Our structure is built around two parts of the book: *Part A: Inside the Classroom* and *Part B: Outside the Classroom*. The objective of the first part is to highlight activities that relate to the specific teaching situation, considerations or issues you need to manage within the classroom. The second part deals with issues that relate to activities before you move into the classroom, or issues that have more to do with the preconditions for learning or teaching. Of course, some of the topics are not that easily directed to one or the other part, because what happens outside relates to inside the classroom or vice versa. But still, the structure will hopefully help you find your way at the smorgasbord.

In short, the content of the book is as follows. *Part I: Inside the Classroom*, is opened by a chapter by Christine Kelly (MIT, US) setting the stage, where the teacher as a facilitator of learning is discussed. The following block of six chapters deal with teaching techniques and approaches. In the first of these chapters, Chapter 2, Mel Silberman (Temple University, US) illustrates techniques that can be used for more active teaching. Mistakes in case-teaching are presented, based on personal experiences, by Kamran Kashani (IMD, Switzerland) in Chapter 3. Pierre Dussauge (HEC, France) argues in Chapter 4 that mini-cases can help teaching 'soft' subjects to MBAs. Pedro Parada and Josep Franch (ESADE, Spain) elaborate on the theme of team teaching in Chapter 5. Transformative management education is the topic of Chapter 6 written by Johan Roos (SSE, Sweden). Göran von Euler (Pocket, Sweden) describes in Chapter 7 how theatre can be used as a learning method.

Part I: Inside the Classroom, also contains a block of six chapters on the theme 'Dealing with Different Contexts'. In the first of these six chapters, Chapter 8, Aswath Damodaran (New York University, US) describes ways to teach large classes. In Chapter 9, Hellicy Ngambi (UNISA, South Africa) explores diversity dynamics in teaching. Seán Gaffney (SSE Riga, Latvia) presents, in Chapter 10, a mild polemic of teaching and learning in a multicultural environment. Some reflections on working with gender issues in the business school classroom are presented in Chapter 11 by Charlotte Holgersson (Royal Institute of Technology, Sweden). Thomas Lavelle (SSE, Sweden) discusses, in Chapter 12, how the challenge of English-medium instruction can be met in international business schools. Tutoring of doctoral students is the subject of Chapter 13, written by Udo Zander (SSE, Sweden).

Part II: Outside the Classroom, comprises three blocks of chapters. The first block deals with designing programs and learning environments. In the first chapter of that block, Chapter 14, Christer Karlsson (Copenhagen Business School, Denmark) suggests tools for program design and management. Kristina Nilsson (SSE, Sweden) shares some experiences from starting programs in Chapter 15. Learning teams and learning managers are explored in Chapter 16 on managerial competency development, written by Peter Daly and Isabelle Sequeira (EDHEC Business School, France).

The second block of chapters in *Part II: Outside the Classroom*, circles around individual development of faculty members. In Chapter 17, Tom Pugel (New York University, US) and Jan Shubert (Babson College, US) illustrate how feedback can be given and received between peers. Philippa Morrison (London Business School, UK) and Pär Mårtensson (SSE, Sweden) elaborate on individual professional development coaching in Chapter 18. Catharina Pramhäll (SSE and Swedish National Accounting Standards Board, Sweden) summarizes, in Chapter 19, pieces of advice given to new teachers by a group of experienced teachers.

In the last and third block of chapters in *Part II: Outside the Classroom*, issues related to leading and developing business schools are focused upon. In the first of these chapters,

Chapter 20, Ferdinando Pennarola (Bocconi, Italy) describes business schools' international networks for faculty development. In Chapter 21, Marie-Laure Djelic (ESSEC, France), Landis Gabel (INSEAD, France) and Andrea Sironi (Bocconi, Italy) share experiences of pedagogical leadership at business schools. Learning styles as vehicles for pedagogical development is the subject of Chapter 22 by Magnus Bild (Bild & Runsten, Sweden) and Pär Mårtensson (SSE, Sweden). Finally, Elena Antonacopoulou (University of Liverpool Management School, UK) elaborates on the theme of mastering business action and the implications for management learning in business schools.

We hope that you will enjoy reading the book and that it will help you in your ambitions to improve teaching and learning at your business school!

Inside the Classroom

Setting the Stage

1 Teacher as Facilitator of Learning

Christine Kelly

In this chapter, we will examine the role of the facilitative teacher: how to get out of the way of learning while helping the learner get the most out of the classroom experience. Often, in academia when we talk about teaching, we focus almost exclusively on the professors, their expertise and their ability to convey their ideas. We can easily overlook what it means to be a learner. This chapter readdresses that balance by focusing on the simple practices, or craft, that all effective professors employ to get out of the way of learning–facilitation rather than pontification.

As we know, learning takes place when students create their own meanings. As John Dewey stated, '... no thought, no idea, can possibly be conveyed as an idea from one person to another. When it is told, it is, to the one to whom it is told, another given fact, not an idea.' Students must wrestle with the facts and conditions to make them their own ideas. Therefore, the role of the teacher is to help students make content memorable and meaningful for themselves.

The intellectual origins of this approach are from such sources as John Dewey, Kurt Lewin, and David Kolb who were astoundingly prescient about the current research on learning and the brain. To fully disclose perspectives and practices, my years as a student of theatre and communication led to bringing theatre practices and experiential exercises to work with faculty and MBA students.

Finally, the foundation for facilitating learning is connection between student and professor. How else to make the classroom a 'safe container' for students to participate fully in their own learning except through connection?

Beginnings

Beginning at the beginning: the professor walks into the classroom, puts down her books, turns on the overhead projector and plugs in her computer. She pulls up the day's agenda on the first page of her slides. At the top of the slide is a welcome to the class, instructions to sit with study teams, and a quote to alert them to today's theme when they come in. She has answered their first question: 'What are we doing today?' They come from another class, or from their jobs. Sometime in the last 48 hours, 90 per cent of the students prepared for today's class. They turned to the assignment—read the case; prepared the problem set, and so on—and then once completed, set it aside. It is then wiped out of conscious memory, replaced by more immediate and 'real' demands of other courses, of work, friends and family. Now as they enter the class, reminded of homework, they retrieve it and hand it in without any thought to today's lecture. The professor, on the other hand, is full of her topic. She has probably spent the last 30 minutes reviewing what took three to six hours to prepare. She turns away from the side of the classroom where she was chatting about an article she saw today on an employer of interest to two students who came in early.

(A colleague notes that he finds a 'gift' for his class almost every day in the news.)

How does our professor begin? The beginning is the most critical moment in the classroom. The students' minds are fresh, relatively open, and willing to tune in. And creating a strong and early emotional connection is crucial—you want to awaken the students and their brains! For example, one renowned professor at NYU Stern, Economist Robert Kavesh, uses a poem at the beginning of each class.

> *As she moves into the center, she senses that the class is relaxed and present. She waits in silence for five to seven seconds while making eye contact with someone in each section of the class. The class is in session. Without a word to the class, she has established control.*

> *She opens with a provocative statement about her topic, and then she reviews today's agenda and delivers the punchline: 'By the end of class today, you will know ___; you will be able to do ___; you will feel ___ about this subject.' The objectives have been established to anchor today's work.*

She began with the end in mind. By providing a proper frame for the course, the day, and the hour, she ensures that the students will be receptive to what she has to say.

All this has been achieved through the use of space, timing, media (blackboard, PowerPoint slides, or an overhead) and the physical presence of the professor. We lead the class in response to our own and our students' expectations about what should occur: the shape of the class, the structure of course material, and the timing of all elements within today's context and the trajectory of the course. By remaining aware of these rhetorical elements to make conscious our choices and our students' needs, we can do more to manage expectations. We are balancing the rhetorical decisions with the cognitive and physical needs of our audience.

To begin, the professor should answer the first five critical questions in the minds of every audience during the introduction:

1. What's the topic?
2. What's your position on it?
3. Why is it relevant to me?
4. Why is it urgent?
5. Who are you to tell me this?

The answers to these questions convey more than the topic, they inform the listener of your perspective and your claim to authority. This opening declares what is at stake for both the professor and the student by citing relevancy and urgency for the listener. Now the student can engage with the problem by making associations with what they already know or believe about the topic. Then they can settle down to listen—perhaps suspending skepticism—but, one hopes, remaining open-minded enough to listen.

Such an opening makes the most of the high levels of attention at the beginning of a session. Attention is at its highest level within the first three to five minutes of class. The audience 'attention curve' shows us that the highest levels of attention occur at the beginning and at the end of a lecture. Making the most of that few minutes of fullest attention will help the student to organize and retrieve material later, moving it from short-term to long-term memory. For this reason and some other important ones, an indirect structure should be used sparingly. The deductive structure can be very useful to approach parts of the topic, but for the class as a whole, deliver the punchline at the beginning. Stating the objective upfront will enhance the student's ability to follow your logic and your thinking while making associations vital to their own.

Creating context

After this set-up will come the context—where today's topic fits into the central thesis of the course, what happened in the preceding class, and how it fits within the scope of the course as a whole—including what was completed last class and where they are in this particular segment of the course. This serves as a review. Likewise, the professor will want to situate the students in the context of today's material.

How they arrive

Most full-time business students' schedules move them from class to class from early morning until late at night. In addition to going to class, our students run organizations, search for jobs, attend company presentations, create C functions ('consumption' functions sponsored by different cultural student groups), manage team projects, international trips, and new businesses, and take courses at two other universities, or across campus. It is an entrepreneurial culture, driving students to micro-manage to thrive in it. In such an environment, how can the professor compete for their attention in class—let alone help them learn? What can we do to bring students fully into the classroom prepared to work despite the demands on them?

Part-time students will run from their jobs where they have been sitting behind computers since early morning until they get up to take a subway to your classroom. I have had many students tell me that it is at this point in the day that their bosses suddenly realize that something vital must be completed. The student has only seconds to determine whether they can juggle the last minute assignment, negotiate a new time for it, or return after class. Even if the student makes it to class, and makes it on time, they are under physical and mental stress and the professor needs to be aware of it.

Capturing the mood of the student

Capturing the mood of the student is essential to capturing a mind. Sometimes, even before setting up the course objective, the professor must first respond to students' moods. For example, one day you might notice that the students are unusually tense. You become aware of a change in rhythm, or the way they entered class. Perhaps it is body tension: sitting with heads down; talking abruptly, loudly; and ignoring your presence. Maybe you overhear the chatter when the students walk in to the classroom.

You ask a question and learn, perhaps, that they just came from an incident in the previous class: a difficult midterm, the announcement of the new business 100K winner (for a start-up), once, a (seemingly) unfairly challenged student. Perhaps, with only 10 minutes between classes, they will not have had time to digest news, or commiserate about an especially difficult test. (In some institutions where departments plan with each other, the professor will have a calendar showing all scheduled exams and papers and can anticipate student stress points.)

Instead of commencing that day with your material, begin explicitly with the students and their mood. Invite them to discuss, briefly, their fears, or the facts, or their excitement. The professor simply acknowledges this mood, hears what is going on, and, perhaps, reflects on it. This moment, in effect, reverses the physiological changes that had occurred in the students' nervous systems. Their reactions have been quieted by their own examination and evaluation.

In a facilitator's guide, it is a checking-in activity. By acknowledging the pressures they feel, or whatever they are feeling, and providing witness to their moods before putting them into the task at hand, the professor will help them put aside the previous incident. From brain research, we know, in effect, that hyperarousal takes over the bulk of a frontal cortex's resources. Once freed up, the frontal cortex can focus on something else. And information obtained in the process of discovering your students' moods will add to your understanding of their needs, your knowledge of who they are, as well as what else is occurring in your institution. It may even lead you to make new connections in your course to the students' interests.

Motivation

Having attended to the mood, the professor will want to explore student motivation. It is not enough to tell students they need to know your subject matter, or that you have some unique slant on what they already know. Telling them the subject is useful is not even enough motivation for the student who already realizes its relevance. The student will need to understand two things: why the material is relevant and what knowledge they are missing. When dealing with adult students who are professionals, this is especially important.

Some courses may lend themselves more towards motivating learning than others. For example, a student's interest in Futures and Options may be obvious. The student may know very little about the subject, and may be totally unfamiliar with the language. This makes it easier to get them to acknowledge that they are missing information. However, they can guess scope and context in order to relate the subject matter to what they intuit or have experienced in their jobs as relevant. In some courses, Human and Organizational Behavior, for example, students tend to take their knowledge for granted. The language is familiar; the solutions posed may sound like common sense—all adding to their sense of competence. Still other courses may seem unique but not fulfilling of a pressing need. One MBA required course, Conceptual Foundations of Business, essentially a course in business ethics, consistently received low course/faculty evaluations. But when alums were asked, three years out, which core course was of most value to them, this one received the highest ratings. The students had by that time experienced the 'startle factor'—its relevance to their security and success. Still, involving the student during the semester proved difficult.

Motivating students to learn

To create an urgent need to learn is a little like trying to arouse someone from sleep. You want to increase alertness. Our brains attend to multiple stimuli, from within and without. 'Novelty and reward are the two primary forces that direct the selection of where to focus our attention. The novelty system takes note of new stimuli. The reward system produces sensations of pleasure, assigning an emotional value to a stimulus, which also marks it for memory' (*A User's Guide to the Brain*, John J. Ratey). An 'emotional' value—key to long-term memory as well as motivating attention—means actively involving the students. The professor will help students 'experience' their needs, or help pinpoint more precisely where they are ignorant: through a case, a discussion, a problem set, an example, or a role play. Recognizing in a graduate level course that some in the class are novices and others are experienced, the professor will acknowledge this difference implicitly or explicitly. The professor's meta-communication, communication about the communication, to the knowledgeable will make clear the relevance of this material to them. Or, she will explain that for them this review and their involvement can be useful to those who are inexperienced. If possible, she will show how their knowledge might need refreshing or updating, or at least, invite them to bring their related practical experiences into discussion.

Motivating students can be simple and practical. One professor I know always brings extra copies of the assignment given out, and when asked about it by someone who missed the previous class, states, 'Would I forget about you?' In other words, her administration and housekeeping role is personal with her students. It is simple awareness, for example, that after 50 minutes of class, students need a stretch break. We can do many things that make it easier to help them manage the learning process.

The locus of learning

Learning is physical and mental. The student needs to be active. Learning is connected to motion. The parts of the brain that coordinate physical movement also coordinate the movement of thought. When I first read this, I thought about where action occurs in a classroom. Often, the action occurs on the dais, or that two foot 'stage' in front of the blackboard. The professor and the professor's media are the center of attention, shaping the flow and delivering the talk. One consultant calls this the 'me and my flip-chart syndrome'. Some people refer to the teacher as actor. In fact, in traditional theatre, action occurs on stage within and behind the proscenium arch. The actors may look out beyond the 'fourth wall' into the audience, but the 'action' takes place on stage. The audience observing the scene may imaginatively project themselves into the scene and identify with the characters, but the 'locus' of the action is on stage. The playwright, the director and the actors control the scene.

If a lecture is about you and your PowerPoint slides, you control the scene. We are often tempted to treat the structure of the class as a drama: we lead the student audience along with us in a kind of treasure hunt, keeping the prize to ourselves until the end. It lends suspense and builds up tension, involving the students in a guessing game, playing them along. My sense is that often this style is unconscious rather than on purpose. For example, I have observed case classes where the professors' questions lead through their logic. The questions are designed to elicit certain answers to lead toward the professor's big surprise at the end, often a kind of 'gotcha', designed to show the professor's superior knowledge. The students are at best involved in a question and answer format and, at worst, involved in guessing what is in the professor's mind. The result of that experience is that the students are getting a fill-in-the-blanks lecture. It tests their preparation and offers a type of modeling of thinking and a rehearsal of material. But is it an effective method to develop students' critical thinking?

Retaining control of pacing and logic privileges the professor's thinking rather than the students' thinking. We reinforce the passive role of student. Not only is the whole constrained by their ability to guess answers, the student who is not inclined to think like the professor is often frustrated.

On this end of the spectrum, the professor controls the material and invites the student to follow along with them as they present material in a lecture. We know that there are advantages to lecturing: basically, the lecture format is most useful to the student when the professor can link disparate source material and/or present material that is new, too new to be readily available in their readings. The skillful lecturer creates the allusion that you are thinking along with them—and learning how to think like the expert is one of the major lessons. The locus of learning is on the 'stage' controlled by the professor.

Somewhere in the middle spectrum is a case presentation. At the other end of the spectrum, the student controls the material. In the facilitated class, the action moves out into the classroom with students. For example, in one kind of active learning, the student solves the problem either alone or in a group and teaches it to others. Here learning occurs in the control of the students.

Ideally, the more neurons fire within the students' heads and within connection with the professor where there is a mutual creation of energy, a mutual exchange, the deeper and richer the possibilities. In the media lab at MIT, the researchers hook up electrodes to the heads of audience members to test the 'credibility of the speaker'. They find that when the speaker is more credible is when the whole parts of the audience's brains are firing. Literally, we talk about connection and how that is discharged by our ability to provoke sparks in the audience. By making the students a part of the field of energy, as it were, through eye contact and the physical focus caused by your stance and relationship to the students, you will change the locus of learning from you to the students. Move the locus of learning into the 'audience'.

'Following the lead of the learner' is a phrase created by faculty attending an international business school seminar on teaching. While observing other professors teach in the ITP—they themselves having returned to the classroom as 'students' for this seminar—and from talking about and researching teaching, these business faculty came to the conclusion that enabling learning requires following the learner—in other words, knowing what the learner needs to learn. To be at the head of that class, we are more than the presenters of content, we are the keepers of the process that follows the lead of the learners as well. To touch that edge means reaching out to the learner.

Stories for learning

Knowing how the student's brain is set off firing means knowing how to organize material to move it from short-term to long-term memory. What we tend to forget as faculty caught up in teaching requirements is that for the students to remember the material they need to map it into their brains. For their maps to be produced, we need to go beyond the Idea to the emotions. We need to capture their values—so, we need a story.

One famous professor of philosophy at NYU begins or ends every class with a story. The subject of the story might be his family or his life, but there is at heart a clear ethical dilemma that reinforces the day's material. A finance professor illustrates concepts with his children's activities. For example, he tells how his daughter persuades her younger brother how he might apportion his allowance or his candy to her benefit in what became a net present value example.

Stories help memory. They give the students a context for their more esoteric course material. They anchor theory in concrete, visual detail, and they change the language of the course. It engages the students. Once listeners hear the narrative structure begin, they are eager to hear what happens next.

The story can open a door for students into the lives of their professors while still making a relevant learning point. Holding out your life to students through a story touches all their senses as well as reinforcing memory through chronology and language. More than a few neurons are firing. From there the student can make associations to the lecture that could not be made from an idea or the facts on a PowerPoint slide.

Pace the class to build momentum.

Chunk up long classes into multiple learning activities and goals.

Begin fast and then build up to a high point.

Create moments of quiet.

Pause for emphasis.

Pause to recapture attention.

Pause for over 5 seconds—longer pauses are effective because most of us are not accustomed to such silence (which is why people will almost always look up when the speaker is silent for a few seconds).

Use active learning activities to help you break up the slow middle (see Chapter 2).

Ask students to think about a question in writing. Using writing activities invites thinking and focuses on material, or helps students prepare an answer to add to class discussion.

Assign a brief reading: a small case, or an example, or a text.

Assign a problem or a question for pairs of students or small groups.

Keeping the students energized

We know that the middle portion of any speech or lecture or class of any length is where attention is at its lowest. The student is most passive. We know we all suffer from a form of attention deficit. My estimate is seven minutes on average is all we can count on for focused attention. Many tricks allow us to work against these habits. Sharpening our awareness of timing as a tool to create and use energy will help shape structure of our lessons.

Thinking about where the action is located and the kind of learning students are being asked to do will keep the class energized—and the professor, too. Shift the learning from the podium to the class and back again. And remember that some play-acting helps. In acting, we learn that energy and enthusiasm can be created by deciding to be energetic and enthusiastic. By our own presence, even following the lead of the learner, we can keep the energy level of the student higher.

Eye contact

How do we follow the lead of the learner? This first rule for following the learner is to see the individual student—'eyeball-to-eyeball'. This eye contact brings the professor in touch with the student and the student in touch with the professor. You are making an emotional connection. One prominent researcher at a business school who consistently received poor student evaluations was often told by his students on the evaluation sheets that he did not care about the students. They said other things as well, but the reaction was emotional and negative. He did care. He spent many hours preparing. The students made comments about his being knowledgeable and that he was a productive researcher; they recognized his scholarship. They just did not realize that he wanted to be in communication with them.

When he invited me to consult with him, I attended his class after our interview (see Chapter 17, 'Getting and Giving Feedback' by Pugel and Shubert), I was astounded to note that after 20 years' teaching, he was not making eye contact with his students. He never looked at them directly. He was turning his head, glancing in the direction of his students, but never actually looking into their eyes or really seeing them.

When the speaker does not see his audience, the audience, without every effort, will involuntarily turn off. This will often take a physical turn: going to sleep, getting restless, or other physical responses to boredom. What interests me is the emotion aroused by it—the angry response. Notice this in yourself when you find yourself listening to a knowledgeable speaker on a topic you espouse interest in, yet find that you cannot pay complete attention;

observe the speaker's eye contact. You may find that the speaker is not really looking at any individual in the audience. This is true of an audience of any size: in rooms of two hundred, if the speaker makes eye contact with a single member of the audience in every section of the room, then all members of the audience will feel that they are being seen as well.

The professor derives many benefits of eye contact: losing self-consciousness, and gaining sustained feedback. Against our intuition, sustained eye contact reduces performance nerves. As important as helping with performance nerves, it provides a feedback mechanism, for example, for pace, volume, and variety.

Feedback from eye contact, careful observation, informs the professor of content issues. The feedback indicates whether a concept was sufficiently explained, or whether the students are tuned out or turned off, whether it is time to move on, 'they've got it', or whether this is really important and they are not quite getting it: say more about that. The feedback loop needs to be completed; during a lecture eye contact is crucial.

In one class I observed, the professor made eye contact with the PowerPoint slides, her computer and then, lastly, the class. The attention of the students flagged, energy in the class was flat, distracted. The more she talked while looking away from them, the more the students had to fight to keep engaged. When she began to focus more on them, she realized that the students were getting only about half of the lecture, if that much. Their feedback signaled their confusion. She began to offer examples, practice sessions, illustrative cases, and so on. In short, she began to teach.

For the student, it assures them that their performance is being observed—the professor is audience for their work. They learn from the professor what it is like to have objective and constructive feedback on their work. We know from playing with our children and from observing their play how much influence is gained from simply being present to them. Eventually, through time in class and time in profession, the students will evolve their own feedback mechanisms. Until then, the professor as witness and model helps them learn to reflect on their learning.

As these examples indicate, eye contact offers much more than might first appear. For the younger student, needing a relationship with the professor is more obvious, but it is no less significant to the older student. Our progress in the course depends upon it.

I am not ignoring the skills of the self-directed learner, the learners who know how to do the work regardless of the teaching. These students are always there, but as we know, learning is much more than just hearing and recalling facts. Eye contact is critical, specifically, for moving forward into practice and application, and supportive connection. It also should be a reminder that learning begins with the emotions, our motor skills are close to our emotional center in the brain, the root of emotion comes from motion, 'e-motion'.

Enhancing the quality of listening

Quality of eye contact supports quality of listening. One tool many professors/speakers often neglect in encouraging good class discussion is listening. Eye contact plays a big role in it. Listening means looking at the student when they are talking, truly focused and hearing what they are saying. Avoid, if possible, the interior chatter: the three items you intended to cover that day in class, or the fact that another student has his hand up—all the class management issues that become apparent when you are not talking. Allow yourself time to get centered and physically open to the student. When the student has completed the comment, wait until the end of the sentence, including the punctuation. Then you can acknowledge them and show them you have listened by summarizing or paraphrasing what they say before you then comment (or make an answer).

> **'Listening'**
>
> Show them you understand that
> They feel strongly and
> Why they feel strongly and
> Pause to let them respond.
> Listening framework: 'From No to Yes'
> Makes the invaluable point that the good
> listener makes it clear to the questioner
> that they hear the feeling and the meaning
> underlying the words.

The whole body is involved in this kind of listening. The effective professor uses this moment to acknowledge the student by turning over the floor to them. Such acknowledgement will support more students to participate and create a sense of safety. After all, we are all aware of how few students actually speak in class. Research indicates that only four students will speak regardless of class size under normal conditions. Accept the student's contribution as a gift that needs to be acknowledged. Once the student has finished a contribution, the professor should begin to respond to the student, but then bring in the rest of the class by looking at them. The temptation is strong to stick with the speaker. If you do that most likely you will get into a discussion with them. Instead, involve the whole class at this point by looking at them. If there is confusion or something needs clarifying on the part of the speaker, they will bring you back to them.

Another common 'listening' problem is to hear only part of the question or answer before beginning to move on—interrupting the student speaker. This cuts off the speaker before they have really finished thinking through their answer. And the speaker is not then acknowledged properly. Once a professor asked me in to observe his class to help him understand why he could not get the discussion started. When I observed him, I could see him cut off student participation by moving quickly from one question to the next, or answering them himself. The students knew that if they waited, he would eventually answer his own question. As we all know from experience, given a choice, students will train us to do their work. By finally really seeing his students, pausing in silence a magic 5–7 seconds after asking a question (at first it took longer until they realized he meant for them to answer this time), they gradually realized that they were meant to do the work.

The physical professor: Voice

Addressing facilitation without commenting on the voice of the facilitator is like discussing food without commenting on flavor. As anyone knows who has spent time with someone whose voice is nasal, tense, too loud, too soft, flaccid, vague, and so on, voice is a critical part of our teaching. After all, when 7 to 8 per cent of communication is attributed only to the sounds of your voice (paralanguage), you can imagine how a clear, open, good tone can affect students in your classroom for an hour or, at times, much, much more than an hour. Voice communicates energy, enthusiasm, warmth, character, and interest. It is a magic tool and an expression of our most personal identity.

To engage the audience, and to feel and express more energy, even when you are tired, having a voice supported by breath and relaxation is as critical to the professor as to the actor. If your throat hurts or is tired after speaking in class, you may be injuring your voice

Some Simple Suggestions for Voice and Breath Work

A. Physical warm up before speaking.

Stretch.

Stand on toes.

Lift arms above head and wiggle fingers.

Take a 10–12"- wide stance and release knees.

Bend from the waist and drop softly between legs like a rag doll.

Relax the neck so head swings loose.

Leaving head down, come up very slowly one vertebra at a time, bringing the head up last.

Shake out hands, arms and shake the leg and arms.

B. Vocal warm up.

Open mouth, drop jaw.

Exhale.

Breathe through nose, exhale through open mouth.

Relax face—soften eyes, brush teeth with tongue, buzz lips, rub jaw.

Open mouth—stretch tongue out, up and down.

Open throat—chew big, silent yawns.

C. Breath.

Notice lower belly out and in: release the lower abdominal muscle and as you release it, breath returns. Repeat.

D. Physical relaxation is the key.

To get the right energy and sound into the words, have a relaxed neck, shoulders with the head lightly floating about your shoulders.

Release any tension in the neck and throat.

For more volume, have the intention of filling the room with energy, allow the breath to support you and project to be heard by seeing students sitting farthest back of the room.

by the way you are using it. Or, you may have a serious problem. No matter how much teaching you do, the voice should not be strained—if you are using it properly. There are many ways to work on voice. A voice lesson is very useful for all who spend their lives speaking.

Classroom space

Use all the space in the classroom: move back and through and around your students to encourage them to look at each other as well as to you and to stir up energy in the others. It will move the focus from the center front to the back and sides of the room. It reinforces their need to participate and to bring other students into discussion with each other.

Being a physical professor in relation to the class means sharpening your observation skills. Notice where you are and where you are in relation to the class. By moving into the circle in front yet close to the class, standing in the center of that circle, you are included in the group, somewhat neutral, focused on membership, somewhat apart from the group. By standing by the board or slides, you are referring students' attention to the material there. By acting as a lightening rod for students' attention, you produce energy—coming in close changes the energy in that section of the room. Your movement attracts the eye, just as light attracts the eye. If you move behind a row of students, the rest of the room will observe that row of students. Students will begin to speak to each other rather than to you. By returning to center stage you are at the center of attention and they are referred to you. You are like a pendulum on a length of cord, a carpenter's weight. You can pull the energy into the center or fling it out in concentric circles or indicate where the action is. By focusing on the students, they will produce the action.

> **E. A solid stance supports the breath and gives the viewer a sense of your confidence.**
>
> Stand with your feet about 10–12" apart under your shoulders.
>
> Flex knees slightly, avoid locking them, and keep hips centered.
>
> Tilt hips forward and back and around to explore the feeling of being centered.
>
> Lift from the breastbone, not the shoulders, keep the shoulders down and loose.
>
> Spread your back to feel the width of it, to give yourself the solid underpinning with a lift and lightness of carriage.
>
> When you move in the room, move toward the students—and if you are making good eye contact this will happen naturally.
>
> Take strong solid steps then 'plant' yourself in a solid stance whenever you stop moving.

Ending class to use a high point of attention

Concluding your class to make the most of the rise in student attention at the end is a delicate matter. You have several objectives: reinforcing the material learned, making the transitions to the next topic, handling administrative details, including preparation for upcoming assignments and, finally, giving the students a sense of completion. Doing all that and closing on time requires preparation as well as an exquisite sense of the moment. You often hear stories about professors who routinely end class with a final thrilling statement just as the bell rings. Films like to show that scene: John Houseman in *Paper Chase* manages to make a provocative statement just as the bell rings prompting students to rise to their feet in excited discussion as they are propelled out the door of the classroom. Few faculty do that routinely.

However, we can plan to end on critical material when we know we have the students' full attention. By handling administrative details and the students' next assignments after the mid-point of class, or right after the break in longer classes, these details are out of the way. Save beginnings and endings for critical material.

Your ending could reinforce what students learned. You can connect to the next topic in concluding the current one. Having a sense of the wider landscape keeps students in mind of their progress, the scope of the subject matter, and a link reinforcing the conceptual, intellectual underpinnings of the subject matter.

When observing time management, and with a little inspiration, you can change the mood at the end. Such a change might be a lighter or a more serious take on our discussion, a side-note, an unusual application, or quote, and so on, that drives home our experience together that day. Of course, the most memorable is ending with a story.

Some of our classrooms are designed with an entrance to the side of the teacher's desk with no center aisle. The most direct way out for students on the far side of the room is behind the teacher's desk. When the energy of the class ends on a high note, students will stop by on the way out, briefly, adding a comment to class discussion, or asking a question, or just wishing the professor a good weekend and saying thanks for the class. In those moments, we sense their connection and recognize how much they lead us to their needs as learners.

This chapter is a reminder and a habit former. I want to remind you of these familiar practices, to offer an explanation of why they are important, and to make them accessible, both to add to our understanding—to reassure doubters of their validity, and to reinforce their importance as habits for learners and professors.

Donald L. Finkel, in a lovely book called *Teaching with Your Mouth Shut*, asks us to think about three incidents where we were aware of having learned something. It is a humbling experiment. Few of the incidents I have heard involve the classroom or a teacher. The exception was when the teacher supported the student's learning process as opposed to telling them what to do. Being facilitative as teachers reminds us of our role in supporting learning.

References

Bransford, J., Brown, A.L., and Cocking, R.R., Eds., *How People Learn: Brain, Mind, Experience and School. Expanded Edition* (Paperback). National Research Council (U.S.) Committee on Learning Research and Educational Practice, National Research Council, 2000.

Christensen, R.C., Garvin, D.A., and Sweet, A., *Education for Judgement: The Artistry of Discussion Leadership*. Boston: Harvard Business School Press, 1991.

Angelo, T.A. and Cross, P.K., *Classroom Assessment Techniques: A Handbook for College Teachers*. San Francisco: Jossey-Bass, Inc., 1993.

_____*Accent on Learning*. San Francisco: Jossey-Bass, Inc., 1988.

DeLoux, J., *The Emotional Brain. The Mysterious Underpinnings of Emotional Life*. New York: Simon and Schuster, 1996.

Dewey, J., *Democracy and Education; An Introduction to the Philosophy of Education*. New York: Free Press, 1944.

Finkel, D.L., *Teaching with Your Mouth Shut*. New Hampshire: Boynton/Cook, 2000.

Fisher, B.M., *No Angel in the Classroom*. Oxford, England: Rowman and Littlefield Publishers, Inc., 2001.

Garner, H., *Multiple Intelligences: The Theory in Practice*. New York: Basic Books, 1993.

Goleman, D., *Working with Emotional Intelligence*. New York: Bantam Books, 1998.

Kolb, D.A., *Experiential Learning: Experience as the Source of Learning and Development*. Englewood Cliffs, NJ: Prentice-Hall, Inc., 1984.

McKeachie, W.J., *Teaching Tips, A Guidebook for the Beginning College Teacher*. Lexington, MA: D.C. Heath and Company, 1986.

Ratey, J.J., *A User's Guide to the Brain*. New York: First Vintage Books Edition, 2002.

Sadker, M. and Sadker, D., *Failing at Fairness, How Our Schools Cheat Girls*. New York: Touchstone, 1994.

Seligman, M.E.P., *Authentic Happiness*. New York: Free Press, 2002.

Silberman, M., *Active Learning. 101 Strategies to Teach Any Subject*. Boston: Allyn and Bacon, 1996.

Video Arts. *From No to Yes*. Video-Based Learning Resources. Virginia Beach, VA: Coastal Training Technologies Corp (www.coastalhr.com).

Inside the Classroom

Teaching Techniques and Approaches

2 Teaching Actively

Mel Silberman

It's not what you tell your students that counts. What counts is what they take away. That's because the more you tell them, the more they will forget. Moreover, you can't learn for them. They must do it themselves. Your role as a teacher, therefore, is to spark and guide their learning and help to make it last. This chapter will present five teaching strategies to spark active learning in your classes:

- **Strategy #1: Engage your students from the start**
  Give your students something to do before a class session even starts to develop a climate for active learning, promote peer interaction, and build immediate involvement in the learning topic. Encourage wide-spread participation, especially at the beginning of a course.
- **Strategy #2: Be a brain-friendly presenter**
  Present information and concepts that maximize understanding and retention through techniques that stimulate students' brains to be mentally alert and receptive to new data.
- **Strategy #3: Encourage lively and focused discussion**
  Structure discussion so that students are motivated to participate and pursue the topic in depth.
- **Strategy #4: Let your students learn from each other**
  Set up effective group learning and peer teaching activities that require peer collaboration.
- **Strategy #5: Make the end unforgettable**
  Close a learning experience so that students review what they have learned, reflect on its importance, and consider future steps.

Engage your students from the start

In order to learn something well, your students need to listen, observe, ask questions and discuss the material with others. Above all else, students need to 'do it'. That includes figuring out things by themselves, coming up with examples, and doing tasks that depend on the knowledge they already have.

The success of active learning depends on your ability to form and sustain an environment in which students take on the responsibility to be 'doers'. Above all, they must be willing to use their brains—studying ideas, solving problems, and applying what they learn. There must be such a climate right from the beginning that supports active learning. The longer you wait to create this climate, the longer your students have to settle into being passive learners. If you want your students to start learning actively, give them a taste of it right away. Get your students to do something before you even start serious teaching. Think of it as the appetizer before the main course. Whet their appetites and they will be hungry learners.

A way to accomplish this is to display a question (for example, how can the company in the case you studied for today's class be profitable with its current level of debt?) in full view of gathering students and ask them to think about the question before class starts. You can also invite them to discuss their response with someone seated next to them. Another idea is to distribute to students a short, fun quiz on today's class topic. Use true/false questions, multiple-choice questions, or short answer questions. Ask students to complete the quiz with the promise that the answers will be summarized when class starts. A final idea is to ask students to write down a question about any reading assignment you have given. Collect the questions. Ask for volunteers to share their question with the entire class. These activities help to introduce a class in a dramatic, active manner that draws students into the topic right from the beginning.

Beyond any structured activities, your class sessions will not spark active learning unless students are eager to participate. The bad news is that only a small minority will actively participate (raise their hands, volunteer, ask questions, and so forth) unless you do something to increase the number of students right from the start. Once the frequent participators are established, it's very difficult to increase the pool of participation.

Many teachers assume that several students do not participate because they are either shy, insecure, or disinterested. Of course, that's true for some students but hardly the majority. Rates of participation are much more influenced by the teacher than determined by the students. Assuming the teacher asks interesting questions, sets a non-threatening climate, and encourages student response, the one problematic behavior I often see is that teachers call on the first student whose hand is raised. The reason this occurs is that it seems rude not to do so, especially if the student in question does not volunteer constantly. In addition, many teachers are grateful that the student is raising their hand when the rest of the class seems disinterested or afraid. The problem that arises is that students (and teachers) get used to a single volunteer (or maybe just a few) and the pattern and rate of participation gets set. Sooner or later, a small minority of students fill the role of responding to teacher requests for participation.

Without realizing it, most teachers even use language that promotes a small pool of students. They say things like: 'Who wants to give his views next?', 'Can anyone tell me what's the solution here?' and, 'I'm looking for someone to ...'

Here are five ways to increase the pool of participation. You don't need to do all of them, but you should get in the habit, as soon as possible, of employing some of them. Also, don't expect great results the very first time you use the techniques you select. The good news is that once the students get the hang of what you are doing, even after one exposure, they will start to respond with greater frequency.

1. **Create the opportunity for 'pre-discussion'**
   - Pose a question and invite students to discuss it with others seated near them.
   - Say: 'Take a few minutes to discuss this question with your partner before we open the floor for discussion.'
   - Next, ask the question again for a total group discussion.
2. **Obtain a commitment to participate**
   - Pose a question and ask: 'How many of you have some thoughts about this?'
   - Encourage several students to raise their hands before you call on any student.
   - Call on students who have not volunteered so far or, if time is available, call on all the hands raised.
3. **Specify how many you wish to participate**
   - Ask a question and open it up to the entire group.
   - Say: 'I'd like to ask four or five students to give me their opinions.'

4. **Establish a 'new' student rule**
   - Pose a question.
   - Say: 'I'd like some new students this time. Who hasn't shared their ideas yet?'
5. **Use a 'call on the next speaker' format**
   - Ask students to raise their hands when they want to share their views and request that the present speaker in the class call on the next speaker (rather than the teacher performing this role).
   - Say: 'When you are the speaker, please talk to other students rather than addressing me.'

Be a brain-friendly presenter

Your students' brains are your best allies. Too often, teachers think that there is nothing going on in their students' heads. Nothing could be further from the truth. Technically speaking, if nothing is happening in students' brains, they are dead. Their brains are alive and working (even when they are asleep). The issue is what are their brains thinking about?

I appreciate the fear that students are thinking about everything but what you want. Yes, students, like all human beings, do a lot of 'mind-surfing'. Your task is twofold: to interest their brains in what you are presenting and to help their brains to really go to work so that they learn and retain the presentation as well. Here are ten suggestions:

BUILDING INTEREST

1. Lead-off Story or Interesting Visual: Provide a relevant anecdote, fictional story, cartoon, or graphic that captures the audience's attention to what you are about to teach.
2. Initial Case Problem: Present a problem around which the lecture will be structured.
3. Test Question: Ask participants a question (even if they have little prior knowledge) so that they will be motivated to listen to your lecture for the answer.

MAXIMIZING UNDERSTANDING AND RETENTION

4. Headlines: Reduce the major points in the lecture to key words which act as verbal subheadings or memory aids.
5. Examples and Analogies: Provide examples throughout the lecture and, if possible, create a comparison between your material and the knowledge/experience the participants already have.
6. Visual Backup: Use flip-charts, transparencies, brief handouts, and demonstrations that enable participants to see as well as hear what you are saying.

INVOLVING PARTICIPANTS IN THE LECTURE

7. Spot Challenges: Interrupt the lecture periodically and challenge participants to give examples of the concepts presented thus far or answer spot quiz questions.
8. Illuminating Exercises: Throughout the presentation, intersperse brief activities that illuminate the points you are making.

REINFORCING THE LECTURE

9. Application Problem: Pose a problem or question for participants to solve based on the information given in the lecture.
10. Participant Review: Ask participants to review the contents of the lecture with each other or give them a self-scoring review test.

Encourage lively and focused discussion

Lively, focused discussions are often the best moments in the classroom. Students are engaged and time flies. All too often, however, a teacher tries to stimulate discussion but is met with uncomfortable silence as students wonder who will dare to speak up first. If you are fortunate to have groups where the participation is strong, a different problem may emerge. There are lots of students participating, but perhaps the discussion goes off on tangents and/or the quality is disappointing. It may feel nice to have so many students involved, but is the time taken really worth it?

There are several things you can do to obtain lively AND focused discussions, time after time. First off, build interest before plunging into the discussion. Merely stating a question is not usually enough to attract students. Here are some engagement suggestions:

*   Survey students. For example, you might ask: Who believes that this company's supply chain strategy gives them an advantage?
*   Distribute a compelling document (a newspaper or magazine article, a cartoon, a chart, or a photo) that connects to the discussion topic.
*   Provide contrasting opinions on a topic.

Merely choosing a topic and tossing it out for discussion can be a recipe for disaster. Think carefully how you want to state the discussion question. There are three things to keep in mind in this regard:

1. Use open-ended rather than close-ended questions.
2. Make the wording of a question clear.
3. Limit the number of questions.

You can assist students to prepare for a high-quality discussion by giving them data that might shed more light than heat in the discussion to follow. Give your students the data before class or right before the discussion. Give them time to read, discuss the information with peers, and ask questions to clarify the contents. Or, invite or require students to collect information that enables them to be an informed participant.

Generally speaking, an open, teacher-led discussion is a poor format for obtaining wide participation and focused conversation. As I discussed previously, open discussion often yields few students. You get to hear from four or five students who do most of the talking in class. Besides, or in addition to open discussion, there are many other options. Here are a few of them:

1. **Spark discussion by using response cards**
    Pass out index cards and request anonymous answers to your question. Use response cards to save time, to provide anonymity for personally threatening self-disclosures, or to make it easier for shy people to contribute. The need to state yourself concisely on a card is another advantage of this method. Say, 'For this discussion, I would like you to write

down your thoughts first before we talk together any further.' Have the index cards passed around the group or have them returned to you to be read at a later point. Be careful to make your question clear and to encourage brief, legible responses.

2. **Form subgroups of three or more**
Use subgroup discussions when you have sufficient time to discuss issues in depth. This is one of the key methods for obtaining everyone's participation. Pose a question for discussion or give the subgroup a task or assignment to complete. It is often helpful to designate group roles such as facilitator, timekeeper, recorder, or presenter, and to obtain volunteers or assign members to fill them. Make sure that students are in face-to-face contact with each other. Try to separate subgroups so that they do not disturb each other.

3. **Go around the class and obtain short responses**
Use this method when you want to obtain something quickly from each student. Sentence stems (for example, 'One thing that makes a good strategic plan is _____') are useful in conducting go-arounds. Invite students to 'pass' when they wish. Avoid repetition by asking each student for a new contribution to the process. If the group is large, create a smaller go-around group. For example, you can obtain short responses from one side of the room, from people who are wearing glasses, or from some other smaller sample.

4. **Create discussion panels**
Invite a small number of students to present their views in front of the entire class.
Use panels when time permits to have a focused, serious response to your discussion questions. Rotate panelists to increase participation. An informal panel can be created by asking for the views of a designated number of students who remain in their seats. Serve as panel moderator or invite a student to perform this role.
A variation of a panel discussion is a 'fishbowl' discussion. A fishbowl is a kind of rotating panel. Ask a portion of the class to form a discussion circle and have the remaining students form a listening circle around them. Use a fishbowl to help bring focus to large-group discussions. Although it is time-consuming, this is the best method for combining the virtues of large- and small-group discussion. Bring new groups into the inner circle to continue the discussion. You can do this by obtaining new volunteers or assigning students to be discussants.

Some of the discussion options just presented allow you to sit back and let the students take charge. Other options require your leadership. In such cases, your role is to facilitate the flow of comments from students. Although it is not necessary to make an interjection after each person speaks, periodically assisting students with their contributions can be helpful. Here is a ten-point facilitation menu to select from as you lead group discussions:

1. *Paraphrase* what someone has said so the student knows that they have been understood and the other students can hear a concise summary of what has just been said.
2. *Check* your understanding against the words of a student or ask a student to clarify what they are saying.
3. *Compliment* an interesting or insightful comment.
4. *Elaborate* on a student's contribution to the discussion with examples or suggest a new way to view the problem.
5. *Energize* a discussion by quickening the pace, using humor or, if necessary, prodding the class for more contributions.
6. *Disagree* (gently) with a student's comments to stimulate further discussion.
7. *Mediate* differences of opinion between students and relieve any tensions that may be brewing.

8. *Pull together* ideas, showing their relationship to each other.
9. *Change* the group process by altering the method of participation or prompting the group to evaluate ideas that have been raised during the previous discussion.
10. *Summarize* (and record, if desired) the major views of the class.

Any of these facilitating behaviors can be used alone or in conjunction with the others to help stimulate discussions within your class. As students become more and more relaxed about contributing their ideas and opinions, you can shift from being a leader to being an occasional facilitator, and perhaps even another person with an opinion. As your role in the conversation diminishes, the students make the discussion their own.

Let your students learn from each other

Your students can learn as much from each other as they can learn from you. After all, they 'speak each other's language'. They can also give each other more personal attention than you can give to each of them. Under the right conditions, learning that is collaborative is more active than learning that is teacher-led.

The best way to let your students learn from each other is to place them in teams. Unfortunately, team learning also has its drawbacks. Chief among these is the fact that teachers have less instructional control than when they themselves are front and center. Have any of the following ever happened to you when you have put students in learning groups for at least 20–30 minutes?

*   *Confusion*: Students don't know what to do because they didn't understand or follow the directions.
*   *Tangents*: Students don't stick to the topic and get off task.
*   *Unequal participation*: Some students dominate; some remain quiet.
*   *One-way communication*: Students don't listen to or respond to each other.
*   *No division of labor*: Some students don't pull their own weight; they let the team down, and are not dependable.
*   *Superficiality*: The team is done before you know it, breezing through the assignment in the fastest way possible and staying on the surface rather than digging below it.

Chances are you have experienced nearly all of these problems, in both short- and long-term groups. When they happen, students and teachers alike get turned off to team learning. What can be done?

First off, who you put with who is often critical to team learning success. Here are several considerations:

1. **Keep the teams small**
    In my experience, productive teams can range from two to six members. Small teams work faster and can manage and coordinate their work with greater ease. Teams that are larger than six members have the advantage of greater knowledge, skill, and perspectives. They can cope with larger projects and can also cover for missing or slack members. But large teams often get bogged down in group process issues that prevent them from moving forward. They are difficult to organize and it can be especially challenging to pull together the work of a large team. If you still wish to use teams larger than six members, be aware that such teams need more structure, more formal meetings, and clearer roles for each member than small teams.

2. **Gain the advantages of random assignment**

    There are two benefits to forming teams by leaving it up to chance. One benefit is that students can't gravitate only to the people with whom they are comfortable. (Although self-selected grouping can work out at times, the greater risk is that friends will socialize more than you prefer.) The other benefit is that students can't exclude one another. Through random assignment, students usually wind up with some peers whom they don't know well or who may be more or less knowledgeable than they are. It's a very powerful message to say to your students that, in effect, they are expected to work with anyone and everyone in the class.

    The simplest way to assign students randomly is by 'counting off'. Count the number of students as soon as you believe that you have full attendance. Then determine how large your subgroups will be by finding a number that easily divides into your total number of students. Be careful. For example, if you have 24 students and you want groups with four members, ask students to count off by 6's (1, 2, 3, 4, 5, 6; 1, 2, 3, 4, 5, 6, etc.). If you count off by 4's, you'll wind up with four groups of six students. If the total number of students is not an even number or a number that can be divided evenly, be aware that typically one or more groups will have one fewer member than the others. For example, in a class of 25 students, you have the possibility of five groups of five students, but, if you want quartets, you will have five groups of four students and one group of five students.

3. **Compose diverse groups**

    When you assign students randomly, there is a likelihood, but no guarantee, that you'll obtain diverse groups (by gender, race, experience level, knowledge, motivation, and so forth). You are more likely to obtain the diversity you may be seeking by deliberately composing the teams yourself. Diverse teams take longer to get started, but often succeed in the long run because of the richness of their resources. There are other reasons to form diverse teams:

    *   You want to be sure that there is at least one skilled or 'responsible' student in each team.
    *   You want different points of view.
    *   You want to make sure that every student has someone on whom they can rely for support. (For example, you can compose teams so that every member has the strong possibility of having one 'friend'.)

    You need to know your class well if you are to use diverse groups effectively. Therefore, it's a strategy that works best after several class sessions. My favorite way to form diverse groups is as follows: Arrange the seating in a teaching session before the students arrive into the group configurations you desire (for example, tables for six students) and place name tents or name cards on the seats or desktops at each team location. As students enter the teaching session, have them 'find their seats'. Some students may grumble when they discover that there are assigned seats (especially if they don't like the group they are placed in), but they usually survive if you are unwavering about your decision.

    If you cannot arrange assigned seating before class, you will need to ask your students to change seats once they arrive. A friendly way to pull this off is to tell your students that you have created teams for today's class (the teams can continue for more than one class session) and these teams are designated by a letter (for example, Team A) or by a name (for example, an animal or a car). Then, announce the names of the members of each team.

When composing teams for diversity, consider any of these possibilities:

- put together students who don't know each other;
- choose students who balance each other in terms of learning style and motivation;
- mix students by gender, race, age, job status, or other significant categories;
- integrate students from different company divisions or functions.

Once learning teams have been assigned, it's probably a good idea to have students experience some initial team building. From everything we know about group development, teams can't perform until they have a chance to form. This axiom applies big time to learning teams. Students need the opportunity to get comfortable with each other before they take on the responsibility of doing their own learning. They also need to bond socially and get accustomed to working as a group without the direct guidance of the teacher.

How much time you allocate to the team-building process depends on your personal circumstances. For some teachers, it may be no more than 20 minutes. For others, it may be several hours. In my view, however much time you take will be recovered many times over once you see the difference that some initial team building makes. Let's explore some ways to spend this time wisely.

1. **Utilize brief team-building activities**
   There are numerous structured activities that help to form teams. These activities help teams to get to know each other rapidly and build a degree of team cohesion early on.

2. **Give students a brief taste of team learning**
   It's important for students to experience learning from each other without the direction of a teacher not only to develop an image of what is expected later on, but also to have some immediate success. Here are some ways to accomplish this:

   - Give teams one simple, but provocative question to answer (for example, 'What is the leading reason a talented person would stay in an organization?').
   - Give teams a quotation to discuss (for example, 'If you never budge, don't expect a push.').
   - Give teams one short task to accomplish together (for example, solve a simple accounting problem).
   - Give teams a brief game (for example, create a tower that is both sturdy, tall, and attractive).

3. **Invite teams to discuss ground rules and responsibilities**
   Talking about ground rules helps long-term learning teams to concretize how they must function in order to reach their goals. You can ask teams to brainstorm potential ground rules or provide them with a checklist such as the following:

   ## Our Ground Rules

   Below are ground rules that are helpful to learning teams. Check the ones most important to you:

   - Start on time with everyone present.
   - Get to know members who are 'different' from you.
   - Let others finish without interrupting them.
   - Be brief and to the point.
   - Be prepared.

- Give everyone a chance to speak.
- Share the workload.

If long-term teams are going to be effective, some crucial jobs have to be done. If no one does them, the teams will drift aimlessly without achieving much. Ask teams to consider assigning themselves (preferably on a rotating basis) some of these important jobs:

- Facilitator: Facilitates learning team sessions.
- Timekeeper: Allocates and monitors time needed and spent.
- Secretary or note taker: Keeps a record of ideas, conclusions, and achievements.
- Checker: Makes sure all members are doing what they are supposed to do.
- Investigator: Finds things out and brings information back to the team.

A wide variety of activities exist that you can give to learning teams. If you utilize some of those, you will find that your students will look forward to the experience of working in such teams. Let's look at some options:

1. **Have students search for information**
   Give teams some questions and provide learning material that contains the answers. Have them find the answers. This method can be likened to an open book test. Teams search for information (normally covered by the teacher) that answers questions posed to them. This method is especially helpful in livening up dry material.

2. **Create study groups**
   Give teams some learning material and ask them to explain it to one another. This method gives students the responsibility to study learning material and to clarify its content as a group without the teacher's presence. The assignment needs to be specific enough that the resulting study session will be effective and the group able to be self-managing.

3. **Jigsaw the learning**
   Jigsaw learning is a creative form of peer teaching. It is an exciting alternative whenever there is material to be learned that can be segmented or 'chunked' and when no single segment must be taught before the others. Each student learns something that, when combined with the material learned by others, forms a coherent body of knowledge. Choose learning material that can be broken into segments. A segment can be as short as one sentence or as long as several pages. (If the material is lengthy, ask students to read their assignments before the session.)

Make the end unforgettable

Many courses run out of steam at the end. In some cases, students are marking time until the close is near. In other cases, teachers are valiantly trying to cover what they haven't gotten to before time runs out. How unfortunate! What happens at the end needs to be 'unforgettable'. You want students to remember what they've learned. You also want students to feel that what they learned has been special.

When you are preparing for the end, there are three areas to consider:

1. How will students review what you have taught them?
2. How will students assess what they have learned?
3. How will students consider what they will do about what they have learned?

Reviewing is a valuable learning activity and can take many forms, from fun games to challenging assignments. Here are some options:

1. Create a review activity based on the format of a television quiz show (for example, Jeopardy) or a popular game (for example, a crossword puzzle). Invite students to be individual game participants or create teams.
2. Use a jigsaw design to create a comprehensive review. Devise a list of questions, problems, key concepts, and so forth that apply to the entire unit or course you want students to review. For example, you might list 20 questions that cover on marketing. Create subgroups of students and assign each subgroup a part of the list. For example, you can create four groups of five students who each receive five questions from the list of 20 questions on the teaching topic. Ask each subgroup to answer the questions, solve the problems, or define the concepts assigned to it. (Decide if you want your students to do this process with or without using reference material.) Redistribute each subgroup so that there is at least one representative from each of the original groups in the new subgroups (called 'jigsaw groups') you have just created. For example, if there were four groups of five students assigned to a portion of 20 questions, have each of those groups count off from one to five. This creates five groups of four students. In each of the five groups will be one student who has worked on the answers to 25 per cent of the questions. By sharing the answers with each other, the entire list of 20 questions will be reviewed.
3. Invite students to summarize the entire unit or course. Explain to students that providing a summary of what you have taught would be contrary to the principle of active learning. Instead, tell them to summarize the unit or course. Divide students into subgroups of two to four members. Ask each subgroup to create its own summary. Encourage the subgroups to create an outline, a mind-map, or any other device that will enable them to communicate the summary to others. Use any of the following questions to guide the students:

    *   What were the major topics we examined?
    *   What have been some of the key points?
    *   What experiences have you had in this teaching? What did you get out of them?
    *   What ideas and suggestions are you taking away from this unit/course?

4. Ask students to perform a variety of tasks. If you have been teaching students skills that can be performed (for example, creating an income statement), challenge them to a performance review. Give students time to prepare for their performance or challenge them to perform without prior preparation. Even if students feel some pressure, try to relax them by labeling the performance as their practice recital. Encourage students to applaud each other's performances.

The end of a course is also a time for reflection. What have I learned? What do I now believe? What are my skills? What do I need to improve? Allowing time for self-assessment gives students the opportunity to examine what the teaching has meant to them. The suggestions that follow are structured ways to promote this kind of self-assessment.

1. Prepare a survey in which students rate themselves on items that reflect the learning they have acquired. You can ask them to evaluate such things as:

    *   the skills they have mastered;
    *   the information they've acquired;
    *   the concepts they have understood;
    *   new or expanded areas of interest.

It's important that students are honest with themselves. They will be if you make the survey something they complete only for themselves. At the same time, consider having students share those responses they want to reveal with a partner or in a small group of students.

2. By the end of a unit or course, after much time has elapsed, your students' awareness of what they have learned may be low. You can counteract that by asking your students to take the time to consider what they are taking away from the class. These may include any of the following:

    *   new knowledge;
    *   new skill;
    *   improvement in _____ (for example, assertive behavior);
    *   confidence in _____ (for example, facilitating group discussion).

At the conclusion of any course that has featured active learning, students will naturally ask, 'Now what?' The success of active learning is really measured by how that question is answered, that is, how what has been learned in the class affects what students will do in the future. Here are some suggestions:

1. **Invite students to consider how to continue learning on their own**
    Point out your hope that students' learning doesn't stop simply because the class is over. Suggest to students that there are many ways for them to continue learning on their own. Indicate that one way to do this is to brainstorm their own list of ideas to 'keep on learning'.
2. **Encourage students to create a plan of action**
    Your students might be more likely to follow up the learning experiences they have had with concrete actions if you invite them to make a contract with themselves. One simple approach is to ask students to write themselves a letter indicating what steps they intend to take to use what they have learned or continue to learn more about the subject on their own. Suggest that they could begin the letter with the words 'I hereby resolve'. Inform them that the letter is confidential. Ask them to place it in the envelope, address it to themselves, and seal the envelope. You can promise to mail the envelope at a later point. Or, invite students to write you an email containing their intentions. You can reply back at a later point with a copy of their message and a friendly note, 'How is everything going?'

Final advice

I hope you are inspired to apply these teaching strategies with your students. I recognize, however, that inspiration doesn't ensure action. So, I would like to end with some final advice.

FOCUS ON OUTCOMES, NOT CONTENT

All too often, teaching is designed around the information, concepts, or skills that appear to be central to the topic at hand. On paper, it seems that the course covered the topic well, but what happens in the actual experience of the students? Most will find that they 'toured' the topic. They went from sub-topic to sub-topic, much like a sightseer goes from city to city or country to country, taking in the tour guide's patter but often forgetting where they were a few days ago. At best, students walk away feeling, 'been there, done that'.

Active teaching focuses on outcomes rather than content. The teaching is designed to achieve a result instead of covering a topic. My suggestion is to look at your current classes and ask yourself if they are focused on content or outcomes. If it's the former, start asking yourself this question:

'What do I want students to do with the teaching they are getting?'

When you make this shift in focus, you will really appreciate the five strategies explored in this chapter and start to use them consistently. As I wrote in the introduction, what you tell and show your students ultimately doesn't count. What they take away is paramount. It makes no difference how eloquent you are or how elegant your presentation slides appear. What's vital is how well they understand what you've taught and how motivated they are to apply it. When the teaching is focused on specific targets, the students must take more active responsibility for the outcome.

SEIZE THE OPPORTUNITY

You have the opportunity to rise above the usual norms prevalent in too many schools today. Far too often, teachers tolerate practices that shut down rather than open up learning. By applying the strategies I have provided in this chapter, there is a strong likelihood that your students will become the active learners who are needed in a rapidly changing world.

Ask yourself if you are truly happy with the current state of learning in your classroom. Do you want to accept the status quo, with students passive and their learning short-lived? We are often reluctant to change our methods because we don't know what will happen if we do. View your attempts to apply the strategies in this chapter as a 'personal experiment in change'. Choose one strategy at a time and stay with it for a while. Try it on for size and see if it fits you. Don't be afraid to tell your students that you are experimenting and want their feedback. Such a move gives you permission to use a new idea and invites them to be your partner in finding approaches that work.

Enjoy your journeys in teaching actively.

References

Jensen, E., *Brain-Based Learning*. San Diego: The Brain Store, 2000.

Johnson, D. W., Johnson, R. T., and Smith, K. A., *Active Learning: Cooperation in the College Classroom*. Edina, Minn: Interaction Book Company, 1991.

Knowles, M., Holton, E., and Swanson, R., *The Adult Learner (6th edition)*. Burlington: Elsevier Inc., 2005.

McKeachie, W. and Svinicki, M., *McKeachie's Teaching Tips*. Boston: Houghton Mifflin, 2006.

Silberman, M., *Active Learning: 101 Ways to Teach Any Subject*. Boston: Allyn and Bacon, 1995.

Silberman, M., *Teaching Actively*. Boston: Allyn and Bacon, 2005.

Thiagarajan, S., *Thiagi's Interactive Lectures*. Alexandria, VA: ASTD Press, 2005.

3 My Biggest Mistakes in Teaching Cases (and Lessons Learned)

Kamran Kashani

This chapter is not about the virtues or drawbacks of using cases in teaching management. There is an ample supply of both[1]. Nor is it meant to be a confessional piece from the serial case-user that I am. I have better things to do than hang my proverbial professional dirty laundry in public (or, for that matter, in private) and engage in an, albeit liberating, self-flagellation exercise. Rather, this paper is about pitfalls in store for all case teachers, young and old, newcomers and old hands, teachers of MBAs, and those in executive development. The 'mistakes' I am about to write about are specific common behaviors that negatively impact a teacher's performance and her ability to use cases most effectively. And it's written with the spirit of 'live-and-learn', to share, with the other practitioners of the case method, what I have learned from my own experiences—especially the bad ones.

The basics

Let me start with some basics of case teaching. Without any doubt teaching cases is difficult. In comparison, lecture-presentations using the evermore sophisticated PowerPoint software (with graphics, sounds, animation, short video clips, and so on) are less complex and, as a consequence, easier on the teacher and the students.[2] The case method's difficulty comes primarily from its inductive nature where a greater wisdom is to be learned from the single sample of a firm and its management challenges. Reaching that bigger truth is made more complex by the tension between the instructor-centered 'teaching', in the traditional sense of the word, and the student-centered 'learning' that case discussion encourages. While we feel an obligation to inculcate our students with useful theories, concepts, and models that often constitute the backbones of our course outlines, student learning follows its own path and logic. A related challenge for case teachers is inherent in the shared control for

---

1   For a sample see the following references:
- Abell, D., What Makes a Good Case? *ECCHO*. Autumn/Fall, 4–7, 1997.
- Barnes L., The More I Teach, The Less I Use the Chalkboard. *ECCHO*. Autumn/Fall, 10–11, 1997.
- Colbert, J., Trimble, K. and Desberg, P., *The Case for Education: Contemporary Approaches for Using Case Methods*, Boston, London: Allyn and Bacon, 1996.
- Gragg, C.I., 'Because wisdom can't be told', (1940) In Andrews, K. *The Case Method of Teaching Human Relations and Administration*, Cambridge, Harvard Business School Press, pp. 3–12, 1953.
- Jennings, D., Strategic Management and the Case Method. *Journal of Management Development* 15: 4–12, 1996.
- Kashani, K., 'How to analyze a case', In *Managing Global Marketing*, Boston: PWS-Kent Publishing Company, pp. 1–4, 1992.
- Romm, T. and Mahler, S., The Case Study Challenge: A New Approach to an Old Method. *Management Education and Development* 22: 292–301, 1991.

2   Some portions of the section on the 'The Basics' have appeared in my article: Kashani, K. How I Teach Cases. *International Journal of Marketing Education* 1(1): 131–146, 2005.

what transpires in class discussion. Sharing control means the instructor relinquishing some of his usual hold over the flow of discussion in the interest of engaging the students and eliciting their contribution including student-to-student exchanges. How a case teacher leads a discussion while creating and protecting an open space for student initiatives becomes critical to student learning, and their ability to gain self-confidence and develop independent judgement.

To manage this complexity, case teachers are well-advised to come to class well-prepared and to orchestrate class discussion with thoughtful lead questions. A good preparation could capture on one page session objectives and the sequence of issues to be covered from the beginning of discussion to the end with a rough allocation of time for each block. It's essential to include in the plan lead questions to direct the flow of class discussion. These questions may be open-ended and broad (for example, *'What is the problem?'*, or focused and narrow (for example, *'Is this organization ready to execute the chosen strategy?'*). Broad questions allow the instructor room to maneuver and selectively pursue those student comments that seem promising; they also let the students seize the initiative and take the discussion in the direction they find appropriate. Focused questions are best for in-depth analysis of issues. A robust teaching plan should typically combine broad and narrow lead questions around different discussion blocks.

No doubt what precedes is good advice: the 'theory' of how effective case teaching works is indeed valid. But putting the theory into practice is another matter. I have found that the complexity inherent in preparing and leading a case discussion often overwhelms most good advice. For example, consider the following everyday scenarios: my new case is untried and untested and I am about to teach it to a demanding class; I have prepared the case under immense time pressure and am going to class unsure if I have fully analyzed all the angles; my students have had a bad day before my session and come to class under-prepared and are in no mood for a 'dialectic' learning experience; my PowerPoint beamer that worked before is dead when I press the 'On' button. I could go on with more such everyday events that can frustrate any good theory of how case teaching should work.

So let me now show you how I add to the real-world difficulties of teaching cases with my own behavior—what I have referred to as my 'mistakes'. I have chosen the five most common ones knowing they are also sources of frustration for many others. After each 'mistake', I draw quick lessons that have helped me reduce their incidence in my teaching.

Mistake no. 1: *Over*-preparation

I often commit this one with a new case that I have never taught before. I prepare the document as if my life depended on it. After hours of working the case over (sometimes after days of thorough analysis and planning) I end up knowing by heart all the facts, the issues and their different angles, the entire analysis, and their conclusions. In other words, I discover everything a teacher needs to know and more. I end up with a well thought out comprehensive teaching plan that hits at every important issue that I have extricated from the case document. At the end, I *know* how to teach the case. And I can't wait till I teach it.

But in class my well-planned teaching strategy, with its dense teaching outline and well-formulated lead questions, falls flat. It fails to excite my students and my initial enthusiasm for the case doesn't rub off on them. I find myself very much in the driver's seat with my students as reluctant passengers. Each time they initiate a new direction away from my teaching plan

I bring them back to it with the conviction of someone who knows the *truth*. Soon, with no space left for them to drive the discussion or improvise, they lose interest, become bored, exchange cynical glances (which drive me nuts) and play the 'let's-feed-the-teacher-what-he-wants-to-hear' game. Before too long my own enthusiasm for the discussion goes the same direction as my students' motivation. We both take deep sighs of relief when the session is over. We survived, but barely.

LESSONS LEARNED

I have learned that my thorough preparation can backfire when the end result is an unyielding teaching plan that stifles student initiative in class discussion. I know that I have *over*-prepared when I end up with a rigidly timed discussion outline, many lead questions and lots of pointers as to what good responses might be. To avoid the mistake, I have learned to allocate open spaces in my teaching plan where I let go of the control and allow the students to lead. These *planned* open spaces are best built around provocative questions with multiple angles, where reasonable students can take on opposite sides and reasonably argue for their positions. By necessity the less important issues would have to be sacrificed to open up time for these debates. There's learning for students even when some of what they initiate doesn't bear fruits. I have also learned that a good discussion combines structure with on-the-spot improvisations. Well-chosen occasional deviations from a good teaching plan could well be the best part of a stimulating discussion.

Mistake no. 2: *Under*-preparation

This error happens when I am under time pressure and don't have the luxury of a full-blown case preparation. Furthermore, I am under the false assumption that because I have taught the case before with some success I could save time by spending a few minutes before my class reviewing the previous case notes and teaching plan.

My light preparation soon shows its limits in class. The first few lead questions that I recall from my notes generate sufficient student comments to have a good start but then the discussion begins to wander off. My teaching strategy becomes a distant memory as the students take full control and take the discussion in seemingly random directions. Here's a student who's interested in the numbers and argues that with the current prices and margins the business is probably making a loss. That comment rings a bell but I can't fully recall the actual case facts on which her numbers are based. Before I can pin her numbers down, another student suggests that the numbers are irrelevant and we must look at the broader company strategy to see if the business is viable. That seems like a good path to pursue, but then he's cut off by another student who's interested in the managerial behavior of the senior executives. He argues that these people are more interested in their own powerbase than what's right for the company. These are all good issues that should be heard, and my old teaching plan had time and space allocated to them, but I am hard pressed to recall their order and rough time allocations. My on-the-spot improvisations don't seem to be good substitutes for what I don't have—a full grasp of case facts and a clear and structured teaching plan with sufficient room for student-led content. Midway through the class I get that sinking feeling that we're spinning wheels, and that only exasperates my sense of a wasted case and class time.

LESSONS LEARNED

I have learned that even tried-and-true cases need sufficient preparation, if for no other reason, than to refresh my own memory of key facts, issues, and the shape of my teaching plan. To make the exercise less boring (re-reading one's old notes is a bore), I try to introduce innovations in the teaching plan to test out alternative structures and lead questions. For example, I may start with a vote on a course of action at the very beginning of the class whereas my old plan called for such a vote towards the end of a discussion. Such deviations from the old plan has at least two benefits: it keeps me alert as I work through an alternative discussion path leading to a revised teaching strategy; and it can actually lead to a better discussion, in which case then the innovation is incorporated in my future plans.

Mistake no. 3: Proving a 'theory'

I like simple but powerful theories. They provide easy answers to complex questions. In my days as a young teacher (students in my first MBA class were my age or older) I found theories in management a big support to my teaching. They gave me confidence that I could deal in my teaching with complicated management issues. If a market was slowing down in growth and becoming increasingly competitive, I could always rely on the theory of *Product Life Cycle* to explain this phenomenon to my students. If a manager was a 'control freak', then I would find an explanation for that behavior in McGregor's *'Theory X'* of management, and if she was a caring and empowering leader then the *'Theory Y'* would be the appropriate explanation. A company in trouble for lack of strategic focus was the victim of Porter's *'stuck-in-the-middle'* theorem of competitive strategy. These concepts were simple, powerful and, most important to me, convincing to my students.

Encouraged by positive student feedback, I went further. Not only did I find these theories useful in my teaching, I actually began to look for cases that would not only illustrate but 'prove' them. In other words I had learned so well to use a hammer that my mission became one of looking for nails to hammer in. Thus the pedagogical tools began to take on the serious role of determining my content. And that was a mistake.

As much as I like my pet theories, even the best of them fail to fully explain the complexity of the real-world management problems. Seriously, how could the world's managers be realistically divided into just two X and Y camps; or the dynamics of a maturing market, or the strategic dilemma of a company, be fully explained by, respectively, the third phase of a *Product Life Cycle* and the Porter's *Generic Strategies*? Building a whole course around such over-simplifying models (including some of my own very good ones) was my way of force-feeding the cases, and student learning, into theoretical abstractions. In doing so I fell into the habit of drawing up teaching plans that had as their endnotes the revealing of a management theory or two. The plans ignored other management issues that couldn't be easily explained by these theories, and my lead questions were, for the most part, hidden clues as to what was to come at the end. The narrow perspective surely undermined student learning by limiting their capacity for analysis independent of my pet theories.

LESSONS LEARNED

I have learned that while theories are highly popular with students, they can be over-relied on to explain the complexity of most real-life situations as described in cases. They offer students a false sense of confidence that much of management problem-solving can be reduced to picking the right theories—a wrong and dangerous conclusion. Today, I avoid building my case syllabus around an inventory of the more popular constructs; interesting and common management problems offer a much better basis for course design. And although I still introduce models and frameworks in my course I also caution the students that as abstract analytical models they tend to over-simplify management reality and that their application to the real-world problems requires good judgement and common sense. Moreover, when they liberally use their acquired theories in case analysis, I challenge them to make sure they have understood their limitations.

Mistake no. 4: Going for 'sound bytes'

Case teaching works when there's widespread student participation in the discussion. At least that's what the theory says. From that often uncontested principle can we then conclude that more student participation is always better than less? Not always, and here was my mistake. Early in my career as a case teacher I sought energizing and highly interactive classes where as many people as time permitted had a chance to contribute to the discussion. Getting everyone to take part in the debate was good for class dynamics; it felt like an accomplishment. But my class time of some 90 minutes wasn't long enough for giving everyone the chance to fully contribute their analysis on important issues. That time limitation meant that everyone who contributed had only a fraction of a minute to make their point. By necessity these 'sound bytes' only scraped the surface of the case and, lacking the backup of a thorough analysis, were increasingly perceived by the students themselves as unsubstantiated opinions. Before long my class had concluded that rigorous case analysis was an overkill when one's output in class discussion was limited to a 30-second comment. From there followed a significant drop in case preparation leading to the vicious cycle of shallow analysis leading to superficial learning and ending up with a deteriorating motivation for case-based learning. My eagerness for a widespread student involvement had led to this counter-intuitive outcome. The blame was squarely on me.

LESSON LEARNED

Over time I have come to appreciate the value of mixing long and short comments during class discussion. Some contributions are best when they are short and provocative. For example, when a student contests a colleague's conclusion with reference to a specific case fact, that contribution doesn't have to take long for its impact to be felt. The point is factual and, as such, effective. On the other hand, when another student tries to develop a coherent line of reasoning why a given course of action isn't necessarily the best way forward, she may need to pull into her argument strands of analysis and fact-based judgement, all taking a good part of class time. Here, that long contribution, with its requisite questions and follow-on questions from the teacher or other students, is time well spent. I have found that long comments are best when delving deep into the key case questions. The short comments come later when, for example, differing perspectives on the issues are being compared and contrasted.

Occasionally I challenge a short but shallow comment and give its author sufficient airtime to come up with the missing facts or analysis. As disagreeable as the experience is for everyone, such a challenge sends a strong signal that with class participation comes the responsibility to be well prepared for follow-on questions or challenges. Needless to say combining short and long comments in a class discussion has a cost: not everyone who wishes to contribute gets a chance to do so. But experience shows that the benefits of better student preparation and more in-depth class contribution far outweigh the cost.

Mistake no. 5: Questions with right-wrong answers

Good discussion questions are the foundations of good case teaching. By good questions I mean those that provoke the students to think beyond a superficial analysis of case issues. Well-chosen lead questions allow the students to take different positions and for the class to hear different answers reflecting alternative perspectives on the same issue. That there are different perceived 'truths', following from different interpretations of the same facts and figures, is a valuable learning in its own right. The students thus learn to view a complex management problem from multiple angles before making up their own minds and committing themselves to a decision.

But not all questions are good lead questions. In earlier times I would choose to ask questions to which there were right or wrong answers: Did Joe correctly calculate the break-even point? (The right answer I was looking for: *No, he didn't and here's why.*) Was the market growing fast enough to meet target sales levels? (Right answer: *Exhibit 5 shows the growth rate for this market is sufficient for meeting the targets.*) And was Mary right insisting on introducing the new product? (Of course not: *Mary had dismissed important research data in the Appendix that showed negative consumer feedback on the features and functionality of the new product.*) Ironically, I would fall back on close-ended questions when I found the class less than prepared to deal with the complexity of a case. I would try to survive this unpalatable scenario with questions to which I knew the answers.

One of the unintended outcomes of such a line of close-ended questioning is the student's growing impression that there's a right or wrong answer to most managerial questions—and that the teacher knows best which is what. Both dead wrong conclusions. Questions with 'correct' answers rarely confront the students with managerial dilemmas; nor do they lead to insightful debates when all one has to do is to refer to the right page or a calculation for the answer. Worst, they deprive the students from developing the mental skills needed to form their own independent judgement in the face of uncertainty—the context for most managerial decision-making.

LESSON LEARNED

While I felt good about my own knowledge of what was right or wrong in the questions I asked, I began to realize that the center of gravity in my classes was around me and not the students. They began to look up to me as the ultimate source of knowledge and the arbiter of correct answers. This was good for my young and fragile ego but I was not helping my students to develop their own independent judgement as future managers and business leaders. And that was a mistake.

So what did I learn? I learned that while some close-ended, right-or-wrong questions could pepper a discussion (where the right answers are already provided by the data in the case or can be derived from them), the more thought provoking ones are those where reasonable analysis could lead to different but still defensible conclusions. I have also learned that good open-ended questions are those which I have myself wrestled with because they don't lend themselves to easy answers. While the easy answer to the question, 'Was Mary right insisting on introducing the new product?' is a negative one, there are no easy answers to the more profound question, 'What motivated her to dismiss the consumer data that so clearly showed the new product's shortcomings?' This latter question could've been one that I might have myself struggled with during my own case preparation. It is thus in delving into the complex mind of Mary and her personal and business motivations that the students begin to see the complexity of a manager's decision-making process and, in that, the potential traps of irrational behavior. There are no easy answers here, but questions around Mary's inscrutable motives offer opportunities for rich student learning.

Mastering case teaching

Let me end this chapter with a brief story. Recently I received a long note of apology from a dear colleague and a star case teacher who had just taught a session in an educational program I was responsible for. The reason for the apology was that his brilliant teaching strategy, a complicated plan involving a couple of cases plus extensive role plays, had fallen flat on its face. Belatedly, he could see what had gone wrong and what he should have done to rescue his class. He wrote that he had committed some basic mistakes exacerbated by poor time management. The star teacher was extremely unhappy with his own performance.

What makes this self criticism noteworthy is that it comes from a person who's been teaching cases for more than 40 years and who is recognized internationally as an authority in the craft of case teaching. Yet, in this recent episode, the master was his own harshest critic, not running away from his poor teaching or ignoring the lessons he learned from it. He was honest with himself, his colleagues, and his students.

This story raises an interesting question: Could it be that what sets the master case teachers apart isn't so much their many successes but their honest self-appraisal and their keen ability to learn from their mistakes? That, I think, is a question worth pondering.

4 The Challenge of Teaching 'Soft' Subjects to MBAs: How Using Mini-Cases Can Help

Pierre Dussauge

No matter how weathered they are and how successful they have been previously, most business school faculty feel a twinge of anxiety – not to mention a rush of adrenalin – as they walk into an MBA class. Indeed, MBAs have the reputation of being difficult students to teach: they usually have significantly more management experience than the instructor and they are paying a high tuition fee. Thus, they have strong opinions about the instruction they are receiving and feel quite legitimate about expressing how good or bad they think a course – or an instructor – is. Within many business schools, a faculty's reputation as an effective instructor is won or lost on how well he or she does when teaching MBAs. This, in turn, will often determine a faculty's opportunities to partake in executive education programs, which clearly can have non-trivial financial implications.

While faculty teaching highly technical – and often also quantitative – subjects such as accounting, finance, statistics or operations management may not generate a great deal of enthusiasm in their students, they are usually respected because of the perceived competence gap between instructor and student: MBAs may not enjoy their statistics course very much, but most of them cannot easily claim to know the subject well and they anticipate that if they do not put in a fair amount of effort they are likely to flunk the course.

'Softer' courses such as organizational behavior, human resource management, strategic management, marketing strategy, and so on do not have the benefit of creating such a perceived 'competence gap' in MBA students. Many MBA students, notably those that have worked in consulting for a few years before enrolling in an MBA program, feel they already know a lot about strategy, for example. Many will also feel that managing people or adequately positioning a brand is primarily a matter of common sense. When the corresponding courses fail to provide them with detailed techniques on how to design a fail-proof strategy, set up an optimal organization structure or efficiently manage people, they feel they are wasting their time, that the course is not worth their tuition money and that, overall, the instructor is contributing very little to their future professional development and success. Indeed, I have repeatedly overheard MBA students refer to their OB, HR or strategic management course as a 'hot air' experience.

Having suffered myself from such a syndrome, I have found that tackling the problem requires first understanding why teaching soft subjects can be such a challenge and then finding ways to overcome the typical MBA student's initial skepticism about why such courses might indeed be useful to their future careers. My personal experience has been that using mini-cases has worked very well for me to achieve this.

In this chapter, I will try to first expose the multiple reasons for which MBA students are not very receptive to soft subjects. I will then suggest some of the things that need to be accomplished in order to overcome the problem. Finally, I will discuss how the case method is a useful tool to achieve this and will argue that mini-cases can sometimes be even more effective in demonstrating that soft subjects provide skills and capabilities that often prove at least as useful to managers all through their career as do harder subjects.

What are 'soft' subjects and why are they so hard to teach?

Most management disciplines are not exact sciences. Indeed, management issues rarely call for an indisputably 'right' or 'wrong' answer. While some 'hard' management courses, such as accounting, finance or statistics, might provide students with the 'right' way of addressing a problem and arriving at a 'correct' answer, most other subjects provide them with perspectives through which to look at a complex issue and, at best, frameworks that will guide their thought process when tackling difficult problems and making tough decisions. For example, provided with assumptions about discount rates and cash flows that will be generated over the years, it is possible to calculate the Net Present Value (NPV) of an investment. There is thus a 'correct' answer to the exercise and students can be shown to have been either right or wrong in their analysis. In contrast, in a strategy class, when examining whether a firm should or should not enter a new business area, there is no way to determine with certainty what the 'right' answer is. In my view, this is what distinguishes 'hard' subjects from 'soft' subjects. I realize, of course, that this soft/hard distinction is somewhat fuzzy, and even artificial. In the NPV example mentioned above, the calculation may be technical and precise but the assumptions on which the calculations are based are not: they are highly subjective and debatable. Nevertheless, the technicality of how to calculate NPV is enough to impress most MBAs and they will perceive finance, accounting or statistics as 'hard' and thus potentially valuable to them, despite the softer – and probably more interesting – aspects of these topics. So 'hard' vs. 'soft' has less to do with the objective nature of each topic than it does with the perception MBAs – and others – have of any particular discipline.

While it does not offer a method to arrive at a right answer, what a course on a soft subject can provide is a set of issues that need to be examined in order to guide the decision. In the above-mentioned example of a firm considering diversification, some of the questions that need to be raised are: How similar is the new business to the firm's existing activities? Will the new business take advantage of the firm's existing assets and strengths? The instructor can also point to empirical evidence suggesting that diversification leads to failure more often than it does to success, especially when the firm's targeted new business is only loosely related to its current activities. However, at the end of the day, the decision to diversify or not diversify is a judgement call. At the closure of the class, there is no way to decide whether those students recommending that the firm diversify, or those favoring the opposite, are right or wrong. The instructor can always point to all the factors that were brought up in class that can help illuminate the decision, but students are nonetheless left in doubt. This tends to be very frustrating and leads to a feeling of 'we learned nothing in this class' and 'my initial intuition was as good as all the fuzzy theories put forth by the professor'.

Obviously, this is almost inevitably going to create a difficult teaching context. If an instructor can provide no clear answers to the issues at hand, his or her legitimacy is called into question. Students with a lot of business experience will feel they know more about the issue than the instructor does, will call on their experience to challenge her/his conclusions, and the feeling most students will have developed at the end of the course is that the entire subject is of little use, that they have learnt nothing valuable for their future careers and that this is one more of the 'hot air' courses that plague business school curricula.

Most faculty, with the notable exception of one or two star teachers, will have a hard time teaching such soft subjects, in particular junior faculty who are less experienced at handling a large group of MBA students. And those star teachers who do succeed at teaching these soft subjects are both envied and despised by their colleagues who claim, behind their backs, that what makes them so popular is that they butter up to their students, that they relax the academic standards on which students are to be evaluated and graded, and that they do not cover the material, but instead perform (this is often referred to as 'belly dancing') in order to entertain the students, oblivious to all the serious and important material these students are supposed to be learning.

My experience teaching strategic management, which definitely falls into the 'soft' subject category and often disappoints MBA students who walk in with high expectations only to realize that the course will not teach them how to think up fail-proof strategies, is that there are a few simple techniques that can help dispel the general student feeling that a soft course is inevitably useless.

How can the legitimacy of 'soft' subjects be established?

The key to making soft subjects appealing to MBA students is to be able to credibly demonstrate that more than common sense is needed in appropriately approaching the issues being discussed and that the concepts presented in the course are indeed useful. In that regard, nothing proves quite as convincing as letting students err when they are left to their own devices, and then show how the use of even simple, seemingly obvious concepts or frameworks, would have made them arrive at significantly different conclusions. Through this process, students will come to recognize the usefulness and value of ideas that, if exposed in a straightforward way, might appear to be trivial.

Of course, raising an issue and creating a context in which most students relying on common sense and/or on their intuition will make a 'mistake' that demonstrates the value of the concepts and theories being presented in the course is not easy. It requires a careful crafting of the issue or question students will be asked to address. And this is where, as I will discuss further along, cases and, above all, mini-cases can be particularly useful.

Along the way, however, this 'trial and error' process can focus on exposing some of the basic fallacies that MBAs relying primarily on intuition and common sense are likely to fall for as they try to address the issue that has been presented to them. Indeed, three fallacies are extremely widespread in the MBA classroom when discussing management issues: substituting analysis with analogies, developing tautological arguments and indulging in wishful thinking.

ANALOGIES

Students often jump to conclusions by observing similarities between the issue which they are being asked to analyze in class and situations they have encountered previously – be it in their professional experience, in other courses or from any other source – and for which they know the actual outcome. They assume that, because of these identified analogies, the same implicit causalities will hold and, hence, the same triggers will produce the same results. However, students often fail to explicitly lay out the chain of causalities leading up to the outcome they predict and may thus arrive at wrong, or at least highly questionable, conclusions. If instructors can frame an issue that invites such misleading analogies and convincingly demonstrate that, by relying on some key frameworks presented in the course, it is possible to explicit the causal relationships at work and thus arrive at a sounder and better supported conclusion, he or she will have gone a long way to proving the value of the concepts presented and discussed in the seemingly 'soft' course he or she is teaching. It will establish the fact that students' initial intuition, their gut feeling, is not enough to 'get it right' and that what they are learning in the course is indeed useful.

TAUTOLOGIES

Another, complementary way to dispel the 'we already knew this' feeling that plagues 'soft' courses is to expose the tautologies that often underpin a lot of the comments put forth by MBAs and offer instead a somewhat deeper understanding of the causal relationships being examined by relying on clearly defined conceptual models. Indeed, when MBAs – and others – are asked to explain, for example, why a particular firm is successful they will often be tempted to emphasize factors that describe success rather than actually explain it: they will often argue that firm 'X' is successful because it has an effective business model or a great strategy. Such a statement explains very little; having a good business model or a great strategy, by definition, is associated with success; what makes a business model or a strategy 'good' is that the firm using it is successful. If it were not, the business model or the strategy would be considered 'bad'. A slightly different version of such statements explaining very little is to attribute success to 'great products or services at low costs'; this is a self-evident truth, and therefore a trivial comment, in the sense that the opposite statement would obviously be absurd: if firm 'X' produced 'bad products at a high cost', it would be very unlikely to be successful, no matter what measure of success were chosen. Exposing such tautological or trivial statements and demonstrating how a more structured approach using concepts from the course can help reach a deeper and more meaningful understanding of the issue being examined is a potentially useful way of dispelling some of the misconceptions students may have about 'soft' courses.

WISHFUL THINKING

When the issues being discussed deal with future actions rather than with the analysis of a past or current situation, tautological statements tend to give way to 'wishful thinking': for example, 'Firm 'X' should introduce better products or services and produce them at lower costs; then its performance will improve.' Once again, exposing such statements as trivial and demonstrating that a more structured approach based on conceptual ideas discussed in the course can provide a deeper understanding of the issues at hand, highlight the crucial trade-offs that need to be made, and can thus usefully guide the formulation of more sensible recommendations, should help establish the value of the course topic, despite it being of a 'soft' nature.

Overall, while 'hard' courses can rely on the technical complexity of the subject to earn the respect, or at least the attention, of MBA students, I am convinced that softer courses need to establish their credibility by demonstrating that relying on intuition, gut feelings or common sense will, at best, lead to superficial and trivial analyses and, more likely, to erroneous conclusions. It is only by exposing the mistakes students make when they lack or ignore the conceptual apparatus underpinning a soft course that the value of that apparatus will become evident and the legitimacy of the course be established. In order to achieve this, the instructor must frame a question or an issue in such a way that most students will indeed rush toward the expected 'wrong' answer without, however, giving students the impression that they have been deliberately 'framed' or manipulated. This is not easy to accomplish and the case method can sometimes be an appropriate means to do so. I will argue, however, that mini-cases may be an even more effective way of achieving the goal outlined above.

How using cases can help

One of the reasons why the case method has been used so extensively in business education is probably that many business disciplines fall into what I have defined above as 'soft' topics. Indeed, those courses that heavily rely on cases are courses that are on the softer side; more technical courses like statistics, finance or economics tend to use cases much less, and rely instead on lectures and exercises. I will not discuss here the general merits and dangers of the case method, referring interested readers to other more relevant chapters in this book (notably Chapter 3 by Kamran Kashani) or to the numerous books and articles that are available on the subject (see among others: Barnes, Christensen and Hansen 1994; Cohen 1974; Ellet 2007). Instead, I will try to show that the case method makes it possible, at least to some extent, to overcome some of the difficulties of teaching 'soft' topics, but that it is by no means a miracle solution.

Who could imagine lecturing for 2 hours in a row, twice a week and for 25 weeks (that is, one semester) on an introductory Marketing, Strategy or Human Resource Management course? Most of the concepts that are to be presented (in Marketing, for example, it would be notions such as 'understanding the customer', 'segmenting the market' or 'making sure products meet customer needs'; in Strategy notions such as 'defining the business', 'analyzing the industry' or 'creating competitive advantage' would form the core of such a course) appear to be self-evident truths and most MBAs will feel they are learning very little from such lectures. Never mind the fact that most managers fail to actually use these notions in their jobs, let alone act according to these basic – but essential – principles! When presented in a straightforward fashion, they appear to be so mundane that no one will pay attention and acknowledge they are getting any value out of the course. What cases do provide is the undisputable evidence that, in real life, applying these principles is far more difficult than would appear.

By describing a business situation in a fair amount of detail, a case provides a setting in which to go beyond merely presenting a set of concepts pertaining to a given management discipline (such as the ones listed above) and stating their usefulness to address determined issues. By analyzing and discussing a case, students must try to apply those concepts in a context that is as close as possible to reality and, hopefully, come to realize that applying even simple notions is not as easy as they had initially thought. The case method is therefore a very useful tool to establish the fact that there is more to many management concepts and frameworks than what their apparent simplicity might suggest.

However, establishing the fact that applying even a very simple concept to a real business situation can be a difficult task requiring more insight and judgement than students initially thought is one thing. It is in fact quite different from creating a perception in these same students that there is a lot of value in the considered concept or framework. Actually, the end result may be exactly the opposite! Indeed, by presenting a complex business situation in a lot of detail, cases also tend to make things fuzzy and ambiguous – which actually helps to establish the fact that applying the concepts or notions from the course is not straightforward – but does not necessarily make the concepts credible and valuable. The very complexity of the issues at hand makes it virtually impossible to arrive at an indisputably 'right' answer; instead, the ambiguity produced by the richness of the information in the case – which is needed to represent reality in an accurate way – implies that it takes good judgement to 'get it right' and, worse still, that the idea of a 'right' or 'wrong' answer is highly subjective. This in turn often leads students to conclude that if the notions studied in the course don't provide access to the 'right' answer, the concepts and methods advocated by the instructor are useless and getting it right is in fact fundamentally a judgement call. This then confirms their feeling that intuition is just as useful, if not more so, then a more structured approach. In that sense, the very advantages of the case method can easily backfire when it comes to establishing the credibility of 'soft' topics.

Revealing how difficult it is to properly address a management issue is different from establishing that the material being exposed in the course is useful in adequately tackling the issue. For example, defining a firm's businesses (what in Strategy is known as 'strategic segmentation') is a conceptually simple idea: when a firm operates in different businesses, each business needs to be considered separately in order to formulate a specific strategy for the firm in each of its businesses; indeed, it would make no sense at all for a firm like Mars to implement the exact same strategy in its candy bar business (Bounty, Snickers, Mars bars, and so on), in its pet food business (Pal, Pedigree, Whiskas, and so on) and in its rice business (Uncle Ben's). Actually coming up with an adequate segmentation of Mars' overall business is much more complex than it looks: should dog food and cat food be lumped together or considered separately? Should ice-cream-based candy bars be included in the overall candy business or should a 'frozen foods' business be identified? Segmentation methods would suggest examining technological factors (do several product lines rely on the same broad technologies? If so, they might pertain to the same broad business line), customers being served, functionalities being provided, groups of competitors, and so on. At the end of the day, however, deciding on a segmentation of a firm's business is a very subjective matter. All the methods discussed in class that may help approach the issue can by no means provide a final and definite answer. This makes the whole topic very frustrating for students and a very hard one for instructors to successfully teach. In that sense, making the complexity and difficulty of the topic obvious to students is only a first step on the way to establishing the legitimacy of a course covering such topics. What is still lacking is the 'trial and error' factor discussed above, complemented by the realization by the students that use of the concepts from the course will notably improve their ability to successfully tackle the issue. Successfully establishing the legitimacy of soft courses requires that students undoubtedly feel better equipped to address a given issue at the end of each class than they did at the beginning, that they come to realize that they have acquired some knowledge that will improve their abilities as managers, that they have become more savvy, more 'intelligent', what others in this book have called the 'aha' factor (see Chapter 8).

Unfortunately, most cases tend to be primarily descriptive and, even if the issue they raise is a complex one, concepts from the course add very little to the intuitive understanding students get from simply reading the case: all too often, in such descriptive cases, these concepts help 'designate' the issue at hand, give it a name, more than they provide means to resolve it. While seasoned case instructors can get away with a situation like this, more inexperienced faculty will have a very hard time, giving students the impression that they are 'rambling on' about the case and about the concepts they believe apply to it, but without arriving at any clear conclusion and without being able to provide a deeper understanding of the issue at hand and hence closure to the discussion.

Obviously, the choice of cases is critical. Not all cases – actually only very few – frame an issue in a way that will drive most students to make mistakes if they choose to rely primarily on their intuition and overlook the key concepts from the course. Identifying 'good' cases is a very difficult and time-consuming task. What instructors of soft courses should be looking for are cases that, read and examined without a structured approach in mind, will suggest answers that a different approach, explicitly drawing on concepts and models from the course, will radically reverse. In other words, a 'good' case is one where the instructor can steer the discussion in such a way that students leave class with a significantly different understanding of the issue than the one they had when entering the class. In addition, this transformation should be the result of applying some conceptual models from the course. I can think of several such cases I have used over the years; they are, however, only a very small percentage of all the cases I have examined and considered using. One of the reasons why so few cases fit the requirements outlined above is the fact that they often try to cover too much ground, address too many issues and provide too much information, without raising any one particular issue for which the use of a clear conceptual approach will drastically change most students' understanding. This is why the use of a mini-case can often be a better way to demonstrate the value of a particular, seemingly obvious concept, model or approach, and hence can help establish the credibility of a soft course.

What exactly are mini-cases? and how can they help even more?

I define a mini-case as a one to two page description of a business situation, often complemented with a limited set of appendices providing quantitative information on the described situation. Many mini-cases are drastically condensed versions of more traditional pre-existing cases. Some mini-cases can be written in that format right from the start and, occasionally, short articles from the business press can be used successfully as mini-cases. Because it is so condensed, a mini-case focuses on one single issue. It must, however, provide all the information – both qualitative and quantitative – needed to be able to satisfactorily address the considered issue by using the frameworks or concepts from the course that it is meant to legitimize.

As all good cases, a mini-case should only contain purely descriptive information; any analysis of the issue it focuses on should be left out of the case itself, be included in a teaching note and be the main topic of the discussion in class. Ideally, a mini-case should drive a somewhat superficial reader toward conclusions that a more structured analysis, based on the data provided in the case itself or in the appendices, will eventually contradict. In that sense, a good mini-case is somewhat like a Sherlock Holmes story: all the information on the murder is provided at the onset; Dr Watson invariably accuses an innocent character of the crime being investigated by jumping to conclusions based on intuition and poor logic; and finally, Sherlock Holmes identifies the murderer by connecting all the available data in a logical way, clearing all the innocent suspects and exposing the culprit. In a similar way, a superficial reading of the information in a mini-case should point in one direction while a more structured approach, using some clearly identified concepts from the course, should lead to a significantly different conclusion.

One such example of what I consider a good mini-case presents the situation of a company whose financial performance is very strong. Quotes in the case from various managers of the company suggest how great this company is, how excellent their products are and what a wonderful job they are doing. The case also provides financial data on the company itself, on its main competitors and on industry averages. When asked to evaluate and explain the firm's performance, most MBAs will repeat the arguments in the case and praise the management for its excellent performance. A somewhat closer look at the data actually reveals that, while the firm's performance may be very good in absolute terms, its performance relative to its main competitors and, more generally, relative to the industry average is in fact quite disappointing. What is the moral of the story? That industry features, more than the company's choices, behaviour and strategy explain its apparently satisfactory performance. And that in fact, aside from being in a 'good' industry, the firm has not done anything worth much praise and that the management should be fired rather than commended, as most students were suggesting at the beginning of the discussion. More generally, it shows that a very simple idea in strategy, that firm performance is driven by both industry features and firm strategy, is important to keep in mind when trying to explain the performance of any company. While a lecture on how industry matters to firm performance would come across as trivial, the 'trial and error' process made possible by the use of a mini-case makes this very simple notion a lot more interesting and valuable to an MBA audience.

In a normal (that is, 'big') case, arriving at the 'right' answer (when there is such a thing) is often a function of stumbling upon the precious little piece of data that was lost in the vast amount of information provided, but which explains it all. Students then tend to feel that they did not get it right, not because their analysis was flawed or because they were not using the right analytical framework, but because they were unlucky not to bump into that important piece of information. What makes mini-cases such a powerful tool to establish the credibility of a 'soft' course is the fact that the available data is very limited; all students have this data under their nose and therefore arriving at a sound conclusion is a matter of using the right conceptual model or framework. In addition, a frequent problem with 'big' cases is that not all students prepare – or even read – them; and even if they all do, the levels of preparation tend to be very different. In contrast, a mini-case need not be prepared in advance; it is so short that it can be read on the spot, during class, thus ensuring that all present have the same level of preparation. The difference in the quality of comments then has more to do with the individual skills of each student and with their understanding and use of appropriate conceptual frameworks. This then demonstrates that the concepts and ideas being discussed in the course are instrumental in shaping the way in which students use the available data to logically build an argument and arrive at meaningful conclusions.

I believe mini-cases also have significant virtues in forcing instructors to clarify what their own teaching objectives are. When using a 'big' case, there usually is so much information available, so many issues that are raised and so many possible avenues for discussion that it is easy for instructors to step into class without being very sure where exactly they are headed. The belief is that student comments will take the class in one direction or another and that the instructor will always find a way to bring up some additional points and wrap up the discussion with a more general closing argument. There is a risk, however, that such a discussion will go nowhere in particular, that it will skip from one topic to the next and that the lessons to be learnt will be lost on most students. With a mini-case, this is not possible. If the instructor does not know very precisely where to take the discussion, it will go nowhere and there will be nothing more to add after just a few minutes – a very uncomfortable situation for an instructor in front of a large class! So when teaching a session with a mini-case, an instructor will need to have a much clearer idea of where he or she is headed, what the points to be made are, and where the discussion should arrive at in order to draw the more conceptual lessons from the whole session. As a result, students usually have a much clearer understanding of what they are to take away from the discussion with a mini-case than they do with a full 'big' case.

Interestingly, I have found that developing and teaching a 'mini' version of an existing large case has helped me improve my teaching of the full version of that same case. It has given me a more precise idea of where I can successfully take the discussion and of the key learning points I can make when wrapping up the discussion.

Obviously, I am not suggesting that 'soft' courses should be taught exclusively with mini-cases. Rather, I believe that a combination of full and mini-cases, and possibly a few lectures, can provide the best learning experience. The mini-cases will demonstrate the value of some key, but seemingly simple notions or concepts; they will, however, also give an over-simplified view of reality by over-emphasizing one issue or set of issues and sweep aside many other relevant questions that would need to be addressed in a real life situation. The full cases will highlight the difficulties of implementing even simple concepts and frameworks and provide a better depiction of the complexities and intricacies of real life management situations; on the other hand, they will leave more room for intuition and judgement. Finally, lectures on 'soft' topics tend to be uninteresting and boring but, if kept short and far enough apart, they can help put the various aspects of a course into perspective and provide a more integrated view of the topic being covered.

Conclusion: A few tips on successfully using mini-cases in 'soft' courses

As a conclusion to this chapter on how mini-cases can be used to enhance the perception that students have of 'soft' courses, I would like to offer some suggestions on how to successfully include such mini-cases in the overall course design and make the best use of them. Indeed, while I strongly believe mini-cases are a useful tool and a nice alternative to other teaching methods, in particular to traditional full cases and to lectures, I am by no means advocating that a course should rely exclusively on mini-cases. Quite the opposite, my experience suggests that mini-cases are most effective when included as complements to other teaching methods and tools. In order to maximize their effectiveness, I would recommend paying particular attention to the following points regarding both the design of the course and the in-class teaching experience:

1. **Schedule mini-cases very carefully**
   Mini-cases should not be included at random in the syllabus. On the contrary, that they arrive at the right moment in the flow of the course is absolutely critical. Because they require no preparation, scheduling them after a session in which a particularly long or difficult 'full' case was discussed is a way to let students recover and give them a little 'breathing space'. Also, mini-cases may be appropriate after a mid-term exam or at a moment when students have a lot of work for other courses. Lastly, I tend to always use a mini-case for the introductory session of a course: having students prepare a full case tends to fail because not all students are aware of what needs to be done, some haven't gotten their course pack yet and the standards in terms of preparation and expectations have not yet been set. A mini-case, in contrast, gets handed out in class so everyone gets it, it is to be read on the spot so dodging is almost impossible and instructions can be delivered as needed during the process. In short, mini-cases are best scheduled when you expect preparation levels to be less than adequate with other teaching methods.

2. **Make sure the teaching objectives being pursued with the considered mini-case are very clear**

   When using a mini-case, it is critical instructors know exactly where they want to steer the discussion. This should include both the paradox or non-trivial outcome that the mini-case was designed to highlight and the conceptual lesson that will be drawn from the discussion. Indeed, while a full case usually offers many alternative avenues to explore and it is possible to let the class discussion go in one direction or in another, a mini-case offers fewer options; lack of a clear sense of direction from the instructor will almost invariably end up in a hollow and purposeless discussion. It can be useful to draft up in advance the sequence of questions that the instructor will raise to make sure the case discussion progresses in the right direction and arrives at the desired conclusion.

3. **Emphasize key learning points**

   In my opinion, it is always a good idea to stress the key learning points after any case discussion or session. It is even more critical when using a mini-case because ambiguity and lack of closure is incompatible with the very focused nature of the issues that are dealt with when using such a teaching tool.

4. **Manage time adequately**

   Many instructors assume that the time needed to adequately discuss a mini-case is proportional to the length of the document compared to that of what they see as a 'normal' case. It is not so. Indeed, I have often taught both the full version and the mini version of the same case and have found that the time needed for each is not significantly different. Indeed, mini-cases often need to be discussed for as long as a full case in order to arrive at the desired conclusion. Because that conclusion to reach is clearer and there should be no ambiguity in what it is in the mind of the students, a superficial discussion will not do the job. So instructors must leave enough time for a thorough discussion and analysis of the issue. Mini-cases require considerably less preparation time on the part of the students, not less time for in-class discussion.

5. **Consider using mini-cases for exams**

   Mini-cases can also be used quite effectively as exams. Indeed, contrary to full cases which are often used as exams for 'soft' courses, mini-cases do not require that the time allocated to an exam include several hours for simply reading the case. They are also much faster and easier to grade than large cases where knowing what to look for in the student responses tends to be fuzzier and the amount of grader subjectivity is often much greater. And, on the other hand, they avoid the over-simplistic nature of a multiple choice questions-based exam which tends to be the preferred choice when grading is to be made easy.

References

Barnes, L.B., Christensen, C.R. and Hansen, A.J., *Teaching and the Case Method (3rd edition)*. Boston, MA: Harvard Business School Press, 1994.

Cohen, P., *The Gospel According to the Harvard Business School*. Harmondsworth: Penguin, 1974.

Ellet, W., *The Case Study Handbook*. Boston, MA: Harvard Business School Press, 2007.

5 Team Teaching

Pedro Parada and Josep Franch

Team Teaching is potentially one of the most rewarding experiences for a scholar. A faculty member learns and gets new insights from the views provided by a team teacher from a different field. They often engage in multidisciplinary research projects. Participants enjoy complementary views and teaching styles and have the chance to experience more diverse learning methodologies. Deans and department directors see how intra- and inter-departmental collegiality improves when faculty 'team teach'. Even programme managers notice how redundancies in content between courses tend to diminish. Building on our experience, we discuss in this chapter when faculty should seriously consider team teaching; we identify different varieties of team teaching; we propose complementary and dividing roles as two basic dimensions for successful team teaching and suggest practical ways to manage team teaching.

To team teach or not to team teach

Team teaching is a topic that is hard to tackle in most business schools and there are those who consider it to be a waste of resources. This is often reflected in the allocation of workload and reward systems. It is not unusual to find some business schools where the total amount of hours in class are split between the faculty who team teach, ignoring the fact that it is more difficult. Some even see a potential danger in having two faculty members working together too closely. Since faculty tend to have big 'egos', putting two of them together for a long period of time has the potential for creating clashes.

Advocates of team teaching argue that there is a lot of value added to the learning process through the real-time interplay of two faculty members working together. Faculty who have a positive experience of the technique argue that some of the best relationships they have struck up with colleagues stem from jointly dealing with students. Some of the most stirring tales of achievement in business schools come from joint in-classroom experiences.

For example, two faculty members decided to step into a classroom to substitute for a colleague who could not turn up to teach. Other teachers scrapped what they had in mind for an in-company training programme after the initial conversation to set expectations with participants revealed the potential to take a very different avenue. Some faculty jointly managed different 'groups' deeply rooted in organisational or national culture inside the classroom, managing conflict in the process. Some even dreamt up a 'wizard' who would answer all participants' questions. Of course the wizard never showed up but participants discovered the wizard in themselves (Husenman and Planellas 1999).

The potential benefits of properly conducted team teaching include: multiple viewpoints for learning; the creation of knowledge and learning synergies in the classroom; fostering creative thinking and allowing participants to explore alternative positions (Helms et al. 2005). Students are able to look at the interlinked nature of the various fields in business management and thus gain a holistic view of the discipline.

Furthermore, greater use of team teaching might help cut out the redundancies in delivering content to participants, thus limiting the so-called 'silo effect' (that is, lack of communication) that arises from repetition of content in business programmes (Helms et al. 2005). Indeed, Nixon, Helms and Pickthorne Fletcher (1997) report an experience where there was considerable duplication of topics in an MBA curriculum. Team teaching was used to pinpoint the topics and help in redesigning the programme. The streamlined course curriculum led to growth in the number of electives offered, thus enhancing value to students through greater opportunities for specialisation.

There is also a major benefit in 'combining a mix of teaching skills and styles' (Helms et al. 2005). Faculty have diverse sets of tools such as multimedia, computer applications, data, cases and examples at their disposition. The wide variety of learning tools arising from team teaching caters better to the wide range of participants' learning and presentation preferences. Furthermore, joint scrutiny reduces the likelihood of commiting sins of omission or commision in preparation, teaching or evaluation (Durcan and Kirkbride 1987). In the light of our generally positive experience of team teaching, we develop the basic ideas that have proven most useful for us and which we believe will benefit others.

What is team teaching?

Team teaching, also known as Shared Teaching, Co-Teaching or Collaborative Teaching (Booth, Dixon-Brown and Kohut 2003), is used in a wide variety of settings. A basic definition is, 'A process in which at least two instructors are responsible for teaching and are present in classroom' (Hatcher and Hinton 1996). However, the concept of team teaching has been used in a wide variety of settings as Table 5.1 shows. Some scholars use the term to refer to squads of faculty teaching different sections of the same course. The simplest variety is having one faculty member who develops the syllabus, schedules the team's rotation, and organises and manages testing, grading and evaluation (Helms, Alvis and Willis 2005). The instructor might also teach the basic concepts and then rely on academic collaborators to guide students through practical applications or exercises. Furthermore, they might teach one or more of the course sections and coordinate other colleagues. In this case, the role is more of a coordinator and the others deliver the content.

Some schools teach core curriculum courses at the same time across different sections, ranging from two to nine sections depending on the size of the programme, with one faculty responsible for each section. This way of team teaching requires flexibility in order to adapt the content and ensure homogeneity across sections. However, the activity of teaching itself is not that challenging. In the end, each faculty member can do their own thing with regard to content and delivery, providing they do not overstep certain bounds. Faculty retain academic freedom and adapt the course to emphasise their own area of expertise and interests (Booth et al. 2003).

Team teaching is also used for courses involving many faculty members from different departments or fields teaching where each one covers a part of the course. This is a popular trend in business schools – as noted by Helms, Alvis and Willis (2005). Usually faculty are selected depending on their content contributions and in some cases on their teaching styles and how they might engage the audience. This approach has been referred to as the Rotational

Table 5.1   Models of team teaching

Source: The authors

Team Teaching Model	Faculty Responsibilities	Teaching Requirements
Squads	Coordination or Delivery	Experience or Teaching Abilities
Parallel	Full Individually with Some Content	Some Degree of Individual Adaptation
Rotational	Full (1), Different Area of Knowledge (2)	Provide Coordinated Unique Content
Colloquium	Full (1), Different Area of Knowledge (2)	Provide Unique Content 'At Will'
Discussant	Full (1), Build Debate (2)	Active Listening
Coaching	Full (1), Feedback on Teaching Content and Process (2)	Ex-Post Meetings
Interactive	Full for Both Faculty	Lively Interactive Dialogue and Debate; Adaptation and Flexibility

(1)   Discussion Leader; (2)   Team Teacher

Model of team teaching (Nead 1995; White, Henley and Brabston 1998). Again, complexity is limited to coordination for ensuring the various sessions are properly linked, and to scheduling faculty members, selecting faculty and briefing them to avoid overlaps or gaps in the course. However, what happens within a session is up to a single faculty member, who decides on content and process, and runs the activities.

In some other cases, several faculty members provide multiple views of a topic in a colloquium-type of session. One topic is usually analysed and discussed from various perspectives in front of students. This might be considered an even simpler setting since everyone tells their story without much need for coordination at all. For participants it is an exercise in listening to different views.

In between, there is the discussion format for team teaching (Lindauer 1990). In this view, faculty interaction of the team teacher is formalised by earmarking time at the end of the session to either build upon what the discussion leader said or to disagree with their views. It is argued that the main advantages of this intermediate approach are that the format disciplines faculty by driving them to prioritise comments and limits tangential topics. It also revives participants' interest towards the end of the session. The presentation retains its dynamic quality given that the comments are prepared during the session.

Team teaching has also been referred to as an activity that helps faculty improve their teaching skills through observation and feedback (Austin, Sweet and Overholt 1991). This approach has been dubbed The Participant-Observer Model (Nead 1995; White, Henley and Brabston 1998). No alternative views are given apart from answers to specific questions raised by faculty and/or participants (Flanagan and Ralston 1983). In this setting, one faculty member observes the preparation and delivery of all or part of the course, evaluates performance and carries out a debriefing. Again, in this case one instructor is performing and the other one observes and eventually provides feedback to the 'performer'. The basic idea is that 'having a friendly colleague observe your teaching' is very helpful (Barnes, Christensen and Hansen 1992), especially when it comes to coaching other faculty members. Nonetheless, there is often no joint interaction in the classroom.

However, some other schools use the term Team Teaching when two instructors perform at the same time in one single class or section of a course. Team teaching in this context – which is often referred to as the Interactive Model of Team Teaching (Helms, Alvis and Willis 2005) or Co-Teaching – is a sophisticated, challenging activity in which business schools invest considerable resources as a way of fostering student participation. It is particularly used in in-company training programmes and executive education for this reason. This is considered by some authors as true team teaching since both instructors participate in most of the scheduled discussion topics with 'lively interactive dialogue and debate' (Helms et al. 2005; Galley and Carroll 1993; Nead 1995).

Even though no team teaching model seems to be best in all cases (White, Henley and Brabston 1998), in this chapter we focus on the Interactive Model of Team Teaching. This kind of team teaching is much more complex given that two faculty members have to run the one or more sessions simultaneously. Consequently, it involves a heavy commitment to adaptation and flexibility in content and teaching style. According to White et al. (1998), this model demands the most effort and time on the part of the faculty but is well received by participants when properly implemented. This chapter refers to team teaching understood as two instructors running a session simultaneously.

The basic dimensions of team teaching: content and learning process

Teaching involves at least two basic dimensions. One is content, which has to be relevant to participants. 'Relevant' here usually means important for business practice, usually effective when applied properly, significant across industries, time and situations, but above all, answering managers' real-world questions and concerns. Content is relevant only if the process is able to elicit the questions from participants and provide alternative answers to them. Thus, the second dimension is process.

The learning process is key for adult students and this is especially so in business education. Participants in this setting usually have lots of experience in their fields and of the learning process. The trick is to incorporate their insights, experience and knowledge together with course concepts and content within an overall framework. In order to run an effective session, faculty should be able to foster emotional commitment from participants. Training managers involves managing both the flow of discussion and debate but at the same time paying attention to the quality and (in particular) the relevance of the content. Normally these two dimensions are managed by faculty acting alone and whose skills improve with practice.

In this context, team teaching is a unique opportunity to enhance both the richness of the process and the depth of content. It requires instructors to split roles: one focuses on deepening the content and the other on enriching the process at each juncture, and with periodic role switching. However, there is also the risk of losing the audience if the roles are too similar. Poor team teaching simply overlooks one or both components. In our experience, one of the key success factors in team teaching is the division of roles to ensure the two instructors make complementary contributions. Team teaching makes no sense if their roles and areas of expertise are similar. These roles are usually played depending on the teaching style of the other person, but multiple roles can be played also at different stages of any given session or course.

Division of roles

Generally speaking, team teaching involves a division of roles throughout the session, in the classroom and throughout the course. There are several possibilities (Table 5.2 shows a few examples). For instance, one instructor could lead the discussion while the other makes notes in order to summarise points on the board or provide general comments throughout the session. One could explain important concepts and the other play devil's advocate, and so on.

One of the basic precepts of team teaching is that it requires much more preparation than solo teaching. Before the session, it is important to design the course jointly so that everyone is clear what their responsibilities are. Such planning embraces course content, grading, teaching style and faculty preferences. In addition, team teaching requires planning that goes beyond the curriculum and considers the space, facilities and technologies needed to accommodate two or more instructors teaching one course.

Even though it is a joint effort, one teacher should lead the discussion at any given moment. Durcan and Kirkbride (1987) have defined two roles, a leader and a follower for each session. In any case, this means that one of the key skills is taking and dropping the lead role. This is not an easy task since not everybody is equally comfortable making the transition. We have seen faculty who know at a glance when the other instructor is about to jump in or out. But some teachers focus more on the participants and therefore do not watch the other instructor. Hence the need to bear in mind instructor positioning in the classroom.

The likelihood of having to step in means there is an ideal position for team teachers in the classroom. In our experience, they should be at the front of the classroom at a point where they can see participants' faces, read students' body language, and be able to jump in and pick up the reins. Figure 5.1 shows some positions from which team teachers could easily assume

Table 5.2   Examples of division of roles

Source: ITP Session Notes, 1991.

Instructor A	Instructor B
Delivers	Conceptualises
Talks	Listens, prepares slides
Elaborates the learning process	Fixes, orders, systematises and links content
Follows the flow of thought	Prepares cells, boxes
Acts	Evaluates
Provocative	Conscious
On the spot	Notices details in the class dynamics
Takes risks in the teaching arena	Corrects 'A' (voice, time management, pointing out those who have lost the thread ...)

leadership of the discussion, as well as possible paths for moving around the classroom. Of course classroom layout and the technology used is key, but most business school classrooms tend to resemble the one appearing in Figure 5.1.

Let us put this idea another way. Generally speaking, effective team teaching cannot be done with one faculty simply sitting at the back. This is the ideal setting for observation and is a common approach used to provide feedback and ideas to faculty members for personal improvement but is totally unsuitable for team teaching.

If the teacher tends to focus on the participants, you might want to sit among them. Sitting in front of the participants (first row) usually lets you stand up and use the equipment or boards in the classroom or simply 'act' (for example, leaving and re-entering the room on purpose). But you might want to sit at the back simply to change your view of participants.

One could also begin from the back and then run to the front of the classroom to shake students up. On one occasion, one of us shaped the context in a negotiations exercise by providing additional information to negotiators by speaking into a microphone from outside the classroom. The other instructor made sure inside that everybody got the instructions properly and used the new information.

On another occasion when team teaching with a partner based abroad, we patched him in through a videoconference, projecting his picture on the screens. We pointed our camera at the participants. But the local instructor was standing up. He was there to highlight key ideas or use body language to emphasise some of the comments beamed in over the video link. Faculty who have taught in a team more than once usually develop their own internal communication protocol. In any case, eye contact among faculty is very important.

Team teaching is a 'joint ride' and that requires faculty flexibility in the classroom. Basically there has to be complementarity and synergy regarding content, style background,

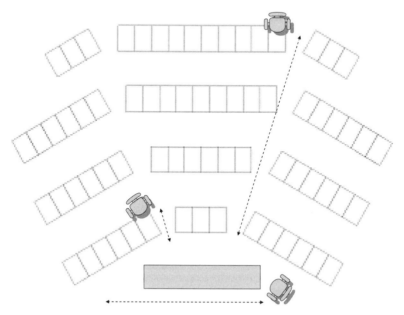

Figure 5.1   Co-teacher positioning: basic options

Source: The authors. Base Chart taken from: http://www.uregina.ca/admin/Faculty_Information/images/class-room_layout_ed616_623_small.gif; October 2006

country, and so on. Commitment to adaptation in tricky classroom situations, some of them unpleasant, is key. Thus, if for any reason one of the team teachers sees that serious clashes are likely regarding content and/or process, they would do well to look for another partner. Team teaching is a learning process. It takes time and experience and a lot of trial and error. In our experience, team teaching becomes easier with practice and after having taught with a wide range of faculty.

Complementarities in content and process

Probably the most evident benefit of team teaching is that of being able to establish different roles for deepening or widening the content. We have seen faculty members who focus so much on the process and on fostering learning-conducive discussion that they overlook the importance of conceptualising ideas. In some other cases, they are just trying to fire students' enthusiasm over a topic or activity. Sometimes it is simply because they really believe that the best way to explain things is to make the audience feel as passionate as they are about the subject. Faculty who play on students' emotions and manage the process to make it dynamic and a constant surprise for participants usually get the best evaluations from their students.

Nevertheless, in many cases participants are simply looking for straightforward answers to their questions. In some cases, even the most passionate instructors receive bad evaluations from participants. This tends to be more common in in-company training programmes where participants are keen to ask questions and get answers.

We once saw a teacher who combined his teaching activities with executive duties at managing relationships for a major consultancy firm. He had a natural tendency to pepper the content with anecdotes drawn from his professional work. At the end of the course, several participants claimed the lecturer was only interested in storytelling. In this context, the learning experience was greatly improved by working with a young faculty member who placed the content within a conceptual framework. The role of the team teacher was one of conceptualising and summarising the discussions they had. It is about explicitly extracting the takeaways in an orderly, brisk manner.

Sometimes teachers jump from concepts to tools or frameworks, implicitly knowing the relationship among them. However, for students the connections are not always evident. It is often very useful for team teachers to place such concepts on a timeline to trace the development of business thinking. Furthermore, this historic view helps students distinguish between management basics from mere fads. Among senior faculty, we sometimes see that they reach far beyond discussion of basic daily management topics. Here, one should bear in mind that a class is not a dissertation and that it is risky to assume that everyone knows what the teacher is talking about.

Sometimes connections are lacking either between concepts or with practice. The relevance or novelty of the examples given are especially important. Not surprisingly, participants in executive education programmes tend to discover ideas when they see them in contexts they understand. Coming from a non-English speaking country, we have often noted the bias that faculty have towards cases or experiences of companies from the English-speaking world. There are many reasons for this, the sheer availability of teaching materials in English being a very important one. However, although almost anyone attending business school knows most of the biggest companies in the USA and UK, foreign students still tend to view them with a certain detachment.

A good way of strengthening student involvement is by building on local examples, cases or news. They bring extra information to the classroom which enriches discussion, but also often makes participants more willing to discuss specific issues they consider especially relevant to the local setting. Sometimes it is just about drawing parallels between foreign cases and local companies. We have seen international faculty who partner with a local faculty member for a number of reasons, one being the local analogies the latter can draw on.

Opportunities sometimes arise for extending or complementing the content. The idea is to provide additional insights. For instance, one of the most interesting experiences is teaching with practitioners. They tend to point out the 'best way' of doing things, 'making decisions' in the classroom. In this case, contextualising is of great value providing one shows a little scholarly caution for understanding why the strategy worked under a given set of circumstances.

Another benefit of team teaching is having different roles for managing the process of discussion and debate in classroom. Indeed, there are multiple roles that two faculty members play to enrich the learning experience of participants. Some instructors create an atmosphere of constructive tension in the classroom. They push students hard to debate the issues. We have seen faculty who, said senior executive participants, 'gave students a headache'. In this case a 'pause' in the session might help the students think and rest before jumping back into the fray. This process is usually very effective when combined with the management of silence in classroom. Once we saw a faculty member who pretended that he had forgotten what he wanted to say. He let 90 seconds slip by trying to 'remember' his lines after standing up to participate in the discussion.

Some faculty love their field so much that they simply focus on delivering the content. Their passion with the subject does not fit the process. In this case, an entertainer is needed to break the inertia in the process of delivering the content. For example, we have seen faculty who have impressed everybody in the classroom, us included, by the quality and depth of their thinking. They have studied every single detail of the situation, compiling and integrating information on all relevant topics. They usually have great slides and have animated PowerPoint presentations. By the same token, we have seen team teachers next to them who simply entertain the audience at given moments. For instance, one of them simply stood up and played a game with a piece of paper to illustrate the ideas. In many situations, they come up with easy jokes. Others introduce a healthy dose of irony. Yet others pose open questions, and some instructors make controversial comments just to provoke the audience. Rotating faculty every now and then is often enough to shake students out of their torpor. For instance, an instructor may lead an activity because he has specific skills for enhancing group dynamics. The instructor might be particularly good at inducing participants to do things, to talk about their experience, to engage in lively role plays or perform other activities.

We have seen faculty carrying out a 'narrating' role, making notes and highlighting take-aways at different phases or stages of the session. Ideally, they should have similar experience to participants in order to understand them and connect with them. They understands participants' points of view very well and this gives them the authority to voice their opinions. Table 5.3 shows some common profiles of complementarity when considering team teaching.

Table 5.3   Basic complementarities for team teaching

Source: The authors

Complementarities	Instructor A	Instructor B
In Content	Passion for subject	Conceptualise
	Introduces toolkit	Historian
	Leader of discussion	Exemplifies with familiar examples
	Leader of discussion	Vision from a different field
	Leader of discussion	Complementor with adjacent concepts
	Reality view	Academic view
In Process	Energises debate	Reflective, brings peace
	Elaborates carefully	Invigorates debate
	Leads discussion	Rotates leadership
	Leads one methodology	Follows with another methodology
	Elaborates the arguments	Cross questions
	Leads discussion	Summarises discussion

Common questions about team teaching

When considering co-teaching, there are some common questions faculty raise. We will try to address them, based on our experience. Usually the first one is: *If an instructor is thinking of inviting a teacher to join, what should they think about, what should they start with and so on?*

There could be at least three approaches to providing a comprehensive answer to this question (see Table 5.4): (1) emotional; (2) knowledge and skills complementarity; and (3) complementarity in teaching style. The first level is emotional. When considering someone, the first thing to bear in mind is: Who do I trust and who do I respect? and – more importantly – Who trusts and respects me? To answer these questions, one usually needs to have previously seen something of the other teacher's style. Let us develop this basic notion.

We have seen many cases of failed team teaching because not enough effort was devoted to choosing the right partner. Faculty, especially junior faculty, sometimes treat the whole thing as a social activity. They invite senior faculty from the school as a pretext for running a joint activity. They sometimes appear to believe that it is a great way to show off.

Something they discover is that senior faculty may not consider the activity as a social event or an opportunity to engage in extended discussions about management ideas or course materials. Sometimes they consider this as a request for help from a junior faculty without much experience, as an offload activity, or sometimes as part of a 'stewardship service' to the school.

Table 5.4   Key success factors in team teaching

Source: The authors

Level	Requisites
Emotional	Trust and Respect
Knowledge and Skills	Complementarity
Teaching Style	Complementarity

Such situations tend to lead to great frustration. Senior faculty might not be interested in talking things through and may well end up going their own sweet way without any attempt to integrate their work with that of the junior partner. The most rewarding experiences junior faculty are likely to have is sitting in on senior faculty sessions and observing, paying attention to how they develop their classes, how they engage the audience, and how they interact and use classroom equipment. Of course, they should also pay attention to the course content. Awareness of the senior faculty's approach tends to increase the junior partner's confidence and competence. This provides a way of complementing senior faculty and creating a positive attitude from the outset – something that in our experience is a must.

Usually when designing a course and considering team teaching, it is very useful to try to imagine what the other instructor can or cannot do. Furthermore, it is useful to imagine what the inviter might do to improve the session. It is a good start when embarking on team teaching for the first time to allocate roles and activities. Later, both will probably come up with ideas to improve or deepen the collaboration.

A second level is complementarity of knowledge and skills. Again, the basic idea behind team teaching is to have two faculty members who deliver more value in the content and process of learning for participants. Complementarity might stem from different sources – for instance, field of specialisation.

Faculty recognition that views may differ is key. The important thing here is that there should be mutual respect. It is also important that participants be made aware of issues to which there are no easy answers, familiarise themselves with different views, and grasp the hidden assumptions underlying the mental models from which the conflicting views arise.

Complementarity is especially valuable when combining faculty with practitioners in the classroom. In our experience, practitioners may play several worthwhile roles in the learning process. The easiest way is to use the practitioner as a guest speaker, who relates their experience on a given subject to students. It is important that participants be debriefed on the class. Here, practitioners provide participants with a real-life case study that might usefully be contrasted with their own experience, the frameworks introduced in the course, and other cases. In this format, it is key that practitioners understand that they are there to share an experience as honestly and openly as possible – not to lecture, teach concepts or contents.

In other situations, practitioners could cover the same topics as the instructor, based on their own experience. We have conducted courses where the faculty member introduces the basics and provides a general overview and the team teacher – a practitioner – goes through it again applying it to their own experience. This approach has proven to be very valuable for participants.

In other cases, we have played two different roles with practitioners. For instance, we conducted courses covering an industry to which the practitioner belonged. This helps provide

Table 5.5   Advantages and difficulties in team teaching

Source: White, Henley and Brabston, 1998

	Advantages		Potential Difficulties
Instructional Synergy	Alternate points of view	**Faculty Inequities**	Mixing tenured and non-tenured faculty
	Mixing teaching methodologies within a single course		Potential for inequitable distribution of work
	Promote creativity		Potential for unnecessary interruptions
	More brainpower in classroom		Effect on teacher evaluation
Functional Integration	Integrating disciplines	**Resource Use**	Takes more time
	Decrease topical overlap		Few books and other materials available on interdisciplinary topics
	Mixing skills		One teacher frequently sits idle
	Smaller student/ratio		Effect on school resources
Team Building	Interdepartmental or inter-school team building	**Faculty Conflict**	Potential for disagreement in class between faculty
	Role models and mentoring for students to work in teams		Hard to reach consensus on course preparation

an overview of the industry, trends, and more broadly for instance, on specific issues such as M&A's. After group work and strategic proposals or negotiation exercises, or simply role plays, the practitioner is able to provide valuable and practical feedback. Finally they could share what they learned in the process. Academic faculty might put it all together within a conceptual framework. In all cases, both faculty and practitioner act as classroom instructors. There are cases of long-term corporate contracts where team teachers are drawn from a business school and a company (Frieswick 2000), providing either face-to-face or distance learning programmes.

The third level is complementarity in teaching style. Once the instructor has decided to team teach a course, they should design the course taking into account the style of the other instructor. If the other person is keen on putting pressure on participants, they might assume the reflexive approach. If the other instructor is keen on sharing anecdotes or discussing a case, they might introduce frameworks.

Another common question is: *How prepared must the team members be to change roles in the teaching situation?* The answer is 'very well prepared'. One of the main contributions of a team teacher is to address issues or dimensions that the other party is unaware of. In many cases, a faculty member may overlook important details because of the focus on managing the situation or the process. This might lead to a situation where the team teacher could weigh in with the arguments their colleague has omitted, and even build a completely different argument. This is why the emotional dimension is so important. One has to assume that the other teacher is acting in good faith and showing due respect, and that the contribution is both worthwhile and being made to support rather than undermine a colleague.

Before stepping in, think carefully about how to go about it. In other words, entry strategy is as important as exit strategy. Entry has to be soft and built on some argument, idea or word used by the other instructor. Usual entries could be 'just to build on the last argument' or 'following up on the final thought' or even 'playing devil's advocate', or any way that shows you simply will elaborate further, or differently from your colleague. You should explicitly show that you back your colleague. Sometimes it is useful just to speak up, some other instructors just raise a hand. For instance, a good way to engage could be simply to stand up and wait. Your colleague will give you the chance to step in when appropriate.

There are various approaches for exit strategies. One is simply to 'dilute' your argument into the overall session by slowly sitting back as you finish your argument. The other is just stay silent once you have finished your argument. You should avoid phrases like 'OK, let's get back to the session' or 'Now my colleague will pick up the thread' since they make it look like you butted in. When all is said and done, the whole process of teaching-learning and team teaching is tantamount to a polite, informative conversation with adults (who often happen to be more experienced in their particular fields than instructors). In daily life, people do not butt in but rather converse naturally in a free-flowing exchange of ideas.

Is team teaching more powerful within areas or across areas? Again, in our experience, team teaching is a powerful tool to enhance the learning experience of participants when building on complementarities. Looking at empirical evidence, Leon and Tai (2004) have shown that team teaching increased the perception of the quality of the final outcome of integrative projects assigned to students and allowed faculty to better understand one anothers' areas of expertise. Participants also perceived that individual performance and team learning improved. They report that team teaching involved a heavier workload for faculty and final evaluations were good, but not as good as experience had led them to expect. This idea leads us to the next question.

How should evaluations be carried out? In principle team teachers have to be ready for common evaluation. Perhaps one of the most difficult issues of team teaching is joint evaluation. Of course, no one likes to get poor evaluations – a danger that instructor pairs incur when team teaching. But the challenging part is accepting that individual evaluations are different. This can be tough on self-confident faculty members who get much lower scores than their partners. If a teacher feels uncomfortable at the prospect, he should not engage in team teaching.

There is the need for commitment from schools in implementing an evaluation system that supports team teaching. In this context, evaluation should be on a team basis covering the course on the one hand and faculty (as a whole) on the other. There is also the possibility of evaluating both faculty members on an individual but confidential basis. It should be a tool for self-development, not career development. Given that team teaching requires more time and effort to prepare, every teaching hour should be treated as taught by each faculty member.

Why should deans, programme and department directors support team teaching?

For faculty, team teaching is challenging. It can be the most rewarding experience or might prove a nightmare. There are several advantages to team teaching that make it worthwhile considering making the extra effort and earmarking the time and resources needed. White, Henley and Brabston (1998) have grouped the advantages into three main categories: Instructor Synergy, Functional Integration and Team Building.

Instructor synergy arises from at least four different sources. First, there is the possibility of giving alternate points of view on the same topic, increasing not only the informative content of a session, but also the depth and scope of knowledge developed in the learning process. Second, mixing diverse teaching methodologies enhances the learning experience of participants. Third, teachers working together enjoy higher instructional creativity that in turn fosters a better response from participants. Fourth, there is simply more instructor brainpower on tap – especially valuable when facing very demanding groups.

The need for functional integration (a major concern for programme directors) is better met when combining faculty from various disciplines to enlarge the management knowledge pooled in the classroom. In a broader perspective, content overlaps in long programmes tend to be cut down when team teaching is widely used. Mixing teaching skills help faculty develop different abilities, whilst combining faculty's student attention time helps reduce the student-to-teacher ratio – features appreciated by departmental directors.

Faculty collegiality, which is of great importance for Deans, is developed in two dimensions, interdepartmental or across departments. Team teaching helps break down departmental barriers and faculty isolation by fostering collegiality. However, there are also difficulties in team teaching which are shown in Table 5.5 together with advantages.

From the perspective of the Dean and Programme Directors, team teaching might be considered as a way to improve the participant's satisfaction with academic programmes. In-classroom experience is greatly enhanced when team teaching is properly conducted. Participants, especially in executive education programmes, realise that the school makes a large commitment of resources in laying on two faculty members and are usually duly appreciative. In the competitive landscape in executive education where every school teaches much the same courses and content (even using the same case studies and readings), team teaching creates an opportunity to surprise participants and the tuition a unique selling proposition. The interaction of two instructors is difficult for other schools to imitate. Thus, team teaching could be considered as a strategic capability, an investment in client and faculty loyalty.

Besides participant satisfaction, team teaching also makes it easier to provide a flexible response to demand for new courses. For instance, in our experience having two faculty members jointly develop and deliver a course let one of them drop their other academic commitments to teach an urgent in-company training programme that proved the first step in building a long-term relationship with a major client. Thus, committing two instructors actually increases flexibility. If this faculty member had not been team teaching he could not have taught the in-company class.

Team teaching requires commitment at different levels of the organisation. In this context, management needs to play a structuring role (this is especially true of the school dean, who might give full credit for team teaching hours, knowing that there is already a hidden penalty in terms of greater preparation time – particularly if it involves coordination from multiple locations). Team teaching requires the participation and involvement of department heads in various academic councils or committees, and of course it also makes additional demands on administrative support (Nixon, Helms and Pickthorne 1997).

Also team teaching 'can lead to the creation of a more collegial and robust faculty' (Helms et al. 2005). Furthermore, it enhances research output, since faculty involved in team teaching often also collaborate at some stage in joint research. Nixon et al. (1997) showed that faculty learn from each others' fields and discover ways to develop interdisciplinary research projects to support their team teaching or cross disciplinary state-of-the-art research articles, the one that counts for the rankings (which have been heavily criticised but nevertheless are a powerful marketing tool for attracting new participants). We have seen many interesting articles and books by faculty from various departments whose written contributions are based on their experience of team teaching.

Team teaching also creates major opportunities for frequent in-depth sharing and discussion of best practice and the problems encountered in teaching and learning (Booth et al. 2003). Once faculty has got used to teaching together, the need for preparation time drops, freeing up more time for research and other activities.

Young faculty develop skills, knowledge and go through an intensive period of socialisation when team teaching. This increases the likelihood of them swiftly integrating into the school's activities and the faculty body. Senior faculty serve as mentors and role models to junior faculty in team teaching settings. It is also 'an opportunity to show appreciation and recognition for achievement to senior, tenured faculty' (Nixon et al. 1997). Perhaps more importantly, as in any organisation, they quickly get a better grasp of the organisational culture, which is key to integrating newcomers. This is important because given the current academic job scene, faculty can easily end up in schools with very different values to the ones they have been used to.

The competitive landscape and the tenure system in some schools has created an aggressively competitive internal dynamic that pulls the faculty apart. Faculty members shut themselves up in their offices trying to get the next publication in on time. Loyalty to the school suffers as a result. After all, scholars can track the resources provided by other schools and move. There is little time to spend together and create a comfortable environment.

Moreover, team teaching may infuse new life and a willingness to take risks into faculty who feel left out or otherwise demotivated. It can give both new and mid-career faculty a renewed zest for teaching (Booth et al. 2003). It is also a possible way to force the pace of change and foster the adoption of new work practices.

If we believe in what we teach, and consider faculty to be a strategic resource of business schools, then we should nurture them and create an environment where faculty identify with the school, team and department, not only with their individual agendas. In this context, team teaching generates culture, socialisation and team commitment.

Basic tips for the reader

If we had to focus on just three points, they would be: First, team teaching requires trust and commitment. If there is mutual trust and respect, team teaching is a huge opportunity. Mutual respect is likely to engender commitment. Junior faculty may trust senior faculty but unless the converse is also true, the road ahead is likely to prove a rocky one. Following Booth et al. (2003), 'faculty must be willing to compromise on every detail of the class'.

Second, faculty should always look to themselves as the team teacher. If they assume that they are there to support the other instructor, their contribution is likely to enhance class discussion. As a helper they must observe, pay attention to the session, and choose the right entry and exit strategies. They should not skulk in the back row with their heads buried in a notebook, simply waiting for their turn to speak.

Third, provide balance to the session through complementarity. Generally speaking, the faculty should provide alternative views of the various topics and styles when conducting the session. Two faculty members playing the same role with a similar approach usually do not contribute much and participants usually notice that.

References

Austin J., Sweet, A. and Overholt, C., (1991). 'To See Ourselves as Others See Us: The Rewards of Classroom Observation' In *Education for Judgement: The Artistry of Discussion Leadership*. Boston, MA: Harvard Business School Press.

Barnes L.B., Christensen, C.R. and Hansen, A.J., (1992). 'A Program for Starting Up and Running a Case-Based Teaching Seminar at Your Institution' In *Teaching and the Case Method*. Boston, MA: Harvard Business School Press.

Booth R., Dixon-Brown, M.D. and Kohut, G., (2003). Shared Teaching Models for Business Communication in a Research Environment. *Business Communication Quarterly*, 66(3): 23–38.

Durcan J.W. and Kirkbride, P.S., (1987). Interactive Team Teaching on Management Courses: Some Personal Experiences. *Journal of European Industrial Training*, 11(8): 17–20.

Flanagan M.F. and Ralston, D.A., (1983). Intra-Coordinated Team Teaching: Benefits for Both Students and Instructors. *Teaching and Psychology*, 10: 116–117.

Frieswick K., (2000). Team Teaching: Partnership Between Companies and Universities are Burgeoning. *CFO*, April: 58–66.

Galley J.D. and Carroll, V.S., (1993). Toward a Collaborative Model for Interdisciplinary Teaching: Business and Literature. *Journal of Education for Business*, 69(1): 36–39.

Hatcher T. and Hinton, B., (1996). Graduate Student's Perceptions of University Team-Teaching. *College Student Journal*, 30: 367–377.

Helms M.M., Alvis, J.M. and Willis, M., (2005). Planning and Implementing Shared Teaching: An MBA Team-Teaching Case Study. *Journal of Education for Business*, September-October: 29–34.

Husenman, S. and Planellas, M., (1999). Las Preguntas de los Emprendedores. *Perspectivas de Gestión*, March: 12–26.

Leon L.A. and Tai, L.S., (2004). Implementing Cooperative Learning in a Team-Teaching Environment. *Journal of Education for Business*, May-June: 287–293.

Lindauer D.L., (1990). A New Approach to Team Teaching. *Journal of Economic Education*, Winter: 71–72.

Nead M.J., (1995). A Team-Taught Business Course: A Case Study of Its Effectiviness at a Comprehensive Community College. *Business Education Forum*, February, 49(3): 33–35.

Nixon J.C., Helms, M.M. and Pickthorne F.L., (1997). Integrating Team-Teaching, Technology and Distance Learning in MBA Programmes: A Case Study. *Industrial and Commercial Training*, 29(7): 218–225.

White C.S., Henley, J.A. and Brabston, M.E., (1998). To Team Teach or Not to Team Teach-That is the Question: A Faculty Perspective. *Marketing Education Review*, 8(3): 13–23.

6 *Transformative Management Education*

Johan Roos

Educational experiences may become transformative when they boost participants' capacity to intuit and improvise, which can be done by combining the benefits of playful construction work with spontaneous drama. In this chapter I ground this claim in humanistic theories and illustrate its practice with two executive education sessions designed for this purpose. Finally, I reflect on these sessions in light of the previous discussion and offer a few simple guiding principles for educators who want to move in this direction.

Transformative education

'... the feeling in the room changed. We moved from profane space to sacred space. The conversation was now more authentic.' Anding (2005, p. 490). According to US organizational scholar, Robert Quinn, teaching becomes transformational when it changes participants' state of being from externally driven and self-focused to internally driven and other-focused. From his terms 'being state', 'expressions of who we are' and 'moral power', it is evident that Quinn thinks of teaching as he thinks of leadership: the success is more dependent on who we are than on the styles and techniques acquired to perform. But, as I will argue in this chapter, acquired techniques matters a lot for creating the context for such transformative education.

I agree with Quinn on the basic assumption that transformation takes the learning experiences to new heights. Like him, I have also observed how people in management education not only gain new skills, but suddenly get a whole new understanding of what they already knew. Moreover, I have come to see and appreciate the tremendous difference between management education that have the look and feel of abstract and austere intellectual reasoning, and ones that engage participants in the same way as sports, arts and other activities where emotions and subjectivity are not only accepted but even demanded.

Over the last decade I have experimented with and developed effective and engaging ways to encourage management education participants to (i) describe, create and challenge (imagination), (ii) quickly access existing knowledge without rational thinking (intuition), and (iii) in the spur of the moment practice this knowledge in new and adequate ways (improvisation) that favors the kind of transformation Quinn observed. The purpose of this chapter is to describe and illustrate how such transformation can spring from boosting imagination, intuition and improvisation among groups of managers. My overall message is straightforward: hands-on construction activity combined with non-scripted drama boost imagination, intuition and improvisation which, in turn, create favorable conditions for transformation. First, I describe what I mean by transformation. Second, I provide two illustrative narratives of management education sessions that manifest transformation. Third, I reflect over these illustrations in view of the theory and offer some concluding remarks and advice for practice.

Framing transformative experiences

Quinn witnessed fleeting, very positive experiences of total absorption in time, space and task, which resemble what in the literature is called 'peak performance.' The literature has described peak performance in terms of *timelessness* (Mainemelis, 2001), *flow* (Csikszentmihalyi 1990), *aesthetic experience* (Sandelands and Buckner 1989), and *collective virtuosity* (Marotto et al. 2007). Such peak performance has enduring consequences, including creativity, heightened self-awareness and increased alertness of what is going on in the immediate environment (Garfield 1987; Lanier and Privette 1996; Thornton et al. 1999). Inspired by this literature I see transformative management education as an example of peak performance.

What causes such peak performances? The group task (Leavitt 1996), the group leader (Bass 1985; Burns 1978; House 1977) and the group members (Kirkman and Rosen 1999) can all play important roles. Marotto et al. (2007) highlighted the intricate interaction among these three agents – the task, leader and group members – for creating peak performance. Their participant observation-based research stressed the important relationship between how group members interact with one another, but also with their task, and found that an aesthetic-oriented transformative state – collective virtuosity – seem to occur during fleeting periods of engaged interaction and deep experience, which are actively catalyzed by group members and/or the leader. But, it is the leader/facilitator who carries the greatest responsibility for creating such circumstances. In spite of careful planning, it follows that the management educator can only hope to have created favorable conditions for such transformation in the particular group, place and time, as there are no guarantees it will happen by default. Hence, the question to address is: *What can we do to create favorable conditions for such peak experience in management education?* One answer is rooted in the epistemology called 'constructivism' and what it means in practice, but the mental state of spontaneity and the intuition and improvisation it enables, complements the picture.

Constructing and expressing from within

In the first part of the 20th century, Swiss developmental psychologist Piaget proposed that learning is an active and constructive engagement with the world, which he called constructivism (see Inhelder and Piaget 1958). The basic idea of constructivism is that we make ideas about the world *from within* as opposed to just getting ideas from the outside. When we reflect on our experiences we generate our own ways to make sense of the experiences.[1] In Piaget's term we make our own meaning by changing our internal cognitive structures to new inputs – accommodating – and not just by assimilating new inputs into pre-existing cognitive structures, that is, our values, beliefs and/or assumptions. Thus, for Piaget, to transform means to accommodate not just assimilating on the surface. Because knowledge is not merely transmitted verbally but must be constructed and reconstructed physically and mentally by

---

1   Piaget framed learning as a development cycle starting when the child first is able to note their action and its effects. Through repeated actions and in different contexts, perhaps involving different objects, the child is gradually able to differentiate and integrate various elements and effects. This is what he called 'reflective abstraction'. The child is also able to identify the properties of objects by the way different kinds of action affect them, which he called 'empirical abstraction'. Over time and with lots of experimentation the child increases their knowledge about what's going on, which forms a new and higher cognitive stage, and so on. This dual process of reflective and empirical abstraction enables the child to construct new ways of dealing with objects, and new knowledge about objects as such. When they become more comfortable with objects, children start to use them to create still more complex objects and to carry out still more complex actions. This process repeats itself and help the child make sense of experience at still higher levels.

the learner, we need our own practical experience ('actions-in-the-world') to accommodate. For example we can make mental models or tinker with objects using our hands. Bruner (1986) further stressed the importance of hands-on problem solving for learning and that instructors should use open-ended questions and extensive dialogue so that students can make connections and discover principles for themselves. To really learn and change we need to interact and strike a balance with the world, people and things included, ideally using our hands and modeling minds to find new ways.

Harel and Papert (1991) added to Piaget the notion that learning happens most effectively when the learner is internally driven in constructing a public entity, whether it's a go-cart or theory of gravity. In the spirit of Piaget, they stressed that the key to learning is that people get the opportunity to project their ideas and feelings from within, rather than repeating what others have prescribed as the correct view or way. The difference from Piaget is in the heavier emphasis on tangible constructions (and the use of computer-based learning). By physically constructing our ideas we both articulate tacit knowledge, and change what we come to know. Hence, constructionism extends the Piagetian constructivism by emphasizing the active process of *physically manipulating materials* to discover new ways or interacting with the world, and potentially, also to accommodate/transform.

Although it is often a whole body experience, most of the manipulation of objects is done with our hands. Already more than 150 years ago the respected anatomist Sir Charles Bell (1840) argued that all serious account of human life simply must acknowledge the central importance of the hand. Recently, Wilson (1998, p. 7) reiterated this message about the critical role of the hand for human intelligence: '... *any theory ... which ignores the interdependence of hand and brain function, the historical origin of that relationship, or the impact of that history on developmental dynamics in modern humans, is grossly misleading.*' These ideas help us further clarify the message from constructivism and its extension in constructionism: to allow for transformation in management education participants in educational experiences should use their hands to experiment, to question and to explore from within. In psychology these beneficial effects have been known since Carl Gustav Jung's experiments almost a century ago and were further refined by subsequent psychotherapists (see Roos 2006).

Acting it out

The hands-on construction activity can be significantly boosted when combined with non-scripted, that is, spontaneous drama (*ibid.*). Whereas theatre is communicating the experience to others (Greek *theatron*: 'a place for seeing/showing'), drama is fundamentally a personal experience (Greek *drao*: 'I do' or 'struggle'). *Non-scripted* drama means internally driven, non-planned but facilitated verbalizing and/or physical movements straight 'from the gut'.

In the 1920s Jacob Levy Moreno created practices and theories for group psychotherapy and personal development. In 'psychodrama' the group focuses on one individual's issues while in 'sociodrama' the group deals with a shared issue. He believed in the positive forces of the inner resources and that a symbolic communication from within, via a creative process that was healing in itself, was beneficial to achieve a healthier future. The desired outcome of this practice is release of ideas, thoughts and repressed material from the unconscious, accompanied by an emotional response and relief (Breuer et al. 2000; Malchiodi 1998; Dayton 2005), in other words, catharsis-like experiences. Thus, non-scripted drama helps people to *act out* their issues in a way that impact them on cognitive, social and emotional levels. Instead of just reason about issues, non-scripted drama nurtures people's imagination, intuition and improvisation capabilities. Combined with the benefits of constructivism (and constructionism), potentially transformative *per se*, non-scripted drama hold the potential to boost imagination, intuition and improvisation. Let's look closer at how these activities favor peak performance.

Imagining *necesse est*

Imagination is an integral part of the wider human experience. Imagination can be seen as the capacity to 'see as', which is a fundamental cognitive faculty through which complex reality is made understandable (Thomas 1999). It can also be seen as the capability to collect from experiences the potential patterns and correlation that can compose a robust representation of the world (Deacon 1997). Others have distinguished different kinds of imagination. For instance, the descriptive one, which allows us to describe the world as we see it right now; the creative one, which allows us to come up with entirely new ways to see the world and the parodic one, which allows us to challenge and even destroy what we do not like (Kearney 1988; Roos and Victor 1999). The very notion of imagination recognizes that we do not experience the world in an unmediated way, but instead experience it 'from within', *mediated* through interpretation.

Although the literatures share a view that imagination mediates perceptions and understanding, imagination is not only a pure intellectual ability to 'image' or 'imagine' something. Imagination has a behavioral as well as material dimension in addition to the much discussed cognitive one. In an organizational context, descriptions, creations and challenges articulated by managers are typically a blend of these dimensions (Burgi and Roos 2006). Thus, what and how we think, what we do (sit, walk about, wave our arms, and so on) and what we use (flip-charts, cases, video, pens, and so on) matter tremendously when we imagine. In the context of management education, when participants physically manipulate materials with their hands, and act out meaning through facilitated role-play, they practice more fully and actively their imagination compared to listening to an instructor, reading a text case, watching a video clip, sitting dialoguing around a table, or even when they jump up and down to place Post-It notes on a wall board. Rather than being story-listener, or storyteller only, participants combine the three dimensions of imagination to take on the additional symbolic roles of handymen and architects (*ibid.*), that is, multi-sensual story-*makers*. By using more fully their imagination, people create favorable conditions for peak performance.

Spontaneity favors intuition and improvisation

When people under favorable conditions combine construction work with non-scripted drama they also nurture a fleeting and creative mental *state* of spontaneity, during which intuition and improvisation happens more easily. Like imagination, spontaneity is essential to the human condition. For instance, Meyer (1941, p. 151) said: '... *the very condition and foundation of spirits, readiness and action ... that which the person may be expected to rise to and to rise with on his own, "sua sponte," ... an all-important characteristic quality of a person.*' Maslow, (1968), suggests that spontaneity is one of a dozen attributes of self-actualized people having a creative, authentic and healthy life. In this chapter spontaneity is defined as an emergent, mental state of heightened attention to the environment combined with increased self-awareness of thought and feelings, during which people are ready to immediately decide to act (Roos and Roos 2006). Thus, spontaneity is *not* automatic, instinctive reflexes, nor is it a disorderly, emotional, uncontrolled or impulsive activity. It is a state of mind, *'a readiness of the subject to respond as required.'* (Moreno 1946, p. 111). Spontaneity enables thoughts and feelings to freely emerge 'from within' the people involved whereby they can become aware of, access and even change their values, beliefs and assumptions. This way, during spontaneity we increase the possibility to accommodate in Piaget's sense, and we also create favorable conditions for peak performance. Intuition and improvisation is how this is done.

The term intuition remains unclear in the literature,[2] but its value has been recognized for centuries. For example, more than a century ago Fitz-James Stephen wrote (Stephen and Posner 1874/1991, p. 270) *'The one talent which is worth all other talents put together in all human affairs is the talent of judging right upon imperfect materials, the talent, if you please, of "guessing right"'*. In this chapter intuition means the process by which people come to immediately know without conscious awareness or rational deliberation.

When we intuit we access deeper levels of cognition and emotions. We use our intuition at many times, but the (state of) spontaneity is particularly favorable for this mental and embodied process. It is through our intuition we just know (and feel) the right answer, the best way of framing a problem, the appropriate next step, and so on. The inherently creative mental state of spontaneity favors intuition – suddenly we just know or feel things are, or are not right. Quinn's (Anding 2005) testimony of 'the light bulbs just went on' may exemplify how his participants suddenly via intuition gained insight.

Improvisation too is a somewhat fuzzy concept in the literature, but in this chapter it means an action with a very short time span between events leading up to the decision to act (or not to act) and the very act. This is similar to Moorman and Miner (1998, p. 702), who defined improvisation as the time gap between *'… composing and performing, designing and producing, or conceptualizing and implementing.'* Thus, while intuition is an internally-oriented (mental) process to know without knowing quite how, improvisation is an externally-oriented action, which the actor, *at the spur of the moment*, knows and feels is appropriate in the particular circumstance. Improvisation is a way to practice knowledge gained from intuition and other sources.

Although we improvise in our daily life, the creative mental state of spontaneity favors improvisation. Out of the blue we 'just do it'. Like intuition, improvisation often coincides with peak performance, and thus, the transformation discussed in this chapter. Quinn's (Anding 2005, pp. 492–3) testimony of how he unexpectedly had to deliver an executive education session exemplifies improvisation and how it can help induce transformation.

RECAP

Let's illustrate how imagination, intuition and improvisation, and the transformation it may cause, may unfold in practice. To this end I will present two narratives of management education sessions that, to some extent, became transformative. In both cases I designed and delivered a similar half-day session for groups of approximately 20 senior executives attending a week-long in-company program. My role was as an external faculty/expert and participant observer.

---

2   For instance, in his review of its philosophical roots, Anderson (1926, p. 377) concluded that 'suddenness' lies at the heart of comprehending intuition and that *'there is no such thing as a faculty of intuition, different in nature from other intellectual processes.'* More recently, Maslow (1968) viewed intuition as a form of cognition along with concrete experience and aesthetic cognition, which characterize self-actualized individuals. Even more recently and in the organizational studies field Crossan (1998; 593) defined intuition as *'rapid processing of experienced information.'* Others have argued that 'hunch,' 'guess' and 'feel' are synonymous with intuition (e.g., Isaack 1978).

The Method

I used a facilitated intervention based on thousands of mixed soft and hard construction pieces of a variety of colors, shapes, textures, smells, tastes and sizes, and following a stepwise process. In the tradition of creative arts therapy (for example, Rogers, 1993) each intervention began with 'warm-up' exercises, followed by the main building experience, role-play and then a subsequent debriefing.

I ran three warm-up exercises with the intention of familiarizing the participants with the task of using playful materials in a serious context at work and analogous to a language. These three warm-ups included: 1) an introductory exercise designed to improve participants' building skills by constructing anything they wished using a small set of pieces/things, 2) an exercise designed to familiarize participants with use of metaphors by inviting them to build and then describe a construction using only metaphoric language, and 3) an exercise designed to improve their ability to give their own meaning to materials by constructing and telling the story of their current job. In the latter exercise I also challenged them to step into their model (expressed meaning) by describing it to others only using first person language.

Following these warm-ups, I shifted the unit of analysis to the organization, and asked participants to individually construct a representation of their organizations that would highlight the issue at hand. In the first case the focus was on post-acquisition integration and in the latter the focus was on customer relationships. In order to reduce the likelihood that they would attempt to capture wishful thinking I encouraged them to build the organization as they 'really saw it' at that moment, rather than as it 'should' be. After some 30 minutes building time, each participant presented their individual representation of the organization to the other members of the group.

In both cases I used the *Thinking from Within* (TfW) approach (Roos 2006)[3] that, in essence, combines Piaget's (playful) constructivism with Moreno's (spontaneous) psycho-/socio-drama. In practice, the TfW approach encourages people to use their hands to construct together meaningful objects and, through non-scripted drama techniques, make the scene come alive and develop symbolic communication. The intended effect is to boost people's capacity to imagine, intuit and improvise for the higher-level purpose of creating a transformational experience.

Illustration 1: UtilityCo

BACKGROUND

A large European utility company, fictitiously called UtilityCo, wanted to help further develop the 'strategic thinking' capability of a group of senior leaders, especially in the area of post-acquisition integration. The company was very successful and had recently gone through a series of more or less successful acquisitions. To this end the senior leadership contracted a business school to design and deliver an in-company program focusing on post-acquisition integration. The program unfolded over 5 days, with pre-program assignments and post-program follow up projects. The purpose of my session was to develop a complementary and shared understanding among participants about the current, rather messy post-merger situation.

THE SESSION UNFOLDED

To achieve the objectives I split participants into two parallel groups and guided them through a carefully designed warming-up process, aiming to make them more open, aware and receptive as well as appreciate the mind-body connection (as described in Roos 2006). Practiced hands-on construction with

---

3   Versions of both examples are published in Roos (2006).

In the next phase I asked participants to work together to build a single, joint version of their organization as they saw it collectively around the table. As facilitator, I intervened occasionally during this process to ask a participant to clarify or elaborate on a statement, or to ask for additional information or underlying stories behind their constructions. Eventually, an integrated representation emerged in each group that included some notions from the individual constructions along with novel elements that emerged during the collective building process. In an attempt to establish the face validity of the representations, at the end of the building process I asked all participants to what extent the finished construction accurately captured the key elements of their organization as they saw it, and they all confirmed it did. Once completed, a volunteer from each group explained the collective model overall and its characteristics and implications discussed.

a broad variety of hard and soft hobby and modeling materials, for example, Play-Doh, Lego, wood, cotton wads, and ready made as well as natural objects, for example, toy cars and fruits. We also practiced role-playing and speaking in first person, for example, taking on the role of a specific object

During the subsequent action phase the participants used various materials to practice their newly developed skills to metaphorically visualize and internalize in three dimensions and improvise dramatic ways to describe their organization from within. After considerable effort and engagement, each group arrived at a shared, elaborate construction they thought and felt portrayed the post-acquisition situation. Using dramatic techniques they shared the essence of their constructions in taking different positions in first person format. The two stories highlight different aspects of their internal, organizational landscape.

GROUP ONE'S STORY

My heart is in (the home country). I have a chain inside, which connects my different parts, but the chain is too short so it does not connect all of them. I have a periscope to look for opportunities, but currently the glass is foggy, so I am not sure what I am seeing. I really appreciate that my various parts are making good progress in their own way. Formally and officially, I am fully 'integrated,' but in reality I am full of holes and gaps. This really concerns me. I need to grow the chain some way to close these gaps before they cause damage to the rest of me. Looking outside I must satisfy customers more than I do now. In fact, I need to remove the barrier between the customers and me, but I am not sure how.'

GROUP TWO'S STORY

I have an outer and inner world. I am firmly anchored to my monopolistic and 'fat cat' past (pointing at two red blocks), which I would like to see reduced in size. Internally, I consist of three regional parts. At my center I have my rational, technical knowledge (green soft apple). From that core I have built many bridges to my various internal parts, but they look different. Specifically, I have a solid bridge to Region A, a thin line to Region 2, and a complex structure connecting Region C, which among the mess consists of a small shining bridge to country X. This unevenness doesn't feel right.

In my outer world I see a prosperous future in Europe, but the financial markets constrain me. I really try to treat my customers well, but there is a barrier between us (fence). Just outside me, and next to the past I want to shy away from, is complicated political machinery, which is spinning around in strange ways. One of the wheels, the most imposing one, is the political system in our home country.

A range of energy issues, like alternative fuels, which I think I understand, circumvents me. Yet, what I cannot really comprehend are the many 'soft' issues (pink mushy brain halves), like attitudes among young people. I am afraid these issues, which I cannot fully grasp, are incompatible with my own technical knowledge and attitudes. Look, I'll show you (illustrates this by moving the pink soft brain halves and fails to connect them with the green apple inside).

Overall, I am concerned about my ability to better connect my inner and outer worlds. I really want to rid myself from my past (illustrates this by removing the chains to it), and open up towards my customers (illustrates this by removing the barrier).

After Group one's presentation not much happened, but early on during Group two's presentation (see Figure 6.1) people in the first group said, 'wow', 'incredibly good', and 'that's fantastic', causing proud smiles among the members of Group two. At the end of their presentation all participants were either laughing or smiling cheerfully. Following the end, some broke out in applause. Others grabbed pieces on the table and began to repeat the moves made by the presenter, like moving the pink brain and trying to connect it to the hard, green apple, or fiddling with the 'spinning wheels' of the political system. And, they did not seem to want to stop doing this. The members of Group one also prompted their colleagues in Group two for more input, calling on them to explain parts of the story over and over again, even the most miniscule parts of their construction. They discussed what their stories revealed about their officially successful post-acquisition strategy, zooming in on the 'gaps' and 'bridges' presented in both models and how this related to 'integration' issues.

Figure 6.1   Group two's construction

Illustration 2: BankCo

BACKGROUND

The country subsidiary of a global bank, here called BankCo, had contracted another business school to design and deliver an executive program for experienced middle executives. The overall purpose of the program was to develop functional managers into high potential general managers, and it unfolded during three week-long modules over 18 months. I was invited to deliver a session during the second module that should help participants identify what they saw as important issues to deal with as (future) general managers. The program director and I agreed to focus on their customer relationships and, as in the case of UtilityCo, my session came midweek and served similar purposes, namely to generate shared understanding of their internal, organizational landscape and to serve as a break from the case-based pedagogy that dominated the program.

THE SESSION UNFOLDED

To achieve the objectives in this session, I split the group into two smaller groups and followed the same three-phase approach of warm-up, action and debrief as I used for UtilityCo. Thus, using a wide range of hard and soft construction material the two groups of bankers eventually constructed together a hands-on model of their subsidiary organization and customer relationships. The objective was to take a 'strategic look' at relevant relationships and how these could be improved.

As participants constructed and conversed with one another, a certain underlying tension in the organization surfaced, prominently featured in the construction of both groups. In the following I will focus on one of the groups. Like in UtilityCo, I applied drama techniques to reinforce the state of spontaneity and make the scene come alive and move forward. The narrative from one of the groups manifests the desired outcome:

> *'I am stretched between three corners: corporate vision, our long-term goals and our short-term goals. Big brother (corporate) is looking down on me, in fact, stressing me. Just below him lies the amorphous IT systems that he imposes on me and which takes up so much of my attention. I feel chained by it (pushed a metal chain into the soft material used). Too close to my heart there is the political knife I use to cut off people I do not like. Sometimes a part of me uses this knife to backstab another part, which I cannot seem to control ... (and so on).'*

The story went on for quite some time and took into account virtually all parts of the construction. Their comments and body language suggested they felt emotionally relieved (insights followed by relief) to have talked about issues that were not usually part of such management meetings.

An important part of their narrative focused on three groups of customers, which cut across the existing and official segments and that they featured in different ways. Instead of accepting the existing definition of segments, they had spent much time constructing new, and to them, meaningful representations of particular groups of customers. Much time was spent on retired people who some of them thought are troublesome. Said one manager, *'They just complain about our service, threatening to take their account elsewhere ... fine with me.'* The feelings were mixed. Eventually they constructed a figure they jointly viewed as these senior customers. It was a strange-looking character pushing a chart full with green stuff (money) and with a 'head' equipped with huge eyes staring at their organization. On top of the head they placed 'horns' that reminded the bank managers of certain aggressiveness these people featured (see Figure 6.2). Unlike other customer groups, the connection between the senior customers and the bank was extremely thin – only a narrow paper strip. Prominently featured next to this symbolic representation was a black cross, indicating that these people were close to death.

When they took turns to act out how the senior customers might regard the bank, the participants had to physically stand at their side of the table to share a story in first person. In this moment they 'were' senior customers. Over the course of creating and telling dramatic stories, the shared view of these particular customers changed. Suddenly one of the bank managers interrupted her story and exclaimed, *'I am not dead yet!'* which led to a deep conversation about demography, health care, life expectancy, wealth management and the role of the bank in the community.

After a short while another participant reached for a candy bar from her bag, placed it near the back cross, and made the point that the senior customers had perhaps another 25 years to live and that both parties could benefit from a more mutually respectful relationship. Silence, then the others gradually offered affirmative statements and body language. The manager who previously was somewhat derogative towards senior customers had now changed his view and contributed actively in the discussion on how to apply the new insights.

During our debriefing participants testified how the session had impacted them. Comments pointed at increased authenticity (*'I was more honest'*), which is similar to what Quinn witnessed during his transformative session, but also included more precision (*'I was forced to be more precise'*) and changed emotions (*'I was terrified at first but when I let go it felt great'*). Specifically, in BankCo participants' simple, but powerful, visualization of a new view of certain customers caused a long discussion about ethical considerations as responsible bankers.

Figure 6.2   Metaphorical BankCo customer

Reflections

So far I have described how clarity emerged from using their hands to construct their worlds from within and act it out in non-scripted, but facilitated ways. Said differently, I have described how participants in management education can engage their imagination more intensively and easily, and reach a state of spontaneity during which they readily intuit and improvise. Imagination, intuition and improvisation favor peak performance and, thus, transformational management education experiences.

How do we recognize a peak performance when we see one? From the literature we have learnt how peak performance makes people lose their sense of time and space, and I have just argued how during peak performance imagination, intuition and improvisation can flow more freely than otherwise. Although I am sure the reader can 'feel' how participants used their imagination and at times reached a state of spontaneity during the two sessions described above, it is tricky to provide hard evidence of such internally driven processes. But, the hunger to continue and develop the scenario further beyond traditional reasoning made them push ahead rather than ask for closure, which may be indicative. It may be equally difficult to observe the outcome of a transformation since any accommodation, perhaps with the exception of near-death experiences, take time to become observable in changed behavior. While acknowledging the methodological challenges involved, there are several indications of transformation, especially of attitudes and opinions.

In both sessions participants gained clarity from designing a construction in real-time and worked together to materialize it in three dimensions. Individually and collaboratively they described the essence thereof in captivating and metaphorical language. Specifically, in terms of *imagination* all participants practised the three metaphorical roles, handyman, storyteller and architect, described in Roos (2006), which suggest they engaged the cognitive, behavioral and material dimension of their imagination to describe, create and challenge the topic and issues at hand. The metaphors used in their constructions and stories manifested their imagination in use.

Recall how UtilityCo managers described their messy post-acquisition organization as a distinct 'inner and outer world' and how BankCo portrayed customer relationships in terms of a thick line. Other UtilityCo metaphors include 'a chain inside', 'periscope', 'holes and gaps', 'fat cat', 'green soft apple', 'solid bridge', 'shining bridge', spinning around' and 'pink mushy brain'. Additional BankCo metaphors include 'three corners', 'big brother', 'amorphous', 'chained', 'political knife', 'cut off people', 'backstab' and 'horns'.

Recall how participants seemed to gain new insights about important matters, for instance, the importance of a previously neglected customer segment of BankCo, and the perceived lack of integration in UtilityCo. UtilityCo group two's story captures several similar insights, for example, the perceived inability to understand young people's attitudes, incompatibility with their technical knowledge and the strong legacy of the past. In BankCo, insights surfaced about the dominance of politicking and the derogative view of certain customers, as well as the sudden changed view about the latter. Hence, *intuition* paves the way for 'aha' insights.

Improvisation is manifested in concrete actions at the spur of the moment. Examples in UtilityCo include suddenly removing the chains to the past, removing the fence to customers and moving the pink brain. Perhaps the most prominent example is when one of the BankCo managers exclaimed '*I'm not dead yet!*' while taking on the role of particular customers, followed by a colleague grabbing and placing a chocolate bar next to these customers, thereby, changing entirely the perceived value of the senior customers for the bank.

During these two sessions people's heightened (external) attention to the environment and (internal) self-awareness of thought and feelings enabled imagination, intuitions and improvisations. People reached the fleeting and creative state of spontaneity during which they intuited and improvised with ease.

The two narratives show how some participants changed their values, beliefs and/or assumptions. The immediate feedback of the respective sessions suggested impact in terms of:

- *Honesty* (for example, 'During my years with the company I have never seen such an honest description of our current state of affairs – nobody held back their critical views ...');
- *Clarity* (for example, 'When you see our complex business constructed like this problems and opportunities are almost obvious ...'); and
- *Creativity* (for example, 'Ideas just flowed when we built our model together ...').
  The depth of this impact remains to be explored.

Concluding remarks

This chapter was triggered by Quinn's account about transformative teaching (Anding 2005). His testimony about 'light bulbs went on,', 'uneasiness disappeared', that participants 'suddenly understood' and 'could see what they could not see previously', that 'lives had been changed,' and that participants 'were on fire', appears to have taken him by surprise. The illustrations in this chapter show similar effects. The literature on peak experiences as well as the concepts of imagination, spontaneity, intuition and improvisation has helped me frame what is happening in more concrete terms.

In my experience, executive education aiming to teach specific knowledge and skills do not necessarily need to be transformative. But, if the objective is to *share and develop experiences* and *cultivate wisdom* among groups of managers, however, learning has to become internally driven more than prescribed from outside the learner. The old teaching-by-instruction model has already given some way to experiential, learning-by-doing models of management education and when these become transformative they move from what Quinn calls a normal reactive state to an extraordinary creative state. In this chapter, and elsewhere, I have proposed that simultaneously involving the hand, the heart and the mind in creating the condition for imagination, intuition and improvisation increases the chances to make management education experiences intentionally transformative.

To readers who want to try out some of these ideas in practice I offer the following simple guiding principles:

1. *Context matters!* As a passionate architect will say, physical surroundings are tremendously important for our mental state. In the same spirit the room, materials and general environment can separate the 'transformational' attribute from management education. Carefully design your mental and physical milieu to be safe and secure and, if possible, attractive.
2. *Warm-Up!* Few people reach the creative state of spontaneity in the same way their car accelerates from 0 to 100 km/h, or in the same time. On the contrary, a 'warm-up' to open up for new ways of thinking and doing should be built into the design. Think cocktail party, not teaching session!
3. *Thinking from within is acting from within!* Consider thinking/acting as two sides of the same coin, just like the famous mind/body or light/particle duality. Address and engage the entire participant, not just the mind-thinking-cognitive part.
4. *Aim for small wins!* Like the famous Dreyfus and Dreyfus (1986) model of gradual learning,

despite (or perhaps because of?) a PhD most of us are novices in the fine art of creating the context for transformational, peak-like experiences and performance. Take one small step at a time and celebrate each small and grand success you enjoy. The rewards are terrific and can transform you too.

Bonne chance!

References

Anderson, F., (1926), 'Intuition'. *The Journal of Philosophy*, 23(14): 365–377.

Anding, J.M., (2005), 'An Interview with Robert E. Quinn – Entering the Fundamental State of Leadership: Reflections and the Path to Transformational Teaching'. *Academy of Management Learning & Education*, 4(4): 487–495.

Bass, B.M., (1985). *Leadership and Performance Beyond Expectations*. New York: Free Press.

Bell, C., (1840). *The Hand, Its Mechanisms and Vital Endowments, As Evincing Design: The Bridgewater Treatises on the Power, Wisdom, and Goodness of God as Manifested in the Creation, Treatise IV*. New York: Harper and Brothers.

Breuer, J. Freud, S. and Strachey, J., (2000). *Studies on Hysteria*. New York: Basic Books/Hogarth Press.

Bruner, J., (1986). *Actual Minds, Possible Worlds*. Cambridge, MA: Harvard University Press.

Burgi, P. and Roos, J., (2006). 'Imagining', In Roos, J. (2006) *Thinking From Within: A Hands-On Strategy Practice*. Basingstoke: Palgrave Macmillan, pp. 41–58.

Burns, J.M., (1978). *Leadership*. New York: Harper & Row.

Crossan, M., (1998). 'Improvisation in Action'. *Organization Science*, 9(5): 593–599.

Csikszentmihalyi, M., (1990). *Flow: The Psychology of Optimal Experience*. New York: Harper & Row.

Dayton, T., (2005). *The Living Stage: A Step-by-Step Guide to Psychodrama, Sociometry and Experential Group Therapy*. FL: Health Communications.

Deacon, T.W., (1997). *The Symbolic Species: The Co-evolution of Language and the Brain*. New York: W.W. Norton.

Dreyfus, H. and Dreyfus, S., (1986). *Mind over Machine; The Power of Human Intuition and Expertise in the Era of the Computer*. Oxford: Basil Blackwell Ltd.

Garfield, C. (1987). 'Peak Performances in Business'. *Training and Development Journal*, 23: 54–59.

Harel, I. and Papert, S. (eds.), (1991). *Constructionism*. Norwood, NJ: Ablex Publishing.

House, R.R., (1977). 'A Theory of Charismatic Leadership', In Hunt, J.G. and Larson L.L. (eds). *Leadership: The Cutting Edge*. Carbondale, IL: Southern Illinois University Press: pp. 189–207.

Inhelder, B. and Piaget, J., (1958). *The Growth of Logical Thinking from Childhood to Adolescence*. New York: Basic Books.

Isaack, T.S., (1978). 'Intuition: An Ignored Dimension of Management'. *The Academy of Management Review*, 3(4): 917–922.

Kearney, R., (1988). *The Wake of Imagination: Toward a Postmodern Culture*. Minneapolis: University of Minnesota Press.

Kirkman, B.L. and Rosen, B., (1999). 'Beyond Self-Management: Antecedents and Consequences of Team Empowerment'. *Academy of Management Journal*, 42(1): 58–75.

Lanier, L.S. and Privette, G., (1996). 'Peak Experiences: Lasting Consequences and Breadth of Occurrences Among Realtors, Artists, and a Comparison Group'. *Journal of Social Behavior and Personality*, 11(4): 781–782.

Leavitt, H.J., (1996). 'The Old Days, Hot Groups, and Managers' Lib'. *Administrative Science Quarterly*, 41: 288–300.

Mainemelis, C., (2001). 'When the Muse Takes it All: A Model for the Experience of Timelessness in Organizations'. *Academy of Management Review*, 26: 548–565.

Malchiodi, C.A., (1998). *The Art Therapy Sourcebook*. Lincolnwood (IL): Lowell House.

Maslow, A. H., (1968). *Toward a Psychology of Being (2nd. Ed)*. New York: Van Nostrand.

Marotto, M., Roos., J. and Victor, B., (2007). 'Collective Virtuosity in Organizations: A Study of Peak Performance in an Orchestra'. *Journal of Management Studies* (forthcoming).

Meyer, A., (1941). 'Spontaniety'. *Sociometry*, 150–157.

Moreno, J.L., (1946). *Psychodrama (Vol 1)*. Beacon, NY: Beacon House.

Moorman, C. and Miner A.S., (1998). 'Organizational Improvisation and Organizational Memory'. *The Academy of Management Review*, 23(4): 698–723.

Rogers, N., (1993). *The Creative Connection: Expressive Arts as Healing*. Palo Alto, CA: Science and Behavior Books.

Roos, J., (2006). *Thinking From Within: A Hands-On Strategy Practice*. Basingstoke: Palgrave Macmillan.

Roos, J., and Roos M., (2006). 'On Spontaneity'. *Working Paper 72*, Imagination Lab Foundation, Switzerland.

Roos, J. and Victor, B., (1999). 'Towards a Model of Strategy Making as Serious Play'. *European Management Journal*, 17(4): 348–355.

Sandelands, L.E. and Buckner, G.C., (1989). 'Of Art and Work: Aesthetic Experience and the Psychology of Work Feelings'. *Research in Organizational Behaviour*, 11: 105–131.

Stephen, F-J. and Posner, R.A., (1874/1991). *Liberty, Equality, Fraternity: And Three Brief Essays*. Chicago: University of Chicago Press.

Thomas, N., (1999). 'Are Theories of Imagery Theories of Imagination? An Active Perception Approach to Conscious Mental Content'. *Cognitive Science* 23(2): 207–245.

Thornton, F. Privette, G. and Bundrick, C.M., (1999). 'Peak Performance of Business Leaders: An Experience Parallel to Self-Actualization Theory'. *Journal of Business and Psychoglogy*, 14(2): 253–264.

Wilson, F., (1998). *The Hand: How Its Use Shapes the Brain, Language, and Human Culture*. New York: Pantheon Books.

7 Acting is Being: Theatre as a Learning Method

Göran von Euler[1]

During the years I have been engaged in *POCKET – theatre4Change*[2] I have become increasingly convinced that the performing arts have such a crucial influence on people's beliefs and imagination that they should be vital to all forms of education and development work, for example, in the following areas:

- Creating greater openness and trust among participants of a teaching group.
- Arousing curiosity and involvement in communicative and human aspects of mergers.
- Concretisation and deepening our theoretical knowledge of leadership.
- Making members of a group better 'improvisers' in their areas of competence.
- Creating full involvement in a process and thus enhancing your enjoyment of life.

If you subscribe to these aims and objectives you should definitely consider the use of theatre next time you plan education in your line of business.

How is this chapter structured?

A few examples and concrete suggestions, based on theory, will show how theatre can be particularly useful in education and staff development. I will primarily draw on my own practical experience as an actor, educator and consultant.

I will begin by giving an example of how theatre can function in education. This is followed by some more general reflections on the usefulness and appropriateness of the method. Some theoretical arguments will help us here. This will lead us to a few further examples from first-hand experience: interesting themes that we have elaborated and suggestions for staging and role play. Finally, a few words about the magic of improvisation.

As a conclusion you will find some references to useful literature on acting exercises.

MBA students participate in interactive theatre: An example

A group of 25 MBA students from all parts of the world have just started their education at the Stockholm School of Economics. Just arrived in Stockholm, unacquainted with the new environment and not knowing each other, they are full of expectations.

One of their first lectures (3 hours) deals with the subject *Diversity and Cross-Culture Communication – Interactive Theatre*. The students enter a room with 27 chairs and a simple stage

1   Göran tragically passed away during the publication process of this book. His chapter was finished and we are pleased that his family has approved its publication. *The Editors.*
2   *POCKET-theatre4Change* is an educational company that supports people and organisations in change, using Interactive Theatre as its most common method.

at the very front. After the three actors/consultants from POCKET have presented themselves for the MBA students and have been chatting for a while the play can begin:

> *The three actors enter in their respective roles: a rather serious young man (Belorussian), a middle-aged Dutch woman and a grey-haired senior citizen from Argentina. They are a newly formed team about to introduce a new revolutionary product for the South-European telecom market. The characters don't know each other and Janek, the team leader from Belarus, immediately takes command and in an authoritarian way lays down the general rules for how to work and communicate.*
>
> *In a number of scenes we get acquainted with their efforts to accomplish their tasks. There are genuine differences of opinion, they mistrust and misunderstand each other and get worked up about their respective (cultural) characteristics. After a couple of months their chief account manager pays them a visit. He wants to see concrete results. In a meeting, arranged by the team leader Janek the following day, a serious conflict is unavoidable. In the middle of the ensuing chaos the character Janek steps down and addresses the audience directly. He asks: What shall I do, this doesn't work, my colleagues don't do as I say, they don't listen, they don't seem to understand – help me!!*
>
> *There is a tentative response from the audience: Perhaps you ought to listen yourself, why don't you tell them to sit down and speak calmly. Janek leaves the audience and walks on to the stage. He tests the suggestions – soon enough new problems arise, he goes down into the audience again. New ideas and approaches are tried out. Suddenly the audience is in disagreement, there are considerable differences of opinion on how to tackle the issues.*

For a while the play is replaced by discussions in small groups. How should we solve the dilemmas revealed in the play? What causes the disagreements? After 5 minutes the actors continue the improvisations and after many suggestions, lively audience discussions, much laughter and smiles of recognition, the play is brought to a credible end.

The last hour is devoted to a joint discussion of what has happened during the session, in what way the situations and characters seem plausible. How can we explain the cultural similarities and differences among the audience? Some are of the opinion that there are already misunderstandings in the group of MBA students. The actors conclude by giving their own reflections on what has happened during this session.

Why theatre?

Let us come back for a moment to the aims and objectives of the arranger/course-leader with this session. Remember this is a group in which the members did not know each other and to whom the course-leader wanted to give a chance to open up, get to know each other and at the same time discuss complex issues which were important for them to understand. The participants are themselves a multicultural group who are going to work together for a year. Through the medium of theatre, the planner wanted to give them an opportunity to see and reflect over these complex matters in an open and easy way.

Because of the various backgrounds of the course members we favoured a case, a story with a common frame of reference. Obviously those involved in the project needed to recognise the relevance of the process.

In the example given above, the advantages gained from theatre as a teaching method are quite obvious from the perspective of the course-leader. Cross-culture communication is a multifaceted subject that involves people's basic values and emotions. The understanding of these vital questions is also a good basis for better communication between the members of the course. It goes without saying that this was a group who would benefit from getting to know one another better in order to communicate more openly.

Generally speaking, when is theatre the most appropriate teaching method? Before we answer this question, let us look at the art of theatre from a more general perspective and consider how it can be used in the life of organisations. Our discussion will include further reflections on the nature of teaching and learning.

Theatre as metaphor and tool

Theatre is a long-standing metaphor for (working) life. Just as in the example above, a play can be used as a metaphor for a better understanding of what is going on in a company or in a group of students. The concept of theatre can be used in the same way. Roles, script, drama, acting are concepts that can be used as metaphors for human (or organisational) activities. Think of such expressions as 'playing private and professional roles', or a leader 'acts' in such and such a way. You can also talk about a person's 'life script'.

Activities in the theatre can be described and used as intervention tools for development work (change management). The objective here is to use theatre to encourage and bring about change in organisations. Drama is used for raising awareness of problematic situations and preparing for change. Techniques and methods in the theatre are also used for the training and learning of new ways of acting and arguing in crucial situations (Meisiek 2002). I am thinking, in particular, of interactive theatre, role play and other techniques for training communication.

Learning theory

These ideas about using theatre in education are based on pedagogical research as well as first-hand experience. I will confine myself to emphasising some of the cornerstones of what is sometimes known as 'learning by doing'. You will find that theatre fits in nicely. My point of departure is a simple and straightforward model of learning (Kolb 1984). The essence of this model describes learning as a cyclic process, in which direct experience leads to observation and reflection, which in its turn leads to abstraction being used as guidance for concrete action (see Figure 7.1).

DIRECT EXPERIENCE

All learning begins with the individual's own experience. We must all start from our own associations and experience. This includes the emotions and values connected with this experience.

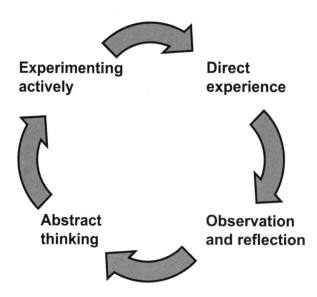

Figure 7.1   Kolb's learning cycle

OBSERVATION AND REFLECTION

Earlier experience is viewed in the light of observation and reflection. You may not at first have words for your experience. It is not always obvious what you have learnt or know. This can especially be the case with values (of which we are sometimes sadly unaware). This is the strength of theatre – providing the mirror in which we can reflect our experiences. The mirror reveals our way of being, our values and emotions.

ABSTRACT THINKING

These reflections can lead to a deeper understanding, including abstractions in the form of generalisations or theories. I would like to stress here that learning is to a great extent a social process, in which everybody, students as well as teachers, must be involved and interact. By actively involving both thoughts and feelings we create opportunities for the individual to assimilate new information and attitudes in a given social setting. (Frijda 1986).

EXPERIMENTING ACTIVELY

Discussions in small groups, greater openness and a willingness to experiment form the last stage of the learning process. During this stage we put our new understanding to the test, making decisions, solving problems – and acting.

The advantage of theatre is its obvious appeal to both head and heart. It involves not only physical expression but also attitudes, values and feelings. By demonstrating these on the stage we can observe what is happening at a distance, as 'second-order' observations, that is, an observation of an observation, which enables us to reflect on different modes of action. During the performance as well as in subsequent discussions we develop a kind of common emotional knowledge, for example, knowledge of how to feel and act in similar situations in real life (Miesiek 2002).

Theatre: When, where and how?

Here are a few examples of situations in which I have found it useful to adopt theatre methods. Of course, there are endless possibilities and approaches but above all we have to consider questions of effective communication, values and how to handle everyday situations.

INTERACTIVE THEATRE: FURTHER EXAMPLES

In the example above which illustrates cross-cultural communication it was obvious that the issue was (the lack of) communication and the fact that values were not immediately apparent. This particular case indicates a field of study where theatre can provide important input into a part of a course comprising theoretical studies of relevant research (see Figure 7.2).

> *This is the most powerful tool for leadership development I have experienced during my 30 years in industry and trade.*

> Bob Onucki, Deputy Managing Director, Customer Development, Sandvik.

With my colleges I have developed interactive theatre programs through the years on related subjects such as equality, work/life balance, ethnic and other discrimination in working life, and so on. All these subjects are related to various aspects of communication. It is very easy for a number of basic assumptions or prejudices to obstruct good communication. They cause conflict and misunderstanding.

During the play and the improvisations the audience can see and become aware of what kind of problems come up in such situations, but also suggest ways of solving such dilemmas.

Figure 7.2   **Interactive theatre**

Another area where interactive theatre can be useful in education is the case of mergers. Organisations face a number of dilemmas. What is the ultimate balance of power between the companies? What will be most successful, merger or acquisition? Do we prefer an abrupt and overt merger or a covert one? The latter strategy may improve the chances of achieving subsequent synergies between the two organisations. Less has been written about the role of the staff and how their reactions influence the outcome. Yet there is much evidence to suggest that this is crucial for the success of mergers.

Together with colleges I have staged a play and set up a program on strategies for take-over and on the merger of enterprise cultures, old hierarchic and new informal ones, the problems of loyalty and the fears that workers experience. This program has been reasonably successful, especially amongst managers. It has helped them identify their shortcomings and understand how to bring about change in their own organisation.

And, again, group reflection within a social framework following the program is essential. This can best be done in a form of dialogue, where the audience has a chance to regulate their emotions and locate their impressions, and it needs to be initiated and guided by us or the group leader.

ROLE PLAY TRAINING

Up until now I have concentrated on drama and interactive theatre. I see these activities as distinct from role play and role play training, which require the more practical participation of group members. Role play as a working method is used extensively in change management. The key requirements here are that group members take on an active role, acting and improvising (within the framework of a number pre-defined constraints).

Role play and traditional plays have a 'case' or a crucial situation in common. The group members are trained in handling the situation. In its simplest form the students are divided into small groups, they are given 'roles' and their task is to train themselves in arguing the pros and cons of a given issue. In a more advanced case study with distinct 'role characters' there will be a greater involvement and a stronger challenge. The case in question may be a staff conflict or the justification for a large investment. This can be done with an audience of 'selected observers' or a larger group of course members. As always you need to reflect carefully on what you have seen and what conclusions can be drawn.

These forms of role play can be used to good advantage for teachers with little experience in the field. Start on a small scale with few participants and observers.

Later on, more complex role play can be used, perhaps with the help of professional actors. These can involve acting out a strategic scenario with successive scenes as in a play. Let me give you an example:

1. The management (that is, a group of students) is faced with a serious business dilemma – sketch and enact the situation!
2. Experts (fellow students or group leader) are called on to account for details.
3. When decisions about the dilemma have been reached, the executive body draws up the strategy and a plan of action.
4. Representatives of the staff (that is, the rest of the students) meet the executive body who explain and justify their decisions.

This comes close to forms of role playing activity associated assessment centre exercises. The difference in that case is that there is a clear element of evaluation in assessment training which is often the basis for selection procedures and recruitment.

You can also involve actors in all sorts of role play to function as difficult characters to generate the right sort of energy and give credibility to the situation. They can either be the manager of the firm, who is arrogant and unwilling to listen, or an employee who has a drinking problem or a patient not following his doctor's orders.

ACTING EXERCISES

So far I have given examples of how theatre can be used in respect of workplaces and themes. Acting exercises are often of a more general character, designed to make amateurs and professionals better actors. This involves, amongst other things, developing your ability to communicate, to listen, to improvise, and to get your message across engagingly. These are qualities that are useful for all of us, colleagues, educators as well as managers.

Courses of this kind will naturally always be part of a greater whole and tailored to specific needs, for example the working climate of a group, where our aim is to create greater openness and tolerance or the training of a professional group to develop and refine their listening capacity when meeting customers and colleagues. The words 'communicate' and 'communication' are often used ambiguously. 'I have communicated this to my colleagues,' is not the same as, 'I have communicated with my colleagues.'

A theatrical 'dialogue' is similarly vague. Dialogue, which originally meant 'through/via speech', is now much more associated with mutuality and improved listening and empathy. This is an ability which can of course be trained.

At the beginning of any course involving drama exercises I invite the group members to explore the nuances of a dialogue. The objective is to grasp what a 'genuine' encounter involves. This is something we have all experienced in life and want to be part of again. But there are repeated obstacles to overcome.

In the first exercise, group members face and look at each other in two pairs. After a few minutes they start talking about the thoughts going through their minds. The most important thing is not to see the other person but to see oneself as a critical observer in the situation. If we then give group members a moment or two to talk about a subject, the listeners will be ready and willing to evaluate what they have seen instead of just listening interestedly. This can lead to an important discussion on the nature of listening.

In various forms of 'mirror exercises', where the task is to act as the mirror image of the interlocutor, group members are given the opportunity of experiencing the essence of listening and of honing their empathy.

Actors are good at communicating messages in an interesting and inspiring way. We can learn a lot from them. There are a number of very important 'techniques' connected with breathing, body language and the way you enter a stage or a room. Most important, however, is the story you want to tell. Which elements are crucial, what is the objective behind the story? This is seldom simply a question of giving facts; in most cases we seek to influence the listeners; as well, to encourage them to commit to a particular project by firing their enthusiasm. If I am well prepared, I will know at once how to get my message across to my students or my audience.

In the theatrical profession as well as other art forms, improvisation is a necessary and useful instrument. We find a direct parallel here to situations in working life. You need to prepare both for the expected and also for the unexpected. Preparation for the unexpected requires an ability to perceive in the reality of an unfolding process, which is sometimes different from what is intended. Theatre makers are skilled at this kind of preparation and perception (Meisiek 2002).

Actors are trained in various forms of improvisation exercises in order to give them presence and help them to read and adjust to the situation and advance the scene dramatically. They are trained to see what is really happening, what is beneath the surface.

Course participants can be trained to use these skills in interactive performances, role play or practical exercises. The focus is on critical situations, involving all the course participants. Suggestions for solutions are tested by the actors as well as the group members.

We have also enacted 'extended' role play scenarios to train participants in various types of significant dialogue, for example, between a manager and an employee. The aim of this training is to develop the ability to handle a) a low standard of achievement of members of the staff; b) loyalty conflicts in change management and; c) an investigation into cases of sexual harassment.

Summary

I have confined myself to a few examples of role play and drama to show the importance of theatre in an educational setting and how you can make such course sections attractive. The forms of theatrical activities I covered were:

INTERACTIVE THEATRE

In which the starting point is a short play, illustrating the actual subject and the dilemma to be confronted. Improvisations follow the presentation of the dilemma. The audience makes proposals for solutions; the actors devise appropriate scenes and act their parts. Group members feel a strong personal commitment in this type of exercise, which arouses strong feelings. There is also a spin-off benefit in terms of new subjects in the group reflections that always should follow. The number of participants can be between 15 and 100, depending on the setting or the aims of the exercise. The use of professional actors is a key requirement.

ROLE PLAY: ARGUMENTATION AND SITUATIONAL TRAINING (EXERCISES)

This is the simplest form of role play, which can be applied in all sorts of groups. You need to allow time for reflection and follow up in small groups following the role play. Start with small groups and clear-cut situations, preferably with a 'for-against' ethic or moral dilemma. Participants represent themselves but take a determined stand on a particular issue.

ROLE PLAY: EMPATHY AND BEHAVIOURAL TRAINING

This is a more demanding form of role play, especially at the initial stage. The roles and their 'background' are just as important for empathy and sympathy as the situation itself. Using an observer to enable reflection and analysis can help draw out the learning. Try outlining the roles clearly (name, age, family, educational background, relation to colleagues, to the boss, special interests and commitments, and so on). Start with dialogues in pairs situations, for example, a difficult conversation between an engineer and his superior. Introduce an observer to delegate distinct tasks to each pair. We suggest you work in small groups of no more than 15 members during the initial stage.

ROLE PLAY: COMPLEX SITUATIONS

The objective of these role plays may be to apply economic theories and strategies in order to build up a cogent argument and to reach a specific goal. This form of role play should involve a complex and involving situation. The number of participants may be five or six. Although all have a common goal, the same priorities and values are not necessarily shared between all participants. It is well worth using professional actors and scriptwriters. Once again – work in small groups initially and remember observing is just as important as acting.

DRAMA EXERCISES

These exercises aim to develop openness, empathy and an interest in different approaches to dialogue. They enhance self-awareness and strengthen the group relations. They serve very well as a warm-up before any actual role play. We suggest you use the following sequence:

- *Encounter* – to develop careful listening, empathy, cooperation. Use pair work, dialogue training and mirroring, with each person offering feedback to the other.
- *Message* – to explore how to get your message across. Traditional drama exercises enable the group to learn the importance of breathing, voice modulation and body language.
- *Improvisation* – to explore how to handle the unexpected. Unplanned events are always a part of acting but the ability to handle them can also be trained separately. Remember to encourage a sense of fun and enthusiasm.

There are a number of good books and articles on the subject, and as an educator I see the great benefits of good examples. Make your own choice or engage a professional actor to inspire you.

It is my strong conviction that the introduction of theatre in management courses and during development can open up new dimensions of creativity and empathy. It is in such encounters that we can appreciate the basis of a better and richer working life.

References

Frijda, N.H., (1986) *The Emotions*. Cambridge: Cambridge University Press.

Kolb, D.A., (1984) *Experimental Learning*. Englewood Cliffs, N.J: Prentice-Hall.

Meisiek, S., (2002) Situation drama in change management. Types and effects of a new managerial tool. *International Journal of Arts Management* 4: 48–55.

Literature and web-links

Boal, A. (translated by Jackson, Adrian), (1992). *Games for Actors and Non-Actors*. London: Routledge, ISBN: 0-415-06154-7.

Boal, A., (1995). *The Rainbow of Desire. The Boal Method of Theatre and Therapy*. London: Routledge.

Berg, M. et al., (2002). *Business Theatre Interactive*. Belz: Weinheim.

Freire, P. (translated by Myra Bergman Ramos), (2000). *Pedagogy of the Oppressed*. New York: Continuum.

Johnstone, K., (1987). *IMPRO – Improvisation for the Theater: A Handbook of Teaching and Directing Techniques.* New York: Routledge.
One of the best books on the art of improvisation

RimÈ, B., Mesquita, B., Philippot, P. and Boca, S., (1991). Beyond the emotional event: Six studies on the social sharing of emotion. *Cognition & Emotion,* 5 (5/6): 435–465.

Spolin E.V., (1999). *Improvisation for the Theatre.* Evanston, Illinois: Northwestern University Press, ISBN 0-8101-4008-X.
This classic book contents more than 200 classic improvisation exercises and traditional theatre games.

Methuen Drama, Improv Encyclopaedia home page: http://www.humanpingpongball.com/index.html
Here you will find tons of stuff related to improvisation theatre. Look for improv. games, handles, concentration exercises, drama techniques, character exercises, warm-ups, long-form improv. formats, improvised show formats, tips for improv. workshops and much more.

POCKET – theatre4Change: www.pocket.nu
Here you will find a more examples of POCKET´s interactive programs and a description of our organisation. You will also find our addresses for contact.

Inside the Classroom

Dealing with Different Contexts

8 Teaching Large Classes

Aswath Damodaran

Budgetary pressures on educational institutions tend to manifest themselves in larger classes at every level. As teachers, we often feel imposed upon when asked to teach these classes and we accept the conventional wisdom that what we do well in small settings cannot be scaled up to larger ones. While this may be true for some teaching styles, it is not the case for others, and there are ways in which we can continue to be effective as class sizes increase and enjoy ourselves, to boot. In this paper, I examine ways in which we can preserve teaching efficiency as class sizes increase.[1]

Teachers at every level, from pre-school to graduate school, are inclined to blame large class sizes for deteriorating teaching quality. If only you would give us fewer students in our classes, they argue, we would do much better. As we hear this lament, it is worth noting that the correlation between class size and teaching quality is tenuous at best, and any correlation that exists can just as easily be attributed to other factors. As the resources that are available for education are scarce, and large classes are here to stay, how can we better adapt to them? In this article, I will begin by first defining a 'large' class, since the number of students that makes a class 'large' will depend upon the characteristics of the students, the subject being taught and the teaching style of the instructor. I will follow up with a series of propositions about behavior in and out of the classroom that can potentially improve how we deal with more students and larger classes.

What is a large class?

So, how large is a large class? The answer, of course, will vary depending upon what you teach, whom you teach and how you teach. A class of 35 may be pushing the limits of a graduate philosophy class, where class discussion is the norm and students are graded on what they contribute to the classroom discussion, but a class of 500 may not be viewed as unusual in an introductory physics course for undergraduates at a large public university. In general, the size of a large class will depend upon the following factors:

- *Homogeneity of students:* The more students have in common, the larger a class can become. As student backgrounds, skills, interests and objectives diverge, class sizes will generally need to shrink to reflect these differences.
- *Subject matter taught:* At the risk of casual generalization, quantitative subjects where answers are more black and white can be taught to larger classes than qualitative subjects where every answer may have shades of gray. Calculus, for instance, should be easier to teach to a large class than theology.

---

1   While much of what I say in this piece is abstract, you can visit the website I have for my classes at http://www. damodaran.com.

- *Teaching style:* Teachers employ different styles, even when teaching the same subject. A lecture-driven teaching style, with relatively little input from the audience, scales up much better than a discussion-driven teaching style. It is much more difficult to employ a Socratic teaching style, when there are 150 students in the room than when there are only 30.

School administrators should consider all of these factors when determining what is an appropriate size for a large class and should not assume that just because one teacher is successful at teaching a large class, other teachers can also be just as comfortable in such settings.

The elements of teaching

While we often tend to think of teaching in terms of what we do in the classroom, the reality is that much of the groundwork for good teaching occurs outside the classroom, as does much of the learning. In fact, the various aspects of teaching are captured in Figure 8.1.

Listed are three questions that students are likely to ask when evaluating a class, and they will judge teachers in the process. First, students want the testing to be fair and the grading to reflect what they learn from the class and the amount of work they put into it. Second, the material that you teach will be examined not only for its interest level, but also in terms of how you connect the material to students' lives and aspirations. Finally, students will make judgements on whether you encourage them to think and keep them engaged in the classroom. You may not be an entertainer, but there is little learning occurring in a classroom where boredom is the dominant emotion.

Testing and grading

Grades may not matter to you but they do matter to your students. Thus, while you may adhere to the teaching proposition that what you care about is learning and not grades, you

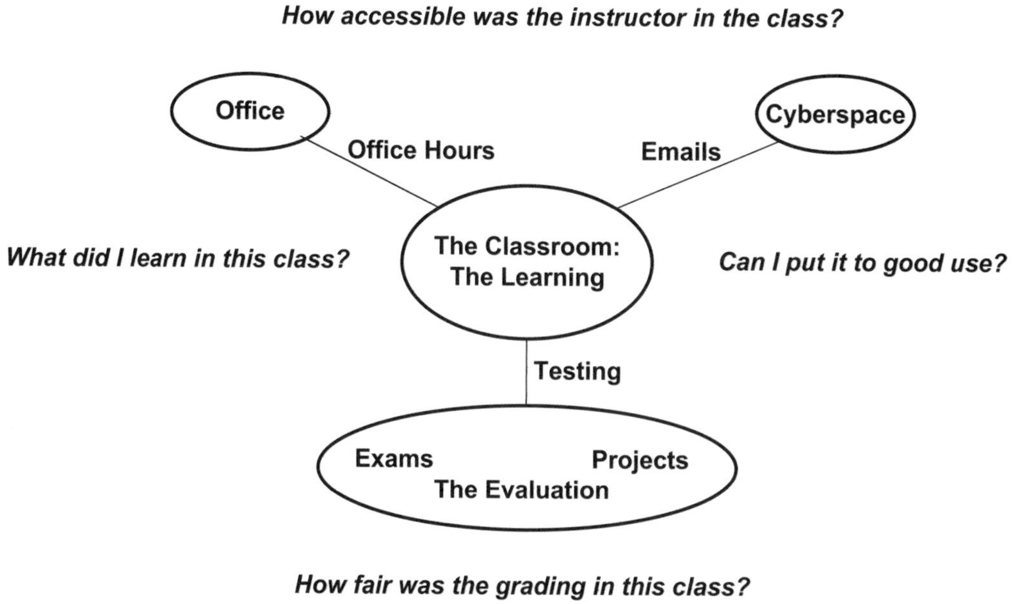

Figure 8.1   The various aspects of teaching

should spend some time establishing how you plan to evaluate the students in your class and what system you will follow. If you fail to do so, you will find your time consumed by questions about testing, and learning will take a back seat to grading issues. While there are a variety of ways you can test your students on whether they understand the material (and follow up by assigning grades), here are some common components of grading systems that work in large classroom settings.

CLEARLY STATED RULES TO WHICH YOU SHOULD ADHERE

It is critical that the rules of the game be laid out before a class starts and that you stick with these rules as closely as you can. While you can be flexible and let the rules evolve, when teaching a class of 20, you will quickly find yourself overwhelmed by requests for exceptions if you allow the same flexibility with larger classes. In particular, the following grading features should be made explicit at the start of the class:

- *How the class will be tested and graded:* If you plan to use a mix of quizzes, exams and projects, specify what the quizzes will cover, when they will be held (unless they are pop quizzes) and to what extent they will be weighted. If possible, also specify what material students can bring in for the quiz (is it open book and open notes?) and the types of questions you will be asking.[2]
- *The grade distribution that you will be using:* Teachers often hate to commit themselves to a pre-specified grade distribution but it is worth considering, especially with a large class. Letting students know up front (in the first class) that only 20 per cent of

---

The Quiz Rules

There will be no amendments, corollaries or other variants of these rules.

1. The quizzes will be on the designated days and during the first 30 mins of the class.
2. The quizzes will be open book, open notes. You can bring in as much supporting material as you can carry.
3. The quizzes are NOT group work. You may not consult with, talk to or pass telepathic messages with anyone else in or out of the classroom.
4. When time is called on the quiz, please stop writing. It is not fair to others to keep working after they have stopped.
5. Each quiz is worth 10 per cent of the examination.
6. If you have to miss a quiz for good reason,[5] you will have to let me know (by email) at least 15 mins before the quiz that you will be missing the quiz.
7. If you miss a quiz for good reason, the 10 per cent weight on that quiz will be reallocated across your remaining exams (quizzes and final). The weighting is not retrospective and previous quiz scores will be unaffected.
8. If you take all three quizzes, your worst quiz will carry the least weighting. It will not be ignored. How much less weighting it receives will depend upon the extent to which your worst quiz score is below that of your other exams. (In the most extreme scenario, you will receive a zero score on your worst quiz and 100 per cent on every other exam. In this case, the worst quiz will have no weight on your grade. If you get a 4/10 (or 40 per cent) on your worst quiz and 90 per cent on all of your other exams, your worst quiz will be weighted only 5 per cent and the remaining 5 per cent will be reallocated across your other quizzes and exam).
9. If you do not take all three quizzes, you will not have the option described in (8), even if you miss a quiz for good reason.
10. I grade all of your quizzes. If you have a beef with the grading (and I do make mistakes), please come to me. I do not bite, chew people's heads off or indulge in similar antisocial behavior. I will listen to your points but I may not agree with them.

---

2   I have always made the exams and quizzes I have given in past classes available to the current one. While that does make my job of writing new exams more difficult, it accomplishes two objectives. First, it ensures that students have a clear idea of how a typical quiz or exam is structured – how many and what type of questions are on it. Second, it encourages more preparation. Students are always more likely to work through real exams and quizzes to get ready for the next one than practice problem sets.

the class will be getting As and 10 per cent will be failing will not only prepare them for what is coming but also allow them to decide whether they want to stay in the class (and play by your rules). In addition, they will be able to assess where they stand in the class at regular intervals and make their judgements on how they improve their standing.[3]

- *The consequences of missing a quiz or a project deadline:* While the decision of what you want to do when someone misses a quiz or a deadline is clearly yours – you may give the culprit a zero or a chance to retake the quiz – it is a good idea to also specify that decision at the beginning of the class. The following is an excerpt from my corporate finance class outline that is both online and provided to students on the first day of class. As you can see, I specify the conditions under which a quiz can be missed and the consequences of missing a quiz.[4]

DO NOT CHANGE THE WAY YOU TEST STUDENTS JUST BECAUSE YOU HAVE A LARGER CLASS

Presumably, you choose particular ways of testing and grading students because you feel that these ways measure learning better. Thus, if you feel that asking open-ended, qualitative questions is the best way to assess learning in your subject, you will construct your exams around such questions. All too often, though, as class sizes increase, teachers switch to different ways of testing, not because they prefer this form of testing but because of grading ease. Multiple-choice questions are a common choice for very large classes since they can be computerized, thus making grading a snap. As a general rule, compromising on testing is never a good idea, since the grades will then not reflect what you want students to learn from the class.

TAKE OWNERSHIP OF YOUR EXAMS

Many instructors use test banks to get questions for quizzes and tests, because of the benefit of the time saved by using pre-written exams instead of writing their own. There is a strong argument to be made for writing your own exams. Not only will this allow you to focus on the concepts that you think matter the most and have emphasized in class, but it will make your grading of the exams easier.[6]

PROVIDE SPEEDY FEEDBACK

Feedback matters in almost everything we do, but it matters even more in classrooms, where a class often lasts only a few weeks or months. As class sizes increase, the importance of getting speedy feedback increases too. A student in a class of only 15 or 20 can assess reasonably

---

3   Many schools are imposing grading distributions on their faculty. If you operate in such a system, you are relieved of the responsibility of coming up with your own distribution. I would still restate the school grading guidelines and my intention to adhere to it in the first session.

4   One reason I always move the points from any missed quizzes to what is left on the class, rather than re-weighting past quizzes, is to prevent game playing. For example, students who have done well on the first two quizzes may be tempted to miss the third quiz in order to get the first two weighted more heavily.

5   *Good reasons for missing quiz:* Physical or mental sickness (you, spouse or child), stalled subway train, important interview (and you cannot change time). *Not good reasons for missing quiz:* Did not have time to prepare, feeling overwhelmed, not quite ready.

6   When I write a question for an exam, I also work through not only the correct solution (as I see it) to this question but as many wrong solutions as I can. If the question is written well, the latter list should not be endless. A badly written or ambiguous question will generate far more possible wrong solutions.

7   I leave the weeks that I give quizzes relatively open – no outside engagements and committee meetings. It does require that I plan ahead several months.

accurately where they stand by keeping tabs or talking to others in the class, but a student in a class of 200 or more does not have that luxury. Consequently, grading quizzes, papers and exams and returning them to students promptly is even more critical when you have a big class than when you have a small one. Since you have far more grading to do with the former than the latter, this may strike you as impractical but it can be done with a combination of well-written exams and good scheduling.[7]

BE FAIR

It is not a bad grade *per se* that leaves a student feeling cheated, but the perception that either the way in which you tested or that you graded was not fair. How do you cultivate this perception of fairness? First, tie your testing, be it exams or papers, to what you do in the classroom. Nothing frustrates a student more than taking an exam where they are tested on concepts that you did not even touch on or emphasize in class. Second, make it difficult for students to cheat; have multiple versions of the same exam if you have multiple sections and use additional invigilators for exams. Finally, be willing to listen to students who believe that they have not been graded fairly. After all, listening to a grievance does not mean that you will need to change a grade.

CONNECT WITH THOSE WHO DO BADLY EARLY IN THE PROCESS

You are drawn to and want to cater to the students who like your class and are doing well, but the group that you should really pay attention to is the group that is not doing well in the class. Some of these lagging students will blame you for their troubles and others will blame themselves, but they collectively will drag the class down, if they feel that their causes are hopeless. You need to reach out to the students in this group early in the class and try your best to bring them back into the fold. This may require you or a teaching assistant spending more time with them or even offering focused review sessions at regular intervals but the pay-off will be substantial. Some in this group will indeed be able to turn around their performance and will be grateful to you for your efforts and even those who fail to pull this off will not blame you for their failure.

Outside the classroom

ELIMINATE ADMINISTRATIVE ISSUES

A significant portion of the time that we spend in class and in office hours is spent answering administrative questions: What is the project? When is it due? What is the page limit? Much of this time can be reclaimed for more productive purposes by being more specific and detailed at the beginning of a class about these and other details.

WATCH FOR AND DEAL WITH REPEAT QUESTIONS

If you assess how you spend your office hours, I will wager that a large proportion of the time is spent answering the same questions (asked over and over again, but by different students).

---

8   A frequently asked question (FAQ) section of my website contains every question that I have been asked in my office hours more than three times and the answer that I gave to that question. The time saved across semesters is significant.

While this is tedious, there are two devices that you can use to reduce these repeat questions. The first is to go back and fine-tune your lectures to remove any ambiguity or uncertainty you may have left behind on individual topics: repeated questions suggest that a large number of students were unclear about something you said. The second is to answer the question explicitly and put the answers up for the entire class to share.[8]

BE ACCESSIBLE

Being accessible to your students is important in any class but it is doubly so in a large class, where students are too intimidated to ask questions in class. While having regular office hours is an obvious solution, having an open door policy where students can drop in at other times is an even better policy. My experience suggests that if students know they can find you when they need you (which is what an open door policy engenders), they are less likely to look for you in the first place.[9]

USE TECHNOLOGY

There is a downside to email, but there is also a substantial upside. Not only can you respond to students when you are away from your office, but you can also keep in touch with them, reminding them of coming deadlines and drawing their attention to interesting news stories.[10]

The classroom experience

OFFER THE BIG PICTURE TO YOUR CLASS

Classes that become laundry lists for topics are difficult to teach, administer and grade. I believe that every well-taught class tells a story that cuts across class sessions and provides a way of linking the topics and subject matter covered by the class. Figure 8.2 shows the one that I use to begin the first session of my corporate finance class and I use it to explain how the class will be sequenced and to anchor all the subsequent classes.

FOCUS EACH CLASS ON ONE OR TWO KEY QUESTIONS

While you may be tempted to cover many issues in a single lecture, the reality is that it is difficult for students to hold on to many different lessons simultaneously. Focusing each lecture on one or at the most, two, major issues is one way to ensure that the lecture is well-organized and students walk away with a few key points. Sometimes, less is more.

MAKE IT RELEVANT

In addition to posing the question around which a lecture will revolve, you should spend some time explaining why answering the question matters. While this may take away from what you feel is more substantive theory or discussion, establishing relevance is a key step in grabbing the attention of your class. To provide an illustration, one of the key questions that you examine in corporate finance is how you measure the risk in an investment. Before I jump

---

9   This may sound counterintuitive but anxious students will monopolize your office hours, because they worry that this is their only chance to get questions answered.
10   On average, I send 4–5 emails a week to my class and put the text of all of the emails online so that they can refer back to earlier emails.

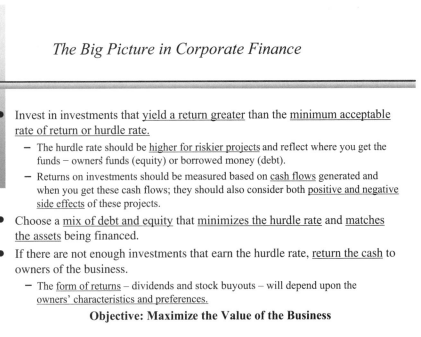

The Big Picture in Corporate Finance

- Invest in investments that <u>yield a return greater</u> than the <u>minimum acceptable rate of return or hurdle rate.</u>
  - The hurdle rate should be <u>higher for riskier projects</u> and reflect where you get the funds – owners' funds (equity) or borrowed money (debt).
  - Returns on investments should be measured based on <u>cash flows</u> generated and when you get these cash flows; they should also consider both <u>positive and negative side effects</u> of these projects.
- Choose a <u>mix of debt and equity</u> that <u>minimizes the hurdle rate</u> and <u>matches the assets</u> being financed.
- If there are not enough investments that earn the hurdle rate, <u>return the cash</u> to owners of the business.
  - The <u>form of returns</u> – dividends and stock buyouts – will depend upon the <u>owners' characteristics and preferences.</u>

Objective: Maximize the Value of the Business

Aswath Damodaran

Figure 8.2   Offer the big picture to your class

into the models for risk and return, I begin by defining risk in the most general terms, note how it is part of every decision that you make as a human being and why it is important to have a model for measuring risk and estimating the expected return.

LOOK FOR WAYS TO EXPAND AND IMPROVE PARTICIPATION

We constantly look for ways to improve classroom participation but the challenge becomes more daunting as class sizes increase, for two reasons. First, there is the intimidation factor where students do not want to ask what they think are silly questions in front of a very large audience of their peers. Second, many students in large classes resign themselves to spectator status and watch those who are quicker on their feet or better versed in the topic step in and answer questions. To improve participation, you can try two techniques. One is to call on specific students and help them work toward an answer, though there is a risk that those students may be embarrassed if they are unable to respond. The other is to provide a focused question and multiple possible answers to make every student in the classroom choose an answer before allowing for a discussion. In my class, I have built into my lectures a series of what I call 'passive' participation exercises, where students get to participate in discussion without putting themselves at risk. Figure 8.3 illustrates this.

With each of these questions, I usually require a couple of minutes of silence where each student can consider the choices and make one. Only then do I open the floor for discussion of the choices. The '2-minute' window ensures that everyone gets a chance to ponder the question, and the subsequent discussion brings out the different opinions on the question.

Seek active participation
Debt as a disciplinary mechanism

Assume that you buy into this argument that debt adds discipline to management.

Which of the following types of companies will most benefit from debt adding this discipline?

- ❑ Conservatively financed (very little debt), privately owned businesses.

- ❑ Conservatively financed, publicly traded companies, with stocks held by millions of investors, none of whom hold a large per cent of the stock.

- ❑ Conservatively financed, publicly traded companies, with an activist and primarily institutional holding.

Figure 8.3   Seek active participation

LOOK FOR MULTIPLE WAYS OF EXPLAINING KEY CONCEPTS

Even the best explanation of a concept or theory will leave some students confused or mystified. Rather than move on and risk losing those students for the rest of the topic, you should consider two or three other ways of explaining the same concept. Hopefully, one of these alternative explanations will allow the concept to click, thus bringing the confused into the fold.

LOOK FOR 'AHA!' MOMENTS

One of the most rewarding aspects of teaching is what I would call the 'Aha!' moment, where people go beyond what you are doing in the classroom and make a connection to a larger phenomenon that they have not understood before or see in a new way now. With large classes, it is more difficult coaxing out these moments, but they will occur and you need to be ready for them.

Conclusion

If teaching is about connecting with your students and making a difference in how they think and perhaps even live, you should welcome the opportunity to have more students rather than less. While much has been made about the administrative headaches and grading burden of having large classes, there is no reason why teaching effectiveness has to decline with class size. It is true that you need to be more organized and structured when you teach a large class, and that you have to prepare far more for your class lectures, but the pay-off is also large. If teaching is about creating magic in a classroom, there is no feeling more magical than being in the well of an amphitheater with 400 students hanging on to every word you say, completely connected with you. For that moment at least, you can see why Mick Jagger and Elton John continue to go on concert tours, even though they need neither the money nor the fame, and why Laurence Olivier, for all his fame as a movie actor, kept returning to live theater. As teachers, in a sense, we are actors, and having a large audience is better than having a small one, especially if you can get them to applaud.

Appendix: Ten tasks for more effective teaching

The points emphasized in this chapter can be converted into a series of tasks or steps that can be implemented in any class. In this appendix, we list ten tasks and steps within each task that can help in making teaching more effective. Note that the difficulty associated with putting each task into practice can vary widely across subjects and across classes even within the same subject.

TASK 1: THE BIG PICTURE FOR THE CLASS YOU TEACH ...

- Think about the big picture/first principles that govern the class that you are teaching now. While doing this:
  - avoid the jargon that is endemic to every discipline;
  - think in terms of the principles that govern how you think through problems in your discipline rather than on tactics or strategy;
  - put first principles in common sense terms;
  - keep it compact (should fit on a page).
- Test it out by explaining what you are trying to do in your class to someone who does not know anything about your discipline and, better still, does not care.

TASK 2: THE QUESTION OF THE DAY IS ....

For each session in your class, outline the key question or questions that you hope to answer. In doing so, keep in mind that:

- most good lectures revolve around one or two questions;
- framing the question correctly will make it easier for your students to follow the class;
- your lecture should revolve around answering the question.

TASK 3: MAKE IT RELEVANT

For each session in your class, explain why answering the question you will be addressing in that session matters to your students. In coming up with the motivation, remember that the following reasons don't usually work:

- you need to know it because it will be on the exam;
- everyone in my discipline (finance, marketing ...) believes that it is important to know this ...

If you cannot find a good reason why students should know the answer to a question, perhaps you should not ask it in the first place ...

TASK 4: GENERALIZE YOUR DISCUSSION

Take each lecture and go through it looking for ways to say things that appeal to those:

- from other countries and cultures;
- from other backgrounds (not finance, in my case);
- with other interests and career plans.

TASK 5: MAKE IT REAL

For at least one measure, model or proposition in your class, follow it up by having students look at a real company. If possible:

- let them pick their own companies;
- make it real time;
- work with the companies in class;
- if not, use a case ...

TASK 6: EXPLAIN WITH EVERYDAY OCCURRENCES ...

Using a key concept in your discipline, see if you can come up with something from everyday life that brings it home. If you can:

- make it personal;
- make it funny;
- keep it connected to what you are trying to explain.

Try it out on an audience. If it does not work, try modifying it. If it does, remember it and keep fine-tuning it.

TASK 7: CREATE ACTIVE PARTICIPATION ...

Take at least one or two open-ended questions that you currently ask in class and see if you can convert them into a multiple choice questions, with each answer representing a feasible answer (albeit with a different assumption needed to get there).

TASK 8: CREATE 'AHA' MOMENTS!

'Aha' moments are, by definition, spontaneous but you can help by creating a non-threatening atmosphere for students to experiment and by avoiding buzz words. Generally the more important the proposition, the greater the payoff to letting students get there on their own.

TASK 9: CONSIDER YOUR MOTIVATION

- Think of what attracted you to your subject matter in the first place (finance, marketing, management, operations, strategy ...) and why. Are you conveying this excitement to your students?
- Think of what bothered you the most when you were learning this subject (The dogma ... the models ... the assumptions ...). Are you repeating the same mistakes?
- Why are you a teacher?

TASK 10: YOU AND TECHNOLOGY

- Make a list of all the technology you use in the classroom and why you use it. Consider what you will do as backup if any aspect of that technology fails during a class.
- Consider which technological innovations make you a better teacher and which ones may get in the way of effective teaching.

9 Diversity Dynamics in Teaching

Hellicy Ngambi

Introduction

While the cultural, ethnic, gender, racial and linguistic student profile has changed relatively rapidly, the profile of staff in the training institutions has not. The racial and gender make-up of teaching staff remain overwhelmingly white, and, at senior levels, male. For example, over 90 per cent of full professors in the Health Sciences Faculty at UCT in 1998 were white men (Health Sciences Faculty, Employment Equity Audit Plan, August 1999). At the University of South Africa, as at January 31, 2007, over 80 per cent of full professors were white (Employment Equity & Transformation Report, 2007). This poses challenges in terms of existing staff being able to introduce new ways of teaching, new role models and new values to support the changing learning environment, to a student body of increasing diversity in experience and background.

Depending on how the teachers handle issues of diversity, their impact on the learning environment may be either positive or negative. However, as may be commonly the case worldwide, most teachers have had little training as teachers. Moreover, where learning takes place in group settings, which is particularly the case in executive MBA and management development programmes, issues of diversity are amplified, simply because students have to work together as part of their training.

Having taught both in culturally and racially as well as linguistically diverse environments, I have faced challenges, some of which will be the topic of this chapter. I will also indicate how I addressed the challenges and my current thoughts on my approach. As well known in literature, diversity is not limited to culture, race, gender and language but includes, among others, religion and age which are important influential dimensions in the African context. In this chapter I will briefly look at literature on teaching in a diverse class, then share my experiences and conclude with lessons on teaching to diverse learners.

Brief literature on teaching in a diverse environment

As alluded to above, teaching in a diverse environment poses challenges which if not effectively addressed can hinder effecting learning. According to Hodgkinson (1997) and Jones (2004), the greatest challenges facing teachers and schools in the years to come include:

*   increase in diversity among the student population;
*   ability to recruit, prepare, support and pay for quality teachers;
*   providing mechanisms by which teachers can recognize, accept and affirm diversity;
*   the number of 'minority' is so large (for example, of 5.6 billion people in the world, 17 per cent are white and 83 per cent people of colour; 52 per cent women and 48 per cent men) if they don't succeed, the global village has a diminishing future!

Some researchers (Knowles 1980; Brown et al. 2000) indicate that a teacher's critical role is to create a positive climate that is conducive to learning 'which causes adults to feel accepted, respected and supported' (Knowles 1980, p. 47). And yet, most of the literature about how to teach and facilitate learning is silent about how teachers' social location and hence diversity is central to these processes in the classroom. This supports the assumption that a teacher's location does not affect the classroom environment in any significant way. Thus the teacher's social identity is ignored as though it has no effect or influence on their teaching and therefore on the students. This myth has begun to be questioned because both research and my personal experience, as will be discussed in this chapter, has revealed that positionality of the teacher is an important factor in the classroom environment.

Gorski (1997) indicates that in teaching to diversity teachers need to answer the following questions to guide them:

- The curriculum content and materials: Does it include contributions made by different ethnic/gender groups and provide models from such groups? Does it provide for discussions on diversity issues and encourage interactions which allow students to bring examples of everyday life into the classroom as part of their learning?
- The Teacher: Do they reflect on personal experiences and assess attitudes and prejudice values as they relate to dealing with different others?
- The student who comes with their own story and level of gender and cultural awareness: Does the teacher empower the students by encouraging them to share those stories and hear those of others? Does the teacher teach students to challenge the information they are presented with?

Teachers must engage their entire personality, how they think, what they know, how they know it, and how they feel and why they feel that way in the teaching process (Apps 1991, p. 1). Each one of us, whether we are always aware of it or not, has a set of diverse values formed by communities in which we grew up, as well as by our religion, social status and ethnic background (Apps 1991, p. 113) which affect teachers' ethical (and any other) decisions in the teaching process (Brown et al. 2000). Teachers have pre-conceived ideas about issues of race, gender, ethnicity and class which will play out in the actions and practices of teachers (Pohan 1996), which if not managed can block the positive learning outcomes. If, for example, one was to teach on leadership styles and approaches of Nelson Mandela, the former president of South Africa; Idi Amin the former president of Uganda; Robert Mugabe, the president of Zimbabwe; Tony Blair, the former prime minister of the United Kingdom; and George Bush the president of the United States, you would get different contents, methodology and responses depending on the positionality of the teacher as well as the students.

What I have learned as a teacher is that one needs an honest self-reflection and critique of one's own beliefs, opinions, values, thoughts and behaviour about different others and how their positionality influence their teaching methodology and student outcomes. What I do is acknowledge how my own world view can shape students' conceptions of self (Howard 2003) – self-fulfilling prophesy. We teach who we are (Palmer 1998). I question whether who I am contributes to the underachievement of students who are not like me. I also evaluate whether consciously or subconsciously I subscribe to the deficit-based notion of gender and culturally diverse students. Let me share some of my experiences as an African black woman.

Personal teaching experiences

In most of my classes I have had to introduce the sessions with a quote that clarifies my position and philosophy in the way I perceive the different or diverse other. I would put up a slide that reads as follows:

FIRST THOUGHTS: You and I

We meet as strangers, each carrying a mystery within us. I cannot say who you are. I may never know you completely. But I trust that you are a person in your own right, possessed of a beauty and value that are the Earth's richest treasures. So I make this promise to you: I will impose no identities upon you, but will invite you to become yourself without shame or fear. I will hold open a space for you in the world and allow your right to fill it with an authentic vocation and purpose. For as long as your search takes, you have my loyalty.

Author unknown

This quote highlights the fact that I am aware that each one of the students is unique and I do not expect any one of them to give up their uniqueness. I emphasize that their worth and value is in them drawing on that uniqueness in participating in the course. I highlight the importance of respect. I do not demand of them to respect me but I promise that I would respect them. In this regard I attempt to teach that respect is not demanded but earned and freely given. I usually talk about our differences whether I am teaching on diversity or any other topic. I reinforce the description of diversity as the mosaic of people who bring a variety of backgrounds, styles, perspectives, values and beliefs as assets to whatever group or organization with which they interact. Whether I am teaching on leadership or diversity I attempt to include the definition of diversity to build an awareness of diverse people that we are. I sometimes use an exercise that groups them into categories of what kind of pets, if any, they own. I ask them how those that own certain kind of pets or don't own any feel about the other group. I ask them how it makes them feel that the other groups feel the way they do about them. Then, I broadly define diversity. In the context of teaching I use the DuCette, Sharpiro and Sewell, (1996) definition. That is:

... encompassing the domain of human characteristics which affects an individual's capacity to learn from, respond to, or interact in a school environment. These characteristics can be covert or overt, recognised by the individual or not recognised, and biologically, or environmentally or socially determined. Some of these characteristics are meaningful only as they describe an individual; others are only meaningful as they describe the entire school climate so that teaching techniques, teacher expectations, discipline programmes and home/school/community relationships will all reflect an atmosphere supportive of learning ...

I also use a scenario I pose to my students in different countries that teach the complexity of our differences in knowledge and experiences we bring to the learning experience, which goes as follows:

An African professor went on sabbatical leave to America where she was lecturing to postgraduate students. She posed a simple problem that she usually puts to her African postgraduates:

There are five birds sitting in a tree. You take a slingshot and shoot one of them. How many birds are left in the tree?

(Ngambi in Smit and Cronje 2002, p. 236)

I would ask the students to write their answers on a piece of paper and give it to the next person. Then that person would share the answer with the class. This same message would bring different interpretations. Most of the American (Western) students said 'four' with certainty. They said, 'One subtracted from five leaves four.' Almost all of my African students said 'zero' with equal certainty. 'If you shoot one bird, the others will fly away,' they said. Then I would ask them who was right. I would proceed to explain to them that we all need to manage our parochialism. I would elaborate that 'different' may be uncomfortable but it is not wrong. Usually depending on who is marking the script, students' learning experience can be blocked by being 'wrongfully' graded. Thus, the positionality of the teacher would play a role in the outcome of the learning experience.

Teaching in South Africa, in an environment where apartheid enforced an inferior education system for the blacks as well as segregation, poses different challenges. Among these challenges is mistrust which leads to misinterpretation and miscommunication and hence misunderstanding. My role as a teacher, especially from the previously disadvantaged group, is to create a positive climate that is conducive to learning 'which causes adults to feel accepted, respected and supported' (Knowles 1980, p. 47; Brown et al. 2000). I attempt to engage my entire personality, how I think, what I know, how I know it and how I feel and why I feel that way in my teaching process. This approach is also supported by Apps (1991). As alluded to above, we all have a set of values, whether we are always aware of it or not, formed by communities in which we grew up, as well as by our religion, social status and ethnic background (Apps 1991, p. 113) which affect us in our ethical, and any other, decisions in the teaching process (Brown et al. 2000). Having been brought up in a typical African village where most of the teaching was done through stories and practical application, my teaching style does reflect that approach.

For example, when I teach on leadership and the importance of having a caring empathetic value system I use a story. One of my famous stories (Ngambi 1999) is entitled: *It Does Not Concern Me*, and goes as follows:

Once upon a time, there was a family who kept animals – a cow, a dog, a chicken and a cat. A rat was seen in the house and the house owner set a trap to kill the rat. The rat then called a meeting with other animals in the house and tried to solicit help from them to remove the trap. All the other animals especially the chicken and the cow told the rat off, saying that the trap does not concern them since it cannot get them. The trap eventually traps a poisonous snake, which had entered the house, which bit the owner of the house, who died! Meanwhile the owner of the house was trying to stop a fight between the cat and the dog when he was bitten by the snake. Therefore, with the death of the owner of the house, the cat and the dog each blaming the other for the death of the master, fought to death. On his death, the cow was slaughtered. On the last funeral rights, the chicken was slaughtered.

The lesson to be learned would be obtained from the answer to the question: 'In the long run, whose concern was the trap?' It was everyone's concern. If Africa, like any other continent, is to come out of its depressing economic condition, including in terms of its leadership, the people of Africa have to work together and value each other's contributions.

Africans have to learn to acquire, share and effectively utilize knowledge to take the continent to a level of excellence.

My instructional approaches and personal philosophy are influenced by my beliefs and cultural background. This in turn impacts on the way that I teach. I was brought up as the daughter of a village headman, one of the senior chiefs in Zambia's Mwenichifungwe chieftaincy. In an African village, the common element in all the activities of the community is participatory democracy, and consensus decision-making based on 'WE' NOT 'I' as is evidenced in most Eurocentric organizations. Members of the community would bond through stories, songs, dances and slogans, thus fostering trust and group care. Hence, my use of stories in teaching. As Pohan (1996) puts it, teacher beliefs influence the type of activities in which students are engaged, the feedback students receive and the degree of interaction that takes place between teachers and students.

Influence of past experience on teaching

THE CURRICULUM CONTENT AND MATERIALS

Since most of the text books available are American, when I teach in Africa I include articles and experiential case scenarios from Africa to bring about relevance. I specifically look for contributions made by different ethnic/gender groups and provide models from such groups. I also ensure that the curriculum content and materials provide for discussions on diversity issues and encourage interactions which allow students to bring examples of everyday life into the classroom as part of their learning process. I have also done some case studies of African chiefs and their leadership styles which I include when teaching on leadership. For example, when I teach on management programmes, I attempt to illustrate that unless you know your employees you cannot effectively manage them. I would pose the following case scenario:

> One of your employees came to you last year to ask for permission to attend her father's funeral and you granted her permission and she went and came back. The same employee comes again this year to ask for permission to attend her father's funeral. You recall she had the same request last year. What would you say to her and why?

Most of the students on the management development programmes and MBA who would be predominantly white males in South Africa, as well as the United States where I have taught, would say no, because she is lying since she already buried her father last year. Then I would explain to them that in the African culture, your father and all his brothers are considered and addressed as 'father'. It could be that one of the two is what in the western culture is known as uncle, but in the African culture referred to as 'father'. Since as managers we have to manage, motivate, retain and evaluate employees' performance it is very important that we know and understand them. Without that knowledge, trust is broken and performance, hence productivity, adversely affected. This approach is influenced by my positionality as an African black female teacher.

When I am teaching I reflect on experiences and assess my attitudes and prejudice values as they relate to dealing with different others. For example I was brought up to believe that as a woman you do not argue with men and your elders. In a teaching environment for learning to be effective you have to discuss and debate ideas and perspectives. When teaching on executive programmes, most of the participants are older and male. By reflecting on my experiences and values I am able to foster a learning environment, which though respectful of cultures, does not hinder class discussion and debate. The debate is not done in a eurocentric way but more in a form of conversations and dialogue. What I then do is empower the students who come with their own story and level of gender and cultural awareness, by encouraging them to share those stories and hear those of others and to challenge the information they are presented with respectfully, not in a judgemental but evaluative way.

Having taught in Zambia and Botswana in an all black student classroom, I realize that issues of diversity (for example, gender, age and culture) arise and need to be considered. Irrespective of similarities most students will assert their differences and need to be given a chance as individuals. The same has been true in an all white classroom in South Africa and the US where I have also taught.

I have learned that the metaphor of the melting pot is no longer functional. We have to switch to either the toss salad or the stew. It allows us to focus both on the differences in the ingredients while at the same time the beauty of the whole. Covert (1995, p. 403) says, 'A good salad does not have a bunch of components that look, taste, or have the same texture. The success of the salad depends not only on its looks but also on a lot of other factors including the taste, the freshness of the ingredients, the smells, the textures and the mixture itself.' This is very true of a learning environment where discovery is encouraged for the students to expand their knowledge and grow. This can be said to be true for the global village.

Research findings (Brown et al. 2000, pp. 277–286) indicate that as a black female teacher, positionality affects my classroom experiences by producing a teaching philosophy based on a history of marginalization; raising issues of credibility based on race and gender; directly affecting classroom interactions and teaching strategies. My instructional approach and teaching philosophy does seem to confirm these research findings. This is also reflected in most of my responses to media interviews. I am inclusive and sensitive, preventing students from being marginalized and empowering all. I invite all learners irrespective of their positionality to participate in sundry ways. I would usually feel that with my exposure, I am an instrument that can bridge students to life-long learning. For example, when I just came to teach in South Africa in 1994, some white Afrikaner male students would say to me that they had problems with me because I am a woman, and a black woman. They would say they had contact with black women only as their maids and never have had a woman in a position of influence over them. It was difficult for them to accept that a black woman would be their teacher. My response to this was more of, 'I better help these students to un-learn this myth.' They had been taught all their lives that a woman, especially a black woman, can neither teach nor manage or lead them. I would thus be involved in motivating them and encouraging them by citing blacks and women who have been leaders, managers, teachers, authors and the like. I believe that everyone can learn. To some extent I do feel, as Brown et al. (2000, p. 278) would put it, that, 'It is my job to give them the time, patience, environment, teaching, and attitude that they may learn.' This again is probably due to my communal upbringing as an African princess taught to be patient and to always encourage people to be positive. My dad used to say, 'People are not paid to be members of the village and chieftaincy. They can always vote with their feet and leave.' He would say, 'Ensure that they don't do that by genuinely caring for them, involving them, being forgiving, and building trust by being trustworthy.'

Students' perception of a good teacher also reveal that both male and female students refer to a 'he' rather than a 'she'. When I ask students who their best teachers were, most of them would refer to a 'he'. In a session at one of the ITP workshops, I asked participants, who are mostly teachers themselves, from different continents to describe their best teacher. The responses were as follows:

Best Teacher:

Male/he = 20 (67 per cent)
Female/she = 3 (1 per cent)
Anonymous/plural on gender = 7 (23 per cent)

This perception confirms that in many cases students question the teacher's credibility based on race and gender by stereotypes such as belief that the best teacher is male, especially white male. My awareness of this perception causes me to be always over-prepared for my sessions and citing other sources for the position that I take to prove that I have done my research and know my 'story'.

Another aspect that has had an impact on my classroom interactions and teaching strategies is my experiences as a student. In most of my classes in Africa, UK and the US, my observation was that male classmates received more feedback and positive reinforcement from both male and female teachers of all races. In this regard I do agree with Sadker and Sadker (1994), that positionality affects classroom interactions and teaching strategies. Having witnessed this in my time as a student I attempt to balance the scales (teacher–student interactions) by calling on the marginalized and reaffirming them. In my culture, women are not supposed to instruct/tell men what to do, which directly influences classroom interactions. In most cases I use humour and stories instead of 'I am a teacher so I must win attitude' in interacting with learners who use verbally abusive words. I also assume an accommodating non-confrontational and gender-specific role of building trust as explained above.

When I first walked into a management development class to teach in the former apartheid RSA, the students' reaction was more like, what is this? Some students whispered to each other as to whether the business school has appointed an AA teacher. As a black African female, I am sensitive as to how I treat the content. I usually would use 'she' rather than 'he', especially when illustrating a positive aspect. In leadership examples I use 'she' and not always 'he' and both female and male role models. I emphasize cultural differences in leadership. Using a participative approach, I call on all, including the marginalized. I use the concept of Ubuntu (African Humanness), *Umuntu ngumuntu ngabantu*: Nguni for, 'A person is a person through other human beings.' *Rintiho rinwe a ri nusi hove*: Tsonga for, 'One finger cannot pick up grain.' *Izandla ziyagezana*: Swazi for, 'The hands wash each other.' Basically emphasizing that all students are important ingredients for effective learning. These experiences provide some lessons for teaching to diversity.

Some lessons for teaching to diverse students

In conclusion, there are some lessons which have helped me as teacher, in this global village where students' diversity is increasingly becoming the norm rather than the exception. Some of these lessons are briefly discussed below.

NEED FOR CRITICAL REFLECTION TO FACILITATE DIVERSITY RELEVANT PEDAGOGY

As a teacher you need to critically reflect on the curriculum content and materials, the student and yourself. What I have come to know as an African black female teacher is that one needs an honest self-reflection and critique of one's own beliefs, opinions, values, thoughts and behaviour about different others and how one's positionality influences one's teaching methodology and student outcomes to facilitate gender and culturally relevant pedagogy. Some of the questions that I have found helpful in my reflection as I prepare to teach to diverse others are those Howard (2003) posed as questions to facilitate critical reflection. That is:

- How frequently and what types of interactions did I have of the different others when growing up?
- Who were the primary persons that helped shape my perspectives of different others?
- Have I ever harboured prejudiced thoughts towards people from different gender, cultural and other diverse backgrounds?
- If so, what effects do such thoughts have on students who come from those backgrounds?
- Do I create negative profiles of individuals who come from different backgrounds?

Responses to these questions would help you to create positive student outcomes. This could, as has done for me, enable you to:

- respond more positively to differences;
- give examples from diverse groups;
- use text books that reflect diversity;
- draw from diverse sources in cases;
- provide some role models;
- understand and support;
- value and include articles and experiential case scenarios from the different countries as well to bring about relevance and equip learners for the global village.

'It is the critical function of the teacher to create a rich environment from which students can extract learning and then guide their interactions with it so as to optimize their learning' (Knowles 1980, p. 56). However, 'regardless of the classroom richness that a teacher may create their gender, race, culture and other differences may still be triggers for negative interactions with their students (Brown et al. 2000)) and hence influence the learning outcome. What might help you as a teacher to be more effective, among other things is to:

- know the law;
- examine your teaching behaviours, attitudes and values;
- clarify your teaching philosophy;
- use appropriate teaching strategies to address the needs of the diverse students;
- become cultural broker: be aware of the gender, cultural and other diverse contexts that shape not only your own but the students' way of knowing; and
- develop meaningful relationships with students, be a team leader – tell your stories.

As president Mbeki would put it, 'We are all condemned to live together and interact with one another, both the unwashed and the perfumed. Divorce is not possible. Inevitably the actions of the one impact on the other for better or for worse, with none in reality being capable of successfully pursuing their purposes without the co-operation of the other.' This is true not only for the African continent but the global village.

Remember, 'Gender, cultural and other diversity is not a choice but a reality.'

References

Apps, J. W., (1991). *Mastering the Teaching of Adults*. Malabar, FL: Krieger.

Brown, A.H., Cervero, R.M. and Johnson-Baily, J., (2000). Making the Invisible Visible: Race, Gender, and Teaching in Adult Education. *Adult Education Quarterly*, 50(4): 3–288.

Covert, J.D., (1995). The Effects of Social Contact on Prejudice. *Journal of Social Psychology*, 135(3): 403–406.

DuCette, J.P., Sewell, T.E. and Shapiro, J.P., (1996). 'Diversity in Education: Problems and Possibilities' In F. B. Murray (Ed.), *The Teacher Educator's Handbook: Building a Knowledge Base for the Preparation of Teachers*. San Francisco, CA: Jossey-Bass. (pp. 136–155).

Employment Equity Audit Plan, (1999). *Health Sciences Faculty*, University of Capetown, South Africa.

Employment Equity & Transformation Report, (2007). University of South Africa, South Africa.

Gorski, P., (1997). *Initial Thoughts on Multicultural Education-Multicultural Pavilion*. New York: Macmillan Publishing Company. (pp. 3–18).

Hodgkinson, H.L., (1997). Diversity Comes in All Sizes and Shapes. *School Business Affairs*, 63(4): 3–7.

Howard, P., (2003). Changing Cultures. *PMJ: Plant Managers Journal*, 30(3): 31, 2p, 2c.

Jones, H., (2004). A Research-Based Approach on Teaching to Diversity. *Journal of Instructional Psychology*, 31(1): 12–19.

Knowles, M.S., (1980). *The Modern Practice of Adult Education: From Pedagogy to Andragogy. 2nd ed*. New York: Cambridge Books.

Ngambi, H.C., (1999). Community Leadership: The Cases of an African village and an American firm. *Southern African Business Review*. 3(2): 27–4.

Ngambi, H.C., (2002). 'Managing Diversity' In Smit and Cronje, *Management Principles: A Contemporary Edition for Africa*. Juta & Co, Cape Town, South Africa.

Ngambi, H., (2004). 'African Leadership: Lessons from the Chiefs' In Meyer, T.A. and Boninelli, I. (Eds). *Conversations in Leadership: South African Perspectives*. Johannesburg: Knowledge Resources. (pp. 107–132).

Palmer, P.J., (1998). *The Courage to Teach: Exploring the Inner Landscape of a Teacher's Life*. San Francisco: Jossey-Bass.

Pohan, C.A., (1996). Preservice Teachers' Beliefs About Diversity: Uncovering Factors Leading to Multicultural Responsiveness. *Equity & Excellence in Education*, 29(3): 62–69.

Sadker, M. and Sadker, D., (1994). *Failing at Fairness: How America's Schools Cheat Girls*. New York: Scribner.

10 Teaching and Learning in a Multicultural Environment: A Mild Polemic

Seán Gaffney

This chapter combines general background material and practical exercises – all easily facilitated by any teacher – to explore and consider issues related to culture and education. The focus is on how these issues may impact on a class of international students. In addition, it provides an overview of the relationship between individual, group and the class as a whole from cross-cultural and group dynamics perspectives. Throughout, it offers practical exercises at individual, small group and class levels, aimed at generating experiential learning of value to both students and their teachers.

Naturally, these potential 'learning outcomes' are partly dependent upon the reader's interest in the subject itself. For teachers, the outcomes are also linked to the teacher's interest in developing a range of classroom skills of particular relevance to working with international student groups. Finally, I am aware that my own presentation of these themes will also impact on the reader's interest, patience and curiosity.

Introduction

Increasingly, Business School classes at undergraduate, graduate and doctoral levels are intentionally international with regard to their composition. In some cases, this internationalism is based on the nationality of the students. In other cases, it is more culturally based: the students may all be formally of the same nationality while, at the same time, culturally diverse in terms of ethnicity and home environments, as can increasingly be the case in many schools. This can be made further complex by issues which are internal to a particular socio-cultural environment. I have met a student who was officially identified by the university as 'Malaysian'. In Malaysia, she is identified as 'Indian'. Within the Indian community in which she lives, she is identified as 'Christian'. As one of her teachers, I needed to learn from her of these complexities in order to relate professionally to her in a manner which was meaningful to her – and therefore supportive of her learning.

I have many colleagues worldwide who regard such information as both unnecessary for them as teachers and even as a problem they can do without. If, on the other hand, colleagues are interested in learning – which I believe is one of the responsibilities of a professional teacher – then the 'problem' provides ample opportunity.

A recent example of my own learning – as a Senior Lecturer on an intentionally international MBA Programme – I had four Chinese students. During my early sessions with the class, it was not unusual for one of them to ask a question or make a comment, followed by a brief exchange between them all in Chinese. These interactions with me slowly faded into a compact silence. My 'exam' for this particular class is in the form of a personal learning paper, reporting on the learning process as it unfolded during the course. Amongst the issues I ask the students to address is to consider what 'cultural aspects' supported or alternatively hindered their learning. One of the Chinese students – explicitly on behalf of the others as well – stated that their learning was hindered early on by the behaviour of a male 'western' student who addressed me by my first name and constantly questioned my input and debated details with me. For the Chinese students, this meant that I would regard the whole class as disrespectful of me, and, in consequence, they – the Chinese group – then felt too embarrassed to engage openly with me.

Whilst this may seem like an issue related only to the Chinese students, in fact it had wider implications. A number of other students in their learning papers referred to the 'distant' and 'uninvolved Chinese'. A behaviour which the Chinese experienced as including them as members of a collective class was having consequences for them which were being experienced by others in a totally different manner. In other words, the social and learning interactions of a whole class were influenced by the experience of four students in relation to the behavioural interaction of one student with 'the professor', and the ripple effect this had on the class as a whole. Part of my learning here is the importance of the issues this chapter addresses, including the classroom exercises – with respect to the example above, this class did not have the opportunity to participate in any of these preliminary exercises. Had they done so, then both the students and I would have had a shared experience and reference for discussing classroom behaviours.

To further focus on this issue, allow me to cite some other recent examples from various MBA Programmes internationally, on which I teach. The names used are fictional in all cases and the nationalities equally anonymous – it is not my intention to provide some checklist of cross-cultural behaviour and teacher interventions, but rather to present issues which the reader can relate to their own experience as a teacher (or even as a student!). As a result, I have deliberately chosen a selection of male and female names in Gaelic (the original language of Ireland and Scotland):

1. Oisín is a member of a project group on an explicitly international MBA Programme. He seems to be under stress during the early modules, and eventually requests a meeting with me. (I am identified as a Gestalt Psychotherapist and Lecturer on the 'Group Dynamics' module). He explains his situation. Oisín comes from a culture where class-group and family loyalty is paramount, though he was born and raised in another country. Having successfully completed his first degree, he quickly got a junior executive position and had been working abroad as a middle-manager. His father had been in constant touch with him, and had recently begun to mention things like 'coming home' and 'settling down'. This had led to a lengthy description of 'suitable' single women within their community. There was, however, a difficulty: the most suitable possible wives had Ph.Ds. Oisín did not. In his father's view, a distinction from a reputable MBA Programme might be a balancing factor. So Oisín was encouraged to find an MBA of sufficient status where a degree with distinction could be used as a bargaining item in marriage negotiations with the parents of suitable daughters with PhDs. He found himself on what he regarded as a MBA Programme of some status – though where group projects and grades were part of the programme, something he had read about in the prospectus and not thought through. Working in a group deprived him, as he saw it, of the possibility of a degree with distinction as a personal and individual achievement. This was an existential issue for him, and deeply private. It took me an hour of conversation with him to get to this point. His need was for a similar goal for all members of his group – which did not seem to him to be forthcoming.
2. Bríd is an ambitious young woman with some professional experience as a junior manager. The international MBA is her first experience of extensive cross-cultural interaction in an international setting. In her Project Group, she pushes a strong ethnocentric line

about how a group 'should' function, how individual members 'must' behave. Any other group member who does not explicitly comply with these apparently obligatory and inevitable 'norms' became the subject of her criticism, both explicit and implicit. She also elicits alliances with other group members around these issues, thus consolidating her ethnocentric expectations into a normative perspective.

3. Eoghan had difficulties from the opening of the programme. Following a day when class members each presented themselves, the faculty introduced the project groups, which had been chosen to ensure a maximum mix of gender, culture, language, academic background, working experience, and so on. The groups were asked to meet and prepare a presentation of themselves as a project group. On the following day, as these presentations were about to begin, Eoghan expressed his frustration at the time-wasting involved – since everyone had already presented themselves earlier, surely this would simply be a repeat of those presentations, in his opinion. As the group work progressed, there were complaints from his group colleagues about Eoghan's behaviour. He did not come to every group meeting about their project. He never came to any social event when, for example, the other group members suggested going out to dinner or for a drink together. On the other hand, he would generally do any task allotted to him, though not always within the agreed time frame. He had little or no interest in reading anyone else's contribution. If he did read the finished group product, it was generally with a stream of critical comments including how *he* would have done it had he been left alone to do so.

4. Daragh was slightly older by about 5 years than any other group member. He also had very specialist knowledge outside of the general economics focus of the MBA. Within weeks, he was openly critical of the comparative youth, lack of working experience and level of knowledge of his fellow group members. He began missing meetings and being openly critical of his group colleagues within the class in general. He refused to participate in contributing to group projects as he was 'not learning anything from the others'.

5. Aislinn seemed to fit in smoothly with her group. Then comments from her group-colleagues began to become complaints. She was generally silent during group meetings, turned in work if the guidelines were clearly stated, and only contributed verbally if 'pushed' to do so.

It is all too easy to see these as examples of individual behaviours, requiring individually-based interventions. However, the reality is that, in each of the above cases, the whole Project Group and its dynamics as a working-group were impacted. Sides were taken; groups fragmented; interpersonal animosities became increasingly central. Deadlines were either missed or managed by last-minute individual actions. The issues internal to the Project Groups leaked out into the class as a whole over time. Other students also took sides; some avoided the students mentioned above. Some blamed the faculty and even the programme itself for disturbing the smooth flow of input and exams by bothering with group projects.

Oisín had difficulties sharing his dilemma with others and became increasingly isolated. He finally confided in one other member and thus – unwittingly – created a secret alliance which led to them both becoming isolated in a more and more fragmented group. Bríd finally became a scapegoat in her group and, by extension, in the class as a whole. Eoghan's consistently 'self-focused' behaviours created compact opposition and he faced being expelled from the programme as an increasingly disruptive presence. Daragh managed to polarise the class as a whole around 'being in a bad group', and found a way to switch groups – though the faculty had expressly stated that the essential learning about group dynamics would be best served by working through individual and group difficulties in each of the three sets of

Project Groups that would be operative over the programme. In a written assignment, Aislinn explained how difficult it was for her to be in her Project Group. She was the youngest and female. Her degree was not of the same 'quality' or relevance as those of her colleagues. Her English was comparatively the weakest. Her experience of groups in her home culture differed considerably from that of the others. She was used to showing respect for those older and more experienced than she, and only speaking when directly addressed. The cultural change was more than she could understand or handle.

Interestingly, those of the faculty who had experience of teaching in the home cultures of the students mentioned above could recognise the patterns of behaviours which were being exemplified. As such, some of these behaviours could be predicted; at the very least, they were not particularly surprising when they did arise.

These examples of the dilemmas of cross-cultural dynamics in our classrooms are further compounded by the trend towards group-work and Project Groups, and even group grades in many cases. This adds the dimension of group dynamics to an already heady mix. It also raises two other issues: 1) to what extent are Business Schools prepared to admit group dynamics as a practical and theoretical subject; and 2) to what extent are the more academically inclined and therefore content-oriented teachers prepared to tolerate that such dynamics are allowed to play a part in the educational programme as a whole. Interestingly enough, there are cultural contexts at work here. In some cultural settings – USA for example – group dynamics and organisational behaviour would not be unusual as integral parts of an MBA. In many countries in Europe, the opposite applies. Further afield, in many Asian and African environments not over-tainted by a post-colonial heritage, groups might be taken as a given.

There is clearly a link between project and/or group work on international MBA Programmes and the growing awareness in the corporate world of the use of multicultural Project Groups and teams: 'Multinational executive teams are coming of age. The days are passing when major multinational corporations (MNCs) such as General Electric or Matsushita, could operate complex, dynamic industries from the unambiguous cultural base of a home country … Resources are likely to flow towards MNCs that know when and how to use multicultural teams as business conditions require them (Bartlett and Ghoshal 1989).' (Maznevski and Peterson 1997, p. 61).

In addition, this complex interweaving of individual, group and class as a whole issues are typical of organisational life – precisely the context for which we are preparing our MBA/Business School students. To offer courses on management and leadership, Business Ethics and HR without acknowledging that our classes, teachers and school management are directly analogous to the realities of corporate life is to miss an opportunity for powerful and realistic learning.

Working effectively with cross-cultural group processes and dynamics in academic settings offers a number of challenges. Does the School Management *genuinely* support innovative practices in an academic setting, or is it merely talking the talk of competitive Business School marketing? Is there sufficient theoretical and practical support in terms of knowledgeable and experienced academics/group practitioners on the faculty? Can other faculty members, whose focus may be more content and examination-based, accept the inevitable impacts of group dynamics and cross-cultural issues? Can faculty function as an integrated whole when cross-cultural group dilemmas emerge? Interdisciplinary tensions are a natural aspect of any faculty: the question here is to what extent any faculty is prepared to accept group dynamics' dilemmas as an organic part of any programme. Part of the dilemma is this: that a cross-cultural group dynamics perspective does not have any easy or standard solutions. It has rather a number of in-the-moment issues which require in-the-moment interventions aimed at student and faculty *learning* rather than the pragmatic removal of anything which 'disturbs' some illusory status quo. MBA students learn little when potential real-life tensions in work-groups are apparently programmed out of existence by rules and regulations which aim at prohibiting or curbing such totally natural dynamics. The opportunities for true experiential learning – by both students and faculty – are considerably more valuable than an often over-optimistic attempt to pre-empt reality.

The remainder of this chapter will therefore focus on some practical supports for both students and teachers in multicultural educational settings. All of the examples which follow have been part of my work with international groups over the past 30 years in graduate, MBA and Executive Programmes, and, as such, are tried and tested.

Cross-cultural generalisations with a practical classroom exercise

'Culture' as a construct is a generalisation, referring to collectives rather than individuals. Individuals may or not be typical or representative of such generalised values, attitudes and their behavioural expressions – under normal circumstances. Under pressure, many individuals will resort to their instinctive cultural perspectives, as this provides security and familiarity. This would seem to be the case in the above examples.

There are as many definitions of culture as there are researchers into and authors on the subject. My intention here is to sidestep any debates around definitions, and focus on the work of Geert Hofstede (Hofstede 1984, 1994), as he has specifically addressed the impact of a cultural environment on education. What follows is an extrapolation of his work in this regard. Please note that using the model explicated below does *not* require any special cross-cultural knowledge by the teacher. All that is required is an ability to allow students to learn for and by themselves through facilitating an in-class exercise well within the competence of any teacher.

The model shown below is used in multicultural classes to raise awareness amongst all students of the differences and similarities they may have in their roles as students as well as in relation to the institution and its teachers. I ask them to work in culturally congruent groups where possible, and to explore their reactions to the model – what patterns do they recognise as representative of their experience in pre-school, school and university settings. To increase the interaction between teacher and students, I suggest that this model is best presented on a whiteboard, one column at a time:

TEACHER SEEN AS:	CONTENT SEEN AS:	STUDENT FOCUS: 1:	2:
Authority figure	The TRUTH	Me	Success
Expert	The latest	My group	Fairness
A resource	A range of possibilities	All students	Non-failure

Some examples of how I may explicate each of these items: to begin with, the first two are both concerned with a double perspective – the teacher's/institution's and the students'. So where any institution or teacher places itself is one side of the coin. At the same time, since this choice may in itself be culturally congruent, it is always relevant to the situation as a whole. How others perceive us can often be a function of how we see ourselves.

As an 'authority figure' I, as teacher, have power and influence both in and outside of the classroom. Students are likely to open the door for me, or at least wait until I have gone through before doing so themselves. Should I happen to walk into a café/restaurant/bar where students are gathered, those who see me as an 'authority figure' are likely to stand up and greet me formally. Whatever I say is important and is to be taken as *the truth* – and passing exams means reproducing my thinking, especially my favourite opinions. Alternatively, the café/restaurant/bar scenario could lead to some students seeing my presence as an intrusion on their personal time, and they are likely to leave and go elsewhere.

As 'expert', I am expected to know most and best. I *should* have the correct answer to any and all questions, and be fully up-to-date with *all* issues related to my subject. No student should ever be able to upstage me on a point of content. Any student who 'over-engages' with me in class can be seen as depriving others of my planned input and therefore impacting on the course content.

As 'resource', I am available for discussion and debate. Questioning my opinions and requesting my guidance are normal: the norm here would be a collaborative form of classroom interaction, exploring alternatives, delighting in differences of opinion, allowing individualised learning according to interest and ability.

As can be seen, each of these descriptors in the first column is directly related to the 'Content' column, so that the first two headings are interrelated as constructs. As touched upon above (Chinese and 'western' students), these distinctions in student/teacher perceptions of their relationship and its relevance for course content, can and do lead to misunderstandings. An additional aspect is that these first two columns may also be indicative of the ethnocentric nature of the Business School teaching/learning culture. To what extent this is implicit or explicit will also have an impact. Far too many students are being lured to schools by an over-enthusiastic use of the word 'international' in the school's marketing, only to find that faculty and management apply a policy of 'our way or the highway'!

When we move to the 'student focus' area, we are moving into a less obvious – or maybe less acknowledged/acknowledgeable – area. Here, students are generally more able to recognise others than they are at describing themselves. Be that as it may, even considering these options opens up areas for discussion. The student whose full focus is 'me' is generally easily recognised. For 'my group', the implications are more easily known. Generally, students with a shared background – whether national-cultural or social – can be distinguished. This can include sharing notes in exams. The 'all students' dimension is generally recognisable where student unions or student representation through, for example, class representatives are essential and active elements.

Where 'success' is concerned, we need only think of students for whom a distinction is the only valid result, or being class valedictorian, or any other such distinguishing honour. 'Fairness' is characteristic of students whose cultural influences include total honesty at exams, totally honest exams where all questions have been adequately covered in lectures or readings and so on. 'Non-failure' can be described as a situation where students focus on minimum requirements for a pass, and no more.

Such simple, generalised descriptions are usually more than enough for students to begin working on a profile of their 'home' culture and educational environment. Groups can report to the class as a whole, and a rough class profile can be created. Students can be encouraged to elaborate on these patterns, comparing and contrasting with each other.

It is not unusual for students to discover that differences in the first two dimensions do not exclude similarities in the latter two. Or that a value on 'fairness' can lead to explicit condemnation of cheating at exams, which may be more typical of a value on 'my Group' and 'non-failure'. An interesting variation can be that 'authority figure' and 'the truth' can be combined equally well with 'me' and 'success', as can 'resource' and 'range of possibilities'.

What is important is that students and teachers share an opportunity to explicate, explore and as openly as possible discuss these issues publicly, so that awareness is being raised on a collective level of some of the underlying and culturally relevant issues in any international class. Issues raised and discussed during an opening session can become a reference when misunderstandings seem to be occurring later.

With an international MBA class, a simple extrapolation can be useful. Replacing the words as follows has an interesting impact. 'Teacher' becomes 'management'; 'content' becomes 'company policy'; 'student' becomes 'career'. Exploring these can add a dimension to the original educational setting, relevant to an international class in any Business School.

From the general to the particular, with a practical individual/ classroom exercise

As educators, our interest is in learning. A number of researchers and authors have explored this subject, amongst them David Kolb (Kolb 1984). Kolb correlated his findings on the process of learning with possible 'styles' of learning or preferences, and developed his Learning Styles Questionnaire (LSQ), with 120 self-evaluated items. In England, two management trainers – Peter Honey and Alan Mumford – adapted Kolb's model and LSQ for easy application in executive settings. This led to an 80-item Learning Styles Inventory (LSI), and four simply understood Learning Styles: Activist, Reflector, Theorist and Pragmatist (Honey and Mumford 1992). Naturally, combinations can and do occur.

In order to promote a more interactive process in class than might usually be the result of an individual pen-and-paper exercise, I have developed a 16-item 'quick and dirty' version. Professors Jane Klobas and Stefano Renzi of SDA Bocconi, Milan, Italy have used this in their classes and correlated the results with the use of the 80-item pen-and-paper version. While there are certainly individual nuances in the results, the overall view of the Learning Style subgroups in any class are sufficiently accurate to be of use to both students and faculty. Anyway, here it is:

I draw the following matrix and ask students to copy it. I then give four learning situations, with four alternative learning preferences. First the diagram:

	A	B	C	D
1				
2				
3				
4				

I then go through the following situations and responses.

SITUATION 1: LEARNING TO RIDE A BICYCLE

(As a metaphor for learning about a new mobile, computer, camera, computer program and so on).

A. You get on the bicycle, wobble around a bit, fall off. You get back on the bicycle, adjust your balance and speed of pedalling and start cycling. You try to turn, and fall off again. You get back on again, hold your balance, pedal firmly, and turn less sharply. It works! You then get bored, hop off your bicycle, and go on to something new. You have, however, now learned how to ride a bicycle and will always remember it.

B. You watch A. You notice – with feeling – the dangers of falling off. You note the connections between balance, speed and careful turning. You go home, think it all through, and the following day, carefully mount a bicycle on a gentle downward hill, and start putting your observations and reflections into practice.

C. You find the best manual you can on 'Riding a Bicycle'. You read it, absorb it. Should you ever need to ride a bicycle, you now know how.

D. You find an expert cyclist, and ask them to simply and clearly show you how. No theory, just hands-on practice.

SITUATION 2: GROUP-WORK ON A COURSE

To explore this, imagine that each lettered group – A, B, C, D – is represented by five members of that learning style.

A. Before the teacher has quite finished introducing the task, you in your A group are up and running, looking for a public place in which to work. It is important for your group to see and be seen, to hear and be heard. Your group members will manage a task focus for about 5 minutes before launching happily into a discussion of everything and anything. With 5 minutes to go before it is time to report back, one member will bring the group to focus on the actual task – this member will probably be the group presenter. The presentation is likely to be highly spontaneous and include many items which others of that group do not explicitly recognise – though agree with as possibilities.

B. You and the other potential members of this group wait until it is absolutely clear that the teacher has no more information to give. You then look for a quiet and private place where you may work in peace. After a couple of moments, you all slowly agree that you are not all fully clear about the task. A reluctant representative is dispatched to find the teacher and clarify the task. Now your group can work! Group B will never be finished on time – it is always too soon to reach a final and safe conclusion. The reporting back will be brief, and focused more on the questions raised than any possible conclusions.

C. You will probably first get clarification of the task, then work with great efficiency to complete it, which you and your Group C colleagues are likely to do with time to spare. You use this time to explore other models and group tasks you have experienced, probably better suited to the current task than that being taught. Your group report will be more about the suitability of alternative models, than the actual task.

D. You will have one question: Why are we doing this? If the teacher answers satisfactorily, then your group will do the task. You are generally finished first, and use the spare time to make phone calls, check mail, watch the news, and so on. Group D reporting will be to the point and practical.

SITUATION 3: ASKING QUESTIONS IN CLASS

A. These are frequent questioners. Any silence can be ended with your questions. You can ask incomplete questions, where the answer comes to you as you ask the question. You can start off with a question which becomes a statement. You can ask the same question twice, apparently unaware that you have already asked it.

B. Asks retroactive questions – on yesterday's class, last week's readings, and so on. Always well-formulated and well-articulated questions (you probably rehearse your questions, to get them absolutely right!).

C. Asks short, concise and analytical questions. You want an answer now – or soon.

D. Your favourite words: 'Why' and 'How'.

SITUATION 4: PRE-COURSE/CLASS READING MATERIAL

A. Received with enthusiasm, fully intending to read it, you manage to find it again immediately before the relevant class, flick quickly through it for a diagram. Come to class with the reading prominently displayed. At the earliest opportunity, you refer enthusiastically to the one diagram you have seen, making intelligent comments about it. Honestly intend to read the material after class, which you never actually do.

B. Experts with highlight-pens, usually green and red or orange. Highlight all texts according to a consistent system. Your course material is always a rainbow of highlights.

C. If the material is clear, logical and complete, you will probably not come to class – too many time-wasting questions, group-works, and general time-wasting.

D. Will check what it is of the material you absolutely *must* read in order to follow the class. Frustrated if you discover that you have read materials unnecessarily!

When the students have completed the matrix, I ask them to identify as '4A', '3A', '2A', '1A' and so on, through A, B, C, D. They are also encouraged to focus on combinations, for example 2, each of any letter. They form groups around similar profiles. As such, the class has now moved from the culturally homogenous groups of the first exercise, to more interpersonally related groups of personal learning styles in this second exercise.

I then add the specific Learning Styles and some general information on them, as shown in Table 10.1:

Table 10.1   Honey and Mumford's learning styles

A	B	C	D
Activist	**Reflector**	**Theorist**	**Pragmatist**
Learns through activity	Learns through observing and reflecting	Learns through theory, models, solid input	Learns through 'hands on' practice
Likes interaction	Prefers listening	Likes structured, focused discussions	Likes realistic exercises
Likes a high tempo	Likes a slow tempo	Expects the 'right' tempo, which they 'know'	Likes varied tempo
Asks questions	Retroactive questions	Concise, logical questions	'Why' and 'how'
'Moves on' quickly	Prefers to consolidate	Moves on when satisfied	Can stick with it until they know how to do it

This is followed by discussion in the Learning Style groups, and then a general open plenary session.

With these first two exercises, both general cultural as well as more specific personal differences and similarities have been explored and explicated around learning – the shared activity of an international student class. Issues of direct relevance to working life in an international career have been explored in the safer and less decisive environment of a classroom – rather than in the stressful and costly world of real business and real organisational life. The next section of this chapter completes this combined learning focus of using the classroom as well as any group projects to provide solid experiential learning of value to both the students and the class during the programme – as well as solid practical training for life after Business School.

Groups and group work, with a practical group exercise

As mentioned above, the use of groups, group projects, group reports and group grading is becoming (or maybe even has become) standard practice in Business Schools. Regrettably, the use of professional group facilitators lags far, far, behind this trend. In what seems like a fit of neo-Taylorism, students are simply expected to be the group robots of trendy faculties. The reality is that people in groups – especially perhaps young, ambitious, career-hungry MBA students – are anything but robots. The Oisíns, Bríds, Eoghans, Daraghs and Aislinns of the opening vignettes are in full focus – including their impact on the groups/classes of which they are members. Cross-cultural and/or interpersonal and/or inter-competence differences are bubbling to the surface. In addition, the development process of any group is also up and running! And this process is particularly complex across cultures, in terms of expectations, attitudes, norms, behaviours and sanctions. This may be the forgotten – or even neglected or disowned – child of international business education.

An additional complexity here is that the most popular models of group development are generally from an Anglo-Saxon perspective and more particularly from an American one. Significantly, in this context, the most commonly-used models are moreover embedded in the dominant WASP (White, Anglo-Saxon, Protestant) and highly individualistic subculture of the USA. As such, these perspectives are fine and fully applicable within the cultures from which they sprung – though less useful in other cultures or with multicultural groups (Gaffney 2006).

My own research has been into testing parameters of group development which may apply cross-culturally inasmuch as culturally heterogeneous as well as homogenous groups can apply the constructs in a manner which supports group development without overt normative elements, other than those projected by members of specific cultures. This latter aspect is one which the proposed model can highlight, thereby providing an opportunity for further process within any group.

First, the Self and Peer Appraisal 'International Group Dynamics Model' (IGDM). This is worked on in two separate steps – Basic Stance and Behavioural Dynamics. It is strongly recommended that the Basic Stance exercise is used as early as the first gathering of a new Project Group.

HANDOUT 1

BASIC STANCE

A Part of the Group...Apart from the Group

Instruction: Please prepare to describe what each of these would mean in *your* home culture; also where *you* would be most comfortable on this continuum. Indicate the latter with an 'X'.

Then, one at a time, each member describes their understanding of these terms, and where they have placed themselves on the continuum.

The purpose of the Basic Stance self/peer appraisal is to explore the underlying assumptions about being a member of a group which each person brings with them. Further, to contrast and compare these assumptions – and first then to find whatever degree of congruence there may be amongst group members' perception of their positions as self- and – later – peer-appraised.

By about the third meeting, the group can be ready for the next step. Start with a current version of the Basic Stance exercise, as follows:

HANDOUT 2

BASIC STANCE

A Part of the Group...Apart from the Group

Instruction: Position yourself in *this group* with an X on the continuum. Use names or initials to position your perception of where the other group members are.

Each member declares their own self-appraised position, followed by listening to each other member's peer appraisal of that member's position.

The teacher can then present the next step, using the Behavioural Dynamics model. This step is best done spontaneously in real time. (Please note that the behaviours to the right might be those mostly associated with maintaining a Basic Stance of being 'A Part of the Group', with the opposite applying for those to the left. However, such generalisations will give way to the specific internal dynamics of any particular group, as self- and peer-perceived).

HANDOUT 3

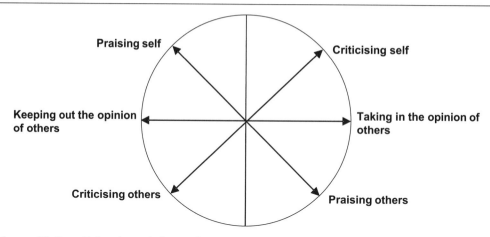

Figure 10.1   Behavioural dynamics

Instruction: Do a self-appraisal by indicating with an X where you see yourself on each continuum. Please note that you may find it appropriate to mark 2 Xs, indicating some situational aspect of your choice – mostly in one place, though sometimes in another on each continuum.

Now do a peer-appraisal by indicating with names or initials your perception of where each of the others are positioned.

Each member first gives their position on each continuum, then receives the peer appraisals.

Discussion.

The model provides an instrument for a) self-appraisal and b) peer-appraisal. Each member of a Project Group, for example, first self-appraises – ascribing whatever meaning to the constructs of the parameters which is relevant to them. They then also do a chart for each of the other members – from whatever perspective the appraiser holds, and whatever meaning the appraiser gives to the constructs of the model.

For example: take the core constructs 'A Part of the Group' and 'Apart From the Group' which here cover an hypothesised universal issue of group membership with a variety of cultural norms and practices. In the vignettes mentioned earlier, it is probable that Oisín, Bríd, Eoghan, Daragh and Aislinn would each place themselves as 'A Part of the Group' from their personal/sociocultural perspectives. Voicing these perspectives and their concomitant self-assessments will open up important issues within their respective groups and allow for discussion of cross-cultural behaviours, their similarities and differences.

When the full three-step exercise has been used, and each group member has voiced their self and peer assessments, these issues may become dynamic and fertile aspects of life in a multicultural work group. Issues which may hitherto have lain under the surface of the group's dynamics will at least be aired, if not immediately resolved. Resolving such issues in a manner which supports the work of the group can be seen as the 'inner task' of the group. It is the group members themselves who dynamically establish, develop and maintain the norms of *that specific group* to which they belong, finding a specific equilibrium between the diverse social, professional and cultural forces at work in the group at any time.

What is often referred to in the Anglo-Saxon literature as a balance between *group maintenance* and *task* (Adair 1986) is a more complex issue in multicultural contexts. In this latter case, a self-created synthesis of values and behaviours is more likely to be consensually developed and maintained by group members than any externally enforced normative system. Such a system may all too often be ethnocentric in origin and aims, thus allying itself from the outset with some, though probably not all, group members and inadvertently already dividing rather than uniting the group as a working unit with a shared task.

To return a moment to the earlier project group vignettes: in the always possible event that these students found themselves in the same group, the following scenario might well be relevant.

At the first meeting, all would probably place themselves as 'A Part of the Group'. Some would do this because, culturally, they 'ought to/should' do so; others because they 'must' as part of the course; others because being 'A Part of the Group' – any group – is a cultural norm and expectation. The discussion which followed this first exercise may well support the members to accept and even explore their differences.

By the third meeting, when the self-appraisals meet the peer-appraisals, then core group issues which were either casually or rationally accepted the first time may now become open to distinctions between theory and practice. Wherever members place themselves on the Basic Stance continuum, they are now faced with hearing how others perceive them – which may or may not be congruent with their self-appraisal. For example, Eoghan's on and off appearances and contributions would not influence his cultural perception of – formally – being 'A Part of the Group'. Others may be likely to place him 'Apart from the Group', as *they* perceive group membership. Aislinn's faithful attendance and obedience to explicit requests may create some confusion: whilst others would place her as 'A Part of the Group' with a touch of 'Apart from the Group', she is likely to place herself firmly as 'Apart from ...' due to her self-criticism around age, experience, contribution, and so on.

These and other issues would become more explicit as the group explored the Behavioural Dynamics exercise in both cases. Eoghan's ability to keep out the opinions of others as well as his generally critical attitude would be up for discussion, as would Aislinn's ability to take in others, be silently self-critical and openly impressed by others' knowledge and experience. Properly facilitated, the discussions that followed this exercise would not only support this Project Group as a working, task-focused unit, it would also provide an invaluable opportunity for all students to experientially learn about group dynamics. This latter would include some notion of the complexity and opportunities of cross-cultural group leadership in the context of international business. Surely such considerations fully belong to the curriculum of any serious international Business School education?

Concluding remarks

I intentionally subtitled this chapter 'A Mild Polemic'. I have far too many experiences of schools, managements and teacher colleagues who hold tightly on to known and proven approaches, while marketing innovation and creativity. Or schools which market 'an international environment' and actually mean the students, not the school. And certainly not the management in its attitude, nor the faculty in either its constitution or attitudes or practices. Neither ethnocentric nor standardised approaches, however explicitly proposed, can fully accommodate or satisfy an international student market. It is my firm belief that, until Business Schools can fully and actively engage in cross-cultural educational practices, then we are not practising what we may like to preach, and certainly not encouraging the very internationalisation of business that we claim to espouse and promote. We are rather continuing the cultural imperialism and dominance that has, in part, created the divided world in which we live.

Concluding recommendations for management and teachers

I am starting with management, as it is impossible for any teacher to attempt anything new without support – both before and after (see 3 below!).

1. Explore the needs of students by encouraging more qualitative programme evaluations rather then the ethnocentric questionnaires of today, mostly geared to reinforce your status quo.
2. Pay more attention to younger faculty, who in terms of age and experience, are closer to your students. Balance their views with those of senior faculty who represent the quality of course content in general.
3. Experiment. And remember that a 'failed' experiment in an educational setting has as much to do with the experiment itself as it has with the outcome. Do not be afraid to try again.

   For teachers:

1. Remember that *you* do not need any major cross-cultural knowledge to facilitate the learning of multicultural classes – your classroom skills are often more than enough!
2. Allow multicultural classes/groups to find their own equilibrium. Neither expect nor impose 'your' norms.
3. Learn to enjoy experiential learning – your own most of all!

References

Adair, J., (1986). *Effective Teambuilding*. London and Sydney: Pan Books.

Bartlett C.A. and Ghoshal S., (1989). *Managing Across Borders – The Transnational Solution*. London: Hutchinson Business Books.

Gaffney, S., (2006). Gestalt with Groups – A Cross-cultural Perspective. *Gestalt Review*, 10:3.

Hofstede, G., (1984). *Culture's Consequences*. London: Sage Publications.

Hofstede, G., (1994). *Cultures and Organizations*. London: Harper Collins.

Honey, P. and Mumford, A., (1992). *The Manual of Learning Styles*. Maidenhead, Berkshire, UK: Peter Honey Publications Ltd.

Kolb, D., (1984). *Experiential Learning.* New Jersey: Prentice Hall.

Maznevski, M and Peterson, (1997). Cross-cultural Work Groups (Claremont Symposium on Applied Social Psychology). Edited by Granrose and Oskamp. Thousand Oaks: Sage Publications.

11 *Damage Control and Tempered Change: Reflections on Working with Gender Issues in the Business School Classroom*

Charlotte Holgersson

Introduction

Management is still a male dominated area today where men and women face different working conditions and career opportunities, despite the increasing number of managerial and professional women in all developed countries (Davidson and Burke 2004). Management literature is still infused by a masculine ethos despite the fact that research on gender and organization today is a discipline in its own right (Wilson 1995; Halford and Leonard 2001; Wahl et al. 2001). It is therefore not surprising to find that mainstream management education also exhibits a non-inclusive culture, dealing with gender-absent theories promoting values and interests which in our Western society are associated with certain men. In fact, scholars have identified management education as part of the explanation to the existence of the 'glass ceiling' women encounter in organizations (Sinclair 1995; Marshall 1999; Wahl 1999; Smith 2000).

As a researcher within the field of gender and organization, I have taught organization and management in one of Sweden's most prestigious business schools both at undergraduate and graduate level, within executive education programs and a full-time MBA program. During these years, I have actively worked together with colleagues within my field to promote more gender-inclusive pedagogy and integrate a gender perspective in the business school curricula.

Drawing on my own and colleagues' experience of working with gender issues in management education, in particular in courses on organizational behavior, initially, I will discuss in which way gender matters in the business school classroom. In the second section, I will account for different examples of how gender issues have been addressed and some of the challenges involved. In a final section I will discuss two approaches when addressing gender issues that I have labeled 'damage control' and 'tempered change'.

In what way does gender matter in the business school classroom? Research problematizing gender in management education highlights the gendered nature of management education. Sinclair (1995) describes two layers of the culture underpinning MBA programs. The outer cultural layer reflected in the curricula and course guides, suggests a preference for quantitative and instrumental approach, stressing efficiency, competitiveness and output, rather than a behavioral approach. Students, in particular women, find that the quantitative and instrumental approach does not recognize or validate their own experience of management as something that is not only about working with numbers. Management curricula and textbooks largely exclude references to women and to research on women in management. The inner cultural layers are, according to Sinclair, reflected in teaching and learning styles, language and assessment methods deny and marginalize women's experience. Sinclair notes that the promotion of masculine values, experience and interests in management education, even if unintentional, has left largely unexplored the contributions and perspectives of women.

Moreover, the politics of gender in the classroom influence students' confidence and contributions (Smith 2000). For example, research shows that men typically speak more than women and women tend to display less assertive behavior in mixed-gender settings and may thus be perceived as generally less powerful or capable than men (Spender 1980; Tannen 1995). Educators' assessment of students' competence may be distorted if students are not able to make their voice heard. Since we attribute dominant linguistic styles more importance, women may find it more difficult to be heard in mixed group settings. Women also face a double bind due to the inherent contradiction between femininity and management (as a result of the correspondence between masculinity and management). If women conform to traditional perceptions of femininity and avoid a dominant assertive style, they are seen as less promising management material. If they conform to traditional perceptions of management, they are perceived as too masculine and too pushy (Sinclair 1995). Either way, women are judged as deficient (Wahl 1995; Wajcman 1998; Holgersson 2003).

Sinclair's (1995) observations that a masculine ethos is evident in management education is confirmed in Smith's (2000) study of postgraduate business students' perceptions of gender issues in the management curriculum and their effects on learning experiences. About a third of the women and a tenth of the men students in Smith's study reported perceptions of male-biased attitudes on the part of male educators, especially through the use of humor. Women were much more likely than men to perceive a gender-disadvantage in classroom learning experience. Most men reported no disadvantage at all. All students found it easier to contribute to class discussions when the educator was of their own sex. Several men and women reported on camaraderie in classes between men students and educators as an advantage for men and disadvantage for women students. More women than men reported that educators had blocked their class contributions. Both women and men students had, however, generally positive evaluations of women educators. A vast majority of women and men students were reluctant to challenge educators' sex-biased attitudes, out of fear of retaliation. Moreover, there was a low awareness of the university's policies regarding bias-free communication and gender-inclusive language. Smith concludes that there is a masculine ethos in management education, reproduced through, amongst others, gendered attitudes and language of male management educators, in particular, contributing to the marginalization, invisibility and trivialization of women's perspectives and experiences. These biases can, according to Smith, directly disadvantage women's learning and indirectly disadvantage men who miss out on hearing and learning about women's insights and experiences.

Not only students are affected by the gendered culture in management education. It also affects the work of women educators. Research shows that male students have difficulties in accepting women educators' authority and credibility (Gallos 1995) and that women educators are more likely to see their performance and competence undervalued and discredited. Sinclair (1995) finds that effective teaching of men by male professors always has a sexual component, where male MBA teachers that are judged 'very good', often leave both men and women infatuated. Women in positions of authority in teaching, on the other hand, are more often stereotyped in pejorative ways, from sexualized and maternalized stereotypes to being dismissed as emulating a man if assertive. However, Sinclair finds that there is often a more positive transference in teaching if teacher and students are of the same sex, since the audience of students wants to identify with the teacher's mastery of the subject matter.

Addressing gender in the business school classroom

How can the above-mentioned problems related to gender in the business school education be addressed? Addressing gender in the classroom, irrespective of discipline, consists of, on the one hand, trying out different methods in different situations in order to minimize the possibility of gender having negative consequences on the students' learning experience and environment and on the other hand, treating gender theories as an important part of the curriculum. In the following section, some attempts of both applying more gender-inclusive teaching methods and raising issues of gender in the business school classroom and some of the key takeaways scholars have highlighted will be accounted for.

DAMAGE CONTROL – SUGGESTIONS FOR GENDER-INCLUSIVE PEDAGOGY

Building on Bondestam (2003), the following key areas can be targeted when working for a more gender-inclusive pedagogy, irrespective of discipline:

- syllabus;
- classroom strategies;
- examination;
- course evaluations.

Syllabus   An important part of designing a course in a gender-inclusive way is to choose or revise the syllabus: Are women and men represented as authors? Are women and men represented in the literature and in what way are they represented?

Classroom strategies   There are many classroom strategies and it is up to every educator to judge what practices can be changed or developed. Strategies can, for example, involve distributing airtime in class more evenly or sometimes dividing students into same-sex discussion groups. However, forcing those who speak the least can counteract one's ambitions. The most quiet are not necessarily the least active. One can also focus on limiting the space occupied by men without depriving them of it (cf. Erson 1994).

Examination   When it comes to examination, teachers who wish to be gender-inclusive should allow for many different learning styles. It is also important to be self-reflective when putting up criteria for grading in order to avoid using criteria that are gender biased and to counteract the teacher's tendency of favoring a certain way of writing or analyzing.

Course evaluations   Altering course evaluation forms in order to be able to analyze if and in which way women and men students experience the course differently.

The measures above aim more at reducing the most obvious factors that cause embarrassment and discomfort for women students, such as gender-biased examples and sexist language and behavior, uneven distribution attention, and space among men and women as well as gender-biased design of seminars and examination. These measures all aim at controlling the damage of the traditional pedagogy applied in the business school classroom.

These suggestions do not necessarily involve teaching gender as a subject or even raising gender as a topic of discussion. According to Bondestam (2003), gender-inclusive pedagogy does not consist of arguing for feminism or gender theories in every situation and it does not consist of always using certain pedagogical methods, or always seeing to it that students are treated in a similar way. It consists more of treating gender theories as an important part of the subject in focus and of trying out different methods in different situations in order to minimize the possibility of gender having negative consequences on the students' learning experience and environment. A damage control approach does therefore not mean teaching gender theories, but requires that a gender perspective be applied in the design of the course and in classroom strategies.

INTRODUCING GENDER

Gender as a subject has, to my experience, been introduced in a number of ways on the business school curriculum. One of the most common ways of integrating gender theory is to have a session on gender in a course that is otherwise gender-absent. Such a session can include, but does not always do so, literature and examination on gender theory. Another strategy used in business schools is to offer a whole course, often elective, on gender in relation to a topic such as organization, leadership, management or economics. A third strategy is to let an entire course be infused by a critical perspective where gender is one of many topics that problematize mainstream management. This strategy is however less common, especially if the course is a compulsory course. The following section outlines three examples of how gender has been integrated in the business school curriculum. The purpose of the accounts is both to provide ideas of how the subject of gender can be integrated and provide some of the faculty's reflections on the challenges that come along with such attempts to alter the curriculum.

The examples are all from the field of organization behavior. Although there is a growing amount of gender research within other areas of business administration and economics, such as accounting and finance, gender research is more established within the field of organization (Wilson 1995; Wahl et al. 2001) and is thus more integrated in the mainstream body of literature. However, texts discussing how gender in management education can be included and the challenges involved are still few.

A SESSION ON GENDER

The first example is that offered by Marshall (1999) who developed a framework for discussing gender within the core organization behavior course in a MBA program in the UK. Knowing that MBA classes are often impatient at conditional knowledge and inquiry-based approaches, a key element in Marshall's framework was to invite the participants to inquire about organizations around them through perspectives that could be associated to gender. She offered a wide selection of questions to feed into discussions about management. Her own role as tutor was to sustain a 'questioning conversation'. She invited people to look at their own experiences and organizations using prompt questions designed to raise key issues. Sometimes she would offer illustrative research findings to broaden potential debate. However, she was careful not to state that there was gender discrimination or that norms and practices might favor men or women.

Marshall looks back at two different occasions that produced two different outcomes. On the first occasion the framework worked very well, her presentational approach allowed contributions from people who had some awareness or expertise in the area of gender and management. During the second occasion, Marshall found that her attempts to invite questioning and reflective discussions failed. Instead, she was sidetracked with questions from the participants that seemed aimed at testing her rather than enhancing their reflections. Marshall felt that the groups were composed of different individuals with different agendas. In the first group, she felt the participants were 'allies, explorers and inquirers'. Even though there were people who were silent, out of resistance, they would not change the overall ambience in the group. In the second group, there was not this sense of cooperation with her and the dynamics were different. She perceived that the group seemed to have formed its own culture and treated her as an outsider, rejecting her attempts to initiate discussions.

Reflecting over her two experiences, Marshall suggests that depending on the group culture, a more authoritative stance may be more appropriate since a participative style can be interpreted as weak if more traditional models of expertise are expected. She also reflects on the fact that addressing the issues of power may put students who feel 'different' in terms of gender, race, sexuality or some other factor in a difficult position. The spaces in which people can voice their experiences and perspectives are not guaranteed safe places. They can create feelings of exposure, vulnerability and may affect these students' group membership. Marshall finds that these are testing issues for a lecturer but does not wish them to deter her from raising difficult topics.

A WORKSHOP NAMING MEN

A second example is offered by Sinclair (2000) who reports on her experience of introducing the topic of masculinities in a MBA course on 'Managing Differences' in Australia. By discussing masculinities, she tried to move away from just focusing on women when discussing gender and actually naming men as norm in management. Moving to topics of gender and masculinities incrementally and through discussion of related topics has proven more successful according to Sinclair. The course started out with the issue of cultural differences and went on to compare with gender and masculinities.

Sinclair notes that the men grew more and more silent once she moved on to the latter subjects. She got signals in the breaks that she should drop the whole topic since there wasn't any problem, it was she who was the problem because she was raising the issue. However, the men gradually warmed up a bit once some men began to share examples of how they felt trapped in traditional corporate masculinities. Sinclair finds that the subject of masculinities is often difficult to discuss in groups of managers or management students unless someone has encountered the experience of discrimination and feels comfortable enough to share it with the group. Unless the participants have this experience, the common response is that there is no problem followed by the belief that women are the problem. Therefore, it is crucial to create an open environment where students can voice doubts and expose vulnerabilities. This may however prove to be difficult to achieve, especially in a competitive environment such as a management education program.

A COURSE ON CRITICAL ORGANIZATION AND MANAGEMENT THEORY

Four colleagues and I (Höök et al. 2005) have reported on our experience of introducing a module on critical organization and management theories within the core course on management and organization in an undergraduate business school program in Sweden. The semester-long course consisted of three modules that followed a problem-based pedagogy mixing traditional lectures and seminars. Each seminar was teacher-led and student participation built on small group discussions, case studies, prepared assignments and presentations of small-scale field studies. We were also well acquainted with the theories taught. The students were assessed through both individual and group assignments. The module on critical organization theories included lectures, seminars, literature, case studies and assignments on gender in management and organization.

In many ways, this was a rather rare attempt to fully integrate gender theories in the 'normal' curriculum and to as far as possible apply a gender-inclusive pedagogy. We found that the students adopted a defensive attitude expressed through ambiguous silence, hesitation and hostility. We interpreted this as a result of a number of clashes. One clash could be traced back to two quite strong and contradictory discourses in present Swedish society: the gender equality discourse versus dominant gender-absent management discourse. On the one hand the dominant ideology in Swedish society advocating equal opportunities – making resistance towards feminism difficult. On the other hand the male dominated, highly competitive and achievement-oriented culture at the present school, and a dominant gender-absent management discourse in business.

We also identified a pedagogical clash. The pedagogy used differed from dominant ways of teaching students at the business school and it also contained a contradiction. Although critical reflection was encouraged, the students were still assessed in a traditional way with a written exam on the course literature. This can be seen as sending contradictory messages to students implying that there was indeed a 'correct' answer. Moreover, the clashes were exacerbated by school management not fully supporting the attempt to introduce a critical approach and openly questioning the approach, thus undermining the module's legitimacy. In sum, we ask ourselves if it is realistic to both challenge prevalent pedagogical ideals as well as the dominant ideological stance in the curricula within a (single) course, especially if support from school management is lacking.

Damage control and tempered change

In the first section of this chapter, I discussed measures that aim at reducing the most obvious factors that cause embarrassment and discomfort for women students. These include avoiding gender-biased examples and sexist language and behavior, distributing attention and space evenly among men and women as well as being aware of different learning styles when designing seminars and examination. These measures all aim at damage control, that is, keeping the damage of the gender order at a minimum.

A damage control approach does not necessarily mean that gender is named or discussed in the classroom. The accounts above, however, show different ways in which gender can be addressed in management education. For example, they all had a gender-inclusive curricula and did not shy away from naming gender as a relevant issue in relation to management. Moreover, the attempts included alternative pedagogical approaches.

However, introducing gender involves a whole new set of challenges, as the examples also showed. First of all, gender is rarely seen as a strategic business issue and students therefore often find discussions on gender a waste of time. Also, naming gender often gives rise to feelings that can become an obstacle for learning. Men may experience that they are as individuals held responsible for all the negative aspects of patriarchy and women may feel singled out as victims. Both reactions can trigger resistance to the subject taught (Wahl et al. 2001). Students feel personally attacked instead of seeing that gender is a social structure that we are active in reproducing through our everyday actions.

Introducing theories that offer students tools to problematize the foundations of mainstream management knowledge can also in my experience give rise to resistance. Introducing an alternative pedagogy itself can give rise to resistance, students not seeing the value of discussions and reflection (Reynolds 1999; Currie and Knights 2003). In addition, instead of taking the opportunity of exploring new discourses on management, students spend time and energy on defending mainstream perspectives, for example, the undisputed manager's perspective and the privileges of men in organizations and society.

Moreover, gender research is often regarded, together with other social sciences, not an exact science compared to more quantitative subjects. It is also seen as more political than other subjects. These perceptions are often held not only by students but also by peers, and undermine the status and legitimacy of gender theory as a subject to be taught at a business school (Smith and Hutchinson 1995).

Even if there is a call for more gender-inclusive curricula and pedagogy among both women and men management students, the above-mentioned examples also show that there are many challenges and difficulties involved when gender is introduced. It is not uncommon that educators introducing gender in teaching and research face hostility from peers and students (Wahl 1999). This contributes to the devaluation of gender as an area of research in management and to the negative working environment for academics openly addressing issues of gender (Smith and Hutchinson 1995).

It is important to be aware that any serious attempt to change targeting gender goes hand in hand with resistance (Höök 2001). Integrating gender therefore requires support from senior levels at the school, especially in compulsory courses. It also requires time for discussion and reflection. A subject like gender that goes against the grain of the dominant management ethos and that touches upon personal issues requires more time in classroom and more support from teachers. The teachers also need to be experienced and knowledgeable in order to be able to convey relevant knowledge and to be able to handle resistance in order to support students in their learning process. Integrating gender theory in a course taught by faculty that have little or no knowledge of gender issues and that are not committed to change, may just as well exacerbate the situation for women students.

These different measures attempt to reform the business school curriculum from 'within' (Sinclair 1995). Radical change is another approach that has also been suggested by scholars. Sinclair (1995) argues that what may be required in order to achieve a reform of management education is a more fundamental reconceptualization of management and posing questions on what kind of managers business schools are active in shaping and whose interests are actually being served. According to Grey (2006), management education socializes students into a certain kind of person deemed suitable for managerial work and encultured into certain managerial values. This may be seen as desirable for some, whilst from a gender perspective it appears much less desirable. Not only does management education typically reproduce a patriarchal gender order, it also contributes to the reproduction of other social power relations such as ethnicity, race, class and sexuality, thus contributing to the reproduction of structures of social inequality in organizations and society.

Nevertheless, implementing radical change is in most cases not an option. The different examples accounted for above are attempts to change the culture of management education from within, both employing damage control measures and introducing gender on the curriculum. Nevertheless, these attempts are still on the terms of existing culture as most other courses are still infused by the dominant management ethos, the pedagogy is still traditional and gender is still regarded as a peripheral subject.

However, changing from within may be a conscious strategy in itself, a 'tempered change-strategy'. Tempered change is a reference to the notion of 'tempered radicals' (Meyerson and Scully 1995) used to describe people who work within mainstream organizations and also want to transform them, seeking moderation at the same time as being flexible in their fight against what they have identified as social injustices (Meyerson 2003). Tempered change initiatives can range from giving an elective course on gender and management to having a couple of sessions on gender within a compulsory course. It can also involve introducing gender under another heading such as 'diversity' or 'masculinities'. The measures chosen all depend on the institutional conditions. Aiming at 'damage control' may in many cases be challenging enough. The point with tempered radicalism and tempered change is that one chooses one's fights without losing sight of the ultimate goal of one's efforts.

Concluding remarks

In sum, there is still a long way to go before men and women face equal conditions in the business school classroom and before gender is regarded as a central business issue. All work for change that is critical in its approach will entail some degree of reproduction of existing power relations (Höök 2001) and this is also valid when addressing gender issues in management education. As Bondestam (2003) writes, every teacher in every teaching situation faces a pedagogical paradox: it is crucial to confirm students as individuals, and at the same time it is crucial to confirm that students have specific experiences as women or men. If we as teachers depart from the assumption that irrespective of gender, students are stimulated by the same learning methods, we exclude the possibility for men and women to learn in different ways. If we instead depart from the assumption that men and women learn in specific different ways, we will as teachers reproduce two separate categories with specific characteristics at the expense of other meanings of gender and at the expense of individual differences among women and men. How can this paradox be resolved? Can it be resolved? Resonating with Bondestam, I argue that this paradox is difficult to resolve given the present gender order in society. However, for a person who myself has emancipatory ambitions both when doing research and teaching, avoiding gender is not an option since that would mean reproducing the existing gender order.

Thus, if one wishes to work for change, the only way forward is to be conscious of the paradox and test different methods and approaches in relation to time and resources available, the student body and the institutional support, and to assess and reflect on one's results. The goal is not to create new, stereotype perceptions of gender, but to use our knowledge of gender consciously and reflexively.

Change presupposes a commitment to change (Wahl 2003). Thus it is crucial when addressing gender issues in business schools, both for faculty, school and program management to have this commitment, especially since change entails resistance. Resistance is not necessarily a result of a badly planned course or seminar but an integral part of change. Thus, both as faculty and management, one should be prepared to face resistance and to take stock from different attempts to address gender issues without giving up.

Faculty wishing to work for change may seldom have the opportunity to implement radical change but are left to try and change small steps at a time applying a tempered change approach. A first step is to assess the institutional conditions in order to choose an appropriate approach.

- What amount of time and resources does the structure allow?
- What level of knowledge and experience do the teachers involved have?
- Is the teaching environment sympathetic to more experience- and discussion-based teaching methods?
- Is there enough support for the course from school management?

Introducing gender as an issue and gender research on the curriculum requires a certain level of openness and willingness to change within the organization. It requires a certain amount of resources both in terms of time and competent staff. If this does not exist, the costs of introducing gender may very well outweigh the benefits. In such cases, it might be radical enough to opt for a damage control approach, targeting to reduce gender-bias in syllabus, classroom strategies and examination.

Change requires acknowledging the importance of gender issues for the learning experience of both men and women and recognizing gender issues as valid and legitimate research issues. This knowledge can be used as a way of not just adding on something new to the business school curriculum but as a way of fundamentally renewing the whole way in which we see and practice management and management education.

References

Bondestam, F., (2003). *Könsmedveten pedagogic för universitetslärare – en introduktion och bibliografi. (Gender-inclusive pedagogy for university teachers – an introduction and bibliography)*. Uppsala: Uppsala University.

Currie, G., and Knights, D., (2003). 'Reflecting on Critical Pedagogy in MBA Education'. *Management Learning*, 34(1): 27–49.

Davidson, M., and Burke, R.J. (eds.), (2004). *Women in Management Worldwide*. Aldershot: Ashgate.

Erson, E., (1994). 'Vad innebär det att vara feministisk lärare?' (What does it mean to be a feminist teacher?) *Kvinnovetenskaplig tidskrift*, 15(4): 54–64.

Gallos, J.V., (1995). 'When Authority = She: A Male Student Meets a Female Instructor'. *Journal of Management Development*, 14(2): 65–76.

Grey, C., (2005). *A Very Short, Fairly Interesting and Reasonably Cheap Book about Studying Organizations*. London: Sage Publications.

Halford, S., and Leonard P., (2001). *Gender, Power and Organisations*. Basingstoke, Hampshire, UK: Palgrave.

Holgersson, C., (2003). *Rekrytering av företagsledare. En studie i homosocialitet. (The Recruitment of Managing Directors. A study of homsociality.)* Stockholm: EFI.

Höök, P., (2001). *Stridspiloter i vida kjolar. Om ledarutveckling och jämställdhet. (Fighter-Pilots in Wide Skirts. On Management Development and Gender Equality.)* Stockholm: EFI.

Höök, P., Gillberg, N., Holgersson, C., Hvenmark J., and Lindgren, M., (2005). Hesitation and Hostility. Faculty's experience of Introducing Critical Approaches in Business Education. Paper presented at *4th International Critical Management Studies Conference*, 4–6 July 2005, Cambridge, UK.

Marshall, J., (1999). 'Doing Gender in Management Education'. *Gender and Education*, 11(3): 251–263.

Meyerson, D.E., (2003). *Tempered Radicals: How People Use Difference to Inspire Change at Work*. Boston: Harvard Business School Press.

Meyerson, D.E., and Scully, M., (1995). 'Tempered Radicals and the Politics of Ambivilance and Change'. *Organization Science*, 6(5): 585–600.

Reynolds, M., (1999). 'Grasping the Nettle: Possibilities and Pitfalls of Critical Management Pedagogy'. *British Journal of Management*, 9: 171–184.

Spender, D., (1980). *Man Made Language*. London: Routledge and Kegan Paul.

Sinclair, A., (1995). 'SEX and the MBA'. *Organization*, 2(2): 295–317.

Sinclair, A., (2000). 'Teaching Managers about Masculinities: Are you kidding?' *Management Learning*, 31(1): 83–101.

Smith, C.R., and Hutchinson, J., (1995). 'Gender as a Strategic Management Education Issue'. *International Review of Women and Leadership*, 1(1): 46–56.

Smith, C.R., (1997). 'Gender Issues in Management Education: A New Teaching Resource'. *Women in management review*, 12(3): 100–104.

Smith, C.R., (2000). 'Notes from the Field: Gender Issues in the Management Curriculum: A Survey of Student Experiences'. *Gender, Work & Organization*, 7(3): 158–167.

Tannen, D., (1995). 'The Power of Talk: Who Gets Heard and Why'. *Harvard Business Review*, September-October: 138–48.

Wajcman, J., (1998). *Managing Like a Man: Women and Men in Corporate Management*. Pennsylvania State University Press.

Wahl, A. (ed.), (1995). *Men's Perceptions of Women and Management*. Stockholm: Fritzes.

Wahl, A., (1999). 'The Cloud – Lecturing on Feminist Research'. *NORA*, 7(2-3): 97–108.

Wahl, A., (2003). Sammanfattande kommentarer. (Concluding remarks) *SOU 2003:16 Mansdominans i förändring. (Changing Male Dominance)* Stockholm: Fritzes.

Wahl, A., Holgersson, C., Höök, P., and Linghag, S., (2001). *Det ordnar sig. Teorier om organisation och kön. (It will be in Order. Theories on Organization and Gender.)* Lund: Studentlitteratur.

Wilson, F., (1995). *Organizational Behaviour and Gender*. Maidenhead: McGraw-Hill.

12 English in the Classroom: Meeting the Challenge of English-Medium Instruction in International Business Schools

Thomas Lavelle

Reflecting on the hundreds of business schools using English as a language of instruction with linguistically diverse students,[1] an observer can find cause for both optimism and concern. The most obvious reason for optimism is that this model works. On one hand, business schools in Anglophone countries attract large numbers of international students every year, whom we must assume reach their educational goals and continue on to professional success despite having studied through a foreign language. Otherwise this international approach to higher education would not remain popular. Similarly, business schools outside native English-speaking countries are offering some or all of their instruction in English. This too is a trend that is intensifying, and again there is no reason to believe the graduates of these institutions have failed to learn in these settings or failed to succeed professionally. In other words, business education in English works.

However, there is cause for concern as well. Business school subjects are at times and in part complex, demanding, abstract and elusive, so we must expect them occasionally to be difficult for students, regardless of linguistic factors. Similarly, some of our subjects frequently involve group projects and thus social interaction both within teams and with external stakeholders such as host companies. This interaction can be difficult even when everyone involved speaks the same language, and even worse when we add a foreign language to the mix, most pointedly if there are doubts about either learners' or teachers' proficiency in that language.

The aim of this chapter is to narrow the distance between extreme optimism and extreme pessimism about English-medium instruction, without either trivializing the difficulty involved in learning and teaching through a second language or denying the history of success that many business schools, students and individual teachers have achieved doing exactly that. Structurally, this chapter frames and discusses a number of questions about English-medium instruction relevant to business school faculty or the academic leaders who manage them. The first of these questions addresses the central pedagogical issue: *Does learning through English as a second language (hereafter ESL) affect learning outcomes?* To answer it, I survey some of the small but growing body of literature in this field and comment briefly on the current state of knowledge.

Like student learning, teaching practice is highly relevant to faculty at international business schools. The most immediate question about this practice asks *How, if at all, does teaching via ESL affect teaching practices?* Here too some published research provides a partial

---

[1]   The focus of this chapter is English-medium instruction for students and by faculty who are not native speakers of English.

answer, supplemented by observations arising from my experience of supporting faculty who do this kind of teaching both at the Stockholm School of Economics and in the International Teachers' Program.

Less immediate, but no less important for teaching faculty and program directors, is the question of standards. In other words, *How good does a teacher's English need to be for her to teach effectively through second-language English?* (hereafter second language is L2 while first language is L1). This question is powerfully context dependent, so answers vary. Therefore I propose a flexible, four-tier model aimed at helping teachers assess their own classroom experience.

A natural corollary to discussing standards is discussing faculty development, the work of helping individuals set goals and meet standards. So the next question is *What can I do to improve?* To answer, we briefly consider L2-acquisition processes in order to help set and maintain reasonable expectations, and in Appendix 1 I describe and explain three language-development activities designed specifically to help improve the English used in classrooms.

The final question we address together here extrapolates on the faculty-development question by considering it from an institutional perspective. If, hypothetically, we grant that instruction through second-language English affects both learning outcomes and teacher performance, *Do business schools share responsibility for helping their teachers meet this linguistic challenge?* If they do, *What development formats best promote this specific type of competence?* This of course, is a question of policy, where answers arise from an inventory of local needs set against local priorities informed by benchmarking and best practice.

Does learning through English as a second language affect learning outcomes?

In the final analysis this will remain an open question. Naturally, experienced teachers often observe that learning processes and outcomes are sensitive to many factors, so language of instruction should be no exception. In fact, an affirmative answer would confirm the intuitive and *a priori* assumption mentioned above that many activities are more difficult when mediated by a foreign language. In a research context of course, assumptions of this kind are strictly speaking unwarranted.

To the best of my knowledge there are no published studies clearly demonstrating that L2 English instruction produces less favorable outcomes than mother tongue instruction in business schools. In fact, while relationships between language and learning outcome is well researched for primary and secondary education (see Washburn 1997, for an overview), studies of higher education lag far behind. I can only speculate about the reasons for this gap, and that speculation takes two directions: conceptual difficulties and practical difficulties.

Conceptually, one reason for caution lies in the current state of knowledge about learning in higher education. As I have argued elsewhere, learning through a second language gives rise to a distinct problem for learning research, so that even though some aspects of student learning are abundantly described, 'little attention has been spent on the problem of concept-formation, much less on the role of second-language mediation in such processes' (Hartman, Lavelle and Wistedt 2004, p. 139).

Practically, it is very difficult to operationalize a research question that speaks directly to language of instruction and learning outcomes. First, the complexity of any given learning process makes it difficult to control for enough variables. Second, among any group of experimental subjects, levels of English proficiency are more likely diverse than uniform.

Similarly, in higher education there is a greater likelihood of prior knowledge skewing the results than in primary and secondary education. Third, language policy is an emotional issue (Nixon 2000; Washburn 1997), which may skew any experiment that is not a blind one.

However, there are published claims of poorer performance by L2 learners in various higher-education contexts. A team of researchers in New Zealand make strong claims about English instruction in mathematics and the results of university students with English as a second language (Barton et al. 2005). They compare students with L2 English to native speakers taught by native speaker instructors and report on a series of studies that examine either the direct results of mock tests or students' self-reported understanding of these test questions. Their key findings are that on direct testing L2 students had a 'mathematics achievement' that is 10 per cent lower than L1 students and that in self-reporting, 'the students were unaware of their disadvantage'. Methodologically, these studies compare two distinct groups of students distinguished solely on the basis of mother tongue. They do not control for prior knowledge, but suggest that the L2 group has above average mathematical skills. There are some efforts to distinguish levels of English proficiency among the L2 students, but what emerges is that while some of them had passed standardized, formally reliable English proficiency tests, others scored below the minimum levels of English language proficiency required to undertake university studies, and in some phases of the study half were 'significantly below' the required level (Barton et. al 2005).

My intention is not to discredit this research or to disregard its results. It is rather to illustrate the complexity of the question that gives rise to some pessimism surrounding ESL instruction in business schools.

Another elaborate study of English-medium instruction in higher education is Klaasen's (2001) doctoral dissertation, set in the context of Dutch engineering education. This well-documented study provides mixed results. First, in an experiment to test the effect of language of instruction on recall-based learning, those students who were lectured in their native Dutch outperformed their classmates who were lectured to in L2 English. Second, in another experiment she finds that students attending lectures in English adopt more learning strategies that reflect deep approaches to learning than do their counterparts attending lectures in Dutch. Deep approaches entail among other things a big-picture perspective on lecture content (see for example, Marton and Säljö 1976 and Ramsden 2003 for discussions). Third, in spite of the learning strategies adopted, Klaassen also reports that in a naturalistic setting, the group following L1 instruction scored higher on questions she categorizes as deep-learning questions and that the groups did not differ on those she categorized as surface-learning questions. In still another study, one that introduced a longitudinal perspective, she found that after one year 'no significant differences could be established between students' learning results of the English group and the Dutch group' (p. 170). In summary, the results from higher L2 education in engineering merit attention, but not alarm.

What may be the most troubling facet of Klaassen's study is the poignant summary she provides of the challenges L2 learners face because of their difficulties with listening comprehension. Summarizing an influential study by Chiang and Dunkel, she identifies the following difficulties among L2 learners following English lectures:

- inability to interact with lecturers;
- inability to detect main points;
- inability to identify discourse markers and the logical relations they signal;
- inability to follow high speech rates;
- poor inferencing abilities;
- unfamiliarity with relevant type of academic discourse.

If this list accurately reflects our students' ability to follow our lessons, it is indeed worrisome. Parts of it probably reflect some of the difficulties facing some of our students some of the time, but Chiang and Dunkel's subjects were students learning English as a foreign language, not functionally proficient students studying another subject through English. Moreover, the Chiang and Dunkel study comes from a research context that aimed ultimately at developing strategies for helping students deal directly with what they saw as a root cause to many of these problems, poor listening comprehension skills. A broad contextualization of this study, therefore, is required to understand what might otherwise be seen as the linguistic foundation for academic failure.

In summary, research findings exist that could cast doubt on the ability of learners to succeed in higher education mediated by L2 English. However, to draw that conclusion a reader probably needs to bring at least some of that doubt with her because in every case there are factors within the research itself or within the research context that support a more balanced view of learners' success.

How, if at all, does teaching via ESL affect teaching practices?

However we interpret our answer on learning outcomes, a second question legitimately follows: how does English-medium instruction affect teaching? The research addressing this question and my experience with faculty courses and coaching both suggest that teaching in L2 English does affect the way teachers work.

One positive effect is that teachers become more sensitive to the roles language and communication play in learning processes and in the construction of disciplinary knowledge. Jones and Sin, for example, modified an accounting course to incorporate writing assignments that check for and activate the language needed to create and manipulate knowledge of accounting clearly and correctly. Similarly, the motivation for the research on L2 maths learners mentioned above (Barton et al. 2005) was partially a performance gap between the first and third years of a degree program, where L2 learners' performance declines as course content becomes more discursive, more linguistically subtle. Finally, Carr and Anderson report on another maths-learning study that examined among other things whether the language of examinations affected students' performance.

Another change in teaching behavior appears to have mixed consequences. This is code-switching, the term linguists and ethnographers use to describe alternation between languages in a multilingual environment. In the South African context, students interpreted switches from English to Afrikaans negatively (van der Walt and Steyn 2004). The code switching I observe and discuss in Swedish contexts is open to both positive and negative interpretations. When L1 Swedish students use breaks, office visits and emails to raise questions with their teachers in Swedish, it almost certainly helps both their learning and their grades. However, their classmates with other mother tongues, typically exchange students or international transfer students, do not have this additional channel for communication with their teachers, and they legitimately raise questions about fairness and equal access. More generally, if code-switching creates a perception of preferential treatment on the basis of mother tongue, it almost certainly will affect the learning climate negatively.

Other reported effects are clearly negative. One is preparation times, which increase for lessons and examinations in L2 English. This is by far the most common problem I encounter among faculty members at SSE actively seeking support for their ESL teaching, and it is reported in the context of Dutch technical education as well (Yusof et al. 2004).

Most changes in the way teachers teach naturally also affect students. In a catalogue compiled by Vinke, we find a series of changes that appear to follow directly from struggles with a second language:

- shorter, less elaborate presentations;
- failure to provide examples;
- failure to define concepts;
- failure to indicate transition between topics and between theory and examples;
- less elicitation of student interaction.

Of course these problems are neither universal nor generalizable to all L2 English instruction. Nevertheless, any one of these five shortcomings would raise concerns. Taken together they are a testimony to the resilience of students studying through ESL around the world, and they could move us to reconsider the question of learning outcomes in a more pessimistic light. If this kind of teaching is widespread (and none of the research cited here attempted to quantify these teaching behaviors), learning is likely to suffer even though that impact is difficult to document.

There may also be more global changes in teacher performance. Teaching through L2 English may alter a teacher's conception of his role as a teacher. We can frame our brief consideration of this change in a four-point taxonomy of teaching roles:[2]

1. *Transmitters:* are content-focused and impart information or skills by telling and repeating.
2. *Developers:* are interaction-focused and promote new skills and understanding by guiding, reinforcing and modeling.
3. *Facilitators:* are also interaction-focused but facilitate learning and understanding by stimulating, questioning and discussing.
4. *Transformers:* are student-focused and support students' cognitive change by providing opportunities and activities.

Presumably the faculty of most business schools combines people who fill all of these roles, and many individual teachers fill different roles at different times. However, in observing English-medium instruction both live at SSE and on videotape from over 20 other business schools, I see colleagues being drawn in potentially disquieting numbers toward the transmitter role. This is not the place to debate passive vs. active learning or teacher-focused vs. learner-focused classrooms, but at the very least, we can regret the narrowing of roles and approaches teachers adopt when teaching in L2 English. This tendency is particularly pronounced among teachers who are relatively new to L2 English instruction. In most cases I cannot say whether these teachers later expand their set of teaching styles and roles in English-mediated classrooms or whether this early emphasis on one-way teaching establishes a long-term pattern.

In summary, we can answer the question on teacher impact affirmatively, and we must also conclude that, with the exception of raised awareness of language and communication, this impact is negative. Just how negative, we can only assess in light of some agreed-upon standard, which is the topic of the next section.

---

2   Of the many approaches to teaching roles and conceptions, I adopt Klaassen's because it is the basis of her interviews with engineering faculty teaching through L2 English.

How good is good enough?

For educators, this question is primarily pedagogical. Ideally, a teacher's English is good enough if it allows her to draw on the full range of teaching strategies she might use in her native language. Similarly, the English used in instruction should also allow students to draw on their full range of learning strategies. This ideal describes a best-case scenario that individual teachers and institutions can use to set long-term goals and to shape their discussion of teaching through L2 English.

However, best-cases rarely work well as standards, particularly in situations where the standard aims to promote professional development. It is preferable to describe success in terms that are graduated, measurable in some way and obviously relevant to the task. However, even though language testing has evolved into a complex science and an extensive industry, traditional tests offer little help in assessing how well a teacher can prepare an introductory lecture in marketing or to develop a case-study board plan in ESL. Therefore, I answer our how-good question in practical terms, and the most practical consideration in a classroom is, of course, understanding.

Mutual comprehensibility therefore provides the minimal standard a teacher and her students need to meet. This is, of course, an intersubjective criterion, and a teacher will best be able to assess whether he meets it in dialogue with students, peer observers or a language coach. To guide preliminary self-assessment and support improvement, I identify here some linguistic and communicative factors that affect comprehensibility.

- *Word boundaries:* Even though words often merge in normal speech, recognizable words are a key to comprehension, and factors that can affect word recognition include stress placement, rate of delivery and accurate word-initial sounds.
- *Verb forms:* English verbs provide a wide range of grammatical information by deploying a small set of resources, primarily a few endings and a small set of auxiliary verbs, so the omission of these forms, particularly the auxiliaries, is likely to cause misunderstanding.
- *Syntactic markers:* These are small words with meanings that often signal relationships, words such as prepositions, articles and determiners, and again the key point is that while errors may cause misunderstanding, omission is likely to do so.
- *Translated idioms:* For our purposes, idioms are more-or-less idiosyncratic expressions with a meaning that is more than, or different than, the sum of its parts; since they are often difficult to learn, the practical lesson for teachers is to be mindful of idioms and avoid translating them directly into English.
- *An open stream of speech:* Students' comprehension of a teacher's English depends upon their hearing it, and even though classroom acoustics are beyond an instructor's control, teachers should make certain to avoid impeding the flow of speech with poor posture, overuse of notes or speaking into a whiteboard or screen.

Mutual comprehensibility provides the foundational stage in a progressive description of adequate English for teaching in international business schools; the second stage, credibility, builds upon it (see Figure 12.1).

Credibility enters a discussion of linguistic standards for ESL among faculty because negotiating credibility is often, perhaps always, one dimension of classroom politics. Ideally, a teacher's credibility would rest exclusively on her or his disciplinary expertise and educational competence. However, age, gender, appearance and nationality each can affect student

CREDIBILITY

MUTUAL COMPREHENSIBILITY

Figure 12.1 Stages 1 and 2 of the good-enough-to-teach model of English proficiency

perceptions of teacher credibility, and so too can language proficiency when English is the instructional lingua franca.

It is difficult, perhaps impossible, to know definitively how students assess credibility. Nevertheless, students do complain about linguistic proficiency through formal and informal channels and with and without justification. We must therefore acknowledge credible English as part of the academic ecology in international business schools

What then can a non-native speaker of English do to help preserve credibility? To begin with, native-like accents are not prerequisites for credible L2 English. What is necessary given the hierarchical nature of this model is of course comfortably comprehensible pronunciation. Beyond that, we can set improvement priorities by distinguishing two aspects of linguistic performance: fluency and accuracy.[3]

The first refers simply to an ability to use a language with ease, and 'non-fluency is discernible in frequent pausing, repetition, and self corrections' (Hedge 1993). While pauses, repetitions and self-correction are perfectly acceptable, even necessary, dimensions of normal speech, listeners tolerate them to varying degrees, and when this kind of verbal behavior becomes noticeable a speaker's credibility can suffer. Fortunately fluency is one aspect of second-language development that does improve through practice. Beyond practicing, because non-fluency often reflects that a speaker is literally lost for words, a teacher can work with vocabulary development to become more fluent, as we see in the next section.

Accuracy concerns errors and their avoidance. Absolutely error-free English is not necessary for successful, credible teaching, but two types of errors do damage speaker credibility. The first of these are recurrent errors. Any error that recurs systematically during a lesson can damage speaker credibility, and here pronunciation typically features more prominently than grammar or vocabulary. Imagine a 45-minute session on some aspect of competitiveness. Imagine further an L2 speaker of English who pronounces his topic word as com-*peat*-itiveness and its root as com-*peat*-itive, two perfectly understandable errors given the pronunciation of the root verb, to compete. He analyzes different firms' com-*peat*-itive positions and their efforts to develop sustainable com-*peat*-itive advantages over their com-*peat*-ators. Initially, most listeners treat this as a slip and think little of it. Each repetition however foregrounds the problem more acutely. Nevertheless, some listeners scarcely hear the problem, and for others it becomes a distraction. For a third subgroup, each repetition erodes authority and becomes a reason to tune out.

For a teacher who wants to meet the credibility standard, there is a practical remedy. It starts by identifying for each lesson that set of key words and phrases that will certainly recur time and again. With the help of a dictionary (and its accompanying CD) or an informant,

---

3   The distinction itself is so well established both among practitioners and researchers that I cannot identify an original source for it (if one exists). For a recent mainstream application of the concepts see Larson-Freeman (2006).

she must be sure to get these key words right. The effort pays off because in any discourse, lexical repetition provides cohesiveness, so when recurrent errors turn this linguistic asset into a liability, a speaker risks losing credibility with some segment of the audience and runs a greater risk of losing attention from a larger segment.

We can call the second dimension of accuracy relevant to credibility high-profile contrastive errors, which are usually only relevant when a teacher and students share a first language. These errors are caused by systematic differences between a target language and a learner's first language, and therefore they are familiar to most learners with a common mother tongue. This type of linguistic environment is common in European business schools, where for instance at HEC a class with a French-speaking instructor can commonly consist largely of French-speaking students combined with a number of international exchange students. English will be the language of instruction, and in terms of high-profile contrastive error, the French-speaking students will be most critical if the teacher should make a common Francophone mistake.

Errors of this kind rarely cause misunderstanding, but because they are familiar and because they are stigmatized through traditional language-teaching methods, they catch listeners' attention. In a classroom, if those listeners have adopted an adversarial posture, this is the kind of error that can erode teacher credibility. So again we can ask, what can a teacher do to avoid this problem and meet the credibility standard? Fortunately, since for any given language the set of high profile errors is finite, with help from a specialist it is possible to identify them and make their reduction a priority.

To sum up, credibility is granted to some speakers/teachers and denied to others, and language proficiency is only one relevant factor among many. However, potential threats to linguistic credibility typically come from two directions. The first and more important of these is non-fluent speech, in other words excessive delays, unwarranted repetition or intrusive levels of self-correction, all of which can be remedied through practice and a richer vocabulary. The second comes from inaccuracy, specifically two types of persistent error. High-profile contrastive errors persist within a language community; for instance native speakers of German struggle with many of the same English grammatical errors. They can affect credibility because they are familiar to students and open a doorway to 'he-can't-even ...' reasoning. Recurrent errors on the other hand persist throughout a conversation or a seminar or a lecture series. They damage credibility simply because their repetition makes them perceptually salient, and once an audience begins to think about a speaker's pronunciation rather than her message, it becomes easier to decide that she is not worth listening to.

Fortunately contrastive errors are systematic and the high-profile set typically small. The strategy for addressing asystematic, but repetitive, errors begins with a teacher's material. These errors occur most often in key terms or expressions that are central to a lesson. By identifying them in advance and making certain that he master them, a teacher can control one of the linguistic factors that may affect credibility.

The next stage in our developing answer to the question of standards marks a milestone. Our first criterion sets a minimal baseline. The second focuses on a potentially negative classroom dynamic. The third, flexibility, turns our attention squarely toward learning.

My teaching works best when I am able to explain the same material many times in many different ways. On the basis of that experience the third stage of our English-standards model is verbal flexibility (see Figure 12.2).

The strongest justifications for this criterion proceed from its opposite. Consider the following example. An operations management teacher wants to introduce the concept *float* in the context of project planning. The students read about it in Chapter 16 of their textbook:

FLEXIBILITY

CREDIBILITY

MUTUAL COMPREHENSIBILITY

Figure 12.2   Stages 1–3 of the good-enough-to-teach model of English proficiency

'the flexibility to change the timings of activities which is inherent in various parts of the project' (Slack et al. 2004, p. 575). The slide students see in class says: *Float – flexibility to change timing of activities*. While this slide is up, the teacher explains that float is the flexibility for changing the timing of different activities. Yet somehow there is a student in the group who didn't catch the definition, or who more likely actually needs help learning how to calculate float; she asks: 'Can you go over float again, please?' to which her teacher replies: 'Yes, of course, float is flexibility. Flexibility regarding timing, you see, of various operations or activities.' This is an example of what Ian Parker calls the curse of triple delivery, the same words delivered by voice, by slide and by text (Parker 2001). The frustration will be familiar to anyone who has experienced this kind of communication.

Some repetition of course is desirable. As we observed in our *Discussion of learning outcomes?*, learning through L2 English carries additional demands for students, and teachers can help by employing purposeful repetition and offering support via static media such as slides and lecture notes.

Returning to our imaginary teacher, in a narrow sense of language usage, she is on safe ground – no errors, little reason for hesitation or self-correction – but her less obvious linguistic limitations carry rhetorical and pedagogical consequences. There is a standard she fails to meet, and the strategy for meeting it requires a broader verbal repertoire. How then can she expand that repertoire?

What she lacks is an ability to paraphrase, to formulate content in other words. So again vocabulary may be an issue, but my primary advice to teachers facing this kind of problem is to work more diligently with rephrasing as a part of preparation. More specifically, in preparing lessons that draw on textbooks or articles, prepare slides and exercises that actively avoid echoing the language of the original. Of course, a teacher should repeat key terms, but highlight their special status as key terms by reframing the other parts of a definition or illustration. By adding a slight verbal focus to traditional class preparation, routine work becomes an additional pathway to meeting a higher standard of classroom English, the flexibility standard.

The fourth stage of good-enough English proficiency is the most subjective, and the criterion that at first glance embodies a narrowly teacher-centered focus. That criterion is pleasure, but I will suggest that when teachers meet this standard and enjoy teaching through L2 English, everyone in the classroom benefits (see Figure 12.3).

Faculty who are enjoying their teaching will do a better job and the quality of learning will rise. Faculty who are enjoying, rather than resenting, their teaching will be better equipped to balance their often conflicting roles as teachers, as researchers and as organizational innovators. Finally, faculty who are enjoying teaching in ESL will probably attain the goals identified at

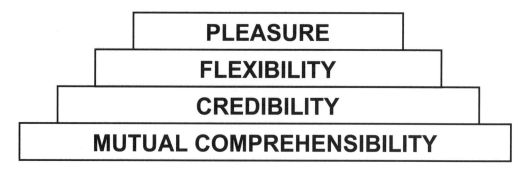

Figure 12.3   All four stages of the good-enough-to-teach model of English proficiency

the start of this section; they will employ their full range of teaching formats and techniques while their students are also free to adopt any approach to learning that matches the material at hand and their personal learning objectives.

Pleasurable teaching in English sits at the top of our ziggurat because enjoying ESL teaching presupposes success with the increasingly restrictive standards mentioned above, comprehensibility, credibility and flexibility. In the next section we consider some specific practical activities through which a teacher or institution can frame and meet reasonable expectations for improved English proficiency in business school classrooms.

What can I do to improve?

This section addresses the conditions governing how individual teachers improve their English in ways that are directly relevant to classroom performance, and thereby it frames the activities described in Appendix 1. There is, of course, a great deal individual teachers can do beyond those examples. But here I want to introduce two concepts imported from research on second language acquisition, fossilization and maturational constraints.[4] First introduced in 1972, fossilization refers to the process by which a second language learner simply stops improving. Since then research and debate have continued, but the key point for us is that fossilization stands in opposition to the common-sense notion that given enough time, exposure and practice, a person's English will eventually get better. Among specialists there are more optimistic and more pessimistic stances, but there is broad agreement that learners avoid these plateau effects only in extraordinary circumstances. In simple terms, once a language learner becomes proficient enough to actually use the language, her attention unconsciously shifts from form to communication, which is natural because people learn languages to communicate, do things with them. The consequence of this shift however seems to be that progress with the new language slows and eventually stops. Happily for business school faculty

---

4   Unfortunately descriptions and discussions of these terms are written almost exclusively for specialists. Ronald Selinker introduced fossilization in his article Interlanguage. *IRAL*, 10: 209–231, reprinted in *Error Analysis: Perspectives on Second Language Acquisition*, Jack C. Richards, ed. Longman, 1974. Michael Long's more recent summary of the field is Stabilization and fossilization in interlanguage development in *The Handbook of Second Language Acquisition*, edited by C.J. Doughty and M.H. Long, pp. 485–538, Blackwell. Eric Lenneberg addresses maturational constraints through his groundbreaking Critical Period Hypothesis, *The Biological Foundations of Language* (1967), but again a good recent summary is in *The Handbook of Second Language Acquisition*, Maturational constraints in SLA by Kenneth Hyltenstam and Niclas Abrahamsson, pp. 539–588.

who want better English for their English-medium teaching, a renewed attention to form can suspend some of the effects of fossilization.

The second concept, maturational constrains, links successful language learning to age. This notion has been discussed since the 1960s and research has focused upon identifying a critical period, after which a learner has little chance of learning a language with native like success. Because ages around puberty are generally accepted candidates for the end of the critical period and because all business school faculty members are adults, we need to set the goals for ultimate attainments in L2 English with some modesty. Klaassen (2001) stakes out a similarly cautious position regarding potential improvement in the English of Dutch engineering faculty, and cites a British study that suggests 4 to 6 months' intensive study are required to raise a subject's score one point on a standardized English proficiency exam, where one point corresponds to the following sorts of differences (see Table 12.1).

Given that both fossilization and maturational constraints offer a generally discouraging prognosis for adults' progress in a second language, a teacher facing the task of ESL instruction can reasonably ask whether there is any hope for improvement. In light of my intention here, I believe of course that there is, and in Appendix 1 there are three English-support exercises that combine features particularly relevant for functionally proficient teachers. These features are: they focus attention on linguistic form; they frame this formal focus in a communicative context; they lend themselves to relatively direct application to classroom situations; and finally they promote fluency and accuracy in ways directly relevant to the standards addressed above. Furthermore, they are only examples, illustrations of many possible pathways to improvement for individual teachers. However, in closing my attempt to balance optimistic and pessimistic reactions to English-medium instruction in international business schools, there remains one final question concerning the role institutions might play in helping their faculty meet this challenge.

Table 12.1   Selected features distingushing bands 6 and 7 on the international English testing exam

Source: International English Language Testing System

Initial state:	End state:
Grammar: Uses a mix of simple and complex sentence forms and makes some errors in grammar, but they rarely reduce communication	Grammar: Uses a wide range of structures; most sentence are error free and infelicities are only occasional
Vocabulary: Uses an adequate range of vocabulary for the task and attempts to use less common vocabulary but does so inaccurately	Vocabulary: Uses a sufficient range of vocabulary to allow some flexibility and precision, including less common words with awareness of style and collocation
Coherence: Arranges information and ideas coherently with a clear overall progression, but cohesion within and/or between sentences may be faulty and may not always use referencing clearly or correctly	Coherence: Sequences information and ideas logically and manages all aspects of cohesion well

What should business schools do?

Of course many faculty members do not find teaching through L2 English to be a challenge. Presumably many already sit atop the four-stage model we developed above and teach with pleasure. The crux of this question, though, concerns our colleagues who are not meeting those standards.

Regarding them, academic leaders have two options. One can say teaching in English is a job requirement and each teacher must find a way to meet that requirement. The legitimacy of this position varies between institutions that have always been international and always used English as a language of instruction and those that have adapted to the growing globalization of business education. At the latter type of institutions, there are teachers whose working conditions have changed and are changing, and I would argue that even business schools with the most draconian personnel policies share a responsibility for helping their faculty adjust to new conditions. The second option is to interpret the challenge of teaching through ESL as a challenge for a school's faculty-development program. Given that option, there are a number of things to say about what forms and formats are likely to be successful.

One approach of course is to treat the problem as a case of traditional language deficit, and outsource the problem completely to a language school or a language department. On one hand, the discussion above of fossilization and maturational constrains make clear that this is not the cheap and easy solution that it might appear to be. Moreover, while such expertise is extremely valuable, divorced from a business school faculty's broader faculty-development mission, traditional language instruction may lack priorities and may fail to inspire teachers.

Another approach, the one we have adopted at SSE and in the International Teachers Program, is to set language-develop targets in a way that matches a teacher's pedagogical vision and then to work toward those targets through activities relevant to day-to-day classroom teaching. This frequently involves classroom observations, and it always involves dialogue about in-class successes and in-class failures. In other words, it integrates linguistic expertise with reflective pedagogical practice. This approach combines small-group courses and individual coaching. The course component is important for a number of reasons: group activity de-stigmatizes language instruction; discussion helps teachers frame problems collectively; courses create new cohorts of peers who share a particular take on their pedagogic practice. The coaching component is also important, largely because language growth is ultimately a personal process. Moreover, a coaching approach acknowledges that progress with English is an aspect of professional development, linked centrally to a teacher's conception of that role. In brief, this approach ties L2 English to the growth and development of pedagogies suitable for global business education.

Closing remarks

In summary, I have answered five questions regarding ESL in the classrooms of international business schools. While there is no direct evidence that L2 English instruction is hurting learning at business schools, conclusive evidence of this kind is difficult to find. However, from other educational settings and from studies of L2 students' general abilities, we have indirect indications supporting the common-sense view that complex and elaborate tasks are more difficult in an L2 than in an L1. We should not exaggerate these indicators, but our review of ESL's effects on teaching practices ought to make us particularly watchful. While additional research is also necessary if we hope to monitor the quality of learning while avoiding blasé optimism or doom-and-gloom pessimism, agreed-upon standards, based perhaps on the model presented above, can provide an immediate, local point of departure. With reference to a small sample of examples in Appendix 1, the section headed '*What can I do to improve?*' illustrates that with guidance there is a great deal individual teachers can do to improve their own performance in English in ways that are relevant to the standards described above and therefore directly relevant to their pedagogical practice. The final section makes a brief case for holistic institutional support for that improvement. In closing, it appears to me that the prospects for and ramifications of teaching through ESL are much more attractive than the most glum among us fear, yet more daunting than the most sanguine among us hope.

References

Barton, B., Chan, R., King, C., Neville-Barton, P., and Sneddon, J., (2005). EAL undergraduates learning mathematics. *International Journal of Mathematical Education in Science and Technology*, 36: 721–729.

Carr, K., and Anderson, G., (2004). 'Taking language into account when teaching ESL students mathematical content'. In Wilson (2004), pp. 419–428 (see below).

Chiang, C. S., and Dunkel, P., (1992). The effect of speech modification, prior knowledge and listening proficiency on EFL lecture learning. *TESOL Quarterly*, 26: 345–374.

Hedge, T., (1993). Key terms in EFL. *ELT Journal*, 47: 275–277.

Hartman, S., Lavelle, T., and Wistedt, I., (2004). 'Learning through English in Swedish professional education'. In Wilson (2004), pp. 137–145 (see below).

Jones, A., and Sin, S., (2004). 'Integrating language with content in first year accounting: Student profiles, perceptions and performance'. In Wilson, pp. 478–492 (see below).

Klaassen, R., (2001). *The International University Curriculum: Challenges in English-medium Engineering Education*. Delft University.

Larsen-Freeman, D., (2006). The Emergence of complexity, fluency, and accuracy in the oral and written production. *Applied Linguistics*. 27: 590–619.

Marton, F., and Säljö, R., (1976). On qualitative differences in learning – 1: outcome and process. *British Journal of Educational Psychology*, 46: 4–11.

Nixon, J., (2000). *Content and Language Integrated Learning and Teaching in Sweden: A Report for The National Agency for Education*. Stockholm: National Agency for Education.

Norell, P., (1991). *Native-speaker Reactions to Swedish Pronunciation Errors in English*. Stockholm: Almqvist and Wiksell.

Parker, I., (2001). Absolute PowerPoint, *The New Yorker*, May 28, 2001: 76.

Ramsden, P., (2003). *Learning How to Teach in Higher Education, (2nd ed.)*. London and New York: RoutledgeFalmer.

Slack, N., Chambers, S., and Johnston, R., (2004). *Operations Management (4th ed.)*. Harlow: Pearson Education.

van der Walt, C., and Steyn, M., (2004). 'Student perceptions and frustrations with bilingual education at Stellenbosch University, South Africa'. In Wilson, pp. 493–507 (see below).

Vinke, A. A., (1995). *English as the Medium of Instruction in Dutch Engineering Education. Delft, Netherlands: Department of Education and Technology*, Delft University of Technology.

Washburn, L., (1997). *English Immersion in Sweden: A Case Study of Röllingby High School 1987-1989.* Stockholm: Stockholm University.

Wilson, R., (2004). *Integrating Content and Language: Meeting the Challenge of Bilingual Higher Education,* Universitaire Pers Maastricht.

Yusof, R. N., Mahamad, T., and Muzainah, M., (2004). 'English-medium instruction in non-English higher learning institutions: Accounting lecturers' experience versus students' perceptions'. In Wilson, pp. 523–535 (see above).

Appendix 1: Three English support exercises

ACTIVITY 1: VOCABULARY DEVELOPMENT

We can set aside some myths about how functionally proficient adults add to their English vocabulary, particularly their active vocabulary. Simple exposure to new words, say through reading or listening, does not help. Looking up words in dictionaries helps only if we are actively engaged in working with the new word and its uses. Instead, learning new words requires that we link them to the lexical networks already stored in our brains,[5] and those networks are organized along two distinct parameters: a word's form and its meaning. Beyond that, if we want to know how to use a new word, we need to know something about the company it keeps, its collocates. This exercise brings all three of these factors into play.

Step 1: While reading or listening to English, or in some other way, identify a set of five or so words you want to master and define them. Ideally, get a mix of verbs, adjectives and nouns, especially the former two. The following set comes from a book about globalization: *penchant*, an inclination, a (strong or habitual) liking; *nimbleness*, the property of being quick and light in movement or action or (of the mind) being able to think and understand quickly; *malign*, to speak ill of; and *bicker*, argue about petty and trivial matters.

Step 2: Look for formal hooks. Play with the English words you already know and identify words that have beginnings or ends similar to your target words. This activates the 'bathtub' effect, the fact that words' first and last syllables are keys we use to store and retrieve them, thus words in the mind have the same visibility profile as a person sitting in a bathtub – high at both ends but low in the middle. For my examples some formal hooks might be:

> **Penchant:** *Merchant, chant,* and members of the *pen-* family such as *pendant, penetrate* and *penitent.*
> **Nimbleness:** Any list of the nouns made from adjectives by adding *-ness*, and here we have a case where a formal hook coincides with semantic matching.

---

5   Jean Atichison's *Words in the Mind* (3rd ed., 2002. Blackwell) is a popular summary of basic research on the mental lexicon.

Malign: *Benign* and *align*.

Bicker: *Ticker, quicker, slicker, thicker* (where the formal match is a pure coincidence and probably not helpful since all of these *–er* endings are comparative endings, unlike the *–er* in *bicker*).

Step 3: Look for semantic hooks. These can be synonyms or near synonyms or antonyms or hyponyms (x is a hyponym of y if it represents a more specific type of x; thus *bicker* is a hyponym of *argue*) or hypernyms (x is a hypernym of y if it represents a more general type or category of which y is an example; thus *vehicle* is a hypernym of *automobile*).

Penchant: *Inclination, tendency; disinclination;*
Nimbleness: *Agility, sprightliness, grace, dexterity; clumsiness;*
Malign: *Defame, slander, vilify, denigrate, disparage; praise, extol; describe, characterize;*
Bicker: *Squabble, quarrel; agree; argue, disagree.*

Step 4: Find your words in context. This is the best way to learn how to use them. My examples are taken from word-based web searches:

Penchant: The key collocational information is that it always take the preposition *for*
*   Her philandering husband apparently has a *penchant* for very young women.
*   The dispute centers on Cheney's *penchant* for secrecy.
*   He related his *penchant* for prevarication, tracing it back to his childhood.
Nimbleness: Some collocational information seems to be that it takes the preposition *in* and that even organizations can be described as *nimble*.
*   Even fewer companies link space and its utilization with core competencies like *nimbleness*, speed or even quality.
*   Newsletter urges *nimbleness* in face of uncertain market.
*   Kroger displays *nimbleness* in adjusting to neighborhood preference.
Malign: I am working with the verb sense of the word, and the key collocational information is that it take personal or personified objects; thus *maligning someone's ideas* might be possible, but I found no examples of that kind of collocation. More surprising was the fact that the adjective usage is far more common than the verb usage, especially in expressions like *malign neglect, malign intent, malign consequences, malign effects*.
*   Parliamentary Affairs Minister Priyaranjan Das Munshi has said that an ex-PMO official was trying to *malign* Presidential nominee Pratibha Patil.
*   Insider trading: attempt to *malign* Pakistan.
*   There has been an orchestrated attempt on Fox to smear and *malign* the Dixie Chicks simply because they do not support George Bush's policies.
Bicker: The interesting fact here seems to be that although only humans bicker, in these examples no specific individuals are named; groups or categories seem to function as the common subjects of *bicker*.
*   Lawyers *bicker* in Ashley Benton trial.
*   Leaders *bicker* over remedy for downtown Miami.
*   Leftwing parties *bicker* ahead of Prodi vote.

None of the illustrative words in this exercise are important in themselves. What is potentially important for business school faculty who want to improve their English vocabulary is the process, the mental engagement with a word, its meaning (as manifest through its semantic relationship with other words), its form and its usage. By working with this process, a teacher can enlarge her active vocabulary in any area and thereby increase her fluency.

ACTIVITY 2: WORD-STRESS PLACEMENT

Accurate placement of word stress is essential for comprehensible pronunciation. Word stress is typically assigned to one syllable per word in English. A stressed syllable is pronounced longer and more loudly than unstressed syllables and the speaker's pitch typically changes at that point as well.

There are some theoretical rules governing stress placement, but most teachers I have worked with prefer to improve in this area by learning words and word groups concretely, rather than learning rules that are cast in linguistic terminology.

Accurate stress placement can be particularly difficult when primary stress falls on different syllables in similar words, as in Equal, eQUALity, Equalize, equaliZAtion; FINal, finALity, FINalize, finaliZAtion; NEUtral, neuTRALity, NEUtralize, neutraliZAtion.

Step 1 of this exercise is to select five 'word families' like those above.

Step 2 is to go through the sets and with the help of a dictionary, its CD or an informant and mark the word stress for each set. I recommend that you type it iconically as I did above because that visualizes the physical distinction more powerfully than the small diacritics most dictionaries use.

* ANalyze, aNALysis, ANalyst, analYTical, analYTic;
* REsolve, RESolute, resoLUtion;
* MObile, moBILity, MObilize, mobiliZAtion;
* PRODuct, proDUCtion, proDUCtive, producTIVity, produce (verb meaning to make or create), PROduce (noun meaning agricultural products);
* comPETE, compeTItion, comPETitive, comPETitor.

Once again the process of doing the exercise adds more value than the lists it produces. However, the lists themselves can be sorted and function as an individualized, quick-search reference work, which some people find easier to use than a dictionary. Finally, the exercise requires a focus on language form, a strategy for resisting or reversing some effects of fossilization.

ACTIVITY 3: TARGET SOUNDS

Different languages have different sound inventories. As a fact this is a commonplace, and as an aspect of language learning it is something beginners frequently struggle with. But for functionally proficient L2 speakers of English (for instance international business school faculty), this is a potential source of the recurrent errors that sometimes erode speaker credibility.

Step 1 is to identify the sound inventories of both English and your first language. You will probably need help with this, which you can find in quality dictionaries and textbooks on English and your language.

Step 2 is to identify the set of English sounds that do not exist in your language. If that is an empty set, congratulations – you are finished. If not, distinguish the vowels and the consonants. At least one study demonstrates that mispronounced consonants attract a stronger negative reaction than mispronounced vowels (Norell).

Step 3 requires you to work with an informant. Find out which of these consonants you can and cannot produce. That information is your starting point for two long-term activities. One of course is to begin practicing those you cannot yet produce. The other refers to stage 2 of our credibility standard. If you are not always meeting that standard because of recurrent errors, these sounds may be the cause. Use your list when you screen material prior to teaching it. Pay particular attention to these sounds when they occur initially in a word; errors in that position catch listeners' attention.

13 *Ascending and Descending with a Dissertation: Images of Tutoring Doctoral Students*

Udo Zander[1]

Doctoral students are almost universally expected to produce a piece of original research, and tutors are expected to make this happen. If originality assumes innovation, and we believe that most new ideas are bad ideas, we can start looking at the odds of writing a successful innovative dissertation. We have convincing data from the world of industry and universities, showing that only one out of ten R&D projects turn out to be a great success, while 20 per cent are moderately successful and 70 per cent are failures (Scherer and Harhoff 2000). To me, there is no reason to believe that the odds for writing a successful innovative dissertation should be dramatically different. This chapter is a playful attempt to inspire tutors to try and beat the odds by focusing on the relational and processual side of doctoral education.

There is no a priori reason to believe that these comments on tutoring doctoral students will contain any new good ideas. First, because my reflections on the topic are by nature self-centered and based on what most scholars would consider a very small sample. Second, because people, including both tutors and students, are different. This means that the variety of processes unleashed by two (or more) people working together, on what is seen (by one or both) as an important project, are endless. Third, the contexts in which the doctoral dissertation project is unfolding vary immensely. Now that this is said, let us quickly move to all our unabashed generalizations (and comfort ourselves with the thought that case studies occupied a central place in the works of Darwin, Marx and Freud).

The role of the tutor is to help the doctoral student in a multi-problem situation. For the student, writing a dissertation is almost always a personal quest to come to terms with privately experienced existential problems, often without realizing it themselves.[2] Ph.D. students are also engaged in a serious exercise of situated learning (Lave and Wenger 1991), meaning that they as 'newcomers' try to emulate the 'old-timers' of the academic profession by observing their behavior in a multitude of situations, like informal research conversations, seminars, conferences, and Ph.D. defenses. Trying hard to be and do like the senior academics (in combination with being totally dependent on the same seniors for a passing grade) leads to a vulnerable position, where the student can easily be exposed to senior academics' whims and become victims of exploitation and abuse. The identity transformation from apprentice/student to colleague that is expected during doctoral studies can be painful, and many are the learning plateaus resulting in frustration among all involved.

1   I would like to thank the editors of this book for their confidence, unfailing support, infinite patience and tutoring, without which this chapter would never have seen the light of day.

2   This fact was brought to me by the lovely Barbara Beuche, the heart and soul of Scancor, Stanford University during a delightful conversation in 1994, when she listened to my stupid questions and suddenly exclaimed: 'But Udo, don´t you know that Ph.D. students never finish their dissertation before they are ready with themselves?'

Selection of the best and the brightest to doctoral studies leads to a serious risk of hubris, where Ph.D. candidates often set out to write *the* ultimate piece on what they (or their tutors) consider the most important problem of all. A predictable consequence of the combination of great intelligence, biting off more than you can chew, and realizing that other great minds have dealt with the problem before is 'over-achiever paralysis', all too often leading to the best students never finishing their degree.

The extremely unstructured nature of the task facing a Ph.D. student in combination with uncertainty about the requirements for achieving a 'pass' lead to the initiation of strong escape mechanisms. It is much easier to engage in sorting piles of paper or routine maintenance of the department's computers than starting to write the dissertation, whatever it is for the moment. Finally, the timing of doctoral studies also often is problematic, as getting the degree in today's society often coincides with major personal 'decisions' on the way to lead one's life, partnering up and belonging.

In the following, I will try to argue that the relational aspects of the process of writing a dissertation matter for the tutor's ability to help in the complex multi-problem situation. The main points will be that the tutor may want to:

- Enter into early and honest discussions with the student about her reasons for being in academia, to find out if this matches the student's approach.
- Continuously make explicit the expectations she has on the student, as a lot of taken-for-granted and unspoken assumptions are present in the old-timer-newcomer relationship requiring situated learning on the part of the student.
- Discuss in some depth the dominant underlying tutoring logic and evaluation criteria applied at the university where the student is active.
- Never lose sight of the ultimate goal of the student writing an acceptable dissertation, make this the only demand on the student and in turn promise to remove all small or big obstacles within the tutor's power.
- As often as possible ask the student what their research question is and expect the student to reasonably early in the process become able to communicate this to non-experts in one or two sentences.
- Attempt to counteract over-achiever paralysis on part of the student by de-dramatizing the exercise of writing a dissertation.
- Protect the student from getting too involved in intra-departmental well-structured tasks.
- Constantly, and from day one, encourage the student to put their ideas and thoughts in writing.
- Encourage the student to expose her ideas to multiple and varied audiences at conferences, seminars, and workshops.
- Weather the storm connected to the student becoming independent with dignity and 'see' the student as being on her journey to become a respected colleague.

If you are aware of the issues outlined in the bullet points above, you can stop reading now and spend your valuable time on tutoring doctoral students instead.

Untangling the immediate context

ON TYPES OF TUTORS

As I have already mentioned, tutors come in different shapes and colors. Perhaps the most fundamental, and often overlooked, taxonomy was elaborated on by Friedrich Schiller in his inaugural lecture at the University of Jena in the eventful year of 1789. He spoke of the fundamental difference between Career Academics or 'Bread-learned' (*Brotgelehrte*) and what he called True Intellectuals or 'Philosophical Minds' (*Philosophische Köpfe*). For his main ideas on dimensions separating the two types of scholars (and tutors) see Table 13.1.

It becomes evident from Schiller's description of the two types, that a doctoral student ending up with a tutor who is in academia to make a living will run into severe problems if she aspires to question or overturn her tutor's world view. Of course, a student in total admiration of her tutor, trying to adapt to her every nod and wink, will have a serious problem inspiring the True Intellectual type tutor to engage in helping with the dissertation work. I would like to suggest that potential doctoral students may want to engage in some introspection and discussion to find out what kind of tutor(s) they want, and assess what kind of tutor(s) they end up with. Ideally, an early discussion of reasons for being in academia between doctoral students and tutors would be helpful. Unfortunately my experience is that these types of discussions are too rare, which sometimes results in taken-for-granted assumptions and unspoken expectations creating problems in the process of doctoral education. In this chapter I will therefore pay some attention to the processual and relational issues in doctoral education.[3]

ON TYPES OF KNOWLEDGE PRODUCTION SYSTEMS

Apart from Schiller's simple taxonomy, there are of course an abundance of historical (and thereby cultural and institutional) factors that affect our views on what a good doctoral student and dissertation is. Despite the remarkable stability of the occidental university system over the

Table 13.1   Schiller on academics: inaugural lecture in Jena, 1789

Career Academics ('Bread-learned')	True Intellectuals ('Philosophical Minds')
Afraid of new ideas; Do anything to stop scientific revolutions	Delighted by new ideas and discoveries
Have 'sunk cost' in education; Novelty destroys the value of knowledge	'Truth' is more important than the own system of ideas
Driven by external criticism and praise	Rewarded by search and diligence
Feel that all other researchers work against them	Feel that all other researchers are working for them

---

3   This means that we will assume that tutors possess the necessary professional skills, including factual knowledge in their area of expertise, and that doctoral students have an appropriate educational background. Obviously one or both these assumptions may sometimes be wrong in reality.

centuries (most certainly one of the most long-lived institutions still around), it has of course evolved since its beginnings in Bologna, Italy, in the late 11th century. I find it very useful to engage in a simple classification of three distinct systems corresponding to time periods, the Medieval system, the Renaissance system, and the Scientific Revolution system.[4] Both tutors and doctoral students will recognize certain aspects of the goals, philosophy, and expectations of their doctoral education being in line with either system. In most cases, the final outcome is a mix of the three systems, artifacts of which have been over-layered as sediments over time. Once again it is of great importance for the doctoral students to figure out in which context they are operating, and what their tutors' preferences and biases are.

In Medieval Europe, the doctorate was a license to teach at a university. In this sense, doctoral studies were a form of apprenticeship to a guild. Interestingly, in some parts of Europe the 'faculty' consisted of the students, who employed the teachers they admired and wanted to be taught by. The earliest doctoral degrees were granted in theology, philosophy, and medicine. Until the mid-1700s the doctoral defense was centered on a *Proponent* with a thesis, debating this with an *Opponent*. The exercise was monitored by a *Professor* seated on a chair (hence 'chaired professor') to emphasize his (always a man in medieval times) authority to judge the discussion. Also present in the room was the *Reader* at a table where he was able to consult the *References* (in those days the Bible, the Philosopher—Aristotle—and possibly *Questiones* written on the topic by the professor) and a crowd of students watching the event. The *Dissertation* was a fictitious written account of the happening at the defense. Although a wide range of topics were tolerated at the defenses, obviously the outcome of the discussion was limited by the content of the references and the presence of an omnipotent professor.

The logic of the medieval system for doctoral education was dramatically affected by societal and technological changes during the Renaissance. The Catholic Church was challenged and Gutenberg's invention of the printing press broke the church's monopoly on book production and opened a possibility for everyone, not just professors, to profess. A good example of the new type of actors was Galileo Galilei who published his 'The Starry Messenger' in 1610 and 'Dialogue Concerning the Two Chief World Systems' in 1632 to promote his ideas on the nature and workings of the universe. He was also a pioneer in receiving research grants, although never getting his doctorate.[5] During the Renaissance, the dissertation as a means of reporting advancements in knowledge was replaced by the essay, an esthetically pleasing and self-contained account similar to a textbook. Obviously, the range of approachable topics widened during the Renaissance, and the ability to address the 'knowing public' was enhanced by Latin's status as a lingua franca.

The appearance of the first scientific journal, the *Journal des Savants*, in the 1630s, heralded the march into the knowledge production system in the age of Scientific Revolutions. The French monk Mersenne regularly copied letters he received from some 400 scholars and circulated them within the group. When he for logistical purposes decided to bundle a number of letters at the time, the *Journal des Savants* was born. The scientific journal was from the 1670s complemented

---

4   I would like to profoundly thank Professor Hans Siggaard Jensen for introducing me to this fascinating area during a most inspiring speech at a meeting with the European Doctoral Programmes Association in Management and Business Administration (EDAMBA), on which this section draws heavily.

5   Galileo never graduated from the University of Pisa, but wanted a university position to be able to tutor students in mathematics. Ironically, it was a lecture on literature that would turn Galileo's fortunes. The Academy of Florence had been arguing over a 100-year-old controversy: What were the location, shape, and dimensions of Dante's Inferno? The question was absolutely serious, and Galileo, asked to answer the question from the point of view of a man of science, treated it with dignity. Extrapolating from Dante's line that '[the giant Nimrod's] face was about as long/and just as wide as St. Peter's cone in Rome,' Galileo deduced that Lucifer himself was 2,000 arm-lengths long. The audience was impressed, and Galileo was remembered with favor. Within the year, Galileo had received a 3-year appointment to the University of Pisa, the same university that never granted him a degree.

with so called 'Transactions', which were reports from meetings at the royal societies. The trend was clearly towards cumulative papers instead of monographs, and the peer-review system was introduced, inspired by the idea of 'blind tests' introduced in the experimental sciences. In essence, the Scientific Revolution system of knowledge production emphasized the accumulation of knowledge around some highly cited 'kernel papers', and the members of Learned Societies through reviewing started deciding who could become a member/peer.

The evolution of knowledge production systems seems to follow the unfreeze-refreeze logic, with the Renaissance being a period of the greatest fluidity. From the perspective of this chapter on doctoral tutoring, the most interesting changes between the three described time periods are in how doctoral work is evaluated and the 'training logic' (see Table 13.2).

As already mentioned, sediments and aspects of all the three systems of knowledge production described in Table 13.2 (where I have tried to reproduce a slide presented by Hans Siggaard Jensen) can be found in most contemporary doctoral education. It is my conviction that doctoral students and tutors could benefit tremendously from discussing and understanding the dominant underlying logic and expectations of doctoral education at their particular university. For a doctoral student it is relatively easy to get a first hunch of the bias of their tutor by exploring their record as to type and style of publications.

The tutor's roles in the process

In the following, I will (well aware of the problems and dangers) try to give some advice to tutors of doctoral students, using the metaphor of mountain climbing. Mountain climbing was initially chosen due to its affinity to the idea of doctoral education being the last step (except for the 'Habilitation' in some systems) in the ascent towards the heavens to reach enlightenment. When invoking mountain climbing I will focus on expeditions involving a team rather than the single climber, in order to capture the social nature of doctoral education and its dependence on certain critical resources provided by universities.[6] I of course leave the judgement of the metaphor's effectiveness entirely to the reader, but its use in a lecturing context seems to always have generated smiles of recognition and certainly sparked interesting debates and hypotheses.

Table 13.2   Three systems of knowledge production

TIME OF ORIGIN	EVALUATION MECHANISM	'TUTORING LOGIC'
Medieval times	Dissertation judged by professor	Trained to debate
Renaissance	Essay or monograph judged by the 'knowing public'	Trained to convince
Scientific revolution	Series of papers judged by Scientific Society	Trained to belong

---

6   The view of mountain climbing expeditions in this chapter comes close to South-Tyrolean alpinist Reinhold Messner's path-breaking view on mountain climbing, where the idea of the large, pyramidal, hierarchically-led expedition is replaced by a small, lightly equipped team operating in a democratic fashion and capable of spontaneous action on the mountain.

To make the connection to mountain climbing, I will try to evoke pictures in the reader's mind. This is done by introducing the different comments on tutors' help by brief descriptions of an image; much like playwrights describe the context of a scene in their texts as a way to influence stage scenery. As a good tutor should be able to envision things like the finished dissertation, as well as the contribution to science and incumbent reactions to the results, I am sure that you as a reader will not have any problems entering the world of mountain climbers.

SIX IMAGES OF MOUNTAIN CLIMBING

Image 1. A cloudy morning in the Himalayan foothills. Strong wind is blowing and a small group of climbers are taking to the mountains. In the foreground collapsed red and yellow tents and piles of left-behind equipment. The first rule for a tutor is to never lose focus of the ultimate goal of the doctoral studies exercise, that is, for the student to finish a dissertation that passes. Much like a mountain climbing expedition leader needs to constantly think about that all coaching, equipment and support is ultimately brought to the mountain to see a single person reach the top, a tutor needs to remember that her first and foremost task is to make sure that nothing hinders the doctoral student's progress towards a finished dissertation. Although it is tempting for a tutor to list all aspects of an academic way of life when asked what is required by the student, it is useful to tell students that their only task is to write a high-quality dissertation in reasonable time, and that you as a tutor will do everything possible to make this happen. This is a simple transparent agreement that makes both parties responsible for success, and the student will figure out the other aspects soon enough by watching senior scholars in action.

Image 2. A lonely gazing climber on a rock, surrounded by hundreds of inviting snow-covered peaks glittering in the sunshine. It is just as difficult for a doctoral student to choose a research question as it is for a novice mountain climber to choose an ascent once they have arrived in a mountainous area. Everything looks different than the map when plans were made, and there is suddenly so much more tangible information available. A tutor may want to spend much time with newly arrived doctoral students, trying to carve out a research question. One useful approach is to challenge students to formulate their research question in one sentence and then try it on people not at all familiar with the topic. Friends, family, and total strangers will do. If they do not understand and get excited, the tutor may want to help the student to phrase the question in a more general way until it works better. The approach bears clear resemblance of the Socratic method of midwifery, since most students as mentioned arrive with an existential but often unformulated question in mind. Having decided on a question, the student has a much easier time choosing literature and theories to study. A number of iterations may be necessary to end up with the final question, but time and effort is saved compared to the 'read-the-whole-library-to-find-what-is-interesting-approach'. If the conceptual literature is still too large to grasp, a viable approach is to focus on empirical studies, asking the question: 'What do we actually know'? This approach almost inevitably leads to a very limited number of studies to start working from.

When doctoral students are thrown head over heels into empirical projects initiated and managed by the supervisor, there is a risk that the students experience a lack of meaning and sensation of slavery. Carefully explaining the underlying research question and calibrating it against the students' research interests is advisable, to avoid later backlashes and apathy on part of the student.

Image 3. A gloomy child, arms on the back, dressed in a raincoat and a rain hat, looking lonesome among some grey, wet boulders, obviously approximately at sea level. Just like in mountain climbing, failure—or at least a less than desirable outcome—is a real option. The challenge for a tutor is to celebrate even the climbing of small hills, as a) not all doctoral student are up to writing a good dissertation; b) most new ideas—certainly most bold ones—are bad ideas; and c) students that venture where no one has gone before often discover that there is a good reason for this. Due to the selection of (generally) smart students to doctoral programs, the tendency towards over-achiever paralysis should be counteracted by a wise tutor.

Image 4. Once again at the foot of massive Himalayan mountains covered in a roaring snow storm. In the foreground some 20 colorful tents clinging to the bare rock in the sun, above which long lines hold rows of small flags of many countries fluttering in the hard wind. In mountain climbing expeditions, there is a clear risk of getting stuck in base-camp. Just like in a base-camp, the academic department or institute offers an abundance of possibilities for doctoral students to feel active, helpful, needed, and appreciated without at all progressing with their dissertation. In the base-camp, there is equipment to maintain and repair, plans to make, news to record, and rumors to evaluate, interpersonal conflicts to get involved in, and always enough people around that appreciate discussing the weather, tutor misconduct, or other pressing matters. A tutor may want to once in a while remind the doctoral student that she will be part of the group going for the peak as soon as conditions are satisfactory. This will keep the student focused on what shape she is actually currently in, and help her start imagining the exciting ascent that lies ahead. This is especially helpful as most base-camp chores are infinitely more limited and structured, and therefore often more attractive, than addressing a research question by venturing into the unknown. In the extreme case, base-camps develop into permanent dwellings that blend in with the local architecture, revealing that the dream of reaching the distant peak lives on in the internal discourse, but the intent to ever actually attempt an attack is no longer there. A wise tutor leaves with her students.

Image 5. A small group of climbers wandering in a seemingly aimless way through a huge field of gravel and sharp rocks. In the background icy slopes against a grey sky. Evening is approaching. As a tutor, you may want to convey to the student that, just like in mountain climbing, the essential thing is to always take the next step irrespective of the surrounding and your internal mood. When writing a dissertation, the next step is often the next written paragraph. One way of encouraging continuous writing on part of the students is to ask for documentation before every meeting. It also saves time for the student as nebulous ideas and concepts almost always are revealed as not useful when an attempt is made to formulate them on paper. Many a non-finishing doctoral student lives under the impression of actually having a whole dissertation in their head, it is just not yet on paper.

Image 6. Two worn-down, half-dressed mountain climbers in a tent, staring past each other at (the usual) freeze-dried food. Only the howling wind is heard. Just like on a mountain climbing expedition, there will be recurrent crises during the cause of completing a doctorate. If there were not, probably very little would be achieved as learning on part of both student and tutor requires a certain degree of increased confusion. Tutors may want to suggest a change of context, a temporary break to make it possible to distance oneself from the situation. Attending and presenting at seminars or conferences often helps, if nothing else, by putting things in perspective and realizing that others are in trouble too. Often, outsiders may see things the tutor or the student do not see or appreciate the value of in the research.

TUTORING DYNAMICS

During doctoral education the student should evolve from being just that to becoming a colleague fully accepted by the scholarly community. This process follows a well-known pattern in the development of groups over time, presented to me first by Seán Gaffney (also an author represented in this book, see Chapter 10). For a simple overview, see Figure 13.1.

From a state of dependence on the tutor, the aim is to let the student and tutor end up in a state of co-dependence. This end-state is desirable as groups of people at this level are highly productive. As can be seen in Figure 13.1, the road to co-dependence unfortunately goes via counter-dependence and independence. Counter-dependence is a state where the doctoral student, much like a teenager, constantly challenges the tutor's position and questions or dismisses her knowledge, advice, and judgement. This period can be very frustrating and painful for the tutor and there is a constant temptation to, by applying means of authority, push the student back into the more comfortable dependent state. It may be advisable to instead 'let go' at this stage and let the student move into independence, where she becomes (temporarily) uninterested in interaction with the tutor. Over time, the model predicts, the now independent student will find her way back to the tutor, much like many teenagers eventually start coming 'home' for Sunday dinners.

Tutoring, like most human endeavors is best done when we realize that doctoral students like other human beings are hardwired to be loss- and risk-avert, emotional, over-confident, prone to simplify and classify, information- and control-seeking, as well as prestige- and power-conscious (Wilson 1988). Especially scholars trained in the Western, Modern-Project, rational scientific paradigm (Toulmin 1990) may be well advised not to underestimate the strong emotional reactions highly present in the doctoral tutoring process on part of both students and tutors.

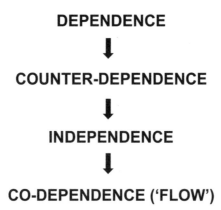

TUTORING DYNAMICS

DEPENDENCE
↓
COUNTER-DEPENDENCE
↓
INDEPENDENCE
↓
CO-DEPENDENCE ('FLOW')

Figure 13.1   Tutoring dynamics

The Swedish poet Hjalmar Söderberg has tried to catch our innermost needs in the novel Doktor Glas from 1905:

> *One wants to be loved, in lack thereof admired, in lack thereof feared, in lack thereof loathed and despised. One wants to kindle some kind of emotion in people. The soul shivers before emptiness and wants contact at any price.*[7]

I would venture a guess that a fair share of relationships between tutors and doctoral students follow the logic of this dynamic.

What tutors may also at this point want to realize is that their efforts will not grant them respect, admiration, or applause from their doctoral students (at least not in the short run). While love and admiration most probably have to be sought elsewhere, tutoring however has the potential of producing a comforting inner feeling of having helped give birth to a new scholar with (hopefully) fresh and original ideas, that in the best of worlds in a Schumpeterian sense will creatively destruct our own.

References

Lave, J. and Wenger, E., (1991). *Situated learning: Legitimate Peripheral Participation.* Cambridge University Press.

Scherer, F.M. and Harhoff, D., (2000). 'Technology Policy for a World of Skew-distributed Outcomes'. *Research Policy*, 29(4-5): 559.

Schiller, F., (1789). *Was heisst and zu welchem Ende studiert man Universalgeschichte?*. Inaugral Lecture at the University of Jena.

Söderberg, H., (1905/1978). *Doktor Glas*. Liberförlag.

Toulmin, S., (1990). *Cosmopolis: The Hidden Agenda of Modernity*. University of Chicago Press.

Wilson, E.O., (1988). *On Human Nature*. Harvard University Press.

---

[7]   *Man vill bli älskad, i brist därpå beundrad, i brist därpå fruktad, i brist därpå avskydd och föraktad. Man vill ingiva människorna någon slags känsla. Själen ryser för tomrummet och vill kontakt till vad pris som helst.*

Outside the Classroom

Designing Programs and Learning Environments

14 *Program Design and Management*

Christer Karlsson

Planning and developing a program – tasks and context

PLANNING A WHOLE PROGRAM

This chapter is about planning and developing a whole program. Other chapters in this book deal with teaching and pedagogical issues but here our focus is at the program level. For the sake of completeness we will ignore any existing program that needs to be developed and look instead at a complete process of planning and developing on the basis of starting a new program from scratch. Business schools often run undergraduate, postgraduate and post-experience programs. This chapters is relevant to them all but relates specifically to Executive Masters programs, including the full time MBA, Executive MBA and Specialized Executive Masters.

A BUSINESS SCHOOL PERSPECTIVE

Planning a complete program cannot be done successfully without first relating the program to the overall strategy and structure of the business school.

The Executive Masters program needs to be positioned within the program portfolio of the whole school. This should be done from an external perspective to ensure that the program portfolio offers good potential for life-long learning for the alumni and other professionals. It also needs to take advantage of the benefits for the school which flow from a modularized (and hence flexible) program and economies of scale.

THE EXTERNAL CONTEXT TO THE BUSINESS SCHOOL

Business schools in common with other businesses have become more global with an increasing number of competitors. In this competitive international environment they have needed to become business-like and improve their own management. Competition is fierce, both with other business schools but also with consultancy firms and corporate universities.

Many universities face the pressures of reduced public financing and faculty shortages. Planning any program must take place in the context of this tough environment. Business school boards and leaders may be tempted to take their lead from those institutions at the very top of the league. However there can only be 20 business schools in the top 20. It may be wiser to reflect on the relevance of your program for regional, national or local markets. A more specialist profile may not deliver the standardized product that matches the ranking criteria of international business papers and magazines but it will offer distinctiveness. Developing and launching a 'me too' product in a mature and highly competitive market has obvious pitfalls. You need to position your product carefully in relation to both supply and demand. Niche positioning is in many cases most appropiate for schools and their programs.

A CONCEPTUAL FRAMEWORK

Developing and planning a program involves both product development and production planning. The concepts and models from the fields of product development management and operations management are as relevant when developing a new business school program as for developing any new product. Product development is a funnel shaped process which starts at a wide a perspective as possible using many ideas from many sources. These are then honed and filtered, leaving you with a manageable number of concrete projects/course modules in your product portfolio.

Operations is a transformational process in which the *transformers* (the teachers and developers) change and develop the *transformed* (the students) into *finished products* (graduates). The role of operations is to achieve this with consistent quality, constant effectiveness, continuous responsiveness and low costs. At the heart of all this is a careful development process and a comprehensive program plan.

PROCESS – WORK STEPS FROM IDEA TO PRODUCT

Start with a plan or schedule for the program development process. The process should lead you through a series of steps from idea to finished product. The first step involves the product concept and requires as comprehensive a description of the whole product idea as you are able to generate. The outcome you are looking for is a product with a clear specification of its constituent components and the relation between each of them. An overview of the process might look something like the following:

- *The concept* – you are aiming for a comprehensive description of the whole idea.
- *Demand and supply mapping* – a visual representation of the whole market. Who are your customers, your competitors and your stakeholders?
- *Profiling and specialization* – focus on your product identity, by defining your USPs (Unique Selling Points), their competitive advantage, and the basis for the overall content and format of the program.
- *Program objectives* – define the learning objectives in terms of knowledge, skills and attributes. What are the program objectives and the learning and development objectives of the program? What are the functional, academic or discipline-related, constraints to the program?
- *Product functionality* – what the program is supposed to achieve for the participants. Describe the process in terms of activities, actors and resources.
- *Product specifications* – write instructions for the development of courses, cases, projects, and so on.
- *Overall curriculum* – create a description of the program process, including brief descriptions of each and every component.
- Define a set of detailed curricula for each program component.

Critical issues in program design

THE MARKET AND THE PARTICIPANT

As in any product development project the most appropriate starting point is the potential customers themselves. There are a variety of different customers in this market. You are able to differentiate between the participant and their employer (who may often actually be funding the course).

From the perspective of the participant you need to consider the strategy that underpins their participation. What role is the program designed to play in their lifelong career plan? This may be complicated by a number of factors. A full-time MBA participant may well be leaving an existing position and, if so, will be taking a considerable risk and making a major investment.

The program needs to provide the participant with considerable new knowledge and experience, networking and job opportunities. A participant on an Executive MBA very likely has a good job and may be seeking to move from a specialized to a general management position. The participant in a specialized masters degree program may wish to prepare himself for a top functional position. Identifying the expectations of potential and recruited participants is an integral step in ensuring the success of the program.

THE PARTICIPANT AND THE WIDER MARKET

The participant works within a market; the job market. The program itself often has a market in terms of those organizations and their Human Resource functions which are planning activities to support their key staff in their lifelong development. A close collaboration with these functions within client organizations which are part of the business school network is important for long-term product planning and development. The success of many programs is often assessed on the basis of the future earning potential of participants before and after their involvement on the program.

PROGRAM TYPES

Some types of programs, such as full-time MBAs, have a high profile but there are many others that are less well known. Potential participants and their employers often find it difficult to identify the defining characteristics of a program. There are MBA programs that are either general- or industry-focused but which should not be function- or role-oriented to qualify as an MBA program. There are specialized masters programs that are function-specific but may also have an industry focus. But there are also many other attempts to develop distinctive, niche programs such as High-Flyers programs, Master of Management Development, Young Leaders programs and Advanced Management programs.

It is important to identify the specific target group(s) for each and to articulate clearly what the program is supposed to deliver for the participant. We will discuss product and portfolio characteristics later in the chapter.

GOVERNANCE STRUCTURE

Governance is an important consideration both during the development and planning of a new program as well as following its launch. Some form of of governing or advisory board may be useful, involving representatives from amongst both academics and practitioners. You may well wish to involve representatives from potential clients, including both professional organizations and employers.

FUNDING

There are a number of different funding models to be considered in product development. Don't forget to consider internal transfer as an option. Cannibalizing existing products to create new ones can be useful even if it is not popular.

There may be a number of courses for possible grants or sponsorship. This approach can be particularly useful as it enables funded development. This classic alternative to straightforward new product development means that an *early adopting* customer is prepared to pay for development of a new type of product. Such new bespoke products, whole programs or modules, may later be generalized to become a new product type in their own right.

FACULTY

Faculty members are an increasingly scarce resource. As a consequence business school faculty members often travel from place to place giving guest lectures. A high level program which uses the best possible resources may well include a healthy mix of 50 per cent external teachers. One risk associated with a high level of external teachers is that the program and its teaching staff may lack identity. This also risks diluting the profile of the school and explains why business schools increasingly seek to restrict the work that faculty members may undertake for competitors.

It is a common mistake to assume that the best teachers are always the most senior professors. Good post-doctoral lecturers may be excellent executive teachers if they have learned how to deal with experienced participants. A useful strategy is to develop a cohort of such teachers at an early stage; encouraging them to shadow more senior lecturers as they gradually assume their own distinct role.

In addition to internal and other academic teaching resources it is important to plan for and develop external resources. These include human resources – practitioners who act as external teachers, as well as teaching resources – good case studies and study visits.

FACILITIES

The facilities are an important part of the product. There is a strong link between the quality of the results, the teaching formats and the physical facilities available. The combination of lecture theatres with or without syndicate rooms and space for informal discussions is crucial to teaching processes and outcomes. A new program may require investment in specific facilities or staff and, if so, this will need to be factored into the budget.

Product portfolio planning

PROGRAM TYPES

You need to consider both the market and the practicalities of design and delivery when planning a program portfolio. A key perspective in planning for the market is the importance of offering a set of programs to address the lifelong development needs of managers and professionals.

Programs may cover general management roles and/or functional roles. General management positions may be split into industry-general or industry-specific positions as well as those that are either global or local. Some of your programs may offer a degree-level qualification whilst others may not. You will also have a mix of short and long programs.

A full-time participant such as a graduate or full-time MBA student may well be giving most of their time to learn as much as possible in the time available and become a valuable asset for a future employer. Candidates of this kind will often be particularly interested in practical management tools and other useful knowledge and skills that demonstrate the participant's potential to any employer.

This is reinforced by activities such as assessment centre-style exercises. An extreme example of this need is visible in MBA advertising using the headline: 'Come and experience more than 200 cases.'

A participant in a part-time program such as the Executive MBA or a Masters student is more likely to focus on knowledge of a higher order; for example, strategic perspectives, reflective analysis or general (rather than functional) management. The format for this kind of student needs to include ample opportunities for covering issues related to their own organization, their own work-related projects and thesis, live case studies and study visits. In addition there may be an exchange of experiences, and the potential to involve participants as complementary teachers and resource persons.

A virtual program is rarely the first option to come to mind. Although this is often the format that best enables worldwide participation there are other more important features too. The key advantage of the geographical dimension is the flexibility it provides. A virtual program enables mobile employees to participate.

Asynchronous is probably a better term than virtual since the participant can work at any time of the day (or night) depending on their work situation and location. You may adopt a virtual format for a complete program or simply for selected modules.

The simplest form of program classification is either general or functional management. The role of the program is often to help the participant make the transition from a functional to a general management position. This makes the program broad in nature, covering all the managerial disciplines. One downside may be that participants may find the program rather basic within their own area. On the other hand the teacher can use the spectrum of knowledge and experience that is available in the classroom in the teaching situation.

More specialized programs will focus on particular applications or industries; for example, the Master of Public Administration (MPA) program. Other examples include industry-specific Executive MBAs such as those designed for the shipping, aviation and automotive industries. The prerequisite for an MBA is that it should be grounded in broad, general management disciplines. Variations include industry-specific Executive Masters such as those for the health and other sectors.

An alternative approach is to develop programs based around a functional area. There are endless variants of Masters in finance, marketing, technology management, and so on.

PROGRAM CHARACTERISTICS

The process of developing and planning a program raises a number of questions about the characteristics of your program. These may be market-related; perspectives such as the positioning and profile of the program. But they will also relate to production characteristics such as quality, efficiency and cost.

Modularization

A key issue both for product development and production is the degree to which the program is modular and the basis for this process. Developing elements of the program as discrete modules enables economies of scale in product development and allows you to present an increased product portfolio by using different combinations of modules.

Modules may be anything from an element that runs for a couple of days in a long program to a complete short stand-alone program. The same module may also be adapted for use in a variety of very different programs for a number of audiences, simply by varying the teaching approach and the degree of candidate involvement. One issue you'll need to consider during program development is whether it is the teacher or the dean who is most skillful in exploiting the benefits of modularization.

Synergies

Synergies between programs may arise from modularization as well as through sharing teachers, teaching materials, administrative staff and support systems. A more focused portfolio of programs should offer advantages in all these areas. One particular application of the approach involves co-teaching of modules between different programs. This may also be enriched by the exchange of experiences between the groups, although you need to be careful to limit its use to avoid the risk of undermining the sense of group identity within each program.

Cannibalization

Setting up a new program may well involve the need to cannibalize one or several activities from an existing product portfolio. There are no general rules about this, but it makes good sense to find out what elements potential participants and their organizations will choose before setting up a new program. The combination between programs will not necessarily risk the negative effects of cannibalization. There are many examples of complementary product *strengthening* the portfolio because the element of choice makes them more attractive to organizations and individuals.

Integration

One important aspect of a program is the extent to which it is integrated with the participant's daily work and with the business of the client organization. Increasingly, participants are sent on a program for their own development but also for the benefit of their organization. A close integration between the program and clients offers many advantages. It provides a source of cases studies, issues, applications and experiences but, be careful: you need to manage client expectations of the extent to which a program will be integrated with the participant's day-to-day work. You are not providing direct consultancy and the advantages to be gained from business development should never sideline the personal development needs of each participant.

Program schedule and length

The length of the program is an important design variable. Participants in full-time programs will often want to graduate as quickly as possible. It has become increasingly popular with a one year *accelerated* version of the full-time MBA. The other side of acceleration relates to the process of reflection, integration and concurrent work. Accelerated programs may result in lower levels of learning. Part-time programs may suffer from a lower level of frequency and intensity which means that participants can lose the connection between modules in the program. More than 2 weeks between activities starts the process of distancing the learner from their material.

Critical issues in curriculum design

As a starting point it is critically important to ask how the program contributes to the development of the participant and their organization. Remember the concept of the production process. How does the participant compare before and after the program? You need to be careful to establish appropriate expectations and plan the program accordingly. The objective is to ensure you end up with a good product and avoid disappointments with expectations that are not met.

Once you have the basic program ideas in place you can consider curriculum planning; the overall content, schedules, formats, teaching material and teachers. You need to have an idea about the courses and other activities we should include in the program. Of course the starting point should be your program objectives and the form of teaching and learning that you have chosen to adopt.

OBJECTIVE

Start by articulating the objectives of the program from the perspective of the graduated participant. We have already discussed the target group and now we need to describe the outcomes for the participant and the level of competence the graduate expects following the program.

ACADEMIC OR VOCATIONAL?

An important distinguishing factor in your objective is the extent to which the program is academic or vocational. One aspect of the objective is to develop the skills of the reflective practitioner within the participant. The vocational training element should develop practical skills without the need for a theoretical background. Any program will contain both components to greater or lesser extent.

DEVELOPING COMPETENCE

In this chapter we will not explore learning objectives or classifications such as Bloom's taxonomy in any detail. However it is important to consider the overall objectives and what the participant requires from the program in terms of knowledge, skills and attributes. Therefore let us go back in history, for a moment; back to classic philosophers such as Socrates, Plato and Aristotle.

They were the first to distinguish between knowledge (*epistêmê*) and craft or skill (*technê*). Episteme or knowledge is built on rational formulae (*logos*). Skill or craft is know-how. An individual may have knowledge without skill, or skill without knowledge. You may understand the laws of motion but not have the skill to play snooker; alternatively, you can play snooker without ever having heard of the laws of motion.

Having distinguished craft from scientific knowledge, Aristotle further distinguishes it from virtue (*aretê*). There may be a number of different approaches that you can take to do the same thing. You can play soccer as a defender or an attacker. Equally, different value systems will guide different behavior, for example risk aversion or entrepreneurship will influence the way you behave when faced with opportunity. If these dimensions can exist independently, they can be said to be *ortogonal*. But the existence of each of them will contribute to the competence of the individual. Consequently competence is the general term to describe a mix of knowledge, skills, and attributes or virtue.

These concepts are important because our objective is to teach knowledge, train skills and develop attributes by way of experience.

LONGITUDINAL PROCESS

If you consider the product as a transformation process in which the participant is transformed by our inputs, then this reinforces the significance of the processes associated with the program. Program development is dependent on an approach that puts processes and process development at its heart. The most common shortcoming of program planning is that of filling a program planning framework with discrete course modules which are only loosely related. If the program delivery involves different teachers who come in to present their sessions without further reference to one another then this shortcoming will be exacerbated.

CROSS-SECTIONAL PROCESSES

Part of the need for a holistic process involves effective integration between concurrent program activities. These may be concordant which each other as well as offering conflicting perspectives. The important thing is to create seamless integration.

Whether you look down or across the program you can see issues for program planning and management. It is extremely important to involve someone of high academic standard who can be responsible for the program as a whole and can make sense of and integrate the various program modules. The role of the program manager is to reflect on, connect, integrate and much more. There is a coordination tool called issue planning which can be used to help teachers to integrate their modules effectively, which we will discuss later.

CONTENT

The content may be the least controversial part of the planning if you have been diligent in positioning your program and your target-group planning. Of course we shouldn't underestimate academic differences on what is important but there are few general conclusions to be drawn about content at this stage. We can offer some guidance on how to organize the content across and down the program.

There are two important dimensions, one relating the sequence in which managerial issues are dealt with, the other to the sequence in which the participants encounter academic disciplines. In an ideal world these two dimensions should be integrated, but inevitably some sequence discord will be unavoidable.

There are four distinct approaches: outside-in versus inside-out; top-down or bottom-up. An outside-in and top-down approach, for example, might generate the following sequence: business context, strategy, product planning, operations, financing, organizing, controlling and auditing. In other words, a structure that follows the logical 'plan, do, review' sequence.

A related issue is the order in which the participants will then meet the various academic disciplines for the first time. You may choose a sequence of strategy, marketing, innovation, finance, legislation, organization, information system, and, finally, accounting. Alternatively, since accounting provides much of the language of communication and performance management, you may prefer to start there and then build up the sequence. Both directions make sense and both are reflected in existing programs. Whilst there is little empiric evidence to support this observation, it does seem as if the accountancy-led approach was more common 20 years ago while today the more fashionable approach is to start the program with an introduction to innovation within an environmental context.

A word of warning: the sequences of various generic disciplines are in no sense ideal models. We try to integrate the various disciplines to create an holistic picture. However, this is by no means easy and you may be advised to continue using the main management disciplines as a means of structuring a number of the modules.

BACKGROUND AND ENTRY LEVEL

The students themselves are a critical factor in the process of transformation..Time spent understanding and defining group make-up is very important. First of all you need the *right* participants. There is a considerable risk in underestimating how hard it will be for an individual, who does not quite fit the profile, to follow the program process and stay the distance. A single individual who does not fit can disrupt the learning process, the group and the teachers. Therefore you need to make considerable effort to test and assess each candidate for any advanced program. This may involve standardized or non-standardized external and internal tests, interviews, as well as tasks such as essay writing.

GROUP MAKE-UP

Simply specifying the entry-level criteria and qualifications of the candidates is not enough. The make-up of each intake for program is also important. You may look for a particular mix of education, nationalities, cultures, genders, ages, industries, functions and organizational roles.

FORMATS

Teaching and examination formats are as much a part of the curriculum as content. There may be similar programs with very different approaches. One may involve considerable academic teaching, whilst another seeks to create experience through written case studies, and a third, uses strongly work-based case studies and projects. Few programs can deliver all of these things, whatever their advertising may suggest. Reflect on the particular mix of resources and opportunities at your school to identify a strategy offering competitive advantage.

Program concept

Before getting into detailed program planning you may find it helpful to create a brief product concept. Your aim is to conceptualize the product idea by creating a comprehensive description of the product. Try developing a description of the whole idea on a single page. This kind of conceptualization often proves helpful because it makes it far easier to communicate the product concept consistently to all the different functions and individuals who will be involved in developing the components at a later stage.

A typical concept description might contain the following:

- What does the program do? What is its function? What are the planned outcomes?
- Who are the likely candidates and what is their level of education and work experience?
- What sort of shape is the career of future candidates?
- How are the candidates selected, grouped and inducted?
- What are the typical positions, roles and career profiles of the candidates?

- What type of program will you be running? How is it positioned in relation to competing programs?
- What does the general structure, content and scale of the course look like?
- What is the intended volume of the program's throughput and how will it develop over time?
- What are the planned teaching formats? What other activities are included?
- What are the admission criteria and what form of selection processes will you employ?
- What are the main internal and external teaching and administrative resources?
- What are the criteria for identifying and selecting teaching staff? Which members of faculty might potentially collaborate?
- What choice of facilities is available and how do they relate to format and style of teaching?

Preparation phase

Before starting on a detailed plan you need to understand the market conditions and other factors in the context of the program. We assume that you will have tested whether there is an existing or potential demand for the type of program. But there are also a couple of other fundamental considerations before going ahead.

Mapping the supply market should give you an understanding of your potential positioning and the likely competition. There are at least three groups of actors you may want to analyze: First, those business schools and programs seen as the market leaders in the style of program you wish to develop. Take time to look at them in depth. They may be a great source of ideas for your own program, equally you may not wish to compete with them directly. Trying to do so may be costly, unrealistic and unnecessary.

Second you have direct competitors; those who offer similar programs aimed at the same target groups in the same markets. These are obvious candidates for competitive analysis. But make sure you take time to look at those schools who offer similar products, for similar target groups but in other markets. There is often a lot to learn from them and they may be potential partners. Gather concise information on these groups around their program types, curricula, content, structure, formats and partnerships.

Now turn to your own profile and specialization. With a clear picture of the market and a genuine understanding of customer demands you can start to define your profile. What is the particular focus of your product? How have you positioned it and how does it relate to other products? How do your plans appear in the eyes of others? What sort of identity does your product have? What are the characteristics of the program? The program title is a starting point but, beyond that, what is it that characterizes your particular approach?

Alongside your product profile and identity you should consider the USPs or Unique Selling Points. What is it that will make a potential candidate choose your program? There are plenty of good, existing products on the market. What is it that will make a candidate ultimately choose your program out of all those on the market?

If you have not spent enough time thinking about your USPs now is the time for careful reflection to identify your competitive advantage. New academic programs are often initiated and developed on the basis of resource, rather than market-thinking; in other words, the starting points are the knowledge and teaching resources that are available. These are important, but will do little to help you define the basis of your competitive advantage.

Planning

During the process of planning activities for the program you need to follow a sequence that matches your program objectives (in terms of participant outcomes). You can then develop learning and development objectives for the entire program, and eventually, functional or academic objectives and objectives for each activity within the program.

There are basically three elements to consider during your planning. The first is those components that will make up the finished product. These may be courses of various kinds; guest lectures, project work, thesis writing, study visits, and so on. The second is the budget and the way in which it can enable as well as constrain your planned program. The third is a description of the process. What are the sequences and the parallel activities in the program? How do the various pieces fit together and how are different activities related? At what stages are different activities designed to fit into the program? You need a list of components with component classifications and specifications, you need a budget and a schedule for the complete program and you need a flow chart to show the relationships between the various elements.

COMPONENTS

There are two elements to component planning: types of component and a list of all components. Each element is best presented with examples. For example:

- Preparations (Prep): A self-study activity (or an optional summer course).
- Foundations (FND): An intensive introduction to the fundamentals of business administration and economics. This may include organization theory, macroeconomics and accounting.
- Longitudinal cases (LC): Developed case studies running over a period of months and involving company documents and employees as the basis for analysis and information gathering.
- Discipline-based courses (DBC): A series of courses that looks at management from the point of view of traditional, function-based disciplines such as economics, managerial economics, marketing, operations, corporate finance, accounting and leadership.
- Managerial-context courses (MCC): These courses complement traditional discipline-based courses. They are cross-disciplinary and designed to support exploration by the candidates; examples of the context behind this kind of course may be humanities, institutions, citizenship and media.
- Issue-based courses (IBC): These are cross-disciplinary courses that explore managerial issues. Typical topics draw upon several kinds of expertise, for example, globalization, branding, innovation, knowledge management, crisis management, entrepreneurship and new ventures.
- Company-based projects (CBP): These are group projects in which students carry out a task for a host company. CBPs offer students both practical experience and a degree of learner autonomy.
- Master synthesis project (MSP): This is the final, individual project. In consultation with an academic supervisor, each student selects both a topic and a format for their work. The output can range from an academic thesis, tutored literature reviews to a company-based project.

- Leadership discovery process (LDP): This is a fully integrated approach to leadership development. It involves coaches and mentors as facilitators to help students improve their professional leadership skills.
- Coaching: Meetings with an academic and practitioner coach to discuss personal and career development.

THE BUDGET

You should now be in a position to create a budget for the full set of activities in the program (see Table 14.1). In this context hours are defined as contact hours (in other words hours where participants are meeting with a faculty member) but you may prefer to use total working hours as a basis for the budget.

FLOW OR PROCESS CHART

Eventually we can allocate the components to different parts of the program. To make it easier to view the program at a glance you may wish to represent everything on a flow chart. See the example in Table 14.2.

Table 14.1   A full set of activities with total working hours

ACTIVITY		STRUCTURE		HRS
CODE	**TYPE**	**WEEK**	**VOLUME**	
Prep	Preparations	Before	Individual	N/A
FND	Foundations	1–2	60 hrs	60
CI	Case introduction	3	30 hrs	30
LC1	Longitudinal case study 1	3–29	200 hrs	200
LC2	Longitudinal case study 2	4–29	200 hrs	200
LC3	Longitudinal case study 3	21–32	80 hrs	80
DBC1 – 10	Discipline-based courses	4–31	10 x 20 hrs	200
IBC1 – 9	Issue-based courses	24–38	9 x 15 hrs	135
MCC1 – 6	Managerial-context courses	05–35	6 x 15 hrs	90
CBP	Company-based projects	29–39	45 hrs	45
MSP	Master synthesis project	29–40	70 hrs	70
LDP	Leadership discovery process	3–40	40 hrs	40
C	Coaching	3–40	40 hrs	40
Elec	Electives	38–40	2 x 15 hrs	30
	TOTAL			

Table 14.2   Activity flow chart

DBC4	OPERATIONS MANAGEMENT AND STRATEGY		
WEEK	VOLUME/ FORMATS	LEARNING OBJECTIVE	CONTENT
8–11	VOLUME: Lectures 20 h, Study visit 1 day, Case discussions 20 h in LC 1 and 10h in LC 2. FORMATS: Integrated lecturing and case discussions 3 days/week at 4 hours/day + 1 full day study visit.	Understanding the different strategic roles of operations and the relations to the business. Knowing different alternative operations system designs and their characteristics. Knowledge of different planning and control philosophies, their applicability and techniques.	• The strategic role of operations • Operations strategy • Design of products • Operations network • Layout and flow • Process technology • Work organization • Capacity planning • Inventory planning and control • Supply chain planning • Lean production • TQM

Development

Finally you can start the development of each detailed component in collaboration with the teaching staff. This will involve intense communication between the program manager and the individual teachers or course designers. At this stage it may not always be obvious for teachers of a single component of the course what the role of their component may be within the whole program. However we do not want to found the development of courses solely on the basis of what is most convenient to the teachers responsible for each specific course.

The following sample template (Table 14.3) may give you some ideas on the specification of each module prior to further development.

You now need to develop a simple but effective method for providing an overview of the whole program and enabling individual teachers to see their role in the process as well as an aid to program management. It is well worth producing a wall version of the flow chart to illustrate all of the module templates in their respective positions. This will give an excellent overview of the program, its components, its process and any relationships (both vertical and horizontal) between program components. There is no software planning program that has proven as effective as a physical wall chart. It is all there at a glance.

There is one more tool worth mentioning at this stage: the issue plan. Ask each person responsible for delivering a part of the course to provide a couple of key words describing the key *issues* covered in each module and include these in the flow chart, either as a table or as a spreadsheet. Give this issue plan to each teacher to help them understand the whole program and the relationship between the respective module and the whole program. The issue plan may also be posted on the wall in the program office. This tool is particularly valuable during program delivery. It will help mitigate the risk of teachers who come and deliver their own session(s) without adequately relating them to the rest of the program. This risk increases over time when the original ideas behind the program may be forgotten or when new teachers join the program.

Table 14.3   Sample module specification

Curriculum flow – Activity location chart

Each cell represents 5 hours per week

Contact hours	WEEK	01	02	03	04	05	06	07	08	09	10	11	12	13	14	15	16	17	18	19
5 hrs/ week						DBC1			DBC3				DBC5				DBC7			
5 hrs/ week						LONGITUDINAL CASE 1														
5 hrs/ week					C															
5 hrs/ week		FND			I	DBC2			DBC4				MCC3			C		DBC6		
5 hrs/ week						LONGITUDINAL CASE 2														
5 hrs/ week					LDP	MCC1			C	MCC2										
Week #		01	02	03	04	05	06	07	08	09	10	11	12	13	14	15	16	17	18	19

Contact hours	WEEK	20	21	22	23	24	25	26	27	28	29	30	31	32	33	34	35	36	37	38	39	40
5 hrs/ week		DBC8				DBC9			DBC10						CBP							LD P
5 hrs/ week		LONGITUDINAL CASE 2						MC 1			LD P	IBC3			IBC6			LD P		Elec		
5 hrs/ week											C	IBC4			C	IBC7				Elec		
5 hrs/ week		C	MCC4		C	MCC5		C	CBP + MSP		MC		MCC6				IBC 8			M		
5 hrs/ week		MASTER CASE 1			IBC1		IBC2		MC3		3		IBC5				IBC 9			S		
5 hrs/ week		LDP		LONGITUDINAL CASE 3											MSP					P		
Week #		20	21	22	23	24	25	26	27	28	29	30	31	32	33	34	35	36	37	38	39	40

Wrap up

CHARACTERISTICS OF THE MODEL

A model for program planning and development such as this one is of course conceptual. It should not be seen as a detailed set of instructions. Each case is special and only some of the discussion and tools may be appropriate. The planning process is both more iterative and concurrent than can be expressed here.

A generic model also has only limited relevance. This model and the given examples provided come from the world of MBAs. Undergraduate programs and short executive programs are two extremes at either ends of the scale. However our advice is designed to be applicable generally and the tools can easily be adapted to your own situations.

The aim of this chapter has been to provide ideas and give you a checklist of issues to be considered. The models and tools presented may give you ideas for your own tools which may be better suited to your own situation. However, the model, as provided, has proven effective in a number of cases of program development in a variety of different business school settings.

KEY ISSUES AND CONCERNS

A number of key issues have featured in this chapter:

- Program planning is different from course planning. The context, sequences, concurrency and resource issues are all of major importance.
- You need to analyze the program within the context of a program portfolio. How does the program fit with a participant's lifelong learning and career?
- Take time for competitor analysis. What characterizes your program and what will make participants choose you?

- Develop a comprehensive program concept. It is important that all the stakeholders, including any who may join later in the process, understand the whole program concept.
- Clarify your program objectives and their value to the participant.
- Remember, your finished product is not the program but the successful graduate.
- The program process is key in program development. Clarify the process you will adopt before you plan the detailed components.
- Develop components within the context of the total program context. Make sure that all components are developed in the context of those that come earlier, concurrently and later to them in the program.
- Simple tools are powerful when planning and developing. Use conceptualization, process charts, budget/resource plans, module templates and issue plans.

15 *Important Considerations When Starting Programs*

Kristina Nilsson

Participants seem to do just as they like. People wander in and out whenever they want. They question the value of most of it; the way the program is run as well as the design. They complain about the content of the course and the workload. They want the course to be delivered to suit them personally. And worse still, the program management seems to be busy satisfying ever changing demands and needs of the group. I get no support at all.

Perhaps you have come across a situation like the one described above where the program is running out of control? The group of students has become stronger than the program management team. A group such as this has probably developed their own set of norms for what is acceptable or not. It is a difficult situation to tackle. If you are in the middle of it you may well be trying to figure out what has happened whilst at the same time struggling to retain control or just limit the damage: trying desperately to keep the group happy until the end of the program. And at the end of the course or program you are probably happier than they are to move on and leave this experience behind you.

If you do encounter a situation such as this, I suspect the causes will be apparent early on in the program. For example, have you managed to establish a mutual contract between you and the participants to cover the rules of the game? Were you clear about the objectives and how you planned to reach them? And, of course, have you been able to negotiate the expectations between you and the participants? These are all issues that I believe need to be managed at the start of a program. This holds especially true for more extensive programs such as MBAs and EMBAs.

This chapter is not about avoiding or changing a problem situation *when it occurs,* rather how you can best prevent the situation occurring. Of course, you can't foresee or pre-plan for every single event that may occur in a program or between people. But you can create a constructive and positive atmosphere in a group so that negative events will not throw everyone off track. This chapter focuses mainly on starting programs because the efforts you make and activities you do or don't do in the early stages of a program will pay handsome dividends later on. Good preparations will directly affect whether or not you will meet the objectives you set beforehand and whether you and the participants enjoy the learning process. Cordeo et al. (2005) equate the importance of getting it right from the start with an Olympic athlete getting out of the blocks. A slow start will be hard to make up later on. Program management and delivery is a lot about expectations management and, if you plan carefully, you can make the learners' expectations work for you.

The value of devoting extra energy into the start of your program

If you are an experienced program or course director you may well have used and tested a number of different ways to start a course or program. There are books with games and tips on how to get a successful start (for example, Epstein 2000). These pre-modular activities and pre-planned exercises have broader purpose than just entertainment. The aim of a well, planned program start is to meet the learning objectives and make the learning experience as meaningful and enjoyable as possible for the learner.

MAKE THE TACIT EXPLICIT

At the very least when you start the program you should communicate your view of the content as well as the learning process. From a program manager's point of view you want to encourage committed individuals who take responsibility for their own learning. If you know enough about your participants' expectations for what they want to achieve and learn, you should be in a better position not only to set and achieve the objectives but also to accomplish a positive learning climate. Can this easily be achieved simply by communicating a clear overview of the content of the program and the learning objectives? This will certainly help you in the process of meeting the objectives, but only partly, due to the characteristics of the learning process as being tacit; not outspoken, very individual, and far from clear to the learner and as such difficult to communicate. An important consideration is also that the learning process is based on trust for you as knowledge producer and learning facilitator; education involves messing with people's minds. Consequently, when you want to facilitate learning you need to encourage the participants to start questioning their existing frame of reference and to question what they already know and have previously learnt. To achieve openness and willingness to explore new areas you need to gain their trust as their learning facilitator and guide. You can earn this trust by being as clear and transparent as possible about your view of the objectives, program design, content and learning processes – how this is evident in the curriculum and learning processes.

What can we gain by making this information overt?

- What you plan for will show in the end: you arrive at the intended results. You will find it easier to evaluate the plan against the outcome if it is out in the open for all involved – it is transparent.
- This transparency forces you to become clearer about where you are standing and why you choose to approach and design the program in a certain way. It will help you articulate your frame of reference.
- I also believe that participants who are aware of what you are trying to accomplish, will better understand and appreciate the various efforts of both the program managers as well as the faculty. You enable them to put themselves in your shoes and understand how you have tried to put yourselves in theirs while designing the program. Your various considerations and assumptions become explicit.
- All involved: faculty, learners and the program management team will find it easier to discuss issues in the program with you.
- If you share your sense of the learning process you will enable the learners to start reflecting on their own view and way of learning and with the help of some facilitation take more responsibility for it. Equally importantly, it may help them accept that there are numerous ways to learn, and all are equally valid and accepted (you can read more about learning styles in Chapter 22 by Bild and Mårtensson).
- You can use this in sense-making when talking about the big picture, and in feedback sessions – you have a shared picture or road map to which you can each relate (you find more about the use of the 'big picture' in Chapter 8 by Damodaran).

• The openness will increase your authority as program manager or if you prefer it will increase the learners' trust in you as their guide and learning facilitator.

I would like to compare the statement and expression about the underlying thoughts and values of the program to the scientific/academic term 'Ontology' – view of the world. In this example, 'ontology' and 'world view' would, for example, be expressed in your or your institution's beliefs, values and views on the education process and program. The other term in common use is 'epistemology'– how knowledge is created (Burrell and Morgan 1979). This concept is also relevant and it may be split into *what* and *how*. In our context *what* relates to the content and learning objectives in terms of the technical knowledge of the facts and figures. This knowledge is measurable and may be assessed. The second part, *how*, refers to the learning process – how you plan to help the learner to acquire knowledge to learn or how knowledge is created within this program or education process. Ramsden (1992) underlines the importance of taking both *what* and *how* into account when you plan and consider people's learning processes. In Table 15.1, I describe both content and learning process in relation to ontology and epistemology, and I refer to both what and how.

Table 15.1   Ontology and epistemology and program planning

	Ontology – world view	**Epistemology – how knowledge is created**
Content	Values, beliefs behind program or on program type	What and That – program and/or learning objectives
Learning Process	Beliefs, position or views on learning and learning processes	How – how the process of learning and acquiring new knowledge is organized by the program team

I refer to ontology when I use the term 'view of the world'. When it comes to epistemology I will talk about content ('what'), for example, a program curriculum or a subject course. When it comes to 'how' I am talking about how the learning process is designed. However, it also is useful to talk about 'view of the world' on learning and learning processes and that this refers to ontology rather than epistemology.

My intention with this chapter is to share and elaborate on some ideas and lessons learned when it comes to starting the program, but some of these lessons relate to activities that should have been managed *before the program start*. Let me start with the big picture – a picture of the whole program planning process.

The big picture – program planning and delivery – input – results – effects

Figure 15.1 shows an overview of a program, from the decision to launch to the long-term effects on those that have been through it and the institution that delivered it. I use a MBA/EMBA program by a way of example but the model can be used for any kind of program planning. The illustration is adapted from the X-model (Lundeberg 1993). The thinking behind the X-model is that: in order to get the intended result and subsequently the intended effects that are successful and effective both from a person and task perspective, you need a

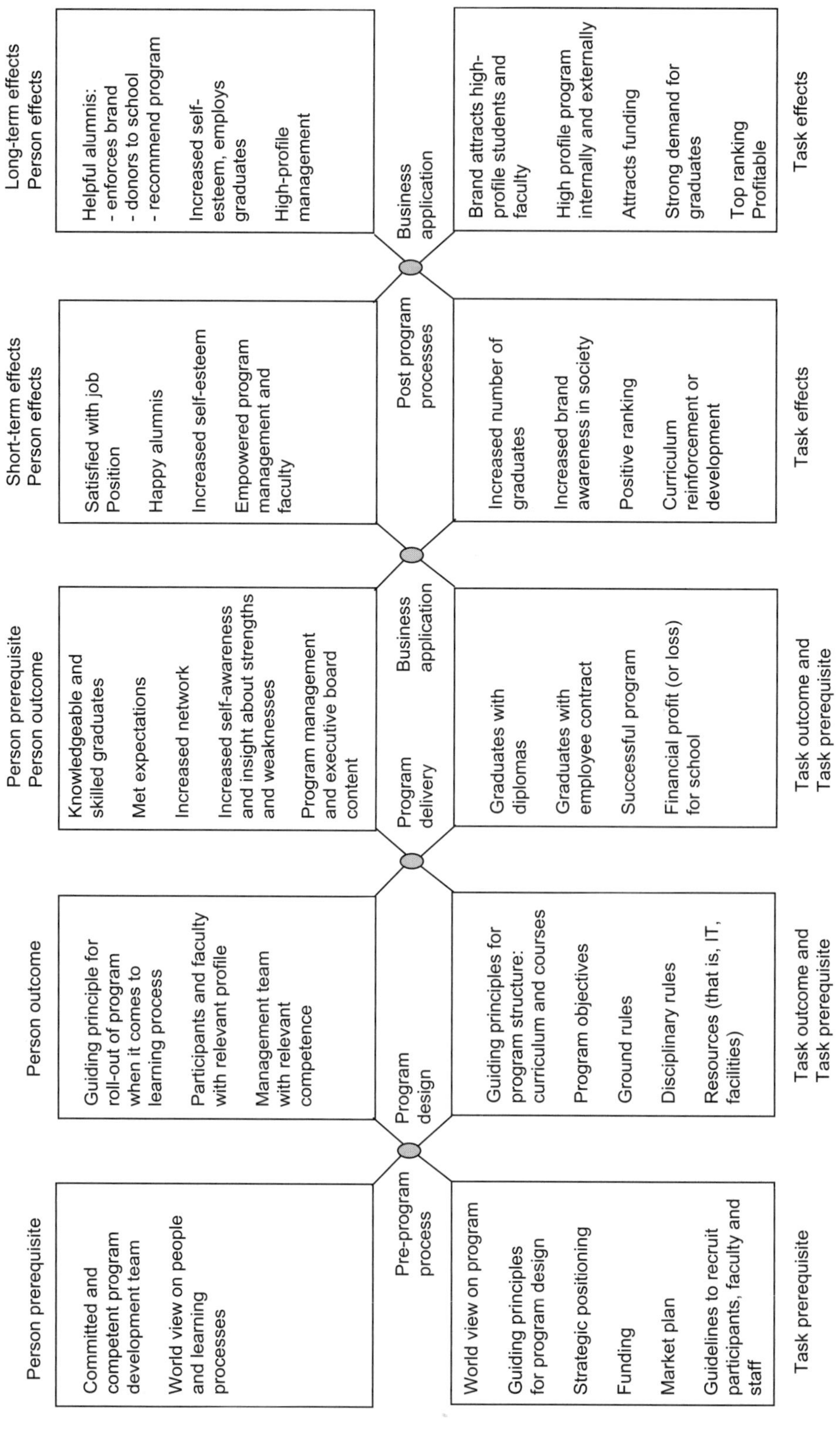

Person prerequisite

Committed and competent program development team

World view on people and learning processes

Person outcome

Guiding principle for roll-out of program when it comes to learning process

Participants and faculty with relevant profile

Management team with relevant competence

Person prerequisite / Person outcome

Knowledgeable and skilled graduates

Met expectations

Increased network

Increased self-awareness and insight about strengths and weaknesses

Program management and executive board content

Short-term effects / Person effects

Satisfied with job Position

Happy alumni

Increased self-esteem

Empowered program management and faculty

Long-term effects / Person effects

Helpful alumnis:
- enforces brand
- donors to school
- recommend program

Increased self-esteem, employs graduates

High-profile management

Pre-program process

Program design

Program delivery — Business application

Post program processes

Business application

Task prerequisite

World view on program

Guiding principles for program design

Strategic positioning

Funding

Market plan

Guidelines to recruit participants, faculty and staff

Task outcome and Task prerequisite

Guiding principles for program structure: curriculum and courses

Program objectives

Ground rules

Disciplinary rules

Resources (that is, IT, facilities)

Task outcome and Task prerequisite

Graduates with diplomas

Graduates with employee contract

Successful program

Financial profit (or loss) for school

Task effects

Increased number of graduates

Increased brand awareness in society

Positive ranking

Curriculum reinforcement or development

Task effects

Brand attracts high-profile students and faculty

High profile program internally and externally

Attracts funding

Strong demand for graduates

Top ranking
Profitable

Figure 15.1   Program overview

process that combines both task and person input; process prerequisites. The centre of the illustration shows the processes that transform all the inputs/prerequisites into outcomes. Thus for example 'program design' and 'program delivery' refer to the processes of designing and later running the program in class. The two processes called 'business applications' describe what happens when graduates are applying their new insights in a work situation.

When you read the model from *left to right* the reasoning is as follows: a number of person and task prerequisites need to be in place in order to design a program. You need to choose the type of program you want, and how to fund and position it in the market. You also need to have a clear view of the customers, who are they, what their needs are and where you will find them. To this you add your view of the learning processes and how you think the students will learn in this particular program. The design process results in a number of task outcomes: guiding principles for the program structure; curriculum and courses, program objectives, resource allocation, and so on. Person outcomes include, for example, guiding principles for the learning process; how you plan the overall learning process; and how you will meet the learning objectives. Added to this is, your requirements on the students that will be accepted, and faculty that are suitable to deliver the courses, and so on. These outcomes of the design and planning process work as input into the run through of the program. On completion of the program, the outcome is more knowledgeable, better qualified graduates, well placed in a company. The figure then highlights the impact, both short and long term, of the graduates as they use their new knowledge, skills and experience in their organization. These may include the effects of increased self-awareness and self-esteem. Thanks to the increasing number of graduates, you will also increase the awareness of your brand in our business community. The first effects will start to show from the day the students are first employed. The longer effects may become apparent at least 2–3 years in post. I have also included in the illustration the individual's relationship to the school and brand after the graduation. You can also read the model from *right to left* – to see how the long-term effects on the right hand side are built up stepwise through a process of deliveries that in turn build on task as well as person prerequisites.

Of course, this is a simplification. The 'delivery process' is a summary of a whole range of sub-processes that in turn need to work properly in order to ensure a successful program. You may, if you wish, represent each single course or each class as a process with its own prerequisites/input and output.

In Cordero et al. (2005), the main focus is on the process once the decision to run the program has been taken. Nevertheless this remains a process model with inputs that transform into outputs that can be expressed in terms of customer value added. The authors call this 'program scripting', and it describes the design process behind the whole learning experience. The authors stress the importance of designing it from the learner's perspective:

> *If you cannot articulate why you are doing an activity from the learner's perspective then it shouldn't be in the design.*
>
> p. 84.

If you want to learn more about program design and planning I recommend the preceding chapter by Christer Karlsson who discusses the different steps you need to go through in detail when you want to launch an MBA program.

My point with showing this picture is to highlight where in the process you find different input and output that should be planned for and managed. As an overview of the program process it highlights that a lot of the inputs/prerequisites, deliveries and effects turn up on the 'person' side of the model. These inputs and outcomes relate to the learners or the learning process which, as I have already pointed out, may be overlooked because these processes risk being seen as implicit in the curriculum. I think it is of utmost importance to bring it into the open in order to help you to get a successful program. This model offers a way to see that from the outset you have anticipated everything and everyone needed in your plans. It is taken into account already from the start.

Starting the program

Starting the program can be seen as a pre-process to the run through of the program in class and, as such, creating the prerequisites for the program delivery. I have pictured this in Figure 15.2.

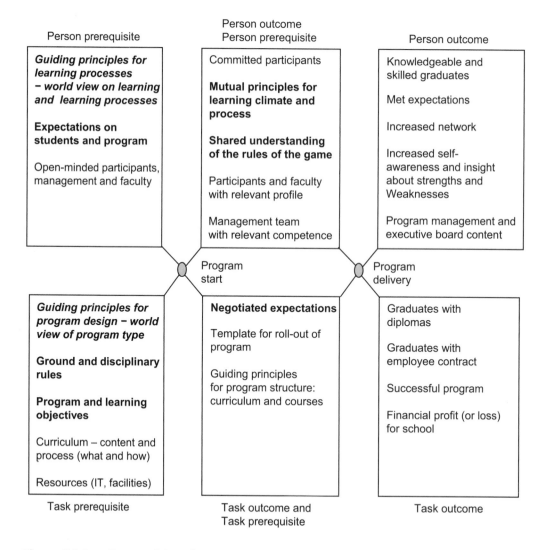

Figure 15.2   Prerequisites for program delivery

I have moved some of the prerequisites from the program planning and design phase in Figure 15.1 into the prerequisites for the program start in Figure 15.2. The repeated text is in italic in Figure 15.2. The aim is to highlight the importance of having transparent frames of references in terms of your view of the world, and learning process and the basis on which you have planned the content as well as the learning process.

Figure 15.2 should be interpreted as follows (*reading from left to right*). The intended outcome or results are as shown in Figure 15.1; in other words, you have met the program objectives, met and hopefully exceeded the students' expectations and the students have managed to get a new job position, and so on. In order to achieve the planned outcome you need to address relevant issues from the start to establish a shared understanding between the program manager and the students as to what is going to happen in the program. This requires that you a) articulate your sense and view of both the type of the program and the learning processes – in other words, the basis for the program design (the guiding principles); b) communicate the program objectives clearly; c) share and negotiate expectations; d) agree a mutual contract with the group to cover the rules of the game. These rules build on two components: i) the basic ground rules and; ii) contingencies that the group add to these. Finally, e) you need to establish a mutual agreement to cover the principles behind the learning climate within the group. I think all these areas are particularly important and I represented them in bold in Figure 15.2. I will explore and discuss these issues in the following paragraphs.

Share your underlying view of the world – the guiding principles for the program

These guiding principles build on your world view and are the underlying values, beliefs and ideas that guide the design of the program. They are made up of elements that are important for you and the school. For example, the values that subsequently influence your decisions around the intake of students or the mix of program participants in respect to their background, age and the size of the group or the way in which you would like to work with the faculty.

Figure 15.3 illustrates the book Editors' view of the faculty development program, International Teachers Program (ITP). We constructed this picture before we started to design our version of the program in detail. It illustrates our core values at the time, and its content guided us in the design and launch of the curriculum, the recruitment of participants and faculty, and finally how we decided to schedule the roll-out of the program.

On the basis of this successful process, I created a similar list of statements once I had accepted the position as program director for the MBA program at Stockholm School of Economics (SSE MBA). I was not part of the initial design process and I felt that I needed a road map when working with the MBA curriculum to help guide my course selection and the design of the learning process. It was also important for me in getting my head around the existing program, which I inherited, as well as the one I was designing and was needed to communicate with others. Table 15.2 includes my take on the thoughts and values that underlie the program.

Although the content of the table has not been discussed and evaluated by the whole MBA team (faculty and administration), I think it captures some important guiding principles. The content of the table is firmly grounded in both the program content and process as I interpreted it during the years I worked as program director.

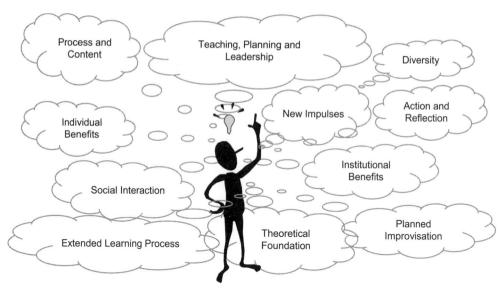

Figure 15.3   Core values of the international teachers program at the Stockholm School of Economics

Table 15.2   Thoughts and values underlying the program

SSE tradition	Theory in practice
Reality rules	Swedish management style
Small-scale and high quality	Flat organization
Knowledge-oriented agenda	Highly committed individuals
Business mentors	Flexibility in content and process
High-profile students – diversity	Moving target
Individual and group leadership	Incremental improvements
Learning in small groups	Double loop – reflective learning
Multinational arena	Process and content
General management agenda	Knowledge and skill
Integration	Self-awareness

There is another model that may be used to capture the essence of the program; the Cogwheel Model (Figure 15.4), which shows the major building blocks of the SSE MBA. The cogwheel depicts the knowledge creation – the epistemology of the SSE MBA. The main focus in this model is on the content (that/what) (see Table 15.1). However, the very process of explaining the model offers insights into the learning process, in terms of how the knowledge will be acquired or produced within the program.

The program represented in the model is a General Management program. It contains a number of courses within business administration. One significant and distinguishing building block is MBA Live™. The program management team firmly believe that the combination of actual cases, from existing companies with real problems and challenges (those companies that themselves open up for students and faculty) when combined with theory, maximizes

Figure 15.4   The cogwheel model

the learning. This approach helps the learner make sense of theory and acquire and apply knowledge on business cases. This set-up also develops the students' ability to manage relationships with external parties and manage projects (Lerpold et al. 2005). To this comes a track named Leadership Agenda (containing courses in leadership, group dynamics and self-awareness, management communication, professional development). Finally, in the curriculum there is also a component that accounts for a deliberate expansion of the students' network within, as well as outside, the school. These statements about the program (in this case the SSE MBA), carry considerable expectations and assumptions which makes it doubly important for the students to understand why this particular MBA program looks the way that it does and why the various components have been organized the way they have. I have used the content of these two frameworks on a number of occasions to help explain the program in terms of activities that have occurred and those that will come, why criticized components, or highly appreciated for that matter, are the way they are and occur at a certain point, and why we have done things in a certain order in the program.

However, I also argue that everyone has their own sense of learning and how people learn, and this view will affect the way you design the learning process. It becomes the guiding principles for the learning processes. This view is visual in the core values but is more implicit in the cogwheel model in the SSE MBA example.

Communicate your guiding principles or world view on learning

In my experience the overall learning objectives may vary between programs. For example, the objectives for an open program will be different from that of an in-company program. By definition, the objectives for an in-company program will be tailored to company-specific needs. Depending on the clients or target group, you may also vary the pedagogy from case to case. By contrast, your sense of the learning process – how people learn – may not vary. Your views may develop and change over time but relatively little between programs or courses. And the participants and students are entitled to understand your views and this transparency will help them understand and follow the principles behind your design of the program. If learners understand your mindset it helps them reflect on their own and other people's learning processes. In Table 15.3 I have incorporated my own paradigms for ('world view' on) learning and learning processes. I may make minor adjustments between programs but these have not changed much over the years. I have included keywords on the left hand side and I have added some explanation after each statement to make it easier for the reader to understand exactly what I mean.

How I communicate my views depends on the context and the group I am talking to. For example, I may stress that 'learning takes time' when I am working with a group of a lot of young managers who may be very stressed and looking for short cuts to save time and effort.

Table 15.3   My world view of learning and learning processes

My view of learning:
• It is a process – learning takes time, it is OK to be confused and stay in this mode for a while.
• You are the owner of the process – I can help you, facilitate, but you are the one who learns.
• A safe environment increases your learning – openness and trust spiral.
• We all learn differently – respect and understand differences.
• Individuals matter, not positions; focus on learning instead of proving yourself.
• Differences in background and learning styles add variety and perspective.
• Small group – center of learning – mirror yourself and expose yourself to other perspectives – the learning is designed to happen during group work.
• Variation is the mother of learning – varied pedagogy to increase your learning and meet more learning styles.

Communicate the program and/or learning objectives

You need to communicate the program or learning objectives not only because they should tell the students what they will learn and achieve but also because they are an important part of the process of negotiating expectations. The objectives help the students to shape their expectations; they provide a clearer picture of what the students will receive in exchange for their time and money.

The left hand column of Table 15.4 includes a set of learning objectives for an open general management program whilst the column on the right hand side provides the learning objectives for an in-company program. The objectives should help you articulate your sense and view of the program, and as such they communicate the curriculum and the basis on which you have planned for the learners to acquire their knowledge.

In-company program objectives are, by their nature, more specific than those for an open general management program. On the other hand, broader, more general objectives are aggregated summaries of a wide variety of minor learning objectives derived from each single course in the program.

Table 15.4   Learning objectives for open and in-company programs

Open program – general learning goals	In-company program
• Knowledge – business administration subject, tools for management, industry and company knowledge, process insights • Skills – interpersonal skills, managing diversity, teamwork, teambuilding, presentation skills, project management • Personal growth/development – self-awareness, responsiveness, adaptability, self-esteem, coachable, demanding excellence • Networking practice and experience – international, national, business, academia, personal, mentor interaction	• Boost understanding of business and value drivers • Identify business critical issues and questions • Support the change to a stronger customer and business perspective • Gain an outside-in perspective • Enhance networking and cross-border cooperation

In the preceding chapter, Christer Karlsson uses an analogy of production to describe the process of creating the program objectives and this analogy underlines the learner-centered nature of the program design.

Establish a mutual contract to cover the rules of the game

As part of the educational institution you need to communicate the rules of the game. These rules frame the acceptable values and norms for each individual. These rules define the basis for grading scales, examinations, working hours, attendance, and so on. These are often the most tedious details to communicate. However, if the behavior starts to deviate in a group, for example students begin to arrive and leave as they please, it may be that the contract with your learners was not sufficiently explicit or agreement was not overt.

BE CLEAR ABOUT THE NON-NEGOTIABLE GROUND RULES

In order for a group to work together, whatever the course, you need a set of ground rules. The school may well have some general rules or guidelines describing actions and behavior that are or are not permitted, some kind of disciplinary code explaining the consequences of cheating, poor attendance, or the basis for dismissal, or how to complain about grades or faculty. The school may also issue guidelines for students on how to manage the studies in general. Typically, these describe the credits system, when and how to apply for courses, grading scales and so on. These basic rules and documents provide the oil to ensure that the system works smoothly. If in Schutz's (1960) terminology the individual has decided to jump on the boat, the decision to join should involve a commitment to follow the ground rules.

Table 15.5 shows some of the principles that I have shared with students when starting programs. These principles are stressed alongside the more general academic policies (credit system, courses, dismissal, and so on) as well as the disciplinary regulations that apply to all programs within the school.

Table 15.5   Principles when starting programs

Our responsibility	To get access to the court and play the game we expect you to:
We supply the resources and infrastructure to facilitate your learning We set the court – you play the game	Attend and participate in all classes and group work Only use allowed help – material, books, and so on. Meet deadlines Respect faculty, fellow students and guests Respect confidentiality Keep updated Keep the premises clean and nice Be online, surf, during class only when teaching faculty says so Keep mobile phones turned off in class
And Joint responsibility to create: Rules of the game The end result A strong brand name	

The aim is as before to ensure transparency, to be overt about norms of behavior and to ensure that everyone has been informed about their responsibilities. If you want to reinforce this process of sharing and communicating rules you may ask the students to sign a written waiver indicating that they have read and agree to be bound by these rules.

This far you have communicated your guiding principles, program objectives and rules of the game. Students should be more familiar with the program and the learning processes so if you haven't done so already it is time to let the students share expectations with you.

Negotiate expectations

From the participants' point of view this is about endorsing their decision to sign up for the program. It is very human to try to validate your previous decisions about a purchase; corroborate that you have made the right choice. This corroboration process may be biased to support your decision; you intentionally or subconsciously look for arguments that support your decision, not the reverse. That is, the more you know about the expectations, the better equipped you are to discuss and manage them at the start of the program. You can help the participants and students to shape their expectations and at the same time make them work for you. The expectations are partly the individuals' own expressions, but they are also a reflection of the brand promise – what your program or school's brand stands for. An MBA program includes more than your school's version of the program: it is a rather old product developed for the American market. You need to decide at an early stage whether to explore the participants' expectations at the outset of the course or program or whether to explore and then meet them once the program is running. I suggest that you start by communicating your own view of the program and then allow the participants to discuss their expectations. This process may be part of an early group forming activity.

I have incorporated a number of more general statements about an MBA in Table 15.6; these are partly derived from a number of accepted attributes of MBA programs and partly from our guiding principles.

The aim of the information in the table is to meet the new MBA students' expectations when they sign up for this type of education, and by making these overt too, make it clear what they have bought into.

At this stage you have shared a considerable amount of information with the students, now is the time for the final important ingredient, essential for a successful start: the learning climate. The aim should be to hand over the responsibility for the learning climate to the participants. Some rules, the ground rules, are not really up for discussion, but other norms of behavior, ways of working and learning, and so on will be far more binding if the participants are involved in drafting them.

Table 15.6   The MBA journey

The journey:	The journey may:
Is challenging – if you want, you can explore new territory Requires time management – prioritizing Requires and or becomes bearable when trusting others – division of labor Means multitasking – planning – requires pro activity rather than reactivity Is being back in school – we set the court; you play the game Requires responsibility – look after yourself as well as your fellow students	Make you frustrated Unfit Tired Put your previous social life on hold Make you wonder why you do this Makes your spouse/significant other and kids wonder where you are

An open and helpful learning climate

Establishing a productive learning climate has much to do with helping people relax and enjoy themselves. In a relaxed learning climate people feel that they belong, they feel appreciated and valued and are encouraged to contribute.

An open and supportive learning climate is the outcome of a process that combines the various ground rules, expectations, learning and program objectives. Learning climates are fluid rather than static. This means that you need to establish a positive environment in which students can learn but that you need to reinforce this throughout the program. A positive learning climate will help program managers, faculty and students to discuss positively how to respond to any difficulties.

I suggest you incorporate a discussion on the learning climate as part of the 'getting to know each other' phase. If you are establishing groups that the students or others will work within during the program you can integrate this activity with the other group forming activities. This could be in the form of a negotiation between the groups; the outcome should be a list of important guiding principles for supporting a positive learning climate in the class. One example of the result of such a negotiation is shown in Table 15.7.

Table 15.7   Learning climate guiding principles

Learning climate – guiding principles
•   Share knowledge and information •   Ground rules in discussion (let everyone in, wait for your turn) •   Be on time •   Show empathy •   Respect, be patient to and help each other •   Come prepared •   Be open for fun •   No bragging •   Openness

It is a good idea to display this list in a prominent place in the classroom or make it easily accessible on your intranet. The principles can be referred to in discussions and faculty can relate to them when presenting their course and should let them guide the design of the learning outcomes and processes.

Wrap up

My intention with this chapter has been to share some lessons learned in program planning in order to inform your program planning. My initial objective was to help you avoid the situation that was described in the introduction to the chapter. As you will have noted by now, I firmly believe that there is a close relationship between your actions and input at the beginning of a program and the results in terms of establishing a positive learning and working environment for the students, the program team and the faculty. This is also closely linked to the final outcome of the program; whether it is successful or not, and how the learning process is brought to a close. Most important in all this preparation is that you create a map that you can use as a benchmark for any issues that arise during the program. This will help you with your sense-making as program director and enable you to respond to any feedback positively.

I have argued that you need to plan for some activities at the beginning of a program, such as negotiating expectations and communicating ground rules, to help you ensure a successful outcome. I have also discussed the need to be transparent about issues that are normally dealt with during the design of the program. Let me close with a salutary lesson for the unprepared. One group developed a reputation for making their own rules. They never concluded the learning climate negotiation because one individual in particular did not want to accept the consensus. Unfortunately this person was selected group representative and as such they started to act on their own in the negotiation. It may not have been this particular student's fault that the group started to go off the rails, but the program manager had nothing to support his position when the problems started to arise; no rules or guidelines that the group had agreed upon.

Recommendations

•   Think about the outcome and the effects; what you want to achieve both in terms of task and individual. Education is about personal development and this is in turn about changing people's minds and sometimes also behavior; make sure that this focus is reflected in your preparations.

- Take time to reflect on and describe your sense of the program in writing, include your view of the learning process, the principles behind the program design and the delivery.
    - Transparency is the key to facilitating, understanding and meeting expectations and goals.
- Running programs is fundamentally a case of expectations management – take your time to investigate, explore, elaborate, negotiate and finally manage the expectations.
    - Help your students or participants to articulate their expectation by sharing yours clearly with them. Managing expectations involves encouraging the students to articulate their views (and ensure you have understood them).
    - It also involves adapting or changing expectations to ensure they are appropriate to the course outcomes.
- Be clear about the ground rules.
    - Make it your task to facilitate a shared contract about the rules of the game.
    - Give the students the chance to express their own opinions and sense of the learning climate.
    - Help them define and agree on the guiding principles for an effective and positive climate within which to learn.
    - Use these guiding principles in any dialogue with faculty and students.

References

Burrell, G., and Morgan, M., (1979). *Sociological Paradigms and Organizational Analysis*. London: Heinemann Educational Books Ltd.

Bild, M., and Mårtensson, P., (2008). *Learning Styles as Vehicles for Pedagogical Development*. Chapter 22 (pp. 271–278) in this volume.

Cordeo, C., Haour, G., Kahwajy, J.L., Kemanian, V., Keys, T., Meehan, S., Robertson, D., Sjöblom, L., Strebel, P., and Vollmann, T., (2005). Program Scripting, In Strebel, .P., and Keys, T., Eds. *Mastering Executive Education: How to combine content with context and Emotion – The IMD Guide*. Great Britain: FT Prentice Hall (Financial Times, Pearson Education).

Damodaran A., (2008). *Teaching Large Classes*, Chapter 8 (pp. 89–100) in this volume.

Epstein, R., (2000). *The Big Book of Creativity Games: Quick, Fun Activities for Jumpstarting Innovation*. New York, NY: McGraw-Hill.

Karlsson, C., (2008). *Program Design and Management*, Chapter 14 (pp. 167–182) in this volume.

Lerpold, L., Mårtensson, P., Mähring, M., and Teigland, R., (2005). MBALive gör Europeiska MBA utbildningar unika, (MBALive makes European MBA Educations Unique). Article in *Management®* *Magazine*, no 4. Sweden: Stockholm.

Lundeberg, M., (1993). *Handling Change Processes – A Systems Approach*. Lund, Sweden: Studentlitteratur.

Ramsden P., (1992). *Learning to Teach in Higher Education*. London: Routledge.

Schutz W., (1960). *FIRO: A Three Dimensional Theory of Interpersonal Behavior*. Will Schutz Associates.

16 *Managerial Competency and Learning Management*

Peter Daly and Isabelle Sequeira

Introduction

Effective management and leadership requires the capacity to think analytically without getting too bogged down in details, to make timely decisions without reacting impulsively, to reach consensus without compromising results, and to get people to perform. These abilities are not necessarily learnt from books on management theory, yet are essential to the future manager. The question that many organisations are asking themselves is, how we can ensure that graduates possess some of these core competencies? It is therefore legitimate that business education has taken up the challenge of fostering competency development in students so that they can compete in an increasingly protean and complex business environment and thereby ensure entry, promotion and even retention in specific organisations. In this chapter, we provide a historical overview of managerial competency in education prior to describing the managerial competency programme at EDHEC Business School, which involves both learning teams and learning managers working together to reflect and discuss academic, personal and extracurricular experience. The four main stakeholders in this learning framework, namely the student, the learning manager, the business school and the company are given a voice to express the benefits and drawbacks of this programme. The chapter ends with practical advice for all those wishing to set up a similar programme at their institution.

Managerial competencies in education: A historical overview

Managerial competence teaching was first addressed in the United States in the early 1980s and at that time, it was predicted to be one of the major issues facing business schools in the years to come (Porter 1983). Defined by Boyatzis (1982, p. 21) as 'the underlying characteristics of a person that lead to or cause effective and outstanding performance' there are a set of competencies that have been shown to predict outstanding manager or leader performance. These competencies include such macro-fields as cognitive and intellectual ability, self-management and intrapersonal capacity, and relationship management or intrapersonal ability.

Competency-based methodology was pioneered by the Hay-McBer company founder David McClelland, a Harvard University psychologist in the late 1960s and early 1970s. McClelland (1973, 1975) identified competencies and performance aspects that were not attributable to the worker's intelligence or degree of knowledge or skill and his research was a key to the development of the competency movement as opposed to the intelligence testing movement. In the early 1980s the focus shifted from an academic setting, where the competency approach was perceived as being rather controversial, to a more management setting.

Researchers such as Boyatzis (1982) popularised the work of McClelland and applied competencies to the sphere of management. He later went on to redefine professional education at Weatherhead School of Management (WSOM) at Case Western Reserve University, in particular at the School of Management, in an attempt to ask key questions concerning the characteristics of superior performers among managers. A management model was developed to encompass 22 abilities and 11 knowledge areas with such headings as 'goal and action management abilities; people management abilities; and analytical reasoning abilities' (Boyatzis et al. 1995, pp. 56–57). The concept of managerial competencies reached its peak in the early 1990s (Kierstead 1998) and since then has been employed in many organisations.

In an extension of the competency-based movement, Goleman et al. (2002) demonstrated that a leader's emotional competence has an enormous contribution to the organisation's bottom line. Goleman (1985, 1995, 1998) in his work has put forward a list of emotional competencies, which are based on emotional intelligence (also known as E.I.) and result in better performance in the workplace. Emotional intelligence considers our ability to learn certain practical skills and consists of 'five elements: self-awareness, motivation, self-regulation, empathy, and adeptness in relationships' (Goleman 1998, p. 24).

Managerial competency development at EDHEC Business School

In the academic year 2002/2003, the French Business School EDHEC[1] set up an academic planning committee to reflect on how the school could develop key managerial competencies. At a macro level, three pillars were seen to underpin learning at EDHEC:

- Inquiry (acquiring knowledge) encompasses basic knowledge acquisition and intellectual creativity.
- Understanding (transforming knowledge) deals with the conversion of that knowledge for the purpose of understanding and the skills that affect behaviour and performance.
- Action (applying knowledge) involves the development of situation-specific competence, which leads to professionalism in the workplace.

Out of these macro learning objectives, seven managerial competencies categories were identified. This list is by no means exhaustive but was identified as those competencies required by our students prior to graduation:

- ethical and cultural awareness;
- initiative and entrepreneurship;
- collaborative thinking and team spirit;
- self-mastery and interpersonal communication;
- leadership;
- managerial communication;
- creativity and decision making.

Kolb's experiential learning (Kolb et al. 1971; Kolb 1984) is the key theoretical underpinning of the managerial competency programme at EDHEC Business School. This learning cycle, which is the most established model of experiential learning, is divided into

---

1   EDHEC Business School is a French *Grande Ecole*, which is ranked 5th in France and has a campus in Lille in the North of France and in Nice on the Cote d'Azur (website: http://www.edhec.com).

four parts: experience (concrete experience) is followed by reflection (reflective observation), the reflection is then assimilated into theory (abstract conceptualisation) and these new (or reformulated) hypotheses are tested in new situations. This model is recurring as the learner tests new concepts and modifies them as a result of reflection and conceptualisation.

If we apply this conceptual framework to the learning events at EDHEC (see Figure 16.1), we see that students acquire concrete experience through school projects, student clubs and societies,[2] gap years, either comprising of work placements (in France or abroad) or foreign exchanges at our partner universities. Reflective observation is enabled via short obligatory internships and a company work-shadowing project in the first year, which requires the students in small groups to observe the daily functioning of a regional company and culminates in the writing of a report and the defence of that report in front of a jury. Abstract conceptualisation is possible through conferences organised by the Chair of Culture and Society, which regularly invites politicians, philosophers, psychologists, sociologists, and so on to speak to the students, and through the core curriculum courses and lectures in marketing, management and strategy, law, accounting and finance, business communication, foreign languages and computer science. Experimentation sees the students get involved in business simulations, student club and society work, and an entrepreneurial project in the second year, where students in groups of up to seven develop a humanitarian, cultural, social or economic project from A to Z. The main objective of the entrepreneurial project is to introduce the students to project management techniques.

LEARNING TEAM AND LEARNING MANAGER

Having identified the key managerial competencies we intended to develop in our students and the conceptual framework underpinned by the Kolbean model, we decided to organise

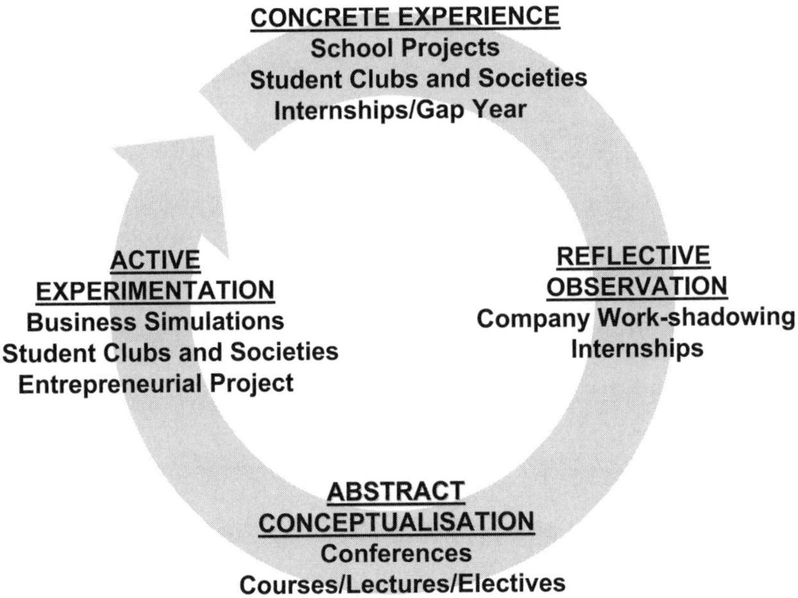

CONCRETE EXPERIENCE
School Projects
Student Clubs and Societies
Internships/Gap Year

ACTIVE
EXPERIMENTATION
Business Simulations
Student Clubs and Societies
Entrepreneurial Project

REFLECTIVE
OBSERVATION
Company Work-shadowing
Internships

ABSTRACT
CONCEPTUALISATION
Conferences
Courses/Lectures/Electives

Figure 16.1   Learning at EDHEC mapped onto Kolb's learning cycle

2   Clubs and societies are extremely important in the life of a French business student, as they are run like small businesses and provide the students with the possibility to put their acquired business theory into practice.

the student cohort into learning teams comprising of 12 students and facilitated by a learning manager (a faculty member but non-faculty are also involved in the process). The main objective here was to enable the students to discuss their experience, observation and conceptualisation, and reflect on their learning in order to make sense of the links between the experience and the managerial competencies. The teams meet regularly with their learning manager and this unit remains intact until the students graduate. The learning manager takes on a very multifaceted role which includes enabling the team to focus on their personal and team competency development; helping the students review their experience; enabling learning and discussion through dialogue within the group as well as ensuring that personal and team objectives are met. The specific objectives of the learning team are set out below:

- To construct and build understanding and conceptualise key managerial competencies and ensure that they are fostered and developed.
- To identify personal and team learning goals and review progress in competency development.
- To engage in frank discussion in order to review and make sense of experience.
- To listen to and question their peers on their critical incidents.
- To provide the student with a support structure in their management studies to evaluate the efficiency of the training and discuss the outcomes.

The students are also asked to keep a written record of their learning and experience in the form of a learning journal (vade mecum). The type of reflective writing serves as a personal journal where students note their questions, reflections, and thoughts of their learning experience. This inductive method enables the students to note critical incidents and identify potential obstacles as well as engage with the different steps of the learning cycle while developing the seven key managerial competencies. The students are free to choose the format of their learning journal. The journal entries are not evaluated but students are asked to provide a summary of their learning at two intervals during the year, which is evaluated by the learning manager.

Stakeholders in the learning event

Here, we would like to give a voice to the different stakeholders involved in this competency development programme. The four main stakeholders: a) Student; b) Learning Manager; c) Business School; and d) Company, were asked to provide feedback on what they perceived as the benefits and drawbacks of this programme.

A) STUDENT

Benefits:

1. Students were given the opportunity to take the time to step back from their learning experience and reflect on it critically at both a group (in the learning team) and individual (in the learning journal and learning summary) level, which few students would undertake on their own.
2. Awareness-raising on the fact that learning and reflection are lifelong endeavours, which do not end when you have graduated or once you have completed a task.
3. Students could start thinking about their qualities, skills and competencies to enable them

to better profile themselves when entering the workplace. Familiarity with your skill and competency set enables the student to match their profile to the advertised position.

4. Space was provided to exchange on students' life choices and experience.
5. Links were made between experience, critical incidents in their lives and managerial competencies.

Drawbacks:

1. Initially the students experienced difficulties conceptualising the managerial competencies as there seems to be a gap between the process they were being brought through and the object of reflection, namely the managerial competencies.
2. Some students have problems with a process that requires collective reflection and discussion in a small group.
3. Some students lack the maturity or concrete experience to benefit fully from this programme and there is an argument for delaying the learning team reflection process until the students have acquired the necessary experience.
4. The inductive approach inherent in this programme proved difficult for students due to their prior learning experience at secondary school and during their post-bac education.[3]

B) LEARNING MANAGER

Benefits:

1. The faculty member called their pedagogical approach and teacher role into question, and was forced to become reflexive about their teaching.
2. The role of the teacher was uppermost in the minds of the faculty, who have to navigate between facilitator, guide, coach, confidante and assessor to provide valuable formative and summative feedback to the students. This required consistent negotiation with the student and with oneself in order to create a comfortable and safe learning space.
3. The faculty members were called upon to appraise the impact of this programme on the student's life. They had to help the student make a successful transition between business school and work life, which involved understanding the students' life choices and learning styles. This led them to better understand the students' learning experience, which could then be fed back into their teaching in the various business disciplines.
4. Some faculty members see the learning team project as an opportunity to connect with the students at a different level and not just via their subject discipline.
5. The process enabled the faculty to become more reflexive on their own comprehension of key managerial competencies, which helped in postgraduate programme management and in their department management functions.

Drawbacks:

1. Some faculty members did not feel that they were professionally equipped to deal with the emotional and affective comments which could arise in discussions with their students.
2. It was difficult to manage student motivation and engagement with the process in the individual groups. While some students embraced the process and proved an asset to the group dynamic, others expressed negativity and demonstrated passive aggressive behaviour.

---

3   *Classes Préparatoires aux Grandes Ecoles (CPGE)* is a post-secondary school programme to prepare students for enrolment in Business and Engineering Schools. The programme usually lasts 2 or 3 years.

3. Not all faculty members were comfortable in the role of facilitator, with some expressing a wish to return to a more teacher-centred expository role.
4. Some learning managers questioned the maturity of the students and their lack of understanding of programme objectives, and this led to faculty confusion.

C) BUSINESS SCHOOL

Benefits:

1. It is an excellent way for a business school to identify pedagogical collaborators within the school and to innovate pedagogically.
2. As the business school model is performance-driven, this type of programme ensures that the faculty and students interact and exchange at a professional level all the while developing their managerial competencies.
3. The business school can communicate to the corporate world that they are preparing and developing managerial competency in their students, which should enable the graduate to become quickly operational in a work environment.

Drawbacks:

1. A large student cohort and the necessity to work in small groups (maximum 12 students in learning team) mean high costs for the institution.
2. The faculty members need to be mobilised to facilitate this programme; they must make themselves available for meetings and training, which is demanding and time-consuming.
3. Such an audacious project requires a lot of administrative support.

D) COMPANIES

Benefits:

1. Nowadays companies are looking to recruit graduates who have already developed key skills such as creativity, adaptability, flexibility, self-management, empathy, and so on, and more importantly, who have already engaged in a reflective process with others in a team setting.
2. Companies believe that it is easier to provide appropriate missions to critically-reflective graduates with increased self-identity and self-knowledge of their skills and competencies. A well-rounded manager who has developed intellectual rigour, and personal and social skills is immediately operational and more productive.
3. The compartmentalisation and fragmentation of knowledge and competencies in our society may mean that the graduates see competency development as a box-ticking exercise and may prove inflexible in a corporate environment as they have one preconceived idea of the individual competencies.
4. Companies also expressed a concern about the time given over to this type of programme as the learning team meetings took place only three or four times in the academic year and this did not allow the students to react to critical incidents in real time or soon afterwards. There was a feeling that reflection on the critical incident should occur within a short time period after it happened.

5. While the initiative was lauded for its innovativeness, there was a concern that students who did not enjoy this type of development programme would be very critical and negative towards similar initiatives within the company as junior staff members.

Advice to faculty and business school

Finally, we would like to offer some advice to faculty members or business schools who may be considering a similar initiative at their institution.

ADVICE TO FACULTY

1. We would suggest that learning managers among faculty are recruited on a voluntary basis as not all faculty members want to get involved in such a project or feel comfortable in a facilitative role. While some would argue that faculty should force themselves into new learning and teaching experiences, the students should not suffer at the hands of an unmotivated learning manager, especially bearing in mind the affective, personal and emotional nature of this programme.
2. Avoid focusing too much on the prescriptive, organisational and procedural aspects of the programme as you risk losing sight of the sense of the learning team and the overriding objectives, that is, the development of managerial competencies via reflection and discussion of critical incidents. The learning managers should therefore have the freedom to choose their own facilitation style in the learning team meetings.
3. Learning managers should work in tandem to reflect on their facilitation of the learning team, share and exchange learning and facilitation techniques and discuss their comprehension of managerial competency development. This could become part of a teaching portfolio for personal and professional development, whereby reflective writing is carried out to make sense of their learning as well as student learning.

ADVICE TO BUSINESS SCHOOL MANAGEMENT

1. Institutions, who may be thinking of implementing such a programme, should try to have a 50:50 mix of faculty and company employees. This ensures that different knowledge, skills and competencies are brought to bear on the learning event.
2. There is a risk that this programme could become just another part of a teacher's workload, and hence lose its edge and originality. Therefore, it is essential that the business schools provide the learning managers with professional development and training such as facilitation/coaching techniques, active listening workshops both initially and at key junctures during the programme.
3. The business school should communicate externally to companies and to the general public, future students, alumni, and so on to ensure that their learning programme is known on the job market. This will enable recruiters to target business graduates from that business school as they know that they have been forced to reflect on their knowledge, skills and competencies.

ADJUSTMENTS TO THE MANAGERIAL COMPETENCY PROGRAMME

By way of conclusion, we would like to comment on how EDHEC has made adjustments to the managerial competency programme following the feedback from the various stakeholders as outlined above. The board of governors decided to suspend the project for undergraduate students and only offer it on post-experience programmes such as executive education, MSc and MBA programmes. This decision was mainly based on the cost (as one hour of learning team was equivalent to one hour of teaching) and the level of maturity and experience required by students (the majority of the students involved were pre-experience). During the course of the 2006/07 academic year, a period of reflection is planned with the aim of offering a similar type or programme, which is more adapted to the undergraduate student population. With many faculty members now familiar with competency development and with training in facilitation/coaching techniques, it should be easy to develop similar projects by capitalising on the existing knowledge and experience within the institution.

Acknowledgements

The authors would like to thank the following people for their feedback and support: Françoise Van Heems, Véronique Bouloucher, Jean-Christophe Meyfredi, Denis Dauchy, Patricia Plichon, Fabienne Labbe and Charles Tondeur.

We would also like to thank our EDHEC students for engaging in this learning initiative.

References

Boyatzis, R.E., (1982). *The Competent Manager: A Model for Effective Performance*. NY: John Wiley & Sons.

Boyatzis, R.E., Cowen, S.S., Kolb, D.A., and associates, (1995). *Innovation in Professional Education, Steps on a Journey from Teaching to Learning*. San Francisco: Jossey-Bass Publishers.

Goleman, D., (1985). *Vital lies, Simple Truths: The Psychology of Self-deception*. NY: Simon and Schuster.

Goleman, D., (1995). *Emotional Intelligence*. NY: Bantam.

Goleman, D., (1998). *Working with Emotional Intelligence*. NY: Bantam

Goleman, D., Boyatzis, R. and McKee, A., (2002). *Primal Leadership: Realizing the Power of Emotional Intelligence*. Boston: Harvard Business School Press.

Kierstead, J., (1998). *Origin of Competency Profiling*. Available from http://www.hrma-agrh.gc.ac/research/personnel/comp_ksao_e.asp, [Accessed 10 May 2005].

Kolb, D., Rubin, I. M., and McIntyre, J. M., (1971). *Organisational Psychology: An Experiential Approach*. New Jersey: Prentice Hall.

Kolb, D.A., (1984). *Experiential Learning: Experience as the Source of Learning and Development*. Englewood Cliffs, NJ: Prentice-Hall.

McClelland, D.C., (1973). 'Testing for competence rather than intelligence', *American Psychologist*, 28: 1–14.

McClelland, D.C., (1975). *Power: The Inner Experience*. NY: Irvington.

Porter, L.W., (1983). 'Teaching managerial competencies: an overview'. *Organisation Behaviour Teaching Review*, 8(2): 8–9.

Outside the Classroom

Individual Development of Faculty Members

17 *Getting and Giving Feedback*

Tom Pugel and Jan Shubert

Introduction

It's a fact. If you teach, you get feedback. Between the two of us we have had more than a half century of experience teaching, reflecting on how it went and, of course, pouring over the evaluations from literally thousands of students. We have gotten feedback from undergraduates, MBA students, and Ph.D. students, along with feedback from participants in Executive Education programs. It has been feedback on our teaching in massive lecture courses, small discussion seminars, case-based courses and practicum or experience-based courses. The feedback has come from men and women, North American students, international students, 18-year olds just beginning their college years and senior executives from multinational corporations. Most of this feedback has been pretty positive, but there have certainly been times when it was painful, surprising or confusing. All of it has definitely given us food for thought, ideas for improvement and even moments of real joy and accomplishment.

As essential as our own insights are and as valuable as student evaluations can be, we have made extensive use of—and taught about—another very powerful way to get and give feedback on our teaching: Ask a colleague.

Observation-based feedback from colleagues isn't a new idea. One of the best pieces written on this process was the eloquent and persuasive essay 'To See Ourselves as Others See Us: The Rewards of Classroom Observation', co-authored by James Austin, Ann Sweet and Catherine Overholt in the 1991 book *Education for Judgment*. (See 'For Further Reading' at the end of this chapter). So while this isn't new, neither is this a widely used process in most colleges and universities around the world. Because it's still relatively unexplored territory, when we teach about this, when we model it, we get a lot of questions, ranging from 'Why in the world would you do this?' to the more hands-on questions about *how* to do it.

We hope that by sharing our answers to the most frequently-asked questions, we can also share our enthusiasm for—and belief in—the power of this process and help you discover ways you could incorporate this into your teaching and into your learning.

Why is feedback from colleagues valuable and powerful?

Tom: Let me begin with the perspective of the instructor who is getting feedback from a colleague and share why I find this valuable.

There are a variety of ways to get feedback on my teaching of a course. I am constantly processing and reflecting on what goes on in the classroom and I also receive feedback from the students or participants. This comes in variety of ways, including mid-course and end-of-course evaluations and surveys. But I can—and do—invite outside observers to class sessions and learn from their observations. Each of these forms of feedback has both value and challenges.

Self-monitoring and reflection happens in real time, while I'm teaching, and so I can make adjustments 'in the moment'. This is part of the performance art of teaching, and it is satisfying when it is working well. I can also take away my observations and make notes to myself about how I might make improvements when I offer that session or topic again in the future. But it also amazes me how much I do *not* see or hear or notice during a class; how impossible it is to be attuned to each students' body language, side comments, or silence. And even when I do see and hear, my perceptions can be colored or biased by something else that is happening in the classroom—the 'selective perception' that results because of what I *do* notice or am sensitive to. As a result, a session that I thought went poorly may actually turn out to be well-received and encourage student's learning or, conversely, a session I thought went well, I later discover confused the students or did not satisfy their needs or expectations.

Written feedback (in the form of course evaluations), along with verbal comments from students or participants, can also be useful, but also presents the challenge of how to *interpret* what they are telling me.

Student evaluations seem to be best at providing a summary measure of what the students or participants thought of the course, overall. But the real information from the evaluations is usually woefully short of providing specific insights into what could be done differently to improve my effectiveness as a teacher. Likert scales are particularly unhelpful, although if there are short written answers to questions about the course I get more information about specific teaching behaviors. For instance, students might write that they like that I hand out hard copies of the slides for the day's topic at the beginning of the session and, if no one else says that this is a bad practice, I will be encouraged to keep doing this. Or if a number of students say that my voice at times is monotone and makes them drowsy and no one else nominates me for a voice award, then I have 'data' that something needs to be changed.

But often there is no clear consensus. The written comments vary from student to student, so that I am not sure what I have. Some students liked one topic and thought the class should spend more time on it, while others thought it was among the least important in the course. Or, some students say that they appreciate that the problem sets are for them to work through on their own to enhance their learning, while other students say that they wished that they had been forced to turn in written answers. More importantly, when students offer an idea for how to improve the course, usually it is only one or at most a few who make the suggestion, while the others are completely silent, so I have no idea what most would think of this change.[1]

Fortunately, given the limitations of self-evaluation and student evaluations, there is a third major way to get feedback: Invite an outside observer into the classroom. Although this does not have to be a faculty colleague, there are significant advantages in asking a fellow teacher to observe.

First, they bring their knowledge of the students and the teaching culture of the school. Second, they often bring knowledge of the content of the course, or at least knowledge of related content areas and ways of teaching in these areas. Third, because this person is also

---

1   At Stern we do have another method for eliciting feedback from students, what we call the Student Small Group Analysis. In this method an outside consultant takes part of a class session to have students work in small groups to develop answers to three questions: What do you like most about the course so far? What do you like least? What specific change(s) could the instructor make? The information from the small groups is then debriefed in full session, and the results are then reported to the instructor. Key advantages of this method are that I receive information from the students directly, and that the discussion of the various points can get at how much agreement there is among the students about the various specific points of feedback. A drawback is that it generally requires me to give up class time (30–45 minutes) to the effort, because it is not possible to get all students together at times other than regularly scheduled class sessions.

a classroom teacher they have a good sense of *what* to look for—they can provide the extra eyes and ears to see and hear how students are responding and what students are doing as the session progresses. And last, but certainly not least, a colleague can make very concrete, very specific comments about what is working well for encouraging student learning, as well as experience-based suggestions on what I could adjust or do differently to enhance my teaching effectiveness.

Jan: What about the value for the person who is doing the observing and giving feedback to a colleague? I can honestly say that every time I have been in the role of observer, I have learned something. Sometimes it is about content, sometimes it is about process. Sometimes it is about the students and how they are looking at the world and how they experience the role of 'learner'. Several years ago I was visiting a young colleague's class and watched as he struggled to get through a very loosely organized lecture he was presenting on some complex material. Sitting there in his classroom, I realized that even though I might suggest a different structure that would better integrate the concepts he was covering, I was actually learning a lot about the content; about things totally outside my field of expertise! This prompted some ideas about how to make what I was teaching in one of my courses more 'connected' to the core course he was teaching.

In another situation, I was observing a very experienced colleague teach a very complicated case involving lots of stakeholder perspectives and a lot of ambiguous numbers. At first I was stunned by the fact that she was using only three questions, repeated over and over, to lead the discussion and engage the students. But the more I listened to the students' responses, the more I watched them dig in and try and provide 'fresh' answers, the more I began to see how powerful that repetition was as a technique for uncovering their very divergent perspectives and understandings of the issues in the case.

As an observer I frequently have those really unsettling moments of watching a colleague, but seeing *myself* and my own teaching. 'Ah, ha!', I realize. 'So it really only *feels* like hours pass when you ask a question and there is a bit of silence'. 'Oh, no!', I groan silently, 'It's not always a good idea to let a student finish a long, rambling answer.'

Watching. Listening. Learning. It really is reciprocal.

Tom and Jan: As teachers, we both find real value in this process, whether observing or being observed. But another often overlooked advantage of colleagues working together in this way is the contribution it can make to overall institutional excellence. Working together on teaching can build and nourish the kind of collaboration and sharing that is fundamental to an academic community. Because teaching is also learning, we can be more productive and build strong cross-disciplinary bridges if we share ideas about content and teaching methods. When these strong collaborative bonds are formed we can more readily ask each other for help and ideas, about not just our teaching, but also about our research, our writing, and about the day-to-day workings of the academy.

Our strong belief in this collaborative feedback process is also shaped by the fact that we both teach in business schools where much of the *student* learning takes place in collective settings: study groups, task teams, group assignments and, of course, the ubiquitous case-discussion classroom. Teaching is, after all, about preparing our students to enter a world where, although individual performance is valued, it is often in the context of a matrix organization, or within cross-functional teams or even cross-organizational partnerships, and where 360 degree feedback is the norm. We can (and should) be role models for the process and the power of collaboration. We should (and indeed must) be able to *demonstrate* that getting feedback is a normal, natural part of being a professional.

How do you organize getting and giving feedback from colleagues?

Like the title of an old Jack Nicholson movie, putting this process in place is all about 'Five Easy Pieces': (1) an invitation; (2) a pre-observation conversation; (3) the classroom visit; (4) the post-observation feedback; and (5) a reciprocal invitation.

WHOM SHOULD I INVITE AND HOW?

Tom: Deciding *whom* to ask may be harder than deciding to ask. For many of us, just having someone else in the room can be intimidating. There is the valid concern about how the observation will be 'used', which can create a particular conundrum for a junior faculty member. Observation by a senior colleague with substantial content expertise and broad teaching experience may be the most beneficial, but also fraught with potential spillover during the faculty evaluation, promotion, and tenure processes. And, despite (or maybe because of) their seniority, seasoned faculty will also feel vulnerable being observed. After all, are they not already good at this? Shouldn't *they* be the ones who model excellent teaching?

Because of these sensitive issues, Jan and I feel strongly that *confidentiality* is the fundamental basis for all observation and feedback. It must be understood that whatever is observed is intended only for the instructor and their development. Regardless of the status or rank of the two colleagues, what happens, happens between the two of them.

I would suggest that a junior faculty member, especially for the first observation or two, invite someone that they believe is safe. This could be another junior faculty member who has suitable skills, interest, and character, or it could be a trustworthy senior faculty member.

Another key question is whether to invite someone *in* your own field or someone from *outside* your discipline or department. The answer depends on what you hope to accomplish with the observation and feedback.

If you are hoping mostly to get insights into the *content* of the session, then you might want to ask someone in your field, perhaps someone who teaches the same or a similar course. If what you want is a broader perspective on the class session and how your students are engaged—the *process*—then you might benefit from inviting someone from outside your field, perhaps someone who is known to be a very good teacher or someone who is very reflective about what makes teaching effective (in promoting student learning).

In addition to adding a valuable 'outside' perspective, inviting colleagues from other disciplines may, at least initially, feel less intimidating; you are still the 'subject expert', and, in many institutions, they will be less involved in any formal evaluation of your work, including your teaching.

Jan: Regardless of who you ask, Tom and I think there are two keys to making this successful. First, it's important to be clear about *why* you would want *anyone* sitting in! You need to have a purpose that their presence can help you achieve.

Asking, 'Can you observe my class and give me some feedback?' is just too broad, too open-ended, and too subject to misinterpretation—and misunderstanding. To help give the visit a purpose and the observer a clear sense of why they're there, I sometimes invite a colleague by saying, 'You do a lot of research and teaching on mergers and acquisitions. It's not my area of expertise and I'd like to get your feedback on how I handle a case (or a module) that covers this.'

If I'm teaching a new case or significantly new material, I always try to invite a colleague to observe the rhythm and flow of the class. Am I moving too fast? Too slow? Am I balancing asking questions (leading the discussion) with letting students talk and explore ideas? And I've also found that asking a colleague to sit in is an extremely useful way to get insights about the students; how they are acting and reacting to me, to the material and to one another.

A second key to making an invitation is more about instinct than hard and fast guidelines. As Tom says, it is essential to feel 'safe'. So invite someone you trust. Someone you trust to be a good listener and watcher. Someone you trust to listen and watch with *your* development in mind. This is *not* about inviting someone who will only tell you that you are doing a great job. It needs to be someone you can trust to be open, honest and candid and to hold up a friendly, collegial 'mirror' so you can get real insights.

WHAT HAPPENS IN THE PRE-OBSERVATION CONVERSATION?

Jan: Obviously, the person you invite to observe you will need to know the basics: The date, time, and location for the class they will be visiting. But there is also a lot of valuable 'contextual' information that should be shared. When Tom and I taught this process for ITP we role-modeled a fairly typical face-to-face pre-visit conversation that demonstrated how to prepare a colleague for a visit to your class. You and your colleagues will develop your own questions, and make this a real conversation.

When we role-modeled this, Tom would tell me about the course overall; the name of the course, the level, where it fit in the overall curriculum, how often he had taught it, how many sections of the course there were, and so forth. We would also go over any reading or homework assignments the students had been given. (Note: As a visitor, it is very helpful to have a copy of the course syllabus, along with the readings and assignments for the session.)

We would also talk about the students. Who typically takes the course? Do they prepare well for class? Do they ask good questions and make solid contributions? Are there any real 'stars' or any students who seem to be falling behind? These kinds of questions (and the answers), help an observer 'see' and understand more. If Tom told me that the class was normally well prepared and lively, but I observe students frantically flipping through the readings or answering only the easy questions, then we could talk about that. What happened in that particular class that was different? How did he react to this and what 'message' did that send about preparation and participation?

But the most important topic is what your colleague, specifically, wants you to watch and listen for. One year, for example, Tom had decided to use an interactive computer technique instead of overhead slides. He wanted me to give him feedback on how well that worked. Did he integrate this teaching tool and handle it smoothly? (He did!) Did it keep the students engaged in the discussion? (It did!)

Tom: To prepare a colleague for observing, I want to provide good background information, but I also want to take responsibility for a visitor in my classroom; I want to be a good host. It may seem obvious, but it is very important to think about and talk about how the 'visitor' will be introduced to the class, being aware that the words you choose can have an effect on how the students behave. And it is also important to talk about the actual classroom, which parts always seem to fill up first (for instance the last row!) and where you would like the observer to sit.

I find it very useful to share my impressions of how the course has gone so far, in terms of student participation in class discussions, how engaged students seem to be, and how challenging they are finding the course concepts and activities. Not only does this give my colleague useful information, it also helps me to reflect on the learning dynamics.

But as Jan has noted, the most important part of this pre-visit conversation is what, specifically, you would like the observer to watch for. In addition to the example Jan gave, here are some questions I have asked my colleagues/observers: What are students who are not participating in the discussion doing? Are there things that I might do to draw more of them in? Am I favoring one part of the room over another when I am recognizing students to ask questions or to add to the discussion? Did the key point of the session actually seem to get across? Of course, I also want to tell my colleague that any insights and ideas will be appreciated, but that these are two or three things that I particularly would appreciate feedback on.

Jan and Tom: Over the years we have also discovered that while these face-to-face meetings definitely provide valuable content and contextual information, maybe more importantly they also reinforce the bonds of trust, which help both parties feel more comfortable and at ease. The person being observed gets to send the message 'I want you to feel welcome in my classroom,' and, 'Here is what I want you to watch and listen for.' The person who will be observing gets to say, ' Thank you for inviting me,' as well as, ' I'm going to do my best to watch and listen for the specifics you've asked for.' We leave the meeting as colleagues, as a team.

HOW DOES THE ACTUAL OBSERVATION TIME WORK?

Tom: At first I am rather self-conscious. Before the class begins I can't help but be aware that a colleague is there. I have already told the students at the previous session that we are going to have my colleague as a visitor and observer of the class session, but I take a minute at the beginning of the class session to introduce my colleague, to remind students that we have a visitor. Then I quickly plunge into what I usually do at the beginning of a class session. That may be one or two administrative announcements, a brief summary of what we did at the previous session, and a request for any questions from students about the course. Then we are off into the day's material and activities.

I do my best to throw myself into the session just like I would without the visitor, and usually I succeed. For long stretches I can forget that they are there, although every once in a while I see them and remember. But, as much as I can, I am not playing to my colleague, rather I am working with the students.

Jan: When I go to a colleague's class I try to arrive just a bit early so I can find where I need to sit and to pick up a bit on what the students say and do as they come in. This is a valuable piece of insight I can share with the person I'm observing, who is often tied up in a conversation with one or two students and may not be able to sense what is going on just before 'the curtain goes up'.

As an observer I take lots of notes, (what Austin calls 'semi-transcription' in his essay) but I try to do this in as unobtrusive a way as possible so that the students don't feel as though I'm 'recording' *them*. A brief example of what my notes might look like is shown in Table 17.1.

Table 17.1   Sample notes

10:10: Tom		
Good morning everyone. Let's get started.	?	A lot of students missing
Everyone take a seat		Seemed a bit rushed
I want to introduce my colleague...		
Before we start today's material, let's review	+	Very good review Good pace
Now, look at supply and demand		
Slide 1: Macro Linkages		
Stay focused on the bottom part today	#	Careful about pointing on the screen and blocking view of information
Slide 2: Exchange		
Oh, I forgot to hand out the slides!	+	Nice handling of this! Good use of humor
Let's find a place to start		
What's the most simple story?	+	Total silence; Good job of giving them time to think
Will this go up or down	+	Good gentle prompt
Allan?	+	Good listening and eye contact
Does anyone want to expand?	+	Good follow-up and you got a couple of responses
Imagine I'm sitting in the U.S. What will I do?	+	Very good! Specific. Got them more focused
Slide: 3 Summary	#	Very hard to read; too much info to process quickly
Remember, I'm an American? What will I do?	#	Good question, but they're still trying to read/think
	#	Less information on slide? More time to process? Ask them to do this in pairs?
=>10:20	?	Energy in room feels 'flat' What could you do to pick it up?
Question from student: 'I don't understand the difference...'	?/#	He seemed ok with response but it was pretty long; also introduced 2 new concepts What if you asked the class to answer his question?

You can see I'm tracking several things: (a) time (so we can talk about the flow of the class); (b) my colleague's comments/questions (a great way to get a glimpse of what moves a discussion along and what might get it off track); (c) how—and how many—students respond (helpful in looking at their level of engagement) and; (d) 'things' I may observe (where my colleague is standing, what students are doing, and so on).

These notes also give me a way to be clear and specific in the feedback session and I always give the notes to my colleague. The 'code' I use also helps me in the feedback session to quickly spot those things I thought worked really well (+), places where I had questions about how things were going or thoughts about trying something else (?), and things I thought could be changed or improved (#).

Jan and Tom: We all learn in different ways. Some of us 'get it' best when we see or hear it. If you are that kind of person (or the colleague you are observing is) then having an audio and/or videotape of the observation is going to be much more powerful than just written notes. But maybe you (or your colleague) really likes to have written data to take away, read, re-read, and mull over. In that case, really thorough notes should work well. And maybe it depends—on the type of class, the newness of the material, the kinds of students. You can't know what kind of feedback will work best unless you ask. And if you don't ask, you can't be a really effective observer.

HOW DO YOU HANDLE THE POST-OBSERVATION FEEDBACK?

Jan: Because I believe that the person receiving the feedback (even if it is 100 per cent positive and glowing) probably feels the most vulnerable in this meeting, I like to let them choose where to meet for this conversation, decide how long the meeting should last, and make the choice about whether or not they want to see my notes in advance (or go over them together) or, if we have done a videotape, to watch it alone first or view it together. The only part of the feedback session I try to be firm on is having the conversation as soon after the teaching session as possible while things are still fresh.

I also think it's human nature for the person who has been the one observed to want to jump right in and ask, 'So, how do *you* think I did?' I know that's the case when I'm getting feedback! But I also know that a powerful and productive place to begin is for the observer to ask, 'So, how do you think the session went?', listen carefully and generously and then follow up with a couple of broad questions such as, 'Are there things you thought went particularly well?' and, 'Was there anything that disappointed you?' or maybe, 'Was there anything that surprised you?' By letting my colleague lead the way on this I can get a lot of clues and cues about what they saw, what they felt, as well as some insights about what is going to be a 'touchy' area or even 'off limits'.

Obviously, the trajectory of this conversation is going to depend a lot on the relationship you and your colleague have established. If you have already been frequent visitors in one another's classes, you may find you can just begin wherever it feels comfortable. But for situations where the collaborative relationship is still new, there are a couple of strategies for keeping the conversation going. The first is, after asking the person who was observed how they felt about the session, move on to the specific things the observer was *asked* to watch for. For example, after observing Tom, I might say, 'Tom, you asked me to pay particular attention to whether or not I thought the students picked up on the key points. Do you want to start there?'

A second strategy is making use of the notes (the more 'objective data'). As the observer I can say, 'I took a lot of notes which you have already seen. Is there a place you'd like to begin, or questions you have about anything I wrote?' If I had a colleague observe me I might say, 'I really appreciated your notes and wonder if we could just go over some of those first?'

The framework that Tom and I have used to guide the *type* of feedback given during the session at ITP is based on the acronym *S-M-A-R-T*: This means that feedback to a colleague should be **S**pecific, **M**easurable, **A**ctionable, **R**elevant, and **T**imely. I've already noted that providing feedback as soon as possible (**T**imely) is important. I want to say a couple of things about the **A**ctionable dimension.

For feedback to be useful, your colleague needs to be able to actually *do* something with it. When I was relatively new to the case-based classroom at Harvard Business School, I asked a well-regarded colleague, known to be a great case teacher, to visit my class and give me his insights about the kinds of questions I asked and the quality of the discussion that resulted. His feedback was some of the most detailed and beneficial I have ever gotten. But one of his primary concerns, complete with quantifiable, relevant examples, was that while I had been doing a pretty good job of keeping a lively discussion going, I had suddenly quit writing on the board and the discussion went flat. Was I aware that I had used only about 75 per cent of the boards?

An accurate observation? Absolutely. Actionable? I wasn't sure. I am just 5'2" tall and I can only *reach* about 75 per cent of the boards! What I needed (and eventually got help constructing) was a very different way to use a very limited amount of board space to track and stimulate lively discussions. The lesson I took away from this was to try and begin where the other person is and point them toward something they could realistically do, almost immediately, that will make a difference in how they teach—and in how they feel about their teaching.

Tom: When getting feedback from a colleague I always try to begin by reminding myself to stay open. To listen. To really try and *hear* what they are saying or asking. It's time for me to *learn* something about my teaching.

The first time Jan and I role-modeled this process for ITP I was not expecting her to begin with the question, 'So, how did *you* think the session went?' As she has mentioned, I was all set to buckle down and talk about the things I *did*, not how I *felt*. I have to confess that I felt put on the spot and unprepared. But then (and in subsequent years) I could see and feel the value of that question: it put me squarely back into the real experience of teaching the class. Thinking about and talking about how that *felt*, actually helps me stay better attuned to observations.

I find it very useful when Jan (or any colleague who has observed me) offers factual observations and comments on what they believe worked well in the session. When they can give me *specific, measurable* examples, it affirms that they were being thorough and thoughtful and saw and heard the many facets of my teaching, not just one dimension. This solidifies the trust between us. I know it is not just flattery.

At the same time, the observer's comments cannot be all positive. Of course I like knowing what went well, but I genuinely want insights into how I might do things differently and suggestions on ways to improve my teaching and the students' learning. I am looking for a *constructive* critique, offered in a way that I can take it in, consider it and ultimately use—in other words, I'm looking for the *relevant* and *actionable* parts of the *S-M-A-R-T* model for feedback.

As we have already mentioned, a lot of what will be effective will depend on the relationship between the two of you and how well you have established some guidelines for the type of feedback you want and can hear. Speaking for myself, it helps me to hear and understand and stay open to ideas when the observer can use a variety of forms to frame what they have seen and heard.

Some of their observations can be presented very straightforwardly ('Several students kept raising their hands, but you called on the same student four times'). Others might be presented as musings ('It's interesting to think about how students react to being challenged'), or as questions ('Have you considered opening the class with a quote or example from that day's business news?'). Concrete, specific suggestions are always welcome, but again, *how* they are offered will affect *how* they are heard. One of the techniques that Jan uses is to phrase her recommendations as musings or questions ('I wonder what would happen if you let the students do the calculations?' or 'Would you feel comfortable being a bit more informal?'). This not only gives me a chance to mull over that idea, but it keeps our interaction on an equal, conversational footing. We are really having a dialog about teaching.

No matter how skillful the observer is, there are times in the feedback conversation when I am tempted to defend what I did, to explain why I always do it that way or why it wouldn't work to do it differently. I have to remind myself to stay in learning mode. This is not the part of my academic life where I need to mount logical, powerful arguments, or defend my ideas and propositions. This is the part of my professional life when I want to listen and learn.

Even if I do not agree with what my colleague-observers say (or what I think they are saying), there is still enormous value in trying to understand the point being made or why they saw the situation that way. If I can stay open, I can ask questions, explore, and gain insights. For instance, a colleague observer once indicated that he found part of one class overly dry and conceptual. He suggested that (perhaps) I should add some lively, provocative examples. My immediate reaction was negative because I was concerned that I was already 'feeding' the students too much and not challenging them to master the conceptual material. But taking a deep breath and staying open to the idea, matching it to my own views about my teaching, and asking him some questions, I came away with a great new idea. I could rework that part of the session so that I started out with a broad opening question and then challenged the students to provide real examples, grounded in the conceptual categories we were covering. It was not the specific suggestion he offered, but it grew into something that worked for me, for my teaching.

Tom and Jan: Perhaps the most surprising thing about these conversations has been discovering how challenging it can be to give a colleague *positive* feedback! Modesty, discomfort with or distrust of praise, a sense of 'collegial equality', and cultural differences can all come into play as we try to find a way, as observers, to say, 'Here is what worked well'.

It is easy—and normal—to be hyper-aware of all the 'negatives', those things we wish we had done better, differently, or not at all! So when we get feedback we understandably want to know how to 'fix' those things. Yet often these negative aspects have taken on a much larger role in our minds than in reality. Moreover, the 'fix' for our less than perfect teaching is actually imbedded in the things we do well, albeit unconsciously. When a colleague can help us be conscious of what is working, to see it, and really understand it, we then have the solid foundation for working on what we want to improve.

A second challenge is always going to be around how *much* to say to a colleague you have observed. How many things can the other person actually hear, take on board, and work on? Our strong view is that less is more. Remember, if you make this an ongoing, reciprocal process there will be opportunities to keep this conversation going, to focus on a particular challenge in more depth, to ask questions, to offer suggestions.

HOW CAN YOU MAKE THE PROCESS REALLY RECIPROCAL AND ONGOING?

- Create the initial invitation so it includes the first pre-observation conversation.
- Make a commitment to one another.
- Let others know what you are doing, why you think it's valuable, and encourage them to try this too.
- Consider how you can contribute to making this an institutional practice that is accepted as normal, natural and important.
- Imagine how you can extend what you are learning about the feedback process and share it with students so they, too, are better prepared for the 360 processes they will encounter in the workplace.

Final words

We can keep this very brief: ***Just do it!***

Don't wait for your institution to create a formal process. Don't wait for someone to invite you to their classroom.

Find a trusted colleague who will make this reciprocal. Invite them to join you in this adventure. Schedule the time. Begin creating what we believe is one of the most powerful teaching and learning tools we have at our disposal. Begin creating strong institutional norms for collaboration. Begin role-modeling, for your students, what it means to be a wise and generous colleague.

References and further reading

BOOKS AND BOOK CHAPTERS

Austin, J., with Sweet, A. and Overholt, C., (1991). 'To See Ourselves as Others See Us: The Rewards of Classroom Observation' In *Education for Judgment: The Artistry of Discussion Leadership*. C. Roland Christensen, D.A. Garvin and A. Sweet, Editors. Boston: Harvard Business School Press.

Davis, B.G., (1993). *Tools for Teaching*. San Francisco: Jossey-Bass Publishers.

McKeachie, W., (2006). *Teaching Tips*. 12th edition. Boston: Houghton Mifflin.

Lucas, C.J. and Murry, Jr., J.W., (2002). *New Faculty: A Practical Guide for Academic Beginners*. New York: Palgrave.

VALUABLE WEBSITES TO VISIT

University of Texas
Peer Observation
www.utexas.edu/academic/cte/PeerObserve.html

University of Minnesota
Classroom Observation
www.umn.edu/ohr/teachlearn/resources/peer/instruments.html

18 *Individual Professional Development Coaching*

Philippa Morrison and Pär Mårtensson

> *Imagine Chris. He is beginning his second year as an assistant professor at one of the top-ranked business schools in Europe. Having completed his Ph.D at a good US school he was recruited to this great position with fantastic prospects. Now the opportunities are there for him to achieve a tenured position and gain respect in his field. What does Chris's everyday life look like? He has a 'seven years to tenure' contract. To get his tenure, he is required to deliver a certain amount of teaching and win in the ever stiffening competition to get papers into 'A' journals. He makes tenure, or he loses his job. He also has to be a good citizen and serve on several internal committees at the school, and attend recruitment talks and seminars. Outside his professional life he moved continents, got married and has having a family at the back of his mind. Taking a break from school at this stage would be highly risky. Could he stop the tenure clock? Could he leave ongoing research projects? Would he be taken seriously in an environment where reputation is everything? Would he lose the courses he taught and have to prepare new courses on his return? There are several young and ambitious assistant professors 'competing' for the rather scarce senior positions in his subject area. Right now Chris is frustrated: teaching is so time-consuming, but also so important. He must get it right quickly so he can get on with what's really important to him. The last course he taught in the MBA program was not a huge success. Fixing his teaching if it gets worse could be very costly in terms of time and effort. The two papers he has submitted to journals based on his dissertation have been sent back with extensive demands for him to revise and resubmit. He starts asking himself questions like: 'Maybe I am not suited to this career? Maybe I am not meant to be a teacher for these demanding and sometimes hostile groups? Maybe my research is not up to 'A' journal standards? Life was so much easier when I was a Ph.D student where at least I had my supervisor to ask for help, in my research and all other issues.*

There are many Chrises (both female and male) at business schools worldwide today. The pressure on individuals at most schools is very tough: faculty members are required to be excellent in both teaching and research, as well as being good citizens at the school. All this is taking place in very competitive environments: the students being taught at the schools are competitive; have usually invested significant amounts of time, money and effort in their education and therefore expect faculty to be of the absolute highest quality; the number of senior positions at a school is most likely limited and there is therefore tough competition between 'colleagues'.

However, in an environment where faculty development is institutionalized, people like Chris can find support. Harvard Business School (HBS) has taken teaching very seriously. With ample resources, HBS led the field by offering help in the form of a teaching and learning center. This center has evolved over the years and now offers an extensive menu of courses and interventions, including coaching for faculty. The *C. Roland Christensen Center for Teaching and Learning* was established in 2004 and offers help with teaching and with other aspects of professional life.

Colleagues are put into teaching groups where they can discuss and reflect upon teaching experiences. Coaching by colleagues and by coaches is 'normal' at HBS and people like Chris are not left on their own. At HBS they have a tradition since the 1960s of observing classes and have regular feedback sessions (see also Christensen et al. 1991, for discussions on the development of discussion teaching). Now, many other good schools, whatever the resources they have, have followed the lead of HBS and invest in their own versions of faculty development.

In this chapter we will discuss aspects of individual professional development coaching. We have both worked with various forms of individual coaching over a number of years with faculty members from business schools in many different countries, as well as of managers in various organizations; Philippa mostly with a broad career/life focus and Pär mostly with a teaching focus for faculty members and a management processes or change project perspective for managers. Given the focus for this volume we will concentrate on the business school setting.

First, we will briefly reflect on reflection. Then we will discuss the context, that is, the business school environment and highlight some challenges in this environment. We then present and discuss four fundamental principles for individual professional development coaching. Finally we discuss some alternatives and conclude the chapter by asking the question: what does it take to do this?

Some reflections on reflection

In this context we work with reflection as a learning tool guiding towards action (see for example, Argyris 1982). Reflection is the starting point and leads towards any preferred learning method and then to action (see also Chapter 23 by Antonacopoulou in this volume). The reflection is also a tool for professionals to review their theories of action with their theories-in-use (Argyris and Schön 1974), and inevitably then be able to learn from this.

Donald Schön (1983; 1987) highlights the distinction between reflection-*in*-action and reflection-*on*-action, where the former means reflection during the action taken, and the latter means reflection taking place before or after the action. In other words, reflection can be seen from the perspective of *timing*.

Another perspective on reflection is whether reflection is taking place *alone*, *with one other*, a coach or similar, or something done *in groups*. That is, the *social context*, is relevant.

In the following section we will take a closer look at the context for reflection in this chapter, the business school environment.

The business school environment

What does the situation facing business schools in the early 21st century look like? A general answer might be to say that it is challenging. But in what ways? What does this challenging situation really look like? We would like to highlight four factors that seem to be present in most of the business school environments that we have come across during recent years.

GLOBAL

The business school market for students and faculty is a global one. Faculty need to bear this in mind when teaching or undertaking research. All the top tiered schools are competing in the same global market.

LIFELONG LEARNING

The relationship between student and school is a long one. There is the need to find appropriate ways of engaging in lifelong learning. The MBA-student, for example, is no longer a student for a year or two at a business school, but part of the alumni and potentially a lifelong learning partner. Seen from a business school perspective this means, hopefully, they will be candidates for several courses in various forms of executive education programs over the years and enjoy a fruitful ongoing relationship.

DIVERSITY

A global school population is of course a diverse population, one that encompasses different culture and religious backgrounds (see, for example, Chapter 9 by Ngambi in this volume). In contemporary business school environments there is the desire to increase and learn from gender, religious and cultural diversity.

RANKINGS

Business schools pay a great deal of attention to their rankings. This has several consequences: First, there is the risk of focusing on short-term actions to improve rankings, that is, trying to break the code of the particular ranking and focus on these aspects without looking at the specific conditions in the business school at hand. Second, there is the risk of implicitly accepting the criteria set up by the rankings, instead of thinking about how to differentiate a particular business school and build upon specific strengths. Third, there is the risk in the longer term that the rankings will commoditize business schools, that is, lower ranked business schools will try to copy the higher ranked one.

What do these factors mean to the people working in the business school environment? We have identified two key characteristics: 'being with self' and 'being with others'.

First, in common now with many other professions, a faculty member's career is a self-managed career. Their career can be seen in terms of how successful the person can be without help or support (see, for example, Dent et al. 1994). The promotion rules in schools are usually transparent: the route through successful teaching and publishing, being a good citizen, having an external profile amongst colleagues includes all these crucial elements which need attention and are jigsaw pieces the individual needs to fit together (see also, for example, Chapter 21 by Djelic et al. in this volume; Boyer 1990). All this with the clock running.

Second, again in common with many other professions, faculty in business schools are members of a community in the school and globally amongst subject colleagues. This is the element of being with others. Whatever a faculty member's tendency to introversion or extroversion, finding stimulation, beneficial networks of professional friends and colleagues can support, invigorate and rejuvenate this professional life over time.

Challenges

Given this context, a number of challenges are apparent.

COACHING DOES NOT FIT IN THE PATTERN

In a business school environment there is most often a cultural pressure to conform by delivering courses and producing research. Individual professional development coaching for faculty members does not fit into this pattern: it is not a course and it is not research. Nevertheless, it may be highly important both for the teaching and the research at the school.

THE PARALLEL TO THE STUDENTS' SITUATIONS

Faculty members should recognize that they are both role-models for students and face similar challenges to the students. In coaching situations they need to open up and abandon their position as role model and instead acknowledge the fact that they are in a similar situation to most of their students. This means that there is a need for faculty members to be able to move between these roles. There is also the need to provide a level of trust that will enable them to open up and fully discuss their situation.

SHORT-TERM DEADLINES ARE TOUGH

When the level of stress reaches a certain point it is difficult to respond to anything apart from the short-term deadlines. If you are about to have a case discussion in an MBA class early one morning and you have not yet prepared sufficiently, it is difficult to have a coaching session late in the afternoon the day before the session. Or if you have a deadline for an important submission of a paper it is difficult to focus on the long-term issues important for your professional development. The timing of a coaching session is thus an important pre-condition for success.

Four fundamental principles

We see four fundamental principles for individual professional development coaching. These are principles that we have found crucial in the context of working with professionals in self-managed careers, specifically academics in business schools. These principles originate from our work in education, how people learn and in psychotherapy, how people think about their situations. Put crudely, the coaching we are discussing is to help people to learn about their situations and thus be as skillful as possible in managing these situations. From our perspective these principles differentiate successful, time efficient, sustainable development from the inadequate, ill-conceived and swiftly forgotten.

IPD COACHING IS NOT REMEDIAL

Our first principle is to make explicit what individual professional development (IPD) coaching is *not* – it is not remedial. In other words, individual professional development coaching or, in this context, faculty coaching, is not like something you take to cure a problem. We propose coaching as a positive process of reflection for the individual in complex self-managed careers. As illustrated by Chris, modern business school life requires a great deal from faculty and regular considered reflection should be viewed as a highly positive, appropriate response to the challenges faculty face.

IPD COACHING IS VOLUNTARY

Our first principle leads to our second. Coaching needs to be voluntary. As with any form of real learning, there is no use trying to force anyone into this type of coaching, even if you can see that the individual will gain from it. Coaching is a positive choice.

IPD COACHING IS CONFIDENTIAL

Our third principle says that the coaching is confidential. Working within an organization with all faculty of course means that the fact that someone is being coached is common knowledge. What is never public knowledge is the content of what is said and worked on within the coaching relationship. The principle of confidentiality underlines that the process is developmental rather than linked to the school's evaluation or promotion systems.

IPD COACHING HAPPENS OVER TIME

Our fourth principle highlights the process aspect of coaching and states that coaching takes place over time. This is not a one-off event, but rather a process over time. Whilst our example of Chris, is of a rookie en route to tenure, our fourth principle clearly states that coaching is something for everyone at every stage of the academic career. You might easily get the impression that individual faculty coaching is of most importance at a certain stage of a career, for example, early in your career. Our experiences are unequivocal – individual professional development coaching is for everyone at every stage. The questions, concerns, preoccupations and challenges vary considerably between different stages, but the need and the potential gains are the same. The development of the individual is about a lifelong learning process and not something you do once or twice and then stop.

Our experience shows that if these four principles are adhered to, faculty soon adopt coaching as a developmental process of choice. If there is reluctance, the first place to look for the reason is not with the individual, but with where these principles are being contradicted.

Alternative forms of coaching

How may the coaching best be done? Our preferred alternative is to use a fairly loose structure where the individual faculty member can choose herself when and how often to meet with the coach. Schools can make an atmosphere where it is good to do professional development and part of that is seeing a coach. At some schools it is assumed that everyone will want to meet with a coach. The real choice is later on, in how much work they then do with the coach.

Another, more drastic, alternative is to not have a coach; remember that the chapter is about *coaching*, not about coaches. The coaching may be done amongst colleagues. (See the example illustrated in the context of feedback on teaching Chapter 17 by Pugel and Shubert in this volume. See also, for example, Chism 2007.) As we have mentioned, trust is an important keyword in individual professional coaching. From this it follows that, if the coaching is carried out amongst colleagues, it is important to have a trusting relationship. Coaching around specific teaching situations may be easier amongst colleagues compared to coaching around future career choices. Remember the potential conflicts related to promotion issues, for example, (as illustrated in the example of Chris) if coaching is carried out between colleagues. But it is worth highlighting that coaching is not only something you can do with a full-time coach, someone entirely dedicated to the coaching role, you can move into the role of the coach amongst colleagues, with a certain degree of care.

Critical success factors

What does it take to do all this? There is, of course, not one single answer to this question, but to conclude this chapter we want to point to a number of elements that we have found to be critical success factors for this type of IPD coaching in a business school environment.

FROM THE PROFESSIONAL'S PERSPECTIVE

Seen from the faculty member's perspective, you need:

1. A *willingness* and an *interest* to participate in the coaching and by extension work on the development of your own professional career.
2. A *commitment* to invest the *time* needed to participate, in spite of other short-term deadlines which may interfere with the series of coaching sessions.
3. An *openness*, that is, to open up and be willing to discuss what may be sensitive issues.

FROM THE ORGANIZATIONAL PERSPECTIVE

Seen from the business school's perspective:

1. *Resources* are of course needed to conduct this kind of coaching. The cost is limited for each individual, but depending on the scope of the coaching initiatives the total amount of resources required may be substantial.
2. A *commitment* is required from school management that professional development is important. This commitment will also serve as a role model for students: the fact that the faculty and the school engage in continuing professional development is a good example to the students.
3. There should be a *coaching culture* within the school where coaching is offered alongside a variety of developmental activities, that is, workshops on various aspects of teaching and research, induction days, courses from external professionals, mentoring systems around the content of their work, the International Teachers Programme, appraisal systems, and so on.

FROM THE COACHING PERSPECTIVE

Seen from the coach's perspective:

1. *Qualifications* for the task are a prerequisite. The coach needs to be skilled for the assignment and to have enough knowledge about the specific context.
2. *Independence* is another keyword for the coach, who should work for the individual and nothing else. The coach should never be involved in any form of evaluation or recruitment processes linked to the individual faculty member.
3. *An interest in the business school environment* is another important factor for the coach. Given the specific context of a business school (as discussed above) it is important that the coach has an interest in both understanding and acting within this type of context.

So Chris and others, no matter how coaching is taking place, and under what circumstances, please keep in mind that *a career involving reflection at a business school is most definitely a career worth having*!

References

Antonacopoulou, E., (2008). *Mastering Business Action: Implications for Management Learning in Business Schools*, in this volume.

Argyris, C., (1982). *Reasoning, Learning, and Action: Individual and Organizational*. San Francisco, California: Jossey-Bass Publishers.

Argyris, C., and Schön, D.A., (1974). *Theory in Practice: Increasing Professional Effectiveness*. San Francisco, California: Jossey-Bass Publishers.

Boyer, E.L., (1990). *Scholarship Reconsidered: Priorities of the Professoriate*, The Carnegie Foundation for the Advancement of Teaching. San Francisco, California: Jossey-Bass Publishers.

Chism, N.V.N., (2007). *Peer Review of Teaching – A Sourcebook (second edition)*. Boston, Massachusetts: Anker Publishing Company Inc.

Christensen, C.R., Garvin, D.A., and Sweet, A. (eds.), (1991). *Education for Judgement: The Artistry of Discussion Leadership*. Boston, Massachusetts: Harvard Business School Press.

Dent, F., MacGregor, B., and Wills, S., (1994). *Signposts for Success: A Guide to Self-Managed Development*. London: Pitman Publishing.

Djelic, M-L., Gabel, L. and Sironi, A., (2008). *Pedagogical Leadership: Experiences from Three European Business Schools*, in this volume.

Ngambi, H., (2008). *Diversity Dynamics in Teaching*, in this volume.

Pugel, T. and Shubert, J., (2008). *Getting and Giving Feedback*, in this volume.

Schön, D.A., (1983). *The Reflective Practitioner: How Professionals Think in Action*. New York: Basic Books, Harper-Collins Publishers.

Schön, D.A., (1987). *Educating the Reflective Practitioner*. San Francisco, California: Jossey-Bass Publishers.

19 *Advice to a New Teacher*

Catharina Pramhäll

Introduction

Within the field of music, it is not that uncommon that some people write the music – the composers – and completely different persons perform the music – the musicians. In contrast, to be successful in the academic world – you both have to write (the research) and to perform (to teach). The majority of teachers in the academic world do both. The research is often well organized with support in the form of courses, tutors and different types of seminars. Unfortunately there is less guidance for teaching.

When the International Teachers Programme (ITP) was hosted by the Stockholm School of Economics 2003–2005, we gave the participants an assignment before we met with them for the first time face-to-face, in the first residential module. The purpose was to encourage the approximately 70 highly experienced teachers and faculty development managers from all around the world to reflect around an important issue. The assignment was the following:

A new teacher is employed at your institution. The teacher knows the subject very well but has no teaching experience. You are asked to give three pieces of advice to this new teacher.

The answers varied enormously, both regarding number of words and content. The shortest answers were:

* *Keep it simple;*
* *Most important first;*
* *Smile.*

The longest answer was two pages and contained many references to relevant literature.

There was a great variety in the answers. Most of the answers were very hands-on (*'practice in front of a mirror'*) but some were more philosophical (*'develop a teaching philosophy'*). You will find a summary of the answers from the 70 teachers in the list below. They are organized in order of appearance, and not presented in order or according to frequency. The list is followed by an elaboration of each piece of advice. Following the advice given by the faculty you will find a short review of some of the guidance available in the literature on teaching.

Summary of pieces of advice to a new teacher

* Develop a teaching philosophy.
* Learn more about teaching.
* Talk to your colleagues.
* Plan the course carefully.
* Be prepared (even over-prepared).

- Visit the location and check all practicalities.
- Have a clear outline of the lesson.
- Use a mix of different teaching techniques.
- Be confident.
- Give feedback to the students.
- Be aware of the power of assessment.
- Don't apologise and never bite off more than you can chew.
- Keep cool if everything doesn't work perfectly the first time.
- Establish a balance.
- Remember students have brains.
- Don't forget to enjoy yourself!

DEVELOP A TEACHING PHILOSOPHY

Successful teachers have a variety of different styles. There is no best way of teaching. Don't try to adopt or copy anybody else's style but build on your own strengths as an individual. One way to achieve this is to reflect on your own experiences of teachers as a student. Who were the good (and bad) teachers that you remember from your own education?

Another way is to observe more experienced teachers teach. Select colleagues on the basis of their experience and expertise in delivering sessions. Ideally, try and look for a mix of different teacher styles. Set up a repertoire of ingredients you may want to try when you develop your own teaching style. But never forget that you have to build on your own personal style.

LEARN MORE ABOUT TEACHING

There are several ways of learning about teaching. You can read the literature on effective teaching strategies. You can also pursue the teaching development opportunities which are available at your school; short workshops ('How to use PowerPoint') and longer sessions (International Teachers Programme) are often provided.

TALK TO YOUR COLLEAGUES

Don't forget that you are not alone. Don't hesitate to talk to more experienced teachers about all kind of questions. Try to find a competent colleague that you trust and teach together with them in a teaching session in order to get some teaching experience and to build your self-confidence. You can discuss lesson outlines, material and problems. The colleague can also sit in while you are teaching to give feedback. Some schools have mentor programs to help new teachers.

PLAN THE COURSE CAREFULLY

Find out how your course (or part of a course) relates to other parts of the program – the position of the course in the portfolio of courses offered by the school. What level of understanding should you expect among the participants when the course starts?

Find out as much information about the audience as possible in order to tailor your course effectively. Keep in mind that every student is a person who uses his or her time to listen to you instead of doing something else, in other words is there by choice. Make sure to have a clear and shared understanding about the expectations with your group of students – what you expect from the students and what can they expect from you.

The next step is to set the learning objectives and to decide which activities and what content will help to achieve them.

BE PREPARED (EVEN OVER-PREPARED)

Each lesson needs to be very well organized and planned. Avoid preparing too many slides. Concentrate on a few well-prepared ones. PowerPoint is a wonderful aid – if used selectively. Prepare all your material a few weeks before the course so that you have the opportunity to review it a week before the class. That will also give you more time to get feedback from more experienced colleagues.

Your will probably speak faster than you expect. Develop a plan A, a plan B and also plans C and D according to the time available. Time management is essential. To practice in front of a mirror could be very useful. There is no substitute for preparation – whatever your level of experience.

VISIT THE LOCATION AND CHECK ALL PRACTICALITIES

Visit the classroom a week before the start of class to get a sense of the atmosphere of the room and decide where to stand during the lesson. First impressions last; decide where you will be in the classroom when the students arrive – the idea is that they will find you happy, confident and well organized.

Try writing on the whiteboard and check the size and legibility of your writing (too small may be hard to read and too large may patronize the class). Check that the text can be seen from all parts of the classroom. Look at the number of whiteboards and plan how, and in which order, to fill them with text. Practice smiling in the classroom and demonstrating a confident demeanour.

Return to the classroom on the day (or the day before) you are due to teach to check lighting, sockets, technology, and so on. If you are using any technology be sure to have the phone number for the technical support team. Always have an alternative ready in case your computer has a bad day.

HAVE A CLEAR OUTLINE OF THE LESSON

One of the great skills of teaching is catching and holding the attention of the students. The first challenge is to get their attention with an opening that has impact. The next is to communicate the learning objectives of the lesson to the students. Identify the key messages of each lesson and build a story around them.

Involve the students in discussion at an early stage so they are engaged from the outset. Don't cram too much information into any one lecture and do not rush. The best teachers have a great ability to explain complex ideas in simple, understandable ways. Allow time during the session for the students to reflect upon what you tell them.

It is important to remain connected to the class. Ask yourself are you immediately aware whenever the class or parts of the class get lost? Do you know why this is?

USE A MIX OF DIFFERENT TEACHING TECHNIQUES

Students have individual preferences for how they learn most effectively. Varying your approach is therefore important to keep them engaged.

Vary the teaching methods used in each session. Twenty minutes is a reasonable time for lecturing before a change of approach is required. Lecturing, small-group discussions, use of the projector and writing on the whiteboard, are just some of the possible approaches. Case studies, computer simulations and practical examples (tailored to the group of students) may also be used.

Students learn best if they are actively involved in the learning process through discussions, presentations, exercises, games, a round robin, and so on. Try to encourage them to participate and share their experiences with the rest of the class.

When you involve the students be aware of cultural differences and how different students may respond.

BE CONFIDENT

Smile! Try to appear confident and relaxed (even if you're not). Any nervousness on behalf of the speaker is transmitted instantly to the audience who automatically start to feel uncomfortable too. Trust yourself – you are the expert!

Be careful not to be over-confident, projecting yourself as an arrogant person. Act with natural authority. Stand straight and establish eye contact. It is important to have eye contact with every single student in the class at least once during the session. One way of doing this is to think of the classroom as split into six squares. Talk to each square in a planned order (see Figure 19.1).

Don't talk to the overhead machine or to the whiteboard – talk to the audience. And again – smile!

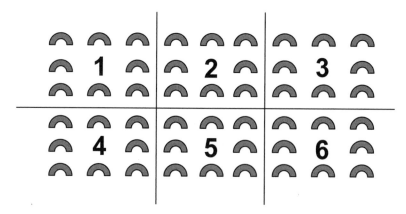

Figure 19.1   Model for splitting the classroom into sections

GIVE FEEDBACK TO THE STUDENTS

Always take time to give feedback on the assignments that the students hand in. This is one of the best ways to help them to learn. Reading a number of papers can be boring – so try to keep the interest with a smile!

BE AWARE OF THE POWER OF ASSESSMENT

Assessment tends to drive most curricula and it is important to incorporate innovative, practical and relevant methods of assessment, which will facilitate deep learning. Deep learning refers to a student's ability to understand, formulate arguments and concepts, relate new knowledge to existing knowledge, apply theory to everyday life, provide evidence, formulate and organize a coherent argument, and internalize the knowledge.

Consider carefully the objectives of the course and design assessments that test if these objectives have been achieved. See the assessment as a way to check if your material is working – is there anything that could be improved in the course?

DON'T APOLOGIZE AND NEVER BITE OFF MORE THAN YOU CAN CHEW

Never start your lesson with an apology or an explanation as to your qualifications.

Do not take on a course with a large number of students until you feel confident in your material and in your ability to sustain the teaching quality for a larger group. It can also be a bad experience to take on a course prepared by someone else and to be asked to deliver it as yours.

KEEP COOL IF EVERYTHING DOESN'T WORK PERFECTLY THE FIRST TIME

Teaching is a question of practice and improving is a trial and error process. Keep a note of what went well and what didn't so you can adjust things accordingly next time. Use the assessments to identify potential improvements.

Your teaching quality can always be improved. Actively solicit feedback from your students. Students can play an important role in helping you to develop your teaching skills and should be actively involved in that process.

Don't try to change everything all in one go. Introduce one improvement at a time: 'This lesson my mission is to establish eye contact with every student (see above).' 'This lesson I will keep all my slides and notes in a good order.'

And don't forget that it is always possible to improve. When you deliver the same lesson in the same way year after year – and don't bother to think about changes – it is probably time to change to another profession.

ESTABLISH A BALANCE. REMEMBER, STUDENTS HAVE BRAINS AND DON'T FORGET TO ENJOY YOURSELF!

It is very important to establish a balance between teaching and the rest of your life. Early in your career, teaching preparation, marking and dealing with student problems can take up a considerable amount of time. Make time for research, administration, family, friends and hobbies.

Remember that the students have brains too. It is your job to make them use them. You are not really there to teach them but to help them in their learning process. They must do the work, not you, but they need your help!

Be yourself when you teach. Enjoy and show engagement. If you cannot develop these facets of teaching – seek another job!

Background theory

There are plenty of books about teaching and learning. For example, *Learning to Teach in Higher Education* by Paul Ramsden (2003). In chapter 6 Ramsden discusses the nature of good teaching in higher education. He also provides a list of the important properties of good teaching seen from the individual lecturer's perspective:

- a desire to share your love of the subject with students;
- an ability to make the material being taught stimulating and interesting;
- a facility for engaging with students at their level of understanding;
- a capacity to explain the material plainly;
- a commitment to making it absolutely clear what has to be understood, at what level, and why;
- showing concern and respect for students;
- a commitment to encouraging student independence;
- an ability to improve and adapt to new demands;
- using teaching methods and academic tasks that require student to learn thoughtfully responsibly, and cooperatively;
- using valid assessment methods;
- a focus on key concepts, and students' misunderstandings of them, rather than on covering the ground;
- giving the highest-quality feedback on student work;
- a desire to learn from students and other sources abut the effects of teaching and how it can be improved.

There is considerable synergy between the advice from the teachers participating in ITP and the properties listed by Ramsden. To be an enthusiastic and confident teacher is important – as is good course planning. Assessment and feedback are also highlighted by the teachers and by Ramsden.

Some of the pieces of advice from the teachers are more overtly hands-on than the features listed by Ramsden, for example the advice to check the location, to smile, to use a different mix of teaching styles and to engage the students. Some of the teachers may have found very specific pieces of advice more useful to a new teacher than generalities. This may also be the reason why no teachers explicitly referred to Ramsden's comments about 'concern and respect for students' and 'to encourage student independence'.

The importance of the school

One important feature, in line with some of the advice from the teachers, is that the school environment should value teaching and provide adequate resources to help a new teacher. In Chapter 12 of his book, Ramsden discusses what it takes to improve teaching in higher education. It is important to create a good climate for teachers and for teaching. The school needs to have clear policies and reward systems that promote good teaching. There should also be resources available for training and for discussions with more experienced colleagues.

Conclusion

A new teacher needs considerable support before their first session. It does not follow that a successful researcher also is a good teacher. I hope that this chapter has provided some useful advice to enable a new teacher to become a self-confident, relaxed, and, therefore, successful teacher. It is important for the teacher to choose a school which has an approach to teaching that resonates with their own.

Reference

Ramsden, P., (2003). *Learning to Teach in Higher Education* (Second Edition). London: RoutledgeFalmer.

Outside the Classroom

Leading and Developing Business Schools

20 Business Schools' International Networks for Faculty Development

Ferdinando Pennarola

Introduction

Business schools are powered by ideas. The essentials of management education are producing and disseminating knowledge, thus responding to a higher goal, that is educating managers. Ideas in business schools are secured in the brains of their people: professors, researchers, management educators are the engine of these organizations. Today, one may argue to what extent these engines are in fact free to circulate in the market for the ideas or they are safely protected inside their home institutions.

In this chapter the extent to which the professors' labour market is a true internationalized arena or still a collection of local needs is not discussed. It may lead to a theoretical debate where boundaries are not defined yet. One factor, indeed, acts as a mediating ingredient in the circulation of ideas: that is organizational networks of schools dedicated to the education of their engines.

For some obscure reasons, partially investigated in this chapter, *'teaching teachers how to teach'* seems to be one of the most long-lasting cooperative examples where a network of leading business schools still prospers. Many other networks, dedicated to research or to joint programme management, for example, have been alive for a given time window. But very few have survived as long as the one that has grown with the International Teachers Programme (ITP).

This chapter collects facts that have developed over almost 40 years of history, related to the International Teachers' Programme story, and frames them in an interpretative skeleton useful to comprehend and interpret why there is so much consideration to cultivating faculty engines.

A useful framework, composed by three

Nothing is as practical as a good theory! In this paragraph a framework is introduced to draw boundaries that will portray the networking efforts initiated by both faculty and their institutions. The main character here is the ITP. The International Teachers Programme is a faculty development programme organized by the International Schools of Business Management (ISBM), a group of ten leading business schools located in Europe and the United States. ITP also welcomes business educators from outside ISBM. ITP has served over 1000 high-calibre faculty and educators from many countries since it started more than 30 years ago. During this period, the Programme has rotated between ISBM Schools. ITP is hosted by the SDA Bocconi School of Management for the academic years 2007–2008 and 2008–2009. Given the enduring cooperation among the ISBM members in running the programme, one can say that the ITP is the epitome of what business schools' international networks have achieved so far.

The objective of this chapter is to demonstrate that the joining of and staying with a network dedicated to 'teaching teachers how to teach' constitutes an adoption of a distinctive ribbon that communicates how mindful the school is to the education of faculty in a core activity like teaching.

Before plunging into facts and figures, it's useful to clarify the theoretical framework within which the story can be read.

THE INSTITUTIONAL PERSPECTIVE

The institutional approach can be considered the dominant perspective for explaining the decision for adopting an innovation. It points out the importance of institutional environments for shaping organizational actions leading firms residing in an organizational field to increasingly resemble each other, resulting in institutional isomorphism (Tingling and Parent 2002).

DiMaggio and Powell (1983) distinguish among three types of institutional pressures: mimetic, coercive and normative.

Mimetic pressure may lead an organization to change over time to become more similar to other organizations in the same institutional environment (DiMaggio and Powell 1983). Therefore it generates conformity with similar organizations in the same organizational field (that is, competitors) (Westphal et al. 1997). The mimetic pressure exerts its influence mostly when innovations are uncertain and ambiguous (DiMaggio and Powell 1983; March and Olsen 1976) which occurs in the early adoption stage (Rogers 2003). For example, firms are more likely to comply with mimetic pressure in order to reduce research costs (Cyert and March 1963), or to minimize experimentation costs (Levitt and March, 1988).

Coercive pressure is defined as formal or informal pressure exerted on organizations by other organizations upon which they are dependent (DiMaggio and Powell 1983). Organizations characterized by dependence in terms of resources controlled by a dominant actor are more likely to comply with decisions made by the dominant actor itself (Teo et al. 2003; Pfeffer and Salancik 1978; DiMaggio 1988). The dominant actor could be: the government, suppliers or customers, and parent corporations (DiMaggio and Powell 1983; Teo et al. 2003). Following Teo et al. (2003) reasoning, we argue that in the context of giving business schools' professors an international exposure, the dominant actor is represented by the recognized leading school in the marketplace of ideas. Indeed, minor schools are compelled to adopt organizational practices, and technologies that are compatible with them (DiMaggio and Powell 1983).

Normative pressure can be considered the sharing of norms and values through relational channels among members of a network. These channels facilitate the agreement about the effectiveness of norms and values which in turn influences the strength of these norms and values in conditioning the organizational behaviour.

Literature takes into consideration different normative relational channels, such as, relational channels with suppliers, customers and organizational associations (DiMaggio and Powell 1983; Burt 1982).

We follow Burt (1982) and Teo et al. (2003) considering suppliers and customers as the main source of normative influence. Indeed organizations having direct and frequent communication are more likely to show similar behaviours (Burt 1982; Rogers 2003). Thus, communication with customers and suppliers that already have adopted a given approach to educating teachers leads the focal organization to be exposed to this approach.

MANAGEMENT FASHION PERSPECTIVE

Management fashion perspective has its roots in New Institutional Theory (Meyer and Rowan 1977; Scott and Meyer 1994; DiMaggio and Powell 1991), and in the production of cultural literature (Hirsch 1972). Green (2004) defines management fashion theory as a variant of New Institutional Theory. Institutional perspective and management fashion perspective have in common the following assumption: the decision to adopt an innovation is not characterized by a rationalistic and independent assessment, but relies on the role played by the external environment in influencing the decision process (Fichman 2004).

Management fashion theory is based on the following assumption: norms both of rationality (Meyer and Rowan 1977) and progress govern managerial behaviour. Norms of managerial rationality are societal expectations that managers will use management techniques that are the most efficient means to important ends (Meyer and Rowan 1977). Norms of managerial progress are societal expectations that, over time, managers will use new and improved management techniques. Therefore, according to management fashion theory, it is important for managers to *cover* adoption decision with an *appearance* of economic rationality and progress. Such an objective can be achieved by adopting management techniques considered rational and progressive (Abrahamson 1996). Decision-makers use management fashion to communicate to organizational stakeholders that their organizations are consistent with institutional environment (that is, norms of rationality and progress) (Meyer and Rowan 1977). Therefore, through this mechanism, firms develop a certain degree of perceived progressiveness.

According to the General Model of Management Fashion Setting (Abrahamson 1996; Abrahamson and Fairchild 2001), norms of rationality and progress create a management fashion market for management fashions. The management fashion market is the arena in which (1) management fashion setters supply management fashions, and (2) management fashion consumers demand management fashions. Management fashion literature (Abrahamson and Fairchild 2001) has distinguished in the supply-side of fashion market a variety of knowledge organizations and idea entrepreneurs that create and disseminate new ideas, new knowledge, and new technologies (for example, business press organizations, professional communities, and so on). In particular, management fashion suppliers create and disseminate management fashions in order to trigger the diffusion of certain innovations. Therefore, they exert pressure over potential adopters.

Following this approach, wearing the distinctive ribbon of faculty development care in an international context may be viewed as a new thing with a management fashion dimension. Indeed, caring about faculty may be considered a rational strategy. Moreover, potential adopters may be exposed to fashion setter pressure in the form of business press articles, conferences in which other academics and consultants promote management fashion rhetoric, and meetings with colleagues (that is, academic research community meetings).

INTRA-ORGANIZATIONAL PERSPECTIVE

Institutional and management fashion perspective focus on the external forces that influence the adoption decision. Other studies point out that organizations adopt innovations to improve their performance (Fichman 2004). These studies are consistent with an efficiency-choice perspective (Tan and Fichman 2002; Abrahamson 1991). According to the efficiency-choice stream of research, the adoption of an innovation is influenced by factors within the organizational boundaries (Greve 1995). In particular it is possible to point out two dimensions: one focused on the economic benefits for the organization as a whole

(Saloner and Shepard 1995; Tan and Fichman 2002), the other focused on the adoption by individuals (that is, users) within the organization (Leonard-Barton and Deschamps 1988). Saloner and Shepard (1995) underscore that the propensity to adopt an innovation is positively related to the perceived benefits. Therefore, if firms perceive that caring about faculty in an international context can improve quality of teaching, they will be more likely to join and stay in a network. Moreover, Leonard-Barton and Deschamps (1988) focus both on primary and secondary adoption process. Primary adoption refers to the adoption decision made by the organization, while secondary adoption is the individual innovation adoption by users (Leonard-Barton and Deschamp 1988; Fichman 2000).

Users may play an important role in influencing the adoption process of innovations (Kettinger and Lee 2002). Indeed, users' informal and potential use of an innovation has an influence on the managers' beliefs about the internal benefits of the innovation (Leonard-Barton and Deschamp 1988). Therefore, managers responsible for taking the decision about organizational adoption should develop a particular attention toward users. Attention toward users/faculty refers to organizational ability to satisfy their needs and to perceive their emergent behaviours (Fichman 2000).

In a nutshell, the life and prosperity of a business school network, like the one developed around the International Teachers Programme, is sustained by the need to follow the leaders (institutional perspective), by the specific competitive environment in which the school operates (fashion perspective) and by its faculty (intra-organizational perspective).

Tracing ITP back to the early 1960s

The consortium that runs the ITP is by far one of the most renowned and extended cooperation examples among business schools networks.[1]

Perhaps, no greater testament to the power of ideas in management education exists than the Harvard Business School, the organization accounted for the 'case method'. And the history of cooperation in management education starts from Harvard, sometime around the mid 1960s, a reference point for many other business schools.

The ITP was created on the initiative of Emeritus Professor Harry Hansen by the Harvard Graduate School of Business in the early 1960s. It developed at a time there was a wide shortage of management teachers at the collegiate level. Support and funding came from the Ford Foundation and the US Agency for International Development. Professor Hansen was Chairman of the HBS International Division under Dean George Baker. The International Division promoted a global view of extending international management education and was responsible for the founding and nurturing of business schools in India, Pakistan, Turkey, the Philippines and Central America, all of which were started during Professor Hansen's chairmanship, who spent most of his time overseas in support of these operations.

A major element in the activities of the International Division was the training of the local staff for the fledging overseas institution. Education included the functional areas, finance, marketing, and so on, HBS philosophy in terms of case-based training as well as teaching skills – usually for a full year. At that time the solution was the ITP as a means for providing career development experience, not only for those schools in which Harvard had a special

---

1   The early days of the ITP re-constructed in paragraphs 3,4,5 and 6 are drawn from the only case study available on the subject by Sonia Heptonstall, *'Faculty Development: The International Teachers Programme. A Case Study'*, Interman – ILO, Geneva, 1991, from which we report ample excerpts.

interest, but also for business teachers from around the world. By looking at the Harvard alumni directories you discover that a high proportion of the participants were from European countries.

The initiative at the time had 'no programme' as such and hence no ITP nominated faculty. Participants themselves designed their own course of studies. There was a great deal of freedom for participants to take part in whatever MBA classes or Doctoral Programme activities they considered best suited for their needs.

Indeed Harvard was facing some critical issues in running the ITP, although faculty showed a substantial enthusiasm for the International Division. One may organize the criticism in the following points.

Since the ITP had been conceived in the sense of an enriching experience, consequently there was no opportunity for participants to earn a Harvard degree. The certificate that was given to participants stated that they simply attended the programme, but it was not considered satisfactory for many of them, since they invested a year in learning activities at Harvard and/or with Harvard faculty.

Faculty experienced mixed difficulties in managing the ITP participants. Some were frequently unprepared in comparison to the majority and required a great deal of faculty time: one-on-one in offices. Although the vast majority of ITP members were fine, hard-working and enriching to the Harvard community as a whole, each class had six or eight who soured the programme's image and cast doubts regarding the legitimacy of all who were associated with the ITP. The lack of selection and the lack of a centrally designed programme was amplifying all these difficulties.

The situation was made all the more complicated by those outstanding profiles that undertook heavy course loads in the MBA programme and received high grades. Some of them decided to stay at HBS and earn a Harvard degree. Some of the ITP applicants had learned about the ITP from HBS faculty members. Professor Hansen himself was active in setting up short-term executive programmes in various European locations – UK, Spain, Switzerland. Others such as Professor Christensen and George Albert Smith were involved with IMEDE as part of a consulting relationship between them and Nestlé Corporation.

The overall value of the ITP experience was under attack. From one side there were pressures to make admission requirements more stringent, to require all participants who attended HBS courses to be graded on the same basis as degree candidates, and to issue certificates to be awarded only in the case of those that received satisfactory evaluations. By the end of 1967 it became clear that ITP would not survive at the HBS unless candidates could marry up to the regular requirements for entry to the School.

The early stages of business schools' networking

In 1969, HBS decided to move the ITP to Europe in order to find out solutions to the mentioned troubles and more. There was a growing sense that the Harvard faculty were not sufficiently international in their outlook, with little hands-on teaching experience in a different culture. This was clashing with the fact that many US corporations were expanding through enlarged operations overseas. Second, HBS was benefiting from a changed business schools environment out of the US; some of the European colleagues in their own institutions were running high-quality respectable management education programmes using the local faculty only. For instance, London Business School was established in 1964 and by the end of the 1960s they gained autonomy and independent status.

Third, the change of the HBS Dean was the occasion to review the internationalization strategy of the School. Time had changed and the benefits of the International Division were less clear-cut, thus turning it down and letting Dr Hansen resume his faculty responsibilities with full-time teaching on the MBA programme.

It was decided to introduce HBS activities directly into Europe, by opening a counterpart of the Advanced Management Programmes in Mt. Pellerin in Switzerland. Full-time HBS faculty were assigned to this initiative and were asked to move to Europe along with their families for longer stays, often more than 1-year long. In parallel, facilities for the ITP were found in Leysin, Switzerland, with major restructuring. From being a generally unstructured 1-year experience, the Programme now evolved into a highly structured 2-month activity. It was during this phase that the ITP began to take on the characteristic of a 'mini MBA', by using both Harvard faculty and some of the best known European school's faculty invited as guest speakers.

It was 1972 when Harvard made a decisive move by inviting seven European management schools to join with them in the further development and management of the ITP. These schools, which subsequently became the 'consortium schools', were:

CESA – Centre d'Enseignement Supérieur des Affaires (subsequently HEC-ISA).
CEI – Centre d'Etudes Industrielles (subsequently IMI).
IMEDE – Institut pour l'Etude des Methodes de Direction.
IAE – Institut d'Administrration des Enterprises.
INSEAD – Institut Europeen d'Administration des Affaires.
LBS – London Business School.
MBS – Manchester Business School.

IMI and IMEDE merged in 1988 and they established the International Institute for Management Development (IMD) located in Lausanne, Switzerland.

Cooperation and networking was done by delegating to an informal board of schools' representatives the management of the ITP and the appointment of a programme director. The reasons for starting a consortium with the above listed organizations are still rather obscure. It seems that Harvard faculty were looking for reputation in local markets and leverage of personal contacts, like the ones that flourished in the past in Switzerland with Nestlé (founder of IMEDE).

It appears clear that 'joining the Harvard community' was perceived as a precious opportunity offered to a few. The institutional pressures and the fact of being considered as a 'fashion setter' was a unique position to undertake, regardless of the difficulties and obstacles to overcome.

The institutionalization phases of business schools' networking

During 1975–1976 it became increasingly necessary to provide ITP activity with a valid legal identity. Harvard wanted to reduce their involvement in the programme and expressed the wish to leave the management in the hands of the European consortium members. In parallel, Ford Foundation decided to cut their funding because they believed ITP was capable of self sustaining. It must be clarified that Harvard was at the time acting as the operating arm of the Foundation: funds were made available from the US School, and the withdrawal of HBS would clearly leave a legal vacuum. To whom should the balance of the funds be transferred? To fill this void a new company was created, International Schools of Business Management, that was incorporated at London Business School on January 7th , 1977 as a charity under the UK law. The inaugural meeting of the Board of Directors under the chairmanship of Professor Peter Moore was held at LBS on Monday, January 24th, 1977.

To reach this end a long negotiation phase was undertaken by the eight schools. By May 1976 a draft Memorandum of Association and Articles of Association for the company were available. The inspiring model was the one of the Case Clearing House of Great Britain and Ireland, incorporated on August 16th, 1973, acting as a management education company limited by guarantee. This was a landing scene of long discussions where it was agreed that the ITP could not be owned but only influenced by the consortium schools. The company would register as a charity in order to avoid any tax on both its profits and its investments, and this was helpful to keep the ITP costs at a minimum for the participating schools.

It was a difficult season for the ITP indeed: when deciding on governance matters like who has the power to call a board meeting, or who will appoint a Chairperson, the discussions were endless. Some institutions challenged the position of others. Each had their internal difficulties with incorporation. In the meantime the European Foundation for Management Development (EFMD) was also invited to sit on the Board. Further matters needed resolving. The tax free nature of the new association excluded any Director from being an employee of the company. CESA, however, had nominated Dr Michel Schlosser who was at the time the Director of the current edition of the ITP. The problem was solved by going ahead with seven schools only but inviting Professor Schlosser to company meetings as an observer.

The old consortium could not be dissolved until June 1977, so a 6-month overlap existed during which the new company had to deal with future policy beyond 1977 and managing the operating arrangement for the 1977 ITP edition.

Membership changes

The first change in the membership of ISBM came later in the fall of 1977 when the Stockholm School of Economics was invited to join, but a major milestone in the development of the charity came in 1979 when the Harvard Business School announced its decision to withdraw completely from the programme. This major change occurred when it appeared clear that management education was approaching a degree of maturity in Europe. The missionary role of the International Division at HBS encouraged confidence that its own case study method was universally applicable, and this role seemed to have come to an end. Second, as it will emerge later in the international scene, HBS had progressively introduced a number of faculty training programmes and seminars that were more attractive for Harvard faculty rather than ITP. Harvard resignation was accepted at the ISBM board meeting in Stockholm on May 19th, 1979.

It is interesting to notice that in this case the intra-organizational pressures of the Harvard faculty caused the detachment of HBS from the ISBM. The cost of stay in the network was perceived as higher than the expected benefits.

The withdrawal of Harvard gave the rise to a lively and prolonged debate as to whether or not ISBM should now be an all-European organization or whether it was desirable to include one or more North American members as Harvard successors. It was stated that although the European experience was a success, a board presence from the Americas would be beneficial to the programme itself by making it more attractive for faculty from US and Canada. Various possibilities were examined, but it was finally decided to invite the Graduate School of Business Studies of the New York University (today Leonard Stern School of Business).

This joining of the Stern School was a brave move for a US school at that time. It definitely demonstrated to the European community that the new American school was as sensible and prepared to manage faculty development as HBS was.

Further additions were examined in the following years. An everlasting debate during many board meetings was often dedicated to the 'Spanish case' in order to explore the cooptation of a leading Spanish institution. These types of cooptation were always examined under the perspective of an expansion of the programme reach to some geographical areas where the ITP was either unknown or not fully attractive.

One explanation of the continuous denial and failure of joining the ITP network by Spanish institutions can be traced back to the lack of the fashion effect for those schools.

Most of these discussions never came to an end. The subsequent addition to the ISBM was Sda Bocconi in 1985. Bocconi had, in fact, had a close relationship with the ITP since the early stages when the programme was held at Harvard. Claudio Demattè, Sda Bocconi's main character in the establishment process of the Italian school took his ITP as the full year at Harvard and then he sponsored the initiative for all of the young established faculty founding team of Sda Bocconi in the early 1970s.

In this case the opportunity of joining such a network and thus entering the 'fashion setters' community as well as the intra-organizational pressures of Sda Bocconi faculty willing to be exposed to international education on teaching worked as key success factors.

The last expansion of the ISBM was in 2002 when the Kellogg School of Management, Northwestern University was invited to join the group. This was due not only to strong personal ties of board members with Kellogg leaders that facilitated the initial talks, but also thanks to a highly reputed image of excellence in teaching and learning of Kellogg. It was a key move made by the ISBM board to deliberately strengthen the image and the presence of the ITP in the US and Canada.

Table 20.1 reports how the ISBM composition changed over the years, since establishment in 1977.

Programme changes

At least two elements must be considered to view the evolution of the programme over the years.

DIFFICULTIES IN SCHEDULING

The summer schedule, a tradition of the ITP since its European landing, was hardly fitting with the personal schedules and research agenda of a young assistant professor and target ITP Faculty. The research agenda was in fact concentrated in the summer time (Table 20.2 reports all annual ITP editions since formation in Europe). Because of this, combined with a decline of participants in the early part of the 1990s, the ITP was progressively reduced in length. From the 2-month summer full-time perspective of the early days when it arrived in Europe, the Insead's edition of 1994 became a 3-week programme in July.

Table 20.1   ISBM member business schools

Founding ISBM Members in 1977
HBS – Harvard Business School
CESA – Centre d'Enseignement Supérieur des Affaires, subsequently HEC-ISA, Paris
CEI – Centre d'Etudes Industrielles (subsequently IMI)
IMEDE – Institut pour l'Etude des Methodes de Direction
IAE – Institut d'Administrration des Enterprises
INSEAD – Institut Europeen d'Administration des Affaires
LBS – London Business School
MBS – Manchester Business School

ISBM Members in 1977, e.o.y.
HBS – Harvard Business School
CESA – Centre d'Enseignement Supérieur des Affaires, subsequently HEC-ISA, Paris
CEI – Centre d'Etudes Industrielles (subsequently IMI)
IMEDE – Institut pour l'Etude des Methodes de Direction
IAE – Institut d'Administrration des Enterprises
INSEAD – Institut Europeen d'Administration des Affaires
LBS – London Business School
MBS – Manchester Business School
SSE – Stockholm School of Economics
EFMD – European Foundation of Management Development

ISBM Members in 1979, e.o.y.
GBA – Graduate Business School of New York University (subsequently, L. Stern NYU)
CESA – Centre d'Enseignement Supérieur des Affaires, subsequently HEC-ISA, Paris
CEI – Centre d'Etudes Industrielles (subsequently IMI)
IMEDE – Institut pour l'Etude des Methodes de Direction
IAE – Institut d'Administrration des Enterprises
INSEAD – Institut Europeen d'Administration des Affaires
LBS – London Business School
MBS – Manchester Business School
SSE – Stockholm School of Economics
EFMD – European Foundation of Management Development

Table 20.1   *Continued*

ISBM Members in 1985
GBA – Graduate Business School of New York University (subsequently, L. Stern NYU)
HEC – ISA, Paris
CEI – Centre d'Etudes Industrielles (subsequently IMI)
IMEDE – Institut pour l'Etude des Methodes de Direction
IAE – Institut d'Administrration des Enterprises
INSEAD – Institut Europeen d'Administration des Affaires
LBS – London Business School
MBS – Manchester Business School
SSE – Stockholm School of Economics
EFMD – European Foundation of Management Development
SDA Bocconi – Scuola di Direzione Aziendale dell'Università L. Bocconi

ISBM Members in 1988
GBA – Graduate Business School of New York University (subsequently, L. Stern NYU)
HEC – ISA, Paris
IMD - Lausanne
IAE – Institut d'Administrration des Enterprises
INSEAD – Institut Europeen d'Administration des Affaires
LBS – London Business School
MBS – Manchester Business School
SSE – Stockholm School of Economics
EFMD – European Foundation of Management Development
SDA Bocconi – Scuola di Direzione Aziendale dell'Università L. Bocconi

ISBM Members in 2002 and today
STERN – NYU L. Stern
HEC – ISA, Paris
IMD - Lausanne
IAE – Institut d'Administrration des Enterprises
INSEAD – Institut Europeen d'Administration des Affaires
LBS – London Business School
MBS – Manchester Business School
SSE – Stockholm School of Economics
EFMD – European Foundation of Management Development
SDA Bocconi – Scuola di Direzione Aziendale dell'Università L. Bocconi
KELLOGG – at Northwestern

Table 20.2 ITP editions prior to the modular format

1994 Insead	1983 SSE
1993 Insead	1982 SSE
1992 IAE – Aix	1981 MBS
1991 IAE – Aix	1980 MBS
1990 IAE – Aix	1979 HEC-Isa
1989 Sda Bocconi	1978 HEC-Isa
1988 Sda Bocconi	1977 HEC-Isa
1987 HEC-Isa	1976 LBS
1986 HEC-Isa	1975LBS
1985 HEC-Isa	1974 Insead
1984 LBS	

RESEARCH CONFERENCES AND RESEARCH AGENDA

The Academy of Management traditionally meets for its annual conference in the second week of August. Given the pressure on research and high academic publication standards, the ITP August week was conflicting more and more with the research agenda of its target population. Moreover, the July/August slot, if not conflicting due to conferences for some, was creating problems for other participants because of personal holiday time or research agenda again. In fact, after the teaching loads ending in May/June, many potential ITP participants were concentrating their research efforts in the summer window of the year.

Thus the programme was conflicting with emerging needs of participants and this resulted in decreasing attendance.

During the progressive shrinking of the length of the ITP there occurred a parallel restructuring of the content. The HEC's editions in the mid-1980s had the 'teaching with the PC' flagship, given the parallel use of spreadsheets and other PC in the classroom initiatives spreading over the business schools' world. The Sda Bocconi editions of the end of the 1980s introduced outdoor training and the use of the voice and standing in the classroom, by leveraging lessons learned from performance theatre professional actors. The IAE at Aix-en-Provence's editions of the beginning of the 1990s brought into class the profound nature of learning processes by including in the ITP faculty prestigious researchers from all over the world. And finally the INSEAD's edition conveyed for the first time the e-learning and learning through simulations message as a culminating approach of leveraging information technologies in teaching.

It appears clear that the ITP network has returned to its 'shareholders' the desired content focus on every edition by continuously updating the themes of learning and teaching and riding the waves of fashion, as interpreted at the beginning of this chapter.

Need to refocus

During the ISBM Board Meeting held in London Business School in January 1994, a major decision was undertaken, that to some extent scared the Board members. The decision was to restructure the ITP from the existing summer residential programme toward a 1-year-long faculty development initiative, with two short residential modules, one in January and the second in July. The proposed solution, that marked the history of the initiative and realigned interest and cooperation of the consortium schools, was the following (drawn from ISBM's board meeting minutes):[2]

For some years now London Business School has had a Teacher Development Programme (TDP) enthusiastically supported by both new and experienced teaching faculty. Now that it is our turn to host the ITP, we have based the design on our own TDP and built upon the strengths of the current ITP.

Proposed innovations in programme design require the involvement of ITP participants throughout the academic year, with two periods of residence at the School in January and again in July. There will be a maximum of forty participants, ideally coming in pairs from the same educational institution. This structure provides teacher development opportunities in each participant's own teaching environment, as well as capitalizing on the resources available in the residential portions of the programme.

Throughout the year participants will be involved in preparing their own Teaching Case Study. This assignment will be structured by the Course Directors and the outcomes will be presented by the participants in January and July at the School. There could be the possibility of publishing these case studies at the end of the programme.

This programme provides the opportunity to show how seriously management educators and their institutions take teaching and to provide an international network of faculty with a common aim of teaching excellence. The proposed model of teacher development could be incorporated into the teacher development programmes already in place in the sponsoring schools'.

'The participants for the 1995–96 programme will be selected by early summer 1995. Selected participants must be teaching sometime during the programme year, and experienced teachers are encouraged to attend'.

'Participants will be interviewed by telephone, and information from the interviews and photos will be circulated among the participants (to allow them to begin making contacts with fellow participants). Participants will receive information about the teaching case assignment and a set of readings; the assignment will include participants' self analysis of teaching needs. They will be asked to observe teaching both in and outside of their teaching area, to give feedback on teaching to the other member of the pair, to be observed and videotaped while teaching an actual class, and to investigate the provision of teacher development and availability of learning technologies in their home educational institution.

One of the immediate consequence of this restructuring was the suspension of the 1995 edition, given that the move toward an academic year-long programme was conflicting with

---

2   Further insights on this key passage of the ITP experience are extensively discussed by Robertson and Morrison (1996).

the new schedule. This caused some worries at the Board level, but everyone agreed that the benefits (in communication terms as well) were far better than the costs of the move.

The restructuring around the modular format turned the ITP into another programme, at least if compared with the way it was implemented in the recent past. According to some interpretation, the modular design was trying to pick up all the best of the original 1-year long at Harvard design of the early 1960s.

In the end this refocusing was perceived as successful and appreciated by participants: they were finally able to limit the time of being away from the home institutions to roughly 2 weeks, but in two different time windows of the year. Moreover, there was the opportunity of investing in a lasting practice teaching project that would be beneficial in their careers.

The restructuring of the ITP embraces to a certain extent the key elements of the institutionalization theory discussed above: participants have to focus both on their learning as management educators and contextualize their achievements in their home institutions, thanks to the modular format.

Institutionalization achieved by rotation of responsibilities: a rejuvenating mechanism

Networking is not done for free. All parties have to invest something in the relationship; if someone perceives that contributions are not equally balanced, a discussion among partners will certainly arise. This takes place always in all networks where all parties have equal access and equal power. On January 20th, 2004, at the ISBM's Board meeting held at INSEAD, a policy document was approved that re-wrote the terms of collaboration and expected cooperation by board members and members schools.

Table 20.3   The modular edition of the programme

✓	2006-2007	IMD
✓	2005-2006	IMD
✓	2004-2005	SSE
✓	2003-2004	SSE
✓	2002-2003	MBS
✓	2001-2002	MBS
✓	2000-2001	NYU-STERN
✓	1999-2000	NUY-STERN
✓	1998-1999	NYU-STERN
✓	1997-1998	LBS
✓	1996-1997	LBS
✓	1995-1996	LBS

The document restated the distinctive characteristic of the ITP: the rotating responsibility of managing and offering the programme from one of the consortium schools is a mechanism that helps to keep the ITP updated. Thus, duties of every Board Member, as representative of their school's commitment to ISBM, include the acceptance of hosting and managing the ITP and other connected initiatives, when the proper moment comes. Among these obligations there is the selection of talented faculty to be proposed as a Programme Director. The ISBM Board will ultimately take the final decision to appoint the ITP's Programme Directors.

The philosophy and the design of the programme are paramount to make the ITP a success. Past experiences say that important ingredients are a) participants, b) faculty, c) programme directorship. Participants come as a result of a) directors' marketing effort, b) programme reputation, c) consortium schools support. At the same time, ISBM is formed by a group of top ranked business schools in the world. Consequently, rotating responsibilities are welcomed as long as the ITP succeeds in ranking as a top programme worldwide. In order to do so, Programme Directors have been counting on an internationally wide and super-talented faculty pool, coming from all the consortium schools as well as from elsewhere.

It is interesting to notice that, over the years, a number of other ITP-competing initiatives have emerged, some with alternate success, some turned out to be a true failure. At the same time, business schools at the ISBM ranking level have progressively articulated their international faculty development needs and expectations. One can certainly say that, in spite of the history and the 'brand name', the ITP is no longer at the heart of the internationalization and faculty networking strategies of major business schools as it probably was before. Nonetheless, the ITP strives for success every year and it succeeds in doing so, collecting an internationally-wide class in every edition. Where is the magic?

Conclusions and lessons learned

As the reader can understand, the described principles, strongly stated and continuously discussed within governance rooms of the ITP case, represents a full convergence of the institutional, fashion driven and intra-organizational causing factors that explain why the ITP network has survived. Like a pendulum, there was a continuous oscillation between two extremes: leave the network or stay. The final result is stay and consequently the joint initiative prospers. As always in reality, there was no magic behind this.

Lessons learned in business schools networks and cooperation say a key variable to keep under control is coordination costs: time and duties that parties have to devote to the joint initiative. As long as the initiative brings value to every single party, and consequently to the interested faculty, and governance keeps coordination costs at the minimum, the relationship continues, for a long time.

References

Abrahamson, E., (1991). Managerial fads and fashions: The diffusion and rejection of innovations. *Academy of Management Review*, 16: 586–612.

Abrahamson, E., (1996). Management fashion. *Academy of Management Review*, 21: 254–285.

Abrahamson, E., and Fairchild, G., (2001). Knowledge industries and idea entrepreneurs: New dimensions of innovative products, services, and organizations. In C.B. Schoonhoven and R.E. (Eds.), *The entrepreneurship dynamic: Origins of entrepreneurship and the evolution of industries*. Stanford: Stanford University Press.

Burt, R.S., (1982). *Toward a structural theory of action*. New York: Academic Press.

Cyert, R.M., and March, J.G., (1963). *A behavioral theory of the firm*. Englewood Cliffs, NJ: Prentice Hall.

DiMaggio, P.J., and Powell, W.W., (1991). Introduction. In W. W. Powell and P.J. DiMaggio (Eds.), *The new institutionalism in organizational analysis*. Chicago: University Of Chicago Press.

DiMaggio, P.J and Powell, W.W., (1983). The iron cage revisited: Institutional isomorphism and collective rationality in organizational fields. *American Sociological Review*, 48: 147–160.

DiMaggio, P.J., (1988). Interest and agency in institutional theory. In Lynne Zucker (Ed.), *Institutional patterns and organizational culture*, 3-22, Boston: Pitman.

Fichman, R.G., (2000). The diffusion and assimilation of information technology innovations. In R. W. Zmud (Ed.), *Framing the domains of it management research: Glimpsing the future through the past*. Cincinnati: Pinnaflex Education Resources, Inc.

Fichman, R.G., (2004). Going beyond the dominant paradigm for information technology innovation research: Emerging concepts and methods. *Journal for the Association of Information Systems*, 5(8): 314–355.

Green, S.E., (2004). A rhetorical theory of diffusion. *Academy of Management Review*, 29: 653–669.

Greve, H.R., (1995). Jumping ship: the diffusion of strategy abandonment. *Adminstrative Science Quarterly*, 40: 444–473.

Hirsch, P.M., (1972). Processing fads and fashions: An organization-set analysis of cultural industry systems. *American Journal of Sociology*, 77: 639–659.

IOSI (2006). *The Diffusion of VoIP in Italy*. Università Bocconi Research Report.

Kettinger, W.J., and Lee, C.C., (2002). Understanding the is-user divide in it innovation. *Communications of the ACM*, 45(2): 79–84.

Leonard-Barton, D., and Deschamps, I., (1988). Managerial influence in the implementation of new technology. *Management Science*, 34(10): 1214–1252.

Levitt, B., and March, J.G., (1988). Organizational learning. *Annual Review of Sociology*, 14: 319–338.

March, J., and Olsen, J., (1976). *Ambiguity and choice in organizations*. Bergen: Universitetsforlaget.

Meyer, J. W., and Rowan, B., (1977). Institutionalized organizations: Formal structures and myth and ceremony. *American Journal of Sociology*, 340–363.

Pfeffer, J., and Salancik, G.R., (1978). *The external control of organizations: A resource dependence perspective*. New York, NY: Harper & Row.

Robertson, T.S., and Gatignon, H., (1986). Competitive effects on technology diffusion. *Journal of Marketing*, 50(July): 1–12.

Robertson, D.C., and Morrison, P., (1996) Professional Development: the Individual Perspective, *Business Strategy Review*, 7(4 – Winter).

Rogers, E.M., (2003). *Diffusion of innovations*. New York: The Free Press.

Saloner, G., and Shepard, A., (1995). Adoption of technologies with network effects: An empirical examination of the adoption of automated teller machines. *RAND Journal of Economics*, 26(3): 479–501.

Scott, W.R., and Meyer, J.W., (1994). *Institutional environments and organizations: Structural complexity and individualism.* Newbury: Sage.

Tan, S.S.L., and Fichman, M., (2002). *Adoption of web-based transactional banking: Efficiency-choice and neo-institutionalism perspectives.* Paper presented at the Twenty-third International Conference on Information Systems, Barcelona.

Teo, H.H., Wei, K.K., and Benbasat, I., (2003). Predicting intention to adopt interorganizational linkages: An institutional perspective. *MIS Quarterly*, 27(1): 19.

Tingling, P.M., and Parent, M., (2002). Mimetic isomorphism & technology evaluation: Does imitation transcend judgment? *Journal for the Association of Information Systems*, 3(5): 113–143.

Westphal, J.D., Gulati, R., and Shortell, S.M., (1997). Customization or conformity? An institutional and network perspective on the content and consequences of TQM adoption. *Administrative Science Quarterly*, 42: 366–394.

Further reading

Abrahamson, E., and Fairchild, G., (1999). Management fashion: Lifecycles, triggers, and collective learning processes. *Administrative Science Quarterly*, 44: 708–740.

Ahuja, M.K., and Thatcher, J.B., (2005). Moving beyond intentions and toward the theory of trying: Effects of work environment and gender on post-adoption information technology use. *MIS Quarterly*, 29(3): 427–459.

Bajwa, D.S., Garcia, J.E., and Mooney, T., (2004). An integrative framework for the assimilation of enterprise resource planning systems: phases, antecedents, and outcomes. *Journal of Computer Information Systems*, 44(3): 81–90.

Carson, P.P., Lanier, P.A., and Carson, K.D., (2000). Clearing a path through the management fashion jungle: Some preliminary trailblazing. *Academy of Management Journal*, 43: 1143–1158.

Chengular-Smith, I., and Duchessi, P., (1999). The initiation and adoption of client-server technology in organizations. *Information and Management*, 35: 77–88.

Chin, W., (1998). Issues and opinions on structural equation modeling. *MIS Quarterly*, 22(1): 7–10.

D'Aveni, R.A., (1995). *Hypercompetion: Managing the dynamics of strategic maneuvering.* New York: Free Press.

Fichman, R.G., (2001). The role of aggregation in the measurement of it-related organizational innovation. *MIS Quarterly*, 25(4): 427–455.

Fishbein, M., and Ajzen, I., (1975). *Belief, attitude, intention and behavior: An introduction to theory and research.* Reading, MA: Addison-Wesley Publishing Company.

Gallivan, M.J., (2001). Organizational adoption and assimilation of complex technological innovations: Development and application of a new framework. *The DATA BASE for Advances in Information Systems*, 32(3): 51–85.

Jarvis, C.B., MacKenzie, S.B. and Podsakoff, M., (2003). A critical review of construct indicators and measurement model misspecification in Marketing and Consumer Research. *Journal of Consumer Research*, 30: 199–218

Orlikowski, W., (1992). The duality of technology: Rethinking the concept of technology in organizations. *Organization Science*, 3(3): 398–427.

Rogers, E.M., (1986). *Communication technology: The new media in society*. New York: The Free Press.

Ryan, S.D., and Prybutok, V.R., (2001). Factors affecting the adoption of knowledge management technologies: A discriminative approach. *Journal of Computer Information Systems*, 41(4): 31–38.

Singleton, R.A.J., and Straits, B.C., (1999). *Approaches to social research*. Oxford: Oxford University Press.

Yao, J.M., Xiaohe, X., Chang, L., and Lu, J., (2003). Organizational size: A significant predictor of it innovation adoption. *Journal of Computer Information Systems*, 43(2): 76–83.

21 *Pedagogical Leadership: Experiences From Three European Business Schools*

Marie-Laure Djelic, Landis Gabel and
Andrea Sironi (interviewed by the Editors)

Introduction

Leadership issues in a business school setting seem to have certain dimensions that are different from many other types of organizations. One example is the issue of balancing research and teaching. Business schools are meritocracies, hence evaluating the performance of individuals in the organization is essential, but challenging: the research produced is often highly abstract and difficult to evaluate, and the teaching is something often carried out in a closed room.

In this chapter we will share experiences from three European business schools regarding what we refer to as pedagogical leadership issues, that is, the delicate task of supporting and developing pedagogy in a research environment. Three individuals with vast experience of pedagogical leadership issues have been interviewed by the editors, in order to illustrate how these tricky issues can be dealt with in practice. The interviewees are:

Professor Marie-Laure Djelic, ESSEC, Paris, France.
Professor Landis Gabel, INSEAD, Fontainebleau, France.
Professor Andrea Sironi, SDA Bocconi, Milan, Italy.

Below you will first find a summary of our interviews and then some brief reflections on what was said during the interviews.

Three interviews on pedagogical leadership

UNIVERSITY AND BUSINESS SCHOOL PROFESSORS ARE OFTEN SAID TO PERFORM MULTIPLE ROLES. WHICH ROLES DO YOU SEE?

Andrea Sironi (AS): I believe there are three main roles a school professor typically performs. The first, and particularly relevant one, is the *educational* one. I consider this a particularly relevant one for two main reasons. The first reason comes from the fact that this is what really distinguishes a school/university from a simple research center. The second reason has to do with the role played by research in the field of management. My opinion is simply that research in the field of management and economics is very important and should be performed with the maximum commitment and care. However, it is not the kind of research that saves lives or changes the prospects of human knowledge as is the one that is generally done in the context of natural sciences such as physics, biology, medicine, and so on.

The second main role of school professors is the one of *researchers*. Research is a vital part of an economics and management professor. More specifically, I believe research in our fields should be seen not only as a means to contribute to the progress of knowledge, but also as a way to contribute to the international academic debate on relevant economics and management issues.

Finally, school professors may play a relevant role as *managers*. While I believe that every professor should achieve minimum satisfactory levels of performance in the previous two roles, it is quite clear that not all professors may be interested or apt to play this third role. Indeed, this is a role usually played on a temporary basis by those colleagues who are generally perceived by the academic community to possess the managerial skills needed to lead and coordinate departments, programs, or entire schools.

Marie-Laure Djelic (MLD): I see four major roles for business school professors:

The first role is the one of creation of knowledge through research. Institutions of higher education all share in the collective responsibility of producing original and relevant new knowledge.

The second role is the one of diffusion of knowledge. This can be done in several ways: in highly formalized ways to academic communities; in pedagogical ways to students; and in practical ways to organizations and to society at large (through, for example, the media).

The third role is the maieutic role in the Socratic sense of the term, that is, structuring learning environments and learning experiences. This is sensibly different from more classical forms of teaching or diffusion of knowledge. It is increasingly becoming, though, what is asked of pedagogues, in the context of in-company programs but also in the MBA classroom or even at the undergraduate level.

The fourth role is the role of managers of knowledge-intensive organizations and of a knowledge-intensive industry. This is done through administrative and/or professional roles within the schools; and through administrative and/or professional roles in the academic community.

In summary, there is a great dispersion and variety of very intense and significant roles that all are at the heart of the construction and development of a knowledge society (and hence at the core of our common European ambition).

Landis Gabel (LG): Business school professors as academics have several roles: *research* and *teaching* being the 'classical' roles. In some business school settings it is sometimes argued that research should be input to teaching, but I also believe that research has its own merits. We have a role of improving the understanding of phenomena, even if it does not rapidly lead to the classroom. One example is some financial models which incubated in the academic community for a long time before they became more common understanding in the classroom. Research and teaching yes, but it is not research to serve teaching, and teaching is not the fundamental objective. The two of them are equally self-standing.

Regarding teaching there are actually two different roles: you can teach the individuals and you can also teach the company, in Company Specific Programs (CSPs). These are two different kinds of teaching.

Another role for academics is to *run academic institutions*. That is part of a life cycle you go through: research and teaching, and then institutional service. Not so much for its own sake but to make possible research and teaching for the next generation.

That links to another role: a senior academic should serve as a *mentor* for the younger ones. That is, mentoring to develop teaching skills and pedagogical skills, as well as research skills. There should be someone taking care of new faculty members.

Another role is the *consultant* to business. At some business schools you get institutional credit for this. INSEAD makes it possible for faculty to do consulting, but it does not actively encourage or discourage it. We have 4-day contracts, so faculty members' consulting work is their private business, something they do on their fifth day. Then towards the end of the year they have to report the number of days they have worked outside the school, but this is not part of the evaluation system. It is confidential, and its purpose is just to enforce the limit of time for private work. We put stronger emphasis on academic research and little less on applied research than some other business schools. This raises the question: should a private business school as an institution (as opposed to professors working independently) be in the consulting business at all? Or is that somehow risky, for example, does it compromise the integrity of the institution? This has of course to do with what reputation the business school wants to have.

Some of these different roles blur, but there are certainly different roles.

YOU ALL MENTION SEVERAL DIFFERENT ROLES THAT UNIVERSITY AND BUSINESS SCHOOL PROFESSORS PERFORM. HOW DO YOU LOOK ON THE PROSPECTS FOR STRIKING A SUCCESSFUL BALANCE BETWEEN THESE ROLES?

LG: You could answer this question in two ways: striking the balance on an individual level, or on an institutional level. Do you expect each individual professor to perform all roles, or do you say that nobody could do all that, and on an institutional level build a portfolio of faculty who can cover all these roles, each professor specializing to some extent in one or two roles at the expense of others? At INSEAD we go round and round this and I do not think that we have a resolution for it. Most of our faculty are good generalists who find synergy between their research and teaching. There are many, however, whose research is highly abstract, with little direct classroom applicability.

There are all kinds of researchers at our school, and the contribution of their research can vary. Some researchers' work enters easily into the classroom. However, some researchers write only scholarly papers, and that contributes indirectly to our reputation, and that reputation contributes to the margins we charge for our programs, even if those who come to these programs do not see the theoretical papers or their authors. I believe that the very best and most prestigious schools can charge high prices because of the aura of the whole school, even if the participants do not see the Nobel Prize winners or would not understand them if they did. People want to go where the smart people are.

I believe that the best model is to be tolerant of all types of contribution, as long as the contribution is significant. There should be some generalists, but also rewards to the top researchers and a willingness to let them do the research. Then complement them with other faculty who can do the teaching and who are good teachers. Institutional contribution can be a burden for older faculty. But do not expect each individual to do all those things.

AS: I believe the balance between the different roles played by a school professor is rather different in the different stages of the academic carrier. While in the early stage of a professor's career, research clearly plays a dominant role, in the later stages teaching and eventually school management tend to become more relevant. The increasing teaching load is generally possible without necessarily reducing research commitments thanks to the increase in productivity a school professor typically achieves through experience in both activities.

Also, I believe a school should do its best to allow different professors to follow their main aptitudes. Indeed, while every professor should demonstrate minimum satisfactory levels in both teaching and research, it is quite natural that – within a school – different types of individual, with different aptitudes, coexist. I do not believe that an excellent teacher should necessarily be an excellent researcher, or that good teaching performances can only be achieved by good researchers. This means that a school should allow each individual professor the option to choose between different tracks where research commitments and teaching loads are differentiated.

Finally, as far as the management or institutional role is concerned, it is quite clear that these special roles often conflict with the previous activities (teaching and research) and should be generally associated with a significant reduction in the teaching load. Also, in the case of professors with good research potential, they should be limited in time in order to avoid a loss of potential.

MLD: The ideal world would be one where the balance between the different roles would be successfully achieved at the individual level. Each individual professor would do all of those activities in parallel and would do all of them reasonably well. There are great cases of that in most faculties. And I strongly believe that the role of an institution and its management team should be to try and help more individuals achieve their own personal balance because those roles are positively related to each other and, I would argue, reinforce each other. In social sciences, broadly speaking, creating knowledge without consideration for its successful diffusion brings forth, after a while, issues of relevance. On the other hand, the diffusion of knowledge without active involvement in its creation and development is, by definition, sterile after a while and in any case it contradicts the very mission of higher education.

In real life, the pressure is high and things are not as simple! Another way to think about balance is at the group or organizational level – through some degree of specialization. Parts of the faculty spend more time and resources on knowledge creation and academic diffusion, for example – other parts focus on diffusion to students/organizations/society. But I do say *more*, not *all* – I do not believe, particularly not in business schools, in tight walls and divisions of labor between teachers and researchers for example. Each faculty member should be involved both in knowledge creation and knowledge diffusion, but possibly to a different extent and with different foci.

IN THE RESEARCH PART OF THE PROFESSION, DEVELOPING THEORIES, METHODS AND KNOWLEDGE IS A NATURAL PART OF THE EVERYDAY ACTIVITIES. IS IT POSSIBLE TO BE AT THE FRONT IN THESE AREAS ALSO WHEN IT COMES TO TEACHING? IF SO, HOW?

AS: I tend to believe that teaching quality has two main components. The first one is in some way 'intrinsic' to the individual professor and to their natural ability to explain in a clear and concise manner, to be sensitive enough to perceive the students' understanding of what they are saying, to their leadership, and ability to attract an audience's attention.

The second one is more related to the degree of preparation and commitment that an individual professor puts into their teaching activity. This second component of teaching quality is highly correlated with the amount of time dedicated to the preparation of teaching material such as effective slides, real life examples, case studies, software simulations, and so on.

This kind of effort becomes more and more relevant the higher the level of education: they are typically more relevant at the executive and MBA level, while they tend to be less relevant for undergraduate programs.

I also believe that a minimum involvement in the professional world, either through consultancy activities or through the direct and indirect participation in real companies management (independent member of an executive board, member of an advisory board, and so on) gives a school professor a significant advantage by allowing them to focus on relevant issues and to keep up to date with real life problems.

MLD: There are several ways to interpret this question: The same individual will be at the top of the league on both fronts at the same time. Why not? It is naturally not impossible but probably quite rare. This is becoming all the more complex, furthermore, that the field of pedagogy itself (its methods, theories and associated research and publication pressures) is becoming more and more difficult and in fact quite parallel to the classical fields of research in management. It is for example becoming more and more difficult and challenging to publish in top 'pedagogically-oriented' journals – the difference is not so great in fact from what is the case with academic research.

One institution *should* (or *could*) be at the top on both fronts. I would say YES for *should* and PROBABLY YES for *could* although it is clearly difficult.

LG: There are often synergies between research and teaching, but there is also a trade-off. That is, one activity may support the other, but there is still the constraint of 24 hours in a day. Therefore you need to decide how much you want your faculty to do one versus the other, even if there is synergy between the two.

I think it is not that often an individual thinks about this balance. The individual typically thinks in terms of two things I have to do: research and teaching. One of these I have to satisfy and the other I have to maximize. For our young faculty it is clear that in teaching you have to meet certain expectations, and you have to get at this point as soon as possible. Once you have reached that point you do not put in more energy in the teaching. You put it into research. You do that for two reasons: research standards rise rapidly in your career and there are long delays in the research process. That is, you have to wait long before you know how well you are doing in research. Second, only research really creates career mobility.

After tenure you find that careers move in different directions because you are no longer up for evaluations in the same way. Your own personality can come in in another way and those more interested in teaching can for example teach more in executive programs and maybe focus more on writing textbooks instead of research articles.

AS: There are different ways to stimulate and promote teaching excellence. One very simple way is based on requiring junior faculty members to attend classes taught by more senior colleagues who regularly achieve excellent performances in their teaching activities. This is regularly done at our School of Management (SDA Bocconi) and typically allows junior faculty members to learn from a wide range of teaching practices, methodologies, and techniques.

A second one is based on the development of initiatives aimed at training school professors in their 'teaching' activities, such as the International Teachers Programme (ITP). These initiatives are not only relevant for their actual content, but also because they allow participants to benefit from the confrontation with school professors from different countries who typically employ different teaching methods and have different experiences. Following this approach, SDA Bocconi has invited the European Case Clearing House (ECCH) to hold case writing workshops in Milan offered to its faculty members.

However, as I already mentioned above, teaching excellence is also based on the intrinsic qualities and aptitudes of a school professor. For this reason, I believe that a sound and rigorous recruiting process, with a significant weight assigned to teaching, remains a key factor in achieving teaching quality at the school level.

Finally, teaching excellence also needs an environment which is clearly recognizing the value of the results achieved by excellent professors. This in turn can be promoted both through annual teaching awards assigned to the best performing professors, and though a system whereby the best practices get widely recognized and clearly communicated to the entire faculty.

MLD: You have (at the institutional level) to design and put in place incentive systems; to define evaluation processes that will stimulate and recognize excellence on both fronts – either for individual faculty members that can do both or for different types or groups of faculty in each case. At ESSEC we have had now for more than 15 years an incentive system with a view to promote and develop research and publication. The main incentive system has essentially three dimensions:

First, whenever somebody publishes something, they get a budgetary allocation. The budget depends upon both the nature of the publication and the quality of the outlet defined through a combination of an internal classification scheme of journals (that was developed in part through benchmarking, in part through widespread consultation of fellow academics in the different fields) and an inside committee made up of several faculty members and the Vice-Dean for Research. This budgetary allocation can be used freely by the individual professor either to buy back some teaching time, to buy for themselves anything they might need for research purposes (a personal computer for their home, printer, software, books, and so on) or to finance exploratory research trips or conferences at which the person is not presenting a paper.

Second, the Research Center covers all the costs associated with participation in conferences and workshops where the faculty member is presenting a paper.

Third, the Research Center sends, twice a year, an internal call for projects to help finance, in particular, new projects (acting as a research angel – if I dare the parallel with business angel).

More recently, we are putting in place a system whereby publication in the very top tier journals is associated with the possibility to 'buy back the fifth day' – our faculty are normally on a 4-day contract; they can use their fifth day for consulting or executive education activities (like at INSEAD as mentioned above). For somebody investing in research and publication with positive results we offer the possibility to buy back the fifth day to focus on research and publication.

Four years ago, we started to turn our energies towards pedagogy:

- We have invested a lot in the ITP – sending regularly up to four faculty members a year and we have found it a very valuable investment.
- We have put together an internal process (call for projects associated with resources of different kinds and help with legal and commercial issues at the end) to stimulate the production of pedagogical material (paper cases, multimedia teaching material, and so on).
- We have put together internally a coaching and teaching program to facilitate the move of

our younger, more research-oriented professors towards executive education – at a speed and with a scope that remains reasonable and compatible with the preservation of a strong research and publication focus.

DO YOU HAVE ANY GOOD EXAMPLES OF SOMEONE WHO HAS MANAGED TO BE AT THE FRONT IN BOTH RESEARCH AND TEACHING?

LG: When you ask about good examples, people who could do anything, one name that comes to my mind is Sumantra Ghoshal. He was one of the few cases we have had who could do anything excellently.

We have at least statistical evidence that higher teaching evaluations go with higher research productivity. It does not say that there is intellectual synergy. It could be that there are certain personality characteristics that make both dimensions successful, or that teachers who don't stress out over teaching can concentrate better on research.

Sumantra illustrates the point that personality traits that make a good researcher can also make a good teacher. What are the research traits? Inquisitive, smart, prepared to expose their ideas to criticism, challenging, and looking for alternative explanations, anxious to engage others in their ideas. There are many of the same personality traits for being a good teacher, although this does not mean that oral presentation is the same as written.

If I had to explain why you have a positive correlation between good teaching and good research I think it is more about personality than it is because you do research and that helps you in the classroom. In some cases that may be true, but mostly it is about personality traits. The people who have the traits can then demonstrate the synergy.

MLD: In a few years, we went from a very limited presence in the pedagogical material world to more than 20 cases deposited with ECCH in three years (2003–2006) with a number of those winning awards and recognition. Those cases are generally highly sophisticated technologically and this level of sophistication has been achieved through the institutional process of bringing together the professors and the technical teams and allocating resources for working together. This has happened without any negative impact on our collective results with respect to research and publication, quite on the contrary, productivity has tended to increase there too.

AS: As any other member of the academic community, I do have in mind both individual colleagues who are consistently achieving excellent performances in their teaching activity, and competing schools which have been more successful in developing the above-mentioned environment, capable of stimulating and promoting excellence in teaching. In the case of individuals, I believe in most of the cases this comes from a combination of a natural gift with a strong commitment to teaching and attention to the students. In the case of schools, I believe that success in teaching mostly comes from a clear and adequate recognition of the role played by this part of our profession in the determination of a professor career.

WHAT SYSTEMS AND APPROACHES DO YOU HAVE TO ASCERTAIN THAT TEACHING EXCELLENCE GOES HAND IN HAND WITH RESEARCH EXCELLENCE?

AS: In recent years, Bocconi has put significant emphasis on research achievements as the basis for recruiting and promotions at the different steps of the academic carrier. While an excellent teaching performance has typically been considered a positive factor, its role has been less relevant than the one played by research. This was mostly the consequence of a clear desire to improve research standards, the second major strategic goal of the entire university together with internationalization.

We are now in the process of redesigning the criteria used for hiring and promotion. While neither de-emphasizing the role played by research nor reducing the goals pursued in terms of research results, these criteria should be based on a more relevant role to be assigned to teaching. More specifically, the idea would be that a professor who is performing poorly in teaching, while they would be supported through the above mentioned 'teaching' courses, they would find it very difficult to progress in their career, just as a professor performing poorly in research would. On the other side, an excellent teaching performance would be considered just as relevant as an excellent research performance as a determinant of promotions.

LG: In most instances I think that most faculty members should either think in terms of I am mostly a researcher and I have to teach and I should do it professionally, or think in terms of being mostly a teacher.

There is, even if you like it or not, a pecking order. Even if you have a teaching-track and a research-track, there is no doubt that if you are in the top of a research-track you are higher up in the hierarchy. We try to break down this hierarchy. One problem is that people in our teaching-track often tried to be in the research-track and were not successful. So that there is a stigma that comes from what we call affiliated professors, people with a heavy teaching load and are not evaluated on their research performance, and typically first tried to follow the research-track and did not make it.

One way we try to get around this is to recruit people to this teaching-track without first having them passing through the research-track. Another way is frankly to ask people to go somewhere else if they fail in the research-track, even if it might have been attractive to the school to keep them in the teaching-track. We have tried to change the titles and call people in the teaching-track, for example, Professors of Management Practice, but it is an uphill battle. It is a publish-or-perish environment.

MLD: Our internal evaluation system that structures the career track of our faculty members is very clear on the importance of both dimensions – research and publication on the one hand, pedagogy on the other hand. We look very carefully within the evaluation committee at the contributions on both dimensions of each of our faculty member.

HOW DO YOU ASSESS AND FOLLOW UP TEACHING EXCELLENCE WHEN HIRING AND PROMOTING?

MLD: During the hiring process, we assess teaching excellence through, essentially, two ways – records available in the file of the candidate (teaching evaluations of courses they have taught before, including as graduate students, and elements to be found in the recommendation letters), and assessment of the pedagogical qualities during the presentation of research that is done in front of the evaluation committee. This evaluation committee is made up of specialists in the field as well as of colleagues from other fields and the capacity to satisfy both types of expectations is something we really look at.

For promotion and evaluation purposes, we rely on several things: the self-evaluation of the professors themselves, going through their pedagogical experience; the course evaluation forms (available after each course); the course documents and materials prepared and used by the professors that are made available by them to the evaluation committee and scrutinized. Those dimensions have on the whole an important impact on the evaluation process.

We try to help with teaching and pedagogy in different ways. We provide training (in particular ITP) for those who wish; we are reactive and can put in place coaching situations at the departmental level (with a senior colleague for example); we have sent some faculty members to theatre workshops or theatre-based training which have proven quite useful; we put in place regular discussions between the young colleagues and the Dean of Faculty.

We have put in place a specific process for executive education together between the Dean's office and our executive education management team. The objective is to familiarize young faculty members progressively and in time with executive education, to allow for a better understanding on both sides (the faculty and the executive education management team); to allow those young faculty members in time to 'dare' to enter into executive education and to do so with more confidence. This process has several stages:

- A systematic 'know each other' meeting: what is executive education? Who are you? What are you working on?
- Collective session on pedagogy in executive education (mini-ITP with a focus on executive education).
- According to needs and wishes, development of specialized workshops (use of PowerPoint slides and different technologies in teaching, handling case discussions ...).
- One on one coaching – pairing senior and more junior faculty members if this is wished for.

In fact this approach has started to generate also, on the side of our executive education management team, a rethinking of their own offer: how can we develop and propose a module or program that would be better fitting our research faculty's particular strengths?

LG: At INSEAD we have a committee of six people who look through the course curricula, the syllabus and development of syllabus, the material used in the classroom, if the person has attended teaching workshops, and so on. If the person has written teaching cases we also look at statistics about how many other schools have adopted the cases.

This is a very time-consuming process and we do it basically at two points: before the tenure-decision (typically year 7) and before the promotion to full professor (typically year 10). We also do a lighter version of the process earlier (year 3) to make sure that things are on track.

Usually we have little information about teaching when recruiting new faculty members. Most of the people we recruit are new Ph.Ds and we let every candidate give a seminar at the school. At least you test if they make any sense at all. Young faculty members are excited and energetic, which in itself is an advantage. Most of them do pretty well.

When talking about hiring faculty we have to keep in mind that faculty is now mobile. The challenge is to keep the people. National borders will decrease in importance.

AS: At Bocconi, teaching performance is currently evaluated using students' evaluations. Indeed, these evaluations are used both by the recruiting and promotions committee as one of the relevant criteria for its decision process, and as the basis for the annual awards for teaching excellence. These are simple prizes generally assigned to those professors who achieved the best teaching performances in the different programs (MBA, MSc, undergraduate, and so on) during an annual meeting of the entire faculty.

However, we are now in the process of revising these criteria. More specifically, while students' evaluations will still represent the main factor, additional elements, such as new program and course development (innovation in teaching), international textbooks writing, new case studies development, a diversified teaching portfolio (being active in more levels: undergraduate, graduate, MBA, executive, Ph.D), and other teaching tools such as simulations and exercises, will be used as relevant factors to be considered when evaluating teaching performance.

HOW DOES THE ASSESSMENT AND FOLLOWING UP OF TEACHING EXCELLENCE DIFFER FROM HOW RESEARCH IS EVALUATED?

MLD: Our assessment of research excellence is, in a sense, using more classical tools – see above our classification scheme that allows us to make a difference between the types of publications. We do 'count' publications (in the double sense of quantity and quality), even though we tend to have an understanding of what is a 'good journal' that is wider than the narrow FT (Financial Times) definition. We also look at ongoing projects and pipelines, at the participation in workshops and conferences, at the various awards and prizes that the faculty member may receive. Naturally, we do pay attention also to things like involvement in the Ph.D program and with Ph.D students.

LG: With both teaching and research you need to have some way of evaluating performance, some sort of standard which is accepted. Both dimensions are difficult.

Regarding research, most business schools do the evaluation in a fairly consistent way. There are publication records, peer-reviews, citations, and so on. There are flaws in that, but at least there is a commonly accepted way of playing that game. The audience for research is relatively large. There is an external and an internal assessment of research and at least the external assessment is relatively objective using external peers, and so on.

Teaching is a lot harder to assess than research. First the audiences are relatively small. Yes, you get the evaluations from the students, but how do your school's evaluations compare to some other school's evaluations? How do you value the non-quantitative elements which we all say are important? For example: creativity in courses, creativity in curriculum, creativity in materials, and so on. Assessing that is a lot more subjective and more internal. It is harder to assess the teaching. It is easy to assess if somebody is a classroom star.

AS: I would argue that evaluating research excellent is easier than assessing teaching performance. Indeed, research performance is generally evaluated based on clear and objective criteria which are mostly represented by the number of publications in the more prestigious and selective international scientific journals. While some disagreement is likely to emerge when trying to identify the journal list (A journals, B journals, and so on), a general agreement is normally present among academicians in terms of which are the main journals where the most relevant results of research activity in each subject typically get published.

Evaluation of teaching performance is more difficult. Indeed, in this case the criteria are more differentiated and diversified and there is less agreement among academics on the methodologies to be adopted. Some tend to believe that students' evaluations are the key factor and the only relevant one. Others tend to think that students' evaluations are significantly biased and strongly affected by factors that have nothing to do with teaching quality. Moreover, they think that students are not able to judge whether a course is really successful in its learning objectives. These colleagues also tend to believe that the evaluation of teaching should be based on a sort of peer-review system similar to the one used for research. More specifically, a committee of peers should analyze an individual professor's teaching performance based on the course syllabus, of the teaching textbook and material produced, and eventually on the attendance of one of their classes.

I personally believe that students' evaluations can be considered as a reliable source of information on a school professor's teaching performance. This is more true the higher the educational level (undergraduate – graduate – Ph.D – executive). However, I agree that these evaluations should not represent the only parameter and should be integrated by the above-mentioned elements (syllabus, textbook, material, and so on).

Some reflections from the Editors

There are obviously many different reflections one can make when listening to the experiences from Professors Djelic, Gabel and Sironi. The following list includes a couple of issues that we want to highlight:

*   Regarding the challenge of balancing research and teaching one has to keep in mind that the balance can be seen both on an individual level and/or on an institutional level. When discussing this balance it is thus important to be explicit about what level is discussed.
*   There seems to be a natural 'life cycle' of different roles in a business school setting. At early stages some sort of combination or sequence of research and teaching roles, and at later stages more managerial/mentoring roles.
*   When assessing teaching there is a major challenge to find ways of assessing the non-quantitative aspects of teaching. This is a challenging task, and if it is done it will take a lot of time and energy, but it is nevertheless an important aspect for the assessment of teaching.
*   Given the complexity of assessing teaching quality some sort of pedagogical portfolios could be useful in terms of capturing the multi-dimensional aspects of teaching (see for example, Fry et al 2003; Chapter 17).

We want to give the final word to Professors Djelic, Gabel and Sironi and we therefore asked them to share some specific advice to people in school management functions and to individual faculty members. Below you find the lists of their advice.

Some advice to school management

The following list of advice to school management is proposed by professors Djelic, Gabel and Sironi.

*   Define as clearly as possible the criteria used for faculty evaluation and promotion and what exactly is expected from a faculty member. While changes to these criteria are inevitable in a dynamic institution, these criteria should be as stable as possible and changes should be made as transparent as possible.
*   Build, over time, a sense of 'elite' among tenured faculty members, who tend to believe that they represent a strictly and toughly selected group of people who very much trust and esteem each other.
*   Create challenges and supplementary rewards after tenure – so that the high value resource represented by your tenured faculty can really express itself.
*   Develop an internal incentive system where high performance in teaching and research is clearly recognized and remunerated.

- Create a protective wall around your young faculty members in the first years of their careers so that they are not solicited for administrative tasks or extra teaching loads. Their only two objectives should be to become a quality teacher and a highly productive researcher.

Some advice to the individual faculty member

For individual faculty members some advice could also be given by professors Djelic, Gabel and Sironi.

- Faculty members in the early stage of their academic career (assistant professor/lecturer) should try to concentrate as much as possible on building a research reputation on their specific field. This is crucial to achieve visibility in the scientific world and gain a 'market value'. This also means trying to work in a research-friendly environment, where cooperation and discussion is normal practice.
- Junior faculty members should not shy away from turning to more senior colleagues for advice on all dimensions of the job as well as for help at critical turning points of their career.
- More senior faculty should try to exploit as much as possible their contacts with the business world – through participation to boards, consultancy activity, and so on – as this significantly improves the relevance and adherence to reality of both their teaching and research activities.
- More generally, the possibility to cooperate (co-authors) with colleagues from business schools located in other countries is very useful as it allows a business school professor to get exposed to different realities, business practices, and cultures. This very often generates extremely productive outcomes both in terms of research (scientific publications) and teaching (case studies, and so on).

References

Fry, H., Ketteridge, S., and Marshall, S. (eds.), (2003). *A Handbook for Teaching and Learning in Higher Education: Enhancing Academic Practice (Second Edition)*. London: RoutledgeFalmer.

22 Learning Styles as Vehicles for Pedagogical Development

Magnus Bild and Pär Mårtensson

Introduction

A business school and its faculty need to fulfil multiple roles. Research and teaching are evidently the pillars, but disseminating scientific findings to a wider society is also important. When it comes to teaching, a basic requirement is that the teacher facilitates students' learning and helps them cope with the demands of their future careers. To realize that aim on an individual student level, it seems essential to provide teaching that helps each student to learn according to her capacity.

It is well known that people learn in different ways (see for example, Kolb 1984). The Learning Styles Questionnaire (LSQ)[1] is one way of investigating individuals' learning style preferences, as is discussed in Chapter 10 of this volume by Seán Gaffney. Although the LSQ developed by Peter Honey and Alan Mumford (1982, 2006) as well as similar tools, is well established and sometimes used in business schools, it seems more uncommon that the outcome of the LSQ is used for pedagogical development.

In this chapter we will share some ideas how the output from LSQ can be used for enriching the pedagogical discussion between faculty, students, and school management. Our experiences are based on work carried out at the Stockholm School of Economics (SSE) and in the International Teachers Programme (ITP).

Some empirical data

Since the freshmen admitted to SSE in the Autumn of 2003 were exposed to the Learning Styles Questionnaire, it has been offered annually. The intake to the school is about 280 students every year. Almost all students have filled in the questionnaire, meaning that the sample consists by now of roughly 1400 students. The distribution for the two most extreme dimensions in the questionnaire is presented in Figure 22.1. The vertical axis shows the number of students, and the horizontal axis shows the number of statements in each dimension that was given the answer 'agree'. To simplify the illustration we have only included the two most extreme of the four dimensions

We see in Figure 22.1 that the M.Sc. students' strongest preference is for pragmatist learning and that the activist learning style is least frequent. Reflector and theorist learning styles come in between the two extremes. What the results suggest is that the M.Sc. students

---

1   The Learning Styles Questionnaire comprises 80 statements where the user should 'agree' or 'not agree'. There are four dimensions (learning style preferences – activist, reflector, theorist and pragmatist) – each of which is assessed by 20 statements.

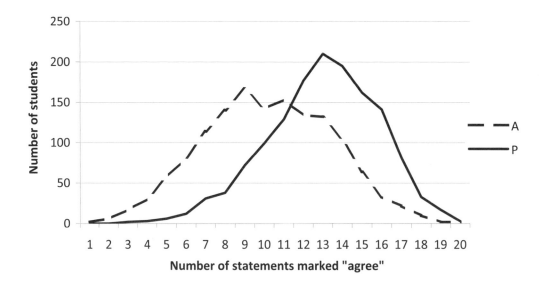

Figure 22.1   The distribution of learning styles among M.Sc. students admitted to the Stockholm School of Economics between 2003 and 2007

have to perceive that the matters taught are relevant and meaningful to them. Reflection and contextualizing is also important. Learning by concrete activities seem less important for this group, which might cast some doubt on methods such as role plays and some forms of group work.

When we compare the groups of the different years, it is striking that the M.Sc. students' preferences are similar over time. This observation might have some implications for the tools used for selecting 280 students out of a cohort of several thousands applicants. But that discussion goes beyond the scope of this chapter.

Since 2002, students enrolled in the Executive MBA and the MBA programs have been exposed to the same LSQ. The intake is considerably smaller than to the M.Sc. program and the total cohort consists of 375 students. We have chosen to present data for the EMBA and the MBA programs together. The distribution for the two most extreme of the four dimensions in the LSQ is presented in Figure 22.2. The vertical axis shows the number of students, and the horizontal axis shows the number of statements in each dimension that was given the answer 'agree'. To simplify the illustration we have only included the two most extreme of the four dimensions

We see in Figure 22.2 that the (E)MBA student cohort has its strongest preference for the pragmatist learning style. The reflector style has the least pronounced preference. Second strongest preference is for the activist style, although the difference between this style and the theorist style is small. This indicates that the group as a whole needs to be working with examples and material that they themselves believe is relevant and meaningful. Furthermore, pre-readings seem to be less appreciated, unless it is turned into an active exercise, for example, a case to be prepared in small groups.

Besides the student groups, we have also offered the questionnaire to SSE faculty. In total 49 faculty members have filled in the questionnaire so far. The distribution for the two most extreme of the four dimensions in the LSQ is presented in Figure 22.3. The vertical axis shows the number of faculty members, and the horizontal axis shows the number of statements in

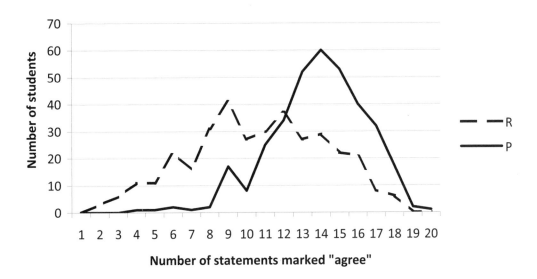

Figure 22.2 **The distribution of learning styles among EMBA and MBA students admitted to the Stockholm School of Economics between 2001 and 2007**

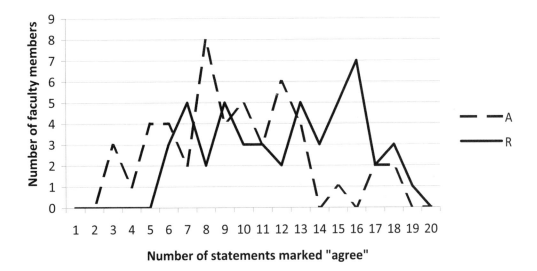

Figure 22.3 **The distribution of learning styles among 49 SSE faculty members**

each dimension that was given the answer 'agree'. For reasons of presentation, only the two most extreme of the four dimensions are portrayed.

We see in Figure 22.3 that the faculty members have their strongest preference for the reflector style. The activist preference is the weakest. The pragmatist and the theorist styles come in between, with the pragmatist style being more pronounced than the theorist style.

We can now compare the data for the three groups. In Table 22.1 below we present the average scores for each of the four dimensions.

Table 22.1   **Averages scores on each of the learning style dimensions for 1400 M.Sc. students and 375 (E)MBA students, and 49 SSE faculty members**

	M.Sc.-students	(E)MBA-students	Faculty members
Activist	10.2	11.4	9.4
Reflector	12.6	10.6	12.3
Theorist	12.1	11.1	11.3
Pragmatist	13.0	13.8	11.7

If we put ourselves in the position of the average faculty member who faces M.Sc. students as well as (E)MBA students, some interesting observations arise. First, the two student categories are different. The difference is least pronounced for both groups' strongest learning style preference, that is, pragmatism. The (E)MBA students have a stronger preference for the activist style, and weaker preferences for theorist and reflector styles. What it all suggests is that our average faculty member has to design a particular session differently if she is going to meet the preferences of the audiences and achieve effective teaching.[2] Second, if there is a tendency for our faculty member to design her teaching in a way that is consistent with her own learning style preference, she has some challenges to overcome. Both student groups have a markedly stronger preference for the pragmatist style than our average teacher. To a smaller extent that difference is at hand also when it comes to the activist style. The teachers' preference for reflection is as strong as the M.Sc. students' she meets, but sessions designed in that way might risk not entirely pleasing an (E)MBA audience. On the other hand, the teachers' preference for the theorist style is compatible with an (E)MBA audience, but the need for theories and models is even stronger among the M.Sc. students.

What our data suggests is that faculty members will meet groups that have different learning style preferences. To be able to offer teaching that is effective to various groups, the teacher needs to be able to design sessions in different ways and at the same time be willing to give up some of her own learning style preferences.

Using learning styles in M.Sc. programs

The LSQ has been presented to all M.Sc. students admitted to SSE since 2003. The decision to introduce LSQ followed from a pedagogical development effort initiated within the school. Early in the process, it was emphasized that just asking the students to fill in the questionnaire would be less meaningful, if the data were not used to explore wider aspects of students' learning. Two such aspects were how well students performed in various courses and what majors they selected later in their studies. We will come back to those aspects after having described how the LSQ was introduced to the students.

The M.Sc. students at SSE meet the questionnaire during their first week at the school. In groups of 30, the students are given a brief description of the purpose of the LSQ. They are however not informed about the learning style theory and the four dimensions that the questionnaire aims at capturing. They are also asked to accept, by signing a form, that the data will be used for further specified enquiries. All students are fully entitled to decline participation,

---

2   See Hawk and Shah (2007) for a discussion of the same topic.

or to participate but not allow their data to be used for the specified purposes.[3] After that introduction, each student is asked to fill in a computerized version of the questionnaire and save it before they leave the room.

At the end of the first week at the school, students get their learning style profile in return during a 45-minute lecture in the main auditorium. The purpose of the lecture is to explain the theory behind the LSQ and to provide the students with an aggregated learning style profile for the entire group. Students are also informed, again, why the LSQ has been introduced in the curriculum and how the data will be used. The last part of the lecture is devoted to students' questions and views.

We hypothesize that a student does better in courses taught in line with her learning style, and worse in courses taught in conflict with her learning style. How well a student is doing is a complex question. We chose to use the examination results as an indicator of performance. It is clear to us that the indicator can be biased. For instance, a particular learning style can be favored by the form of examination as much as by the teaching format, for example, to examine students by asking them to perform a role play probably suits activists better than reflectors. It is possible that another examination form, for example, a reflection paper, would have given the opposite result. Further, asking questions at a particular level in Bloom's taxonomy (1956) might disfavor some students more than others.

Instead of immediately engaging in thorough analyses, we decided to explore the courses piecewise. We started with a mandatory course in Business Statistics, since we believed it had a clear and stable pedagogical philosophy and an examination format well in line with the teaching format. Further, rather prejudiced, we thought that the subject as such would attract students with a theorist learning style preference more than those with a weak such preference. We then created two groups of students, one consisting of the 10 per cent scoring highest on the theorist dimension, and one consisting of the 10 per cent scoring lowest on that dimension.[4] The results are presented in Table 22.2. The examination percentage stretches from 0 per cent to 100 per cent.

There is a difference between the two groups in Table 22.2, although it is not as marked as we would have expected. There are some potential explanations for this, one being that the students with the lowest preference for theorist learning struggle harder since they realize there is a risk of failure. In contrast, the students with the strongest preference for theorist learning might realize that they will pass the exam and therefore do not put as much effort into their studies.

Presenting results like those for Business Statistics for all courses and all four learning styles would be an important feeder to a lively pedagogical discussion at the school. Curriculum redesign, introduction of new pedagogical tools, intensified pedagogical training for faculty

Table 22.2   Examination results in Business Statistics for the students scoring highest and lowest on the theorist dimension in the LSQ

	Lowest 10 % of students	Highest 10 % of students
Business Statistics	59.2 %	64.7 %

---

3   More than 99 per cent of the students have filled in the questionnaire and accepted the way the data will be used.
4   In Honey & Mumford's terminology that means we are comparing those with a *very strong* preference to those with a *very low* preference.

and students, and greater variation in examination formats are potential outcomes of such an effort. We do, however, need a larger sample before such discussions would reach their full potential.

Another use of the learning styles data has been to analyze whether there is any pattern in what major students choose for the last 2 years of the curriculum. Again, we contrasted the 10 per cent of the students with the highest score on the theorist dimension to the 10 per cent with the lowest score on the same dimension. The analysis generated some interesting tendencies, although the sample is yet too small to allow firm conclusions. Anyway, the two student groups included 13 students that later chose Marketing as their major. Eleven of the 13 students had a very low preference for theorist learning. The pattern was the opposite when it comes to the 16 students that later chose Accounting as their major. Twelve of them had a very strong preference for theorist learning.

The outcome from this latter analysis has partly different recipients than the former one. Of course, it is still interesting for faculty members, but it seems unlikely that it will generate any of the positive consequences that were identified as outcomes of the examination study above. It is probably more interesting for school management and administration if data like these can be used for making estimates of how popular various majors are likely to be. It can also have impact on the size of faculty in different departments and where recruitment might be needed in the nearby future.

Using learning styles in (E)MBA programs

Since 2002, a total of 375 students enrolled in EMBA and MBA programs at SSE have been exposed to the LSQ. It has normally been introduced during the first week of the program. The set-up has typically been as the following seven steps:

1. The students are asked to fill in the paper version of the questionnaire immediately before lunch.
2. The instructors prepare the feedback during the participants' lunch.
3. After lunch, the theory behind the questionnaire is introduced and the four dimensions of the learning styles are exemplified.
4. Then the students are asked to go out in their ordinary working groups and fill in a simple sheet of paper. The paper is a matrix, with the group members' names on one axis, and the four learning styles dimensions on the other axis. The assignment is that each group member should tell the others about a typical learning situation she has been exposed to. After each 'story' the group discusses which learning style the 'storyteller' most likely has the strongest preference for.
5. After the group discussion, all groups meet in the plenary room. We then ask all with a tendency for the activist learning style to raise their hands. The number (but not the names) is noted on the whiteboard. The procedure is repeated for the other three learning style dimensions. By doing that, we and the participants get an idea of which learning styles are *believed* to be most frequent in the group.
6. In the next step, we hand out the learning style profile to each individual and let them look at it for a while. We then open the floor for reactions and questions. One evident discussion topic is the similarity between the students' self-expected learning style and the style indicated by the questionnaire.
7. In a next last step, we send out the students again and ask them to discuss three questions

in their working groups. One question is what impact the profile of the group has for the program. Another question is what it means for their work as (potential) managers. A third question is what it means in their private lives.

The learning styles results are made public to the faculty on an aggregated level. The belief is that it would stimulate more effective teaching. The results are also used later in the program to form homogeneous and heterogeneous groups and to reflect on how well they work.

Using learning styles for faculty

It goes without saying that the results presented above would be inspiring enough for self-reflections about teaching for most faculty members. But we have also developed two session formats that could be used for ensuring that the learning styles results are converted into real pedagogical development.

The first session format was developed for the Department of Accounting at SSE. All faculty members were gathered for a 2-day kick-off where the learning style session was devoted one half-day. Above, we described our seven step approach for an EMBA group. The faculty members were exposed to the first six steps of that approach. The seventh step was however different. We asked the teachers to form homogeneous groups, that is, all reflectors in one group, and so on. We then provided them with a one-page description of a 2 hour session that most of them have taught several times in their career and that they were hence well familiar with. The reflectors were then asked to redesign the session in a way that they thought would appeal to the pragmatist learners. Similarly, the activists were asked to redesign the session to fit with the preferences of the theorist learner.

After doing that, the reflectors were asked to team up with the pragmatists, and similarly the theorists were asked to team up with the activists. The idea was that each group should present the building blocks of their redesigned session to the intended recipient.

Finally, all groups gathered in a plenary session to discuss how the group work proceeded, how the proposals were received, and what the consequences will be for the accounting curriculum at SSE. It is probable that the session was one important ingredient in a process that led to a radical redesign of the Introductory Accounting course and that also changed the order between what was taught during the first 2 years in the M.Sc. program and what was taught during the latter 2 years.

The second session format was developed for the ITP when hosted by IMD 2006/07. The time allotted to the session was 3 hours. Again, we used an approach very similar to the one presented above for the EMBA classes. The six first steps were represented again. But we also added a very first step by asking the participants to hand in, and circulate among their class-mates, a description of a session that they currently teach.

After the sixth step in the EMBA description, we asked the participants to form pairs freely. The assignment for each pair was a) to draw a learning style profile of the existing two courses of the pair, b) to articulate in what way they wanted to change their course, for example, make it more oriented towards the activists, and c) to present their findings during a poster session in the plenary room.

The session was ended by a plenary discussion where participants were asked to discuss what they would do on their return to their home institution.

Advice to faculty and school management

In this chapter we have illustrated some paths for initiating a discussion on pedagogical development in a business school. Using questionnaires is evidently only one way to reach the goal. If a questionnaire is used, then the LSQ by Honey and Mumford (1982) is of course only one alternative among many. We want to end the chapter with some specific advice to school management and individual faculty members:

Some advice to school management:

- Initiate LSQs, or any other type of questionnaire that you believe is better, as a vehicle for pedagogical development.
- Make sure that the instruction format of each course is varied in order to satisfy as many learning style preferences as possible.
- Do not issue stereotyped rules and standards for what a course should look like and how it should be examined, since that will probably lead to favoring some students at the expense of others.

Some advice for individual faculty members:

- Learn about your own learning styles preferences.
- Sit down with a colleague that has a radically different learning style preference than you, and discuss each others' courses.
- Prepare by trying to figure out students' learning styles. If it is not possible to use the Honey & Mumford questionnaire, go for the quick version presented by Seán Gaffney in Chapter 10 in this volume.

References and further reading

Bloom, B.S. (Ed.), (1956). *Taxonomy of Educational Objectives: The Classification of Educational Goals: Handbook I*. New York: Cognitive Domain, David McKay.

Gaffney, S., (2008). 'Teaching and Learning in a Multi-cultural Environment – A Mild Polemic', in this volume.

Hawk, T.F., and Shah, A.J., (2007). Using Learning Style Instruments to Enhance Student Learning. *Decision Sciences Journal of Innovative Education*, 5(1): 1–19.

Honey, P., and Mumford, A., (1982). *The Manual of Learning Styles*. Maidenhead, England: Peter Honey Publications Limited.

Honey, P., and Mumford, A., (2006). *The Learning Styles Questionnaire: 80-item version*. Maidenhead, England: Peter Honey Publications Limited.

Kolb, D.A., (1984). *Experiential Learning: Experience as the Source of Learning and Development*. Englewood Cliffs, N.J.: Prentice-Hall.

23 Mastering Business Action: Implications for Management Learning in Business Schools

Elena P. Antonacopoulou

Introduction

That Management Learning (ML) has become big business is without a doubt both the cause for the challenges it faces and the opportunities it needs to explore if it is to continue to add value to the range of stakeholders' groups that it is intended to serve. This chapter engages with one of the most central aspects in ML – understanding and supporting purposeful action. ML can be defined in a number of different ways however, at the core of what ML seeks to achieve is to integrate different learning opportunities that are available in a range of education programmes, training events and development initiatives. Whether ML happens in Business Schools, in Corporate Universities, in Training fora or as part and parcel of the day-to-day experiences practising managers engage with at work, at the core of all these activities is *action*.

In this chapter, ML is put under the microscope in order to better capture its role in shaping managerial action. It is argued that ML is an integrative mechanism connecting a range of dispersed learning practices. ML however is not only a means of synthesising learning across different activities. The core purpose of ML is to support practising managers to become *Masters of Business Action*.[1]

It has been acknowledged in recent years that management education has to be better aligned with the experience of managing if it is to be relevant (Pfeffer and Fong 2002). The obvious arena for accounting for the relevance of ML for management practice is the impact it can have towards informing business action. Understanding the complexities of managing demands an engagement with *Practice, Practitioners* and their *Phronesis* (practical judgements). This means that understanding what managers do when they manage needs to inform how ML is conceptualised and designed.

This chapter unpacks three of the current challenges in ML and presents three opportunities for rethinking ML to better support business action. The three ML challenges discussed are: Globalisation, Pedagogical Practice and the complexity of the learning (formal and informal) process. Three opportunities are also discussed in relation to each of these challenges that help us to rethink ML in supporting the development of *Masters of Business Action*. The latter is seen as a central priority in rethinking the future development of Business Schools.

The chapter is organised around these three challenges and opportunities. The discussion begins by defining ML and outlining the main themes that it seeks to address. The second

---

1   I acknowledge the contribution of Mr Paul Oliver, Ex-Strategy Director of British Telecommunications who as an active member of GNOSIS – an initiative that fosters the co-creation of knowledge between business professionals and academics – has articulated the notion of 'Masters of Business Action' during one of the many sessions that have formed our interaction and collaboration over the last 3 years.

section presents and discusses the three challenges of ML. The third section presents and discusses the three opportunities for ML. The discussion section outlines ways in which the opportunities to rethink ML can also reflect the three main principles of Mastering Business Action – *Practice*, *Practitioners* and their *Phronesis* (practical judgements). The paper concludes with a summary of the main themes and outlines the implications for leading and developing Business Schools.

Rethinking management learning

ML has evolved over the years as an umbrella term under which a number of themes are addressed. Unlike other terms however, it has the capacity to show how bridges between concepts such as, management education, development and training, can be built. As a holistic term seeking to integrate these different concepts, ML seeks to respond to the lack of agreement as to how education, development and training are conceptualised and defined by exposing the criteria employed when distinctions are drawn between them.

In a review of the state of the field, Antonacopoulou (2000) showed that some conceptualisations concentrate on process, others on the orientation, method, content and the degree of precision involved. It is commonly agreed however, that education is broader and generic rather than specific. Training on the other hand, is perceived to be more narrow and focused to specific needs, while development is perceived to entail both education and training and to encapsulate the notion of continuous improvement. A review of the various definitions of education, training and development also reveals that there is little discussion of the objectives, time, methods, content and context of learning (with very few exceptions e.g. Reid et al. 1993). Considering that education, training and development are aimed at different levels of insight, it is difficult to draw a line between where one stops and another begins given that each of these processes have elements of each other, something which some commentators have acknowledged (Buckley and Caple 1990).

It would appear that the context in which education, training and development take place influences their purpose, the way they are defined and the role they play in relation to individual learning. Therefore, when reference is made to education, training and development in the context of a society the emphasis on individual learning might be quite different from the same processes taking place in the context of organisations. It appears that the broader the context the bigger the number of stakeholders and the more difficult it would be to maintain a common definition and a shared set of objectives. Therefore, the organisational context may have a stronger impact on individuals' learning, as it is the more immediate context in which the individual learner interacts (see Antonacopoulou 2006a).

These issues help explain why ML over the years has accommodated a number of themes and has not been defined clearly. ML explores the interdependencies between learning and different forms of education within different contexts. ML covers a broad spectrum of issues ranging from individual and workplace issues through to social, economic and political issues. For the purposes of our analysis ML is defined as an integrative mechanism allowing different learning opportunities to support managers in mastering business action.

This definition allows us to also begin to explore more fully the themes with which ML has engaged over the years. Grey and Antonacopoulou (2004) in their overview of the main debates in Management Learning over a 10-year period (1994–2004) provide a range of themes that have underpinned the focus of ML over the years. Unquestionably, the main themes that have sustained attention and will remain relevant in future debates could be summarised as the following three: firstly, the role of ML in relation to globalisation; secondly, reflections and developments on pedagogical practice and thirdly, the complexity of learning within formal (organisational, classroom) and informal contexts. Each of these themes presents both a set of challenges and opportunities for the way ML can develop in the future to support the development of managers especially in Business Schools. Each of these themes are discussed in turn both for the challenges they present and the opportunities they generate in rethinking ML. We begin by discussing the challenges first.

Challenges in management learning

THE ROLE OF MANAGEMENT LEARNING IN GLOBALISATION

This theme captures many of the recent developments in ML not least in terms of the way ML has been affected by globalisation, at the same time as it is also one significant means through which globalisation has occurred. Thus, on the one hand, the globalisation of trade and of corporations has carried with it, like seeds in the wind, the provision and practice of ML. It has also necessitated and facilitated the migration of students and organisational members and has required ML to be attentive to the requirements and effects of globalised capital and globalised corporate reach. The global distribution of management ideas, concepts and techniques, whether through education and training or through other means, is one of the things which makes the global distribution of goods and services possible, if only through the provision of a structure of shared understandings and vocabularies. Indeed, the very growth of concepts and practices of, for example, organisational learning is itself partly the basis upon which ML, generally, globalises.

Thus, the globalisation of ML is both a condition and a consequence of globalisation more generally. This observation points to a series of other trends in ML. One such trend is the homogenisation of ML in the way in which management ideas and practices have been developed within the West, and in particular North America, and transported or translated into other contexts. The agents of this process have in many cases been management developers and trainers, consultancies, Business Schools and other parts of the institutional apparatus of ML. Globalisation produces a need for new kinds of managerial capacities which can be learned by, amongst other things, Business Schools (Richards 1997). Globalisation, then, emerges as having conflicting or even paradoxical effects upon ML that cannot be captured simply through an image of homogeneity.

China and India are perhaps particularly interesting sites given the very rapid transformations which are taking place in these countries and the extent to which these are informed by Western management ideas. The transfer of Western management ideas to China and India has been spearheaded by the influence of Western multinationals and their joint ventures with Chinese and Indian partners. However, it is also increasingly a feature of indigenous state-owned enterprises particularly as local knowledge is exploited in the process of securing outsourcing contracts (Fan 1998).

Other contexts, and Eastern Europe is a good example, are rather different because, amongst other things, these countries experience the rapid loss of existing political structures (Kostera 1995). These counties and their entry to the European Union is a reflection of what some would describe as the colonisation of management-speak and management technique as a route to economic and political emancipation.

Globalisation and ML therefore, sensitise us to the process of commercialisation and marketisation of ideas and pose several key questions about the implications of this for the governing pedagogical values that underpin a range of ML initiatives most dominant of which is the MBA product. In ML in particular we see clear evidence of this globalisation in the growth of international programmes that are intended to provide exposure to practising managers to different realities and perspectives in the world. The question that is often not asked however, is how are these experiences coupled with day-to-day experience and how can they inform the practical judgements managers make that influence their actions. This point reflects that at the core of ML lie several pedagogical assumptions that guide how ML programmes are designed. Several assumptions about the way ML broadly conceptualises the process of learning also underpin how ML is delivered. These are two further challenges worth exploring.

REFLECTIONS AND DEVELOPMENTS ON PEDAGOGICAL PRACTICE

While globalisation trends in ML may appear to flow with minimal resistance this in no way leaves space to assume that this has been an uncritical and unreflective exercise at least on the part of the learners and educators themselves. A concern with pedagogy and educational process has revivified the study of the practice of teaching and has created new avenues for supporting learning over and beyond the formal classroom approaches typical in Business School ML programmes. For example it is notable that the trend of digitisation has introduced a number of innovative approaches to teaching via e-learning. The latter has also repositioned the importance of learner-centeredness in education and flexibility as a condition for learning.

Moreover, these trends in relation to pedagogical developments have also transformed traditional conceptions of the relationship between teaching and learning and provided scope for rethinking the identity of management scholars as conduits for learning. The more active accent on the learner as having both responsibilities and rights must perforce recast the role of the teacher.

Whether approached using a critical theory (critical management studies) lens or simply a reflective perspective, this process of taking a good look at the relationship between pedagogical practices and the implications for learning, has provided a renewed attention to the relevance debate with a greater emphasis on engagement and knowledge (Pfeffer and Fong 2002; Starkey and Madan 2001). In relation to the latter, this marked an important repositioning of the relationship between learning and knowledge away from the traditional view of learning as the acquisition of discrete bodies of knowledge (Antonacopoulou 2006b; Spender 1994).

There is a growing appreciation of the need for a more engaged understanding of learning if it is to support effective, responsible and accountable action. For that engaged understanding to emerge the role of 'knowing' and 'not knowing' has also been acknowledged. The latter introduces inquiry, humility and self-awareness as critical foundations for both teaching and learning.

Donald Schön's notion of the reflective practitioner gains a renewed sense of meaning and importance and helps rebuild the relationship between teacher and student on the basis of a common practice – learning. These perspectives are significant in that they also help move the debate on actionable knowledge (see Argyris 2004) forward. A more relational view of actionable knowledge is propounded that better reflects the learning capability of the individual and the organisation to connect heterogeneous elements (social, political, economic, technological).

The focus of actionable knowledge is on *learning-in-practice* as a form of self-organisation that is fluid, dynamic and emergent. Actionable knowledge becomes a pragmatic engagement with the social complexity of organising (see Antonacopoulou 2007a).

Actionable knowledge advocates a partnership between academics and practitioners with a commonality of interests and purposes founded on respect for the distinctive capabilities on each side.[2] It bears saying, however that this vision is somewhat at odds with at least some version of the critical approaches to ML, which question and problematise received wisdom and power relations within and beyond the classroom and issues of diversity (see Sinclair 1997; French and Grey 1996). This latter concept entails a move away from traditional attempts in ML to give neat, simplified and idealised solutions towards opening up the paradoxical, messy and contested nature of management and organisational situations. This point further challenges us to review how learning as a complex phenomenon has underpinned the way ML is conceptualised.

COMPLEXITY OF LEARNING IN FORMAL AND INFORMAL CONTEXTS

The nature of individual/managerial learning has been at the core of the ML agenda. Representing different modes of learning as well as styles of learning by individuals were among the earlier attempts to explain how, what and why individuals learn. Individual's learning goals and strategies for addressing these has also shed light on the modes of knowing and types of knowledge (William James' 1950 'knowledge about' and 'knowledge of acquaintance' and Polanyi's 1962, tacit and explicit knowledge) that constitute the 'experience' learners derive from learning. These experiences place the socio-political dynamics that underpin and define individual learning more centre stage, showing how learning at the individual level is a social process shaped by inter-subjective forces (Gherardi et al. 1998).

The social view of learning draws even more attention than any previous analysis to *learning practices* and to learning as a 'practical accomplishment'. In doing so, it shows the role of routines, artefacts and other situated characteristics that constitute a 'practice' and their impact in shaping the way people interact and through that interaction constantly re-discover the *dynamics* of learning. Through the contextually specific learning practices, members of a community are socialised and this helps to perpetuate the community itself enabling individuals to participate actively in the co-construction of their own learning.

The importance of acknowledging individual learning as a social process, with the individual as an active participant in the co-construction of the meanings and importance of learning, is also central in the relationship between individual and collective/organisational learning. The latter has been another central theme in ML research and has sought to uncover the relationship between micro and macro learning processes.

The idea of organisations as learning systems and of 'learning organisations' as a new image of the ideal form of organisation, have been key themes that have influenced thinking in ML. Despite the lack of agreement as to whether it is possible to talk of organisations as possessing learning capabilities or indeed identifying 'learning organisations', these ideas challenge us in the way we understand learning in relation to ML.

---

2   An initiative that has been leading the way in developing such a perspective is GNOSIS (www.gnosisreseearch. org) which identifies *re-search* as a common practice which can usefully integrate knowledge and action, theory and practice by providing a space for connecting different communities and perspectives (across the sciences and across communities). This focus on interconnectivity calls not only for exploring effectively the interdependencies between theory and practice, action and knowledge. It also calls for a commitment to learning from and through collaboration.

Problematising the relationship between individual and organisational learning draws attention both to their similarities and differences, as well as to the difficulties presented in fostering learning in organisations. The role of social forces in shaping interpretation mechanisms, transparency and accountability are brought to the fore as forces shaping the feasibility of workplace learning. By emphasising the role of social structures like that of the learning culture these perspectives move the debate of learning and organising beyond behavioural and cognitive perspectives. They also help challenge the ontology of the idea of the learning organisation through these various meanings and problematise the political aspects of legitimisation in the use of the term rather than the application of the idea.

More importantly this perspective challenges the restricted understanding of learning in organisations often equated with training (see Antonacopoulou 2001). This helps explain why indeed the learning organisation remains an undelivered promise (Elkjaer 2001); particularly, when training interventions are the main method for developing a learning culture (Cook and Yanow 2003). Ironically, the focus of the training interventions tends to be individuals' change and development. This observation makes even more critical the need to pay more attention to individuals' experiences and consistent with John Dewey's (1938) principles of inquiry and reflectivity, to explore the relationships between actions in response to problematic situations.

Opportunities to rethink management learning

Although the ML debate is rich in perspectives and themes, projecting into the future there is scope for addressing in each of the three main thematic areas not only in the challenges they present but also the additional issues that could help strengthen the impact of ML across the spectrum of platforms it seeks to engage. This would be particularly pertinent in our efforts to improve ML through a careful rethink of the core principles of ML.

For example, in relation to the global nature of ML there is a need to engage in critique so that we can not only reflect critically on some current practices, but also systematically seek to change and improve our critique and our reflective practice as well as our actions. This principle would be particularly relevant if we are to better understand one of the more recent trends in ML, the domestication of management education since the emergence of Corporate Universities (see Antonacopoulou 2002).

In relation to the pedagogical underpinning of ML it could be argued that a return to the fundamental principle of *paideia* might be a useful way of sustaining the reflexivity in teaching and learning practice. Finally, in relation to the complex nature of learning and its implications for individual learners as practising managers on ML programmes there is a need to conceptualise learning in ways that better reflect its complexity and in doing so to examine the implications for rethinking the role of learning as part of working and living. Each of these opportunities are briefly elaborated next.

THE ROLE OF REFLEXIVE CRITIQUE IN GLOBAL ML

Whilst being critical has been central to critical perspectives in management studies, the role of *critique* towards analysing management still remains relatively unexplored particularly in ML. At the most basic level, being critical in its broader sense encourages reflection and questioning of one's reason and practice so that one can be both informed and accountable of one's actions. This broader definition extends what it is to be critical beyond principles of emancipation, inequalities in power and control and the significance of systematic and insightful thinking (see Alvesson and Willmott 1992). It does, however, elevate an important distinction between *being critical* and *critique*. The former often implies criticism and scepticism, whereas the latter is about emphasising *critique as reflexive praxis*. This means that greater emphasis is given to systematically unpacking core assumptions and competing perspectives so that new possibilities can lead to informed and purposeful action.

If the challenges of globalisation in ML are to be truly engaged with, *reflexive critique* would be paramount. Reflexive critique seeks to draw the emphasis on reflexive practice rather than criticism or scepticism. Critique is also about reflecting and questioning one's practices when one is being critical. After all, to be critical one must start from being critical of the critical orientation one applies in assessing any situation including one's own reason and practice. This view extends current forms of critique beyond *the critique of rhetoric*, the *critique of tradition*, the *critique of authority* and the *critique of objectivity* (see Mingers 1999). The idea of reflexive critique, introduces the *critique of simplification* and the *critique of identity* (see Antonacopoulou 2008).

The *critique of simplification* would seek to highlight the limitations of the assumed linearity of management and the reductionist analysis of the process of managing which fails to capture the full extent of the social and political dynamics. The *critique of identity* promotes the significance and reciprocity of the interaction between emotion and patterns of thought. Such critique takes as central to the analysis of issues one's own subjectivity, the identity reflected in the lived reality, the significance of self-awareness both in relation to one's way of thinking, as well as in relation to the associated emotions that support the security sought.

Instilling *reflexive critique* would be essential in engaging with the challenges globalisation presents us with. It could prove particularly helpful in addressing new fads in ML. One example could be the way reflexive critique could help us understand the implications of trends like commercialisation and marketisation of ML.

For example such a position would encourage a critique of the current transformation of Higher Education Institutions from places of intellectual development to sites of capital accumulation and intellectual property which can be bought and sold in an increasingly competitive market (Noble 1998). The trend towards the commercialisation of education is not only reflected in the initiatives of institutions of Higher Education but in the initiatives of management consultancies and corporations as well. The latter have had probably the most significant impact on ML in recent years with the massive growth of what are now being referred to as Corporate Universities (Meister 1998).

Corporate universities have instilled a new paradigm in ML which is fast shaping a new ideology emphasising corporatisation and domestication of learning (Antonacopoulou 2002). It is this new dominant ideology, which in turn has generated a new set of pressures and measures of quality in ML. The emphasis on consumption, relevance, performativity and short-terminism are manifestations of this new ideology. Such ideology in global ML characteristically removes reflection from action, encourages a tendency to 'bank' (Freire 1972) on qualifications instead of continuous learning and promotes an instrumental approach to addressing knowledge and skills gaps. Moreover, this new ideology in ML operates in direct contradiction to the principles of lifelong learning and education so central in many organisational and societal debates promoting images of 'learning organisations' within 'learning societies'.

It appears that the drive behind the investment in corporate universities is not education for its own sake, but education for the organisation's sake, often not even for the development of the individual given that the curriculum of corporate universities is defined by business goals and the perceived relevance of knowledge for what often might be short-term operational agendas. This point returns to the long-standing debate of the imbalance between individual and organisational development and the tendency for organisational objectives to supercede and determine individual's learning, even under best efforts to develop learning organisations. It is therefore, of paramount importance to carefully consider the implications of the current ideologies and assumptions in ML as these define the expectations from ML programs.

Some of the most criticised implications include the intensification of academic labour, the increasing power and control that administrators gain, with the associated pressures exerted on those who have to perform in line with the new standards and requirements and in general a return to Tayloristic principles of mass production and consumption of education offerings (see Clarke 2001). Moreover, another set of implications is the nature of the knowledge that underpins the new education trends. In particular, the extent to which this knowledge facilitates learning at the individual, organisational, as well as, wider social level. This issue is much less discussed in the existing literature, yet it could be a defining distinction between education provided in public universities by comparison to the education provided by corporate universities (Blass 2001).

Consequently, corporate universities stimulate a number of changes in the way education is conceptualised, ML is supported and power and political dynamics in individual development are renegotiated. The business ideology of *domesticating* knowledge for organisational ends hardly approves of questioning, experimenting and critical thinking, all of which reflect more aptly the meaning of ML. If one is only expected to attend learning events with the intention of acquiring job-specific and organisationally-focused knowledge and skills, then could this be called learning?

Acknowledging that such an ideology may be detracting from the essence of what learning is provides the necessary foundation for considering ways in which all those involved in learning (and education more broadly) need to reflect on their contribution to the current state and the future that they can help create. It is critical when we think about the future of ML that we focus our efforts not to justify the value of ML because of its consequences, but because of its principles.

REVISITING PEDAGOGICAL PRACTICE: THE POWER OF PAIDEIA

Instilling *reflexive critique* within the business curriculum could help address the role of critical reflection in providing a synthetic analysis of management in the light of participants' experiences of managing. Moreover, reflexive critique in the business curriculum would emphasise that more attention be given to the learners' experiences and problems creating also the space for faculty teaching on ML programs to be reflective and reflexive of their teaching and learning practices. Conscientised (from Freire's (1973) concept of *conscientisation*, that is, a critical reading of commonsense reality) ML teachers and learners could seek to reflect on why does ML (and education more broadly) continue to fail so many learners? And what can ML teachers and learners do about it?

Perhaps a start can be made in appreciating that any form of reflection as to what lessons our experiences hold calls for a more careful rethink of how and whether we actually learn from the experiences we encounter. Placing learning in the context of our experiences as educators invites us to retrace education through the notion of *paideia*.

What the ancient Greeks viewed as paideia, was the cultivation of each individual's natural, in-born potential in every domain of social activity, which cannot be achieved through fixed programmes. As the Jungian theorist Luigi Zoja (1997) has argued, paideia was a major innovation of the Ancient Greek polis, representing an institutionalised form of the psychological process of individuation. Indeed what makes paideia so significant as a concept and so central in ML is that it is a psychological, as well as a social, process of shaping the person as a member of a community to which the person contributes and is shaped by.

Paideia is a much broader notion than education. Education is one of the products of paideia. Paideia lies at the core of what education is. From the Greek word education – εκπαίδευση – (ekpaidevsi, ek-paidevo – παιδεύω) – meaning I nurture from young age, I guide one's development, I provide opportunities for learning, I contribute to the development of the person as a social being; see Maratheutis 1986; 1995). Paideia does not draw boundaries to childhood from adulthood (pedagogy and andragogy see Knowles, 1980) when it comes to development and learning. What is central to paideia is the whole person as a free spirit in search of its own self-fulfilment. This search for self-fulfilment and self-actualisation is not restricted by time or space. This means that paideia in ML would support learning across multiple contexts (ML programme in universities, training events provided by the organisation, development programmes provided by other external bodies).

In the Greek language, paideia (paidevo – παιδεύω) also means struggling, exerting great effort to achieve something. The struggle that paideia implies is when one strives for something with passion – it is *a labour of love*. This reflects what Heidegger (1968) had in mind when he argued that teaching is more difficult than learning. Learning, as the Greeks realised, is ultimately a labour of love, for one's teacher, for one's community, for oneself and for truth; yet, love itself must be cultivated and developed through learning. When it comes to supporting learning therefore, distinctions such as pedagogy or andragogy become unnecessary. What really matters is not whether we have a child or an adult learner but whether we care deeply enough to work with the individual needs of that person, which ultimately make them individual (unique).

If we are prepared to embrace fully the challenge that learning and education present us as educators and educated, then we are more likely to invest in becoming more successful *pedagogos* (παιδαγωγός from the words – *paideia* (*paidi* – child) and *agogos* – (conduit/root)) a source and resource for learning. This is perhaps where the ultimate of what being a scholar is all about – supporting learning by being prepared to learn, embracing existing experiences as foundations for existing and future learning and fundamentally nurturing that unique human (child-like) quality of inquisitiveness and aporia towards that which is taken as reality and truth.

These virtues are also central to the notion of *phronesis* – practical judgement – propounded by Aristotle. In rethinking how we can support the development of managers we need to carefully review whether recipes of success through the adoption of 'best practice' is the way to go. This view seems to dominate the current 'xenomania' (the opposite of xenophobia) that characterises what is perceived to be relevant and important to learning for business success. The tendency to copy 'best practices' unreflectively is highly problematic and potentially one of the sources of the lack of innovation and productivity in businesses. Learning to exercise practical judgement in distilling one's course of action is less often discussed and certainly much less supported in existing ML programs. Paideia without phronesis is inconceivable for without phronesis the virtues of learning if not practised are forgotten and worse still ignored in the realm of unthoughtful responses to short-term bottom line priorities.

ML based on the principle of inquiry (*phronesis*) and the ideology of paideia could widen its scope beyond the education of managers and executives as members of organisations but as members of the society at large. Its objective should not be to provide just knowledge and skills relevant to a specific organisational need but to provide an educational experience which sensitises managers to the challenges and dilemmas of managing in different contexts (cultural, economic and political) and conditions.

Taken together these opportunities invite us to rethink ML as a means of supporting the development/nurturing of managers who have the consciousness to be responsible for the decisions they make and accountable for the actions they take. ML would promote greater responsibility to the active role managers play as educators (by bringing diverse practical perspectives, which enrich the educational experience) and not just as those to be educated. This opportunity to reposition ML in these terms could also provide better scope for maximising the impact of ML in supporting managers in the actions they take.

LEARNING, PRACTICE AND PRACTISING

Our tendency to simplify learning so that it can be managed to deliver predetermined outcomes removes the essence of learning as a complex force helping us address many of the challenges working and living present us with.

Appreciating the complexity of learning implies a need to understand the inter-connections between the multiplicity of forces that constitute learning. Learning as a complex integration of biological, psychological, social, cultural, emotional and other forces is part of an ecosystem. This means that all the various forces learning is part of and interacts with co-exist and co-evolve in relation to internal and external conditions.

This point suggests that the institutionalisation of learning practices within any (social) system, are subject to the ongoing institutional transformations which are caused by learning practices (cf. Giddens 1984). The social structures are also constantly negotiated as diverse social forces interact in embracing the emerging nature of learning and organising (see Clegg et al. 2005). Therefore, if learning is about connecting, inter-connectivity implies the co-existence of heterogeneous forces. Diversity is what feeds learning in the way conditions that underpin interactions and connections between systems create tensions.

That multiple dimensions exist in tension is to reflect the multiplicity of possibilities each dimension can create by being attracted to different possibilities. Tensions dissolve into the space of possibility and become *ex-tensions* of current reality. These *ex-tensions* reflect the elasticity of processes like learning as multiple possibilities emerge in the way inter-connections are explored or rediscovered through practising attempts. Seen this way, learning emerges from multiple possibilities previously not explored. Such possibilities may be interpreted as *surprise* or *serendipity* depending on whether they are considered relevant or attainable. No single experience determines learning practice, which is unpredictable and uncontrollable.

The political nature of learning remains one of the biggest challenges in learning research (Lawrence et al. 2005). The political nature of learning reminds us that learning does not take place in a vacuum. Learning is a connection of possibilities stimulated by the signals received within the context in which learning takes place. These signals however, are subject to multiple interpretations, which define the actions one takes to make life and work more meaningful. This point however, reveals a key dimension of the political nature of learning that we have so far neglected partly because we have paid insufficient attention to the power of learning.

The power of learning is at the core of what makes knowing political. To learn therefore, is to make viable connections between a diverse set of emerging dimensions that affect action and interaction with others. To be accountable for one's actions is one of the defining characteristics of those who chose to lead a life of learning.

The characteristics of learning as a complex set of forces renew the importance of embeddedness and situatedness of learning in action (in practice) (Antonacopoulou 2006b). This is consistent with a growing shift towards a practice-based view which has been marked in recent years (see Orlikowski 2000; Schatzki et al. 2001; Gherardi 2006). Learning in relation to practice is conceptualised as a set of actions in flow, dynamically connecting structures, actors and artefacts together. The practical judgements of practitioners define their practices – including their learning practices – and the way they seek to master the business actions that constitute the core of their world. It is important to understand the actions themselves if we are to understand learning. Practising becomes a way of re-conceptualising ML in action.

Practising must not be confused with improvising. The engagement of a practitioner in the practice through active participation and listening as well as openness to ideas and possibilities is not enough. Practising also entails visualisation and immense concentration in rehearsing again and again parts of a practice differently. It also involves a process of losing the structure once in the act. This means that the practice becomes a second nature for the practitioner to the extent that they *are* their practice. Practising therefore, does not only require engaged participation, it demands embodied participation. The latter includes over and beyond engagement the identification and unity of the practitioner with the practice in the course of enacting it.

Practising therefore, is as much a process of repetition as it is a space embracing the multiplicity of possibilities as different (new) dimensions are (re)discovered in a moving horizon where past, present and future meet. Repetition therefore, in the context of practising, is not a mechanistic process of replication. *Replication* implies institutionalisation in the process of re-presentation and re-production. *Repetition* on the other hand, implies re-hearsing, re-viewing aspects of a practice (Antonacopoulou 2007b).

This means that at the core of practising a practice is actively learning and unlearning different aspects of a practice in a proactive way that does not only rely on routines of habit but different ways of embodying a practice. Learning and practising therefore are not outcomes nor accomplishments but a flow through order and chaos in the endless journey of becoming.

Mastering Business Action: implications for leading and developing business schools

The opportunities and challenges discussed in the previous paragraphs could form the key foundations for supporting the development of practising managers through ML programmes. Perhaps in agreement with Mintzberg (2004) it could be argued that ML supports the development of Managers not MBAs yet, if MBA implies **M**astering **B**usiness **A**ction the very essence of ML can be transformed.

Mastering Business Action in the context of ML in particular could provide a renewed focus on three dimensions of action that are not hitherto fully explored. In relation to the issues discussed in the previous sections we would highlight the importance of better aligning the practitioner and their phronesis with the practices they engage in. Considering that one of the practices managers engage in during ML programs is learning, then developing their capability to be responsible learners 'in control' of their learning would be a key priority. To support managers to do that it is critical to support the development of practical judgment – phronesis. The latter is not simply a case of building capabilities and competencies in a range of 'soft skills' such as communication, interpersonal skills and emotional intelligence. Considering the previous opportunities in rethinking ML, practising managers could usefully develop the capacity to think critically, to exercise critique in forming their judgements and to be responsible and accountable for their actions. Moreover, providing them a safe space in which they can practise (re-hearse) these various capabilities will provide them with confidence, courage and compassion to also seek to improve their business practices. To do that they would need to be supported to learn to respect and value the challenges and opportunities of mastering their learning practice first.

Mastering Business Action therefore may be the core of future Executive Education based on ML that engages practising managers to learn through reflexive critique and the principles of paideia how to develop virtuous modes of practising the development of actions that shape their business practices to serve better ends by exercising consciously their practical judgement. This view encourages all those responsible for developing and leading Business Schools to carefully consider not only the underling structures on which ML programs are founded upon. Perhaps more fundamentally, it calls for an engaged approach to developing and leading that reflects the core values, challenges basic assumptions and reflects a commitment to learning practice as a critical resource to ongoing renewal.

Summary

In summary, developing a future agenda for ML that can effectively serve the development of practising managers, calls for a careful rethink of issues that form the core of ML and the way learning can inform and mobilise action. Mastering Business Action could form the core focus of future ML.

Responding to the macro/global issues that business practitioners are concerned with at the same time as they are encouraged to develop a phronetic response to micro/local issues they have to address is central to Mastering Business Action. To achieve this there is a need to embrace the task of educating managers as a process of co-creating knowledge for action. This means that the model of presenting ready-made solutions which place some (for example, educators) as producers of knowledge and others as consumers (for example, learners on ML programs) of knowledge needs to be abandoned. Equally critical is the need to abandon the uncritical and unreflexive approach to learning that looks for answers rather than asking questions.

The model propounded in this chapter as we rethink ML for Mastering Business Action invites us to consider a partnership model where there is mutual effort by learners and educators to inform each others' agenda by co-creating a framework for action that extends personal experiences into promising practices that can be explored and practised without rude imitation and unreflective replication. This point implies a model of learning founded on critique, reflexivity and action. These principles can also form the basis of developing a strategic learning agenda that can support practising managers in their efforts to respond to the challenges they face and to embrace the opportunities that are available to them as they become *Masters* of Business Action in their ongoing pursuit to embody their values for personal improvement and collective growth.

Acknowledgements

These ideas have grown as part of the AIM International Project 'Practice and Practising: A Comparison across Organizations, Industries and Countries' under grant number RES-331-25-0024 financial supported by the ESRC/EPSRC Advanced Institute of Management Research.

References

Alvesson, M., and Willmott, H., (1992). (Eds.). *Critical Management Studies*. London: Sage.

Antonacopoulou, E.P., (2000). Reconnecting Education, Training and Development Through Learning: A Holographic Perspective, *Education + Training*, Special Issue on 'Vocational Education and Training in SMEs', 42(4/5): 255–263.

Antonacopoulou, E.P., (2001) The Paradoxical Nature of the Relationship Between Training and Learning. *Journal of Management Studies*, 38(3): 327–350.

Antonacopoulou, E.P., (2002). Corporate Universities: The Domestication of Management Education. In DeFillippi, R. and Wankel, C. (Eds.) *Rethinking Management Education*, pp. 185–207. New York: Information Age Publishers.

Antonacopoulou, E.P., (2006a). The Relationship Between Individual and Organisational Learning: New Evidence from Managerial Learning Practices. *Management Learning*, 37(4): 455–473.

Antonacopoulou, E.P., (2006b). Working Life Learning: Learning-in-Practise, In Antonacopoulou, E.P., Jarvis, P., Andersen, V., Elkjaer, B. and Hoeyrup, S. (Eds.) *Learning, Working and Living: Mapping the Terrain of Working Life Learning*, pp. 234–254. London: Palgrave.

Antonacopoulou, E.P., (2007a). Actionable Knowledge. In Clegg, S. and Bailey, J., *International Encyclopaedia of Organization Studies*. London: Sage.

Antonacopoulou, E.P., (2007b). Practice. In Clegg, S. and Bailey, J., *International Encyclopaedia of Organization Studies*, pp. 1291–1298. London: Sage.

Antonacopoulou, E.P., (2008). Reflexive Critique: An Innovation in Life Long Learning. In Wankel, C. and DeFillippi, R. (Eds) *A Lifetime of Management Learning: University and Corporate Innovations in Life Long Learning*. USA: Information Age Publishers.

Argyris, C., (2004). Actionable Knowledge. In Tsoukas, H. and Knudsen, C. (Eds.) *The Oxford Handbook of Organization Theory: Meta Theoretical Perspectives*, pp. 423–452. Oxford: Oxford University Press.

Blass, E., (2001). What's In a Name? A Comparative Study of the Traditional Public University and the Corporate University. *Human Resource Development International*, 4(2): 153–172.

Buckley, R., and Caple, J., (1990). *The Theory and Practice of Training*. London: Kogan Page.

Clarke, L ,(2001). Why Do We Need Coolclass? *The Coolclass Chronicle*, 1(1): online.

Clegg, S. R., Kornberger, M., and Rhodes, C., (2005). Learning/Becoming/Organizing. *Organization*, 12(2): 147–167.

Cook, S.D.N., and Yanow, D., (1993). Culture and Organisational Learning. *Journal of Management Inquiry*, December, 2(4): 373–390.

Dewey, J., (1938). *Experience and Education*. New York: Collier Books.

Elkjaer B., (2001). The Learning Organization: An Undelivered Promise. *Management Learning*, 32(4): 437–452.

Fan Y., (1998). The Transfer of Western Management to China: Context, Content and Constraints. *Management Learning*, 29(2): 201–221.

Freire, P., (1972). *Pedagogy of the Oppressed*. Harmondsworth: Penguin.

Freire, P., (1973). *Education for Critical Consciousness*. New York: Seabury Press.

French, R., and Grey, C., (1996). *Rethinking Management Education*. London: Sage.

Gherardi S., Nicolini D. and Odella F., (1998). Toward a Social Understanding of How People Learn in Organizations: The Notion of Situated Curriculum. *Management Learning*, 29(3): 273–298.

Gherardi, S., (2006). *Organizational Knowledge: The Texture of Organizing*. London: Blackwells.

Giddens, A., (1984). *The Constitution of Society*. Cambridge: Cambridge University Press.

Grey C., and Antonacopoulou E.P., (2004). (Eds) *Essential Readings in Management Learning*. London: Sage.

Heidegger, M., (1968). *What is called Thinking?* (Translated by J. Glenngray). New York: Harper & Row.

James, W., (1950). *The Principles of Psychology*, Vols I and II. New York: Dover Publications.

Knowles, M.S., (1980). *The Modern Practice of Adult Education: From Pedagogy to Andragogy*, 2nd Edition. N.Y: Cambridge Books.

Kostera M., (1995) The Modern Crusade: The Missionaries of Management come to Eastern Europe. *Management Learning*, 26(3): 331–352.

Lawrence, T.B., Mauws, M.K., Dyck, B., and Kleysen, R.F., (2005). The Politics of Organizational Learning: Integrating Power into the 4I Framework. *Academy of Management Review*, Vol. 30, No. 1: 180-191.

Maratheutis, M. I., (1986). Η Αγωγή του Προσώπου, Θεωρία της Παιδείας, Μιχαλάκη Ι. Μαραθεύτη, Λευκωσία. (ISBN: 9963-7558-2-8)

Maratheutis, M. I., (1995). *Μελετήματα Ελληνορθόδοξης Παιδείας*, Θεωρία της Παιδείας, Μιχαλάκη Ι. Μαραθεύτη, Λευκωσία. (ISBN: 9963-7558-9-5)

Meister, J.C., (1998). *Corporate Universities: Lessons in Building a World-Class Work Force*. New York: McGraw-Hill.

Mingers, J., (1999). What is it to be Critical? Teaching a Critical Approach to Management Undergraduates. *Management Learning*, 31(2): 219–237.

Mintzberg, H., (2004). *Managers Not MBAs: A Hard Look at the Soft Practice of Managing and Management Development*. San Francisco: Berrett-Koehler.

Noble, D.F., (1998). Digital Diploma Mills: The Automation of Higher Education. *First Monday*, 3(1): online http://www.firstmonday.dk/issues1_3/noble.

Orlikowski W., (2000). Using Technology and Constituting Structures: A Practice Lens for Studying Technology in Organizations. *Organization Science*, 12(4): 404–428.

Pfeffer, J. and Fong, C.T., (2002). The End of Business Schools? Less Success Than Meets the Eye. *Academy of Management Learning and Education Journal*, 1(1): 78–95.

Polanyi, M., (1962). *Personal Knowledge: Towards a Post-critical Philosophy*. Chicago, IL: The University of Chicago Press.

Reid, M.A., Barrington, H. and Kenny, J., (1993). *Training Interventions: Managing Employee Development*, 3rd Edition. UK: IPM.

Richards D., (1997). Developing Cross-Cultural Management Skills: Experiential Learning in an International MBA Programme. *Management Learning*, 28(4): 387–407.

Schön, D., (1983). *The Reflective Practitioner*. New York: Basic Books.

Schatzki, T.R., Knorr-Cetina, K, and von Savigny, E., (2001). *The Practice Turn in Contemporary Theory*. London: Routledge.

Sinclair, A., (1997). The MBA through Women's Eyes: Learning and Pedagogy in Management Education. *Management Learning*, 28(3):313–330.

Spender JC., (1994). Knowing, Managing and Learning: A Dynamic Managerial Epistemology. *Management Learning*, Vol. 25, No. 3: 387–412.

Starkey, K., and Madan, P., (2001). Bridging the Relevance Gap: Aligning Stakeholders in the Future of Management Research. *British Journal of Management*, Vol. 12: 3–26.

Zoja, L., (1997). Individuation and Paideia. *Journal of Analytical Psychology*, 42: 481–505.

About the Contributors

Elena P. Antonacopoulou is Professor of Organizational Behaviour at the University of Liverpool Management School and Director of GNOSIS, a dynamic management research initiative. She is Senior Fellow of the Advanced Institute of Management Research. Her research interests include change and learning processes in organizations. Her work is published in international journals such as *Organisation Studies*, *Journal of Management Studies*, *Academy of Management Review*. She is currently Subject Editor for Organizational Learning and Knowledge for the *Emergence: Complexity and Organizational Journal* and has completed a 5-year term as joint Editor-in-Chief of the international journal *Management Learning*. She serves on the editorial board of several journals. She has served in numerous positions at Board and Executive levels at the Academy of Management (USA). (E.Antonacopoulou@liverpool.ac.uk)

Magnus Bild is founding partner of Bild & Runsten AB, a financial training company that specializes in developing and delivering tailor-made programs for managers as well as financial specialists in the area of accounting and finance. Magnus has been Head of Pedagogical Development at the Stockholm School of Economics (SSE) and served as Program Director for the International Teachers Programme (ITP) when it was hosted by SSE during the period 2003 to 2005. Magnus holds a Ph.D from SSE and has been elected Best Teacher by MSc and MBA students. (Magnus@bildrunsten.se)

Peter Daly is Associate Professor and Head of Business Communication & Language Studies at EDHEC Business School, Lille, where he teaches Managerial Communication. He also teaches Literature and Celtic Civilisation with the Chair of Culture and Society. Having worked in Managerial Communication education since 1995, mainly in Germany and France, his primary teaching and research interests revolve around management communication, learning and pedagogy in business education and ICT in Higher Education. He is currently undertaking Doctoral Studies in Higher Education at the University of Sheffield. (Peter.daly@edhec.edu)

Aswath Damodaran is Professor of Finance and David Margolis Teaching Fellow at the Stern School of Business at New York University. He teaches the Corporate Finance and Equity Valuation courses in the MBA program. He received his MBA and Ph.D from the University of California at Los Angeles. His research interests lie in valuation, portfolio management and applied corporate finance. He has published in the *Journal of Financial and Quantitative Analysis*, the *Journal of Finance*, the *Journal of Financial Economics* and the *Review of Financial Studies*. He has written and co-edited numerous books on equity valuation, corporate finance and investment management. He received the Stern School of Business Excellence in Teaching

Award in 1988, 1991, 1992, 1999 and 2001, and was the youngest winner of the university-wide Distinguished Teaching Award (in 1990). (adamodar@stern.nyu.edu)

Marie-Laure Djelic is Professor at ESSEC Business School, Paris, France where she teaches Organization Theory, Business History and Organization Theory. From 2003 to 2007, she was Dean of the Faculty at ESSEC. Her research interests range from the role of professions and social networks in the transnational diffusion of rules and practices to the historical transformation of national institutions. She is the author of *Exporting the American Model* (Oxford University Press, 1998), which obtained the 2000 Max Weber Award for the Best Book in Organizational Sociology from the American Sociological Association. She has edited, together with Sigrid Quack, *Globalization and Institutions* (Edward Elgar 2003) and together with Kerstin Sahlin-Andersson, *Transnational Governance* (Cambridge University Press 2006). (djelic@essec.fr)

Pierre Dussauge is a Professor of Strategic Management at HEC-School of Management (Paris). He has held visiting positions at the Ross Business School of the University of Michigan (Ann Arbor), at INSEAD (Fontainebleau), IESE (Barcelona), the Indian School of Business (Hyderabad), Tsinghua University (Beijing), and INCAE (Costa Rica). Pierre Dussauge was a finalist for the Best Teacher award in the Michigan MBA in 1996, 1998 and 1999, and received the Best Teacher award at HEC in 2002. Pierre Dussauge is the author or co-author of several books in the field of strategic management and of many articles published in academic or practitioner-oriented journals (*Strategic Management Journal, Journal of International Business Studies, International Studies in Management and Organization, Long Range Planning, European Management Journal, the Financial Times*, and so on). Lately his research has focused on the topic of global strategic alliances formed by competing firms. (dussauge@hec.fr)

Göran von Euler tragically passed away during the publication process of this book. His chapter was finalized and we are pleased that his family has approved its publication. Göran von Euler had a BA and MA degree in psychology and pedagogy in addition to his degree from the National Academy of Mime and Acting (Stockholm, Sweden). Göran worked with adult education during thirty years. He started at the Stockholm Institute of Education, continued at the Ministry of Education, and finally founded the interactive theatre *POCKET,* an educational company supporting people and organisations to change. Göran served as process leader, actor and CEO of *POCKET* until his death in September 2007. "I would like the theatre to be a mirror that helps clients and participants to reflect, see themselves, and from there take another step – in dialogue with others", was a guideline for Göran. He followed his guideline in numerous plays for in-house executive programs in management.

Josep Franch is Associate Professor of the Department of Marketing Management. He is the Director of the CEMS MIM and MSc Programs at ESADE. He is expert in international marketing and global marketing, and his main area of specialization is marketing strategy design, and product and brand management in multinational and global companies. He is one of the main experts in the case study method and author of numerous practical cases in the field of marketing He has also won Ruth Green Memorial Award for the best case presented by a non-American author at the Annual Meeting of the North American CASE Research Association (NACRA) in 2004. He has previous experience as Marketing Director in companies such as Fujifilm, providing consultancy services to companies including Novartis, Sony and Xerox. (josep.franch@esade.edu)

H. Landis Gabel is the Novartis Chair in Management and the Environment and Professor of Economics and Management at INSEAD. He holds BSc, MBA, and Ph.D degrees from the University of Pennsylvania and a MSc degree from the London School of Economics. Before joining INSEAD in 1982, Professor Gabel was on the faculty of the University of Virginia. Professor Gabel's research focuses on microeconomics and public policy, in particular industrial, trade and environmental policy. He has written or edited six books and has published academic papers in economics, legal, environmental and business journals. Professor Gabel was Dean of Faculty and Deputy Dean of INSEAD from 2001 to 2006. He founded INSEAD's Center for the Management of Environmental Resources and directed it until 2005. (landis.gabel@insead.edu)

Seán Gaffney was born and raised in Dublin, Ireland, lived in Great Britain for 8 years and has been a resident of Sweden since 1975. He has an MA in Gestalt psychotherapy from the University of Derby/Gestalt Academy of Scandinavia and teaches in Gestalt Training Institutes around the world. He is a Senior Lecturer in Cross-cultural Management on graduate and MBA programs in the Stockholm School of Economics, SDA Bocconi, IMI Teheran and SSE Riga. He has published articles/chapters on groups, organizational behaviour and also social change. He is currently completing his Ph.D in multicultural group/organizational dynamics and leadership. (seangaff@gmail.com)

Charlotte Holgersson is researcher and teacher at the Department for Gender, Organization and Management at the Royal Institute of Technology in Stockholm, Sweden. She defended her dissertation on the recruitment of managing directors, 2003. She has several publications in Swedish on theories in gender and organization and an article on homosociality. Among her publications in English are *The social construction of top executives* (2000), *Irony as a Feminist Strategy for Women Managers* (2005, together with Wahl and Höök), *Male managers' reactions to gender diversity activities in organizations* (2003, together with Wahl), *Narrating Gender and National Identity: Nordic Executives Excusing for Inequality in a Cross Border Merger Context* (2005, together with Tienari, Söderberg and Vaara). Her current research projects focus on management, sexuality and change practices in organizations. (charlotte.holgersson@itm.kth.se)

Christer Karlsson is at Copenhagen Business School, Professor of Innovation & Operations Management and Dean for CBS Executive which includes Executive Masters, short Executive Programs and Diploma Programs. He is concurrently Professor and Vice President at the European Institute for Advanced Studies in Management (EIASM), Brussels and Professor at the Stockholm School of Economics. He has been teaching Program development and Planning in ITP. He holds a MSc and Ph.D from Chalmers University of Technology, Gothenburg. His main research interest is in strategy and management of technological development and production networks. He is a member of several editorial boards of professional journals. (ck.om@cbs.dk)

Kamran Kashani is Professor of Marketing and Global Strategy at IMD. He teaches topics in marketing, brand building, global strategy and international management. His special interests span across industrial, business-to-business and consumer marketing. Professor Kashani has worked as Management Educator with a large number of international companies. Professor Kashani graduated from the University of California, UCLA, and gained his Doctorate in Business Administration at Harvard Business School. He has written extensively on the subject of marketing and global strategy. His publications have been translated into more than a dozen languages around the world. He is the winner of several awards for best paper and case writing.

In addition to his teaching responsibilities at IMD he is currently researching the topics of marketing innovation and brand building in a cross-national business. (Kashani@imd.ch)

Christine Kelly holds a Ph.D and teaches workshops and coaches faculty for the International Teachers Program and at MIT Sloan. For 3 years, she co-directed the ITP at New York University, Stern School of Business. At Columbia Business School and at New York University, she initiated, designed and developed teaching and learning programs. She teaches courses in Management Communication and Team Facilitation. She offers workshops on leadership as acting, facilitation, coaching and dialogue. She serves as coach in the Sloan Executive Program and in the Sloan Fellows Program in Innovation and Global Leadership. Christine Kelly is formerly director and creator of Management Communication Programs at Columbia University and New York University business schools. (ckelly@mit.edu)

Thomas Lavelle teaches Management Communication and Business English at the Stockholm School of Economics, where he also offers a number of faculty-development courses. He received a Ph.D in English from Stockholm University after doctoral studies there and at University College London and the University of Wisconsin, Milwaukee. He has published on topics ranging from English syntax to public language policy. His current research interests include the use of English in higher education and second-language academic writing. (thomas.lavelle@hhs.se)

Pär Mårtensson is Head of Pedagogical and Faculty Development at the Stockholm School of Economics (SSE) and currently responsible for the development and launch of a new 2-year master program in General Management at SSE. He is an Associated Researcher at the Center for Information Management and at the Institute for Business Process Development. He holds a Ph.D from SSE and his research concerns management processes and their relation to change activities, and methods for integrating theory and practice. Pär has written or co-edited four books and published his research in for example *MIS Quarterly*. Pär served as Program Director for the ITP when it was hosted by SSE 2003–2005. (par.martensson@hhs.se)

Philippa Morrison is Faculty and Senior Staff Development Advisor at London Business School. She has a background in teaching and in Existential Psychotherapy. Philippa works both inside business schools and outside academia, using her model of philosophical questioning, specifically in the supervision of other coaches. The overall aim is to focus on current preoccupations in order to clarify and self-motivate the client. Philippa was part of a team which won a UK Government grant to work with other universities to adopt this style of individual professional development. She has been involved for many years with the ITP, firstly as co-director, and redesigned the programme along the lines of her work at London Business School. (pmorrison@london.edu)

Hellicy Ngambi is Professor at the Graduate School of Business Leadership and currently the Deputy Executive Dean of the College of Economic and Management Sciences at the University of South Africa (Unisa). She was the Executive Director and CEO of Unisa's Graduate School of Business Leadership. She was previously the Principal and Managing Director of the Academy of Business Management in Botswana. She holds the following degrees: a doctorate in Business Leadership, Unisa, RSA; a Master of Science in Management,

USF, USA; a Master of Business Administration, BSU, USA; a Bachelor of Arts degree, UNZA, Zambia; Chartered Institute of Marketing Certificate and International Teachers Programme certificate, LBS-UK. She conducts research and has written, presented and published various articles and book chapters on workforce diversity, leadership, alternative work arrangements, job sharing and emotional intelligence with emphasis on the African context. (ngambhc@ unisa.ac.za)

Kristina Nilsson is Business and Program Director at IFL Executive Education at Stockholm School of Economics. Previously to that she was Program Director for SSE MBA (full-time MBA). Kristina has extensive experience of running programs and courses at different levels and in different international contexts; undergraduate (SSE Riga, Latvia), graduate (MSc), executive (Executive MBA), faculty (ITP). Her research area and interest is now mainly focused on change processes, adult learning and learning processes in a Business School context. (Kristina.Nilsson@hhs.se)

Pedro Parada is Associate Professor of the Business Policy Department at ESADE. He is Visiting Professor at HEC School of Management in Paris and SDA Bocconi in Milano. He serves as Academic Co-Director and Professor of the Global Executive MBA jointly offered by ESADE and Georgetown University. He has written articles, cases and book chapters in English, Spanish, Catalan, French, German, Portuguese and Chinese. He taught for and collaborated with private companies from different sectors such as banking and insurance, telecommunications, consultancy and auditing, service companies, industrial companies and pharmaceuticals, among others. He also works with entrepreneurs in Incubators in Catalonia and Andorra, and Enterprise Associations in Catalonia and Valencia. Previously, he was a Lecturer of Strategy at the Universidad Católica de Bolivia; worked at the cement industry, and served for the UN in the Ministry of Finance. (pedro.parada@esade.edu)

Ferdinando Pennarola is tenured Associate Professor of Organization and Management Information Systems at L. Bocconi University, Milano (Italy). He teaches: Organization Design, Management Information Systems, Change Management and Management Consultancy. In February 2005 he was appointed Delegate Rector for E-Learning at Universita L. Bocconi. His main research work is in the field of service management and professional service firms where he has published books and articles in Italy and internationally. In 1993 he joined the Board of Directors of ISBM (International Schools of Business Management), that runs the ITP (International Teachers Programme) as a representative of SDA Bocconi. From January 2005 he is Chairman of the Board of ISBM. He earned his ITP in 1987 from HEC-ISA. He is also a member of the Editorial Board of *Organization*. (ferdinando.pennarola@ unibocconi.it)

Catharina Pramhäll holds an MSc and is a lecturer in accounting and finance at the Stockholm School of Economics. She has been teaching since 1992. She is Course Director for Introduction to Accounting and Finance (first-year course for 300 students) in which problem-based learning is used extensively. She also teaches in executive education programs. Catharina participated in ITP at INSEAD 1994. She was part of the faculty when the program was held at SSE (2003–2005). She is the Head of the ITP alumni network. Catharina also works as an Accounting Expert at the Swedish National Accounting Standards Board. (catharina. pramhall@bfn.se)

Tom Pugel began his teaching as a graduate student at Harvard University and has taught at New York University Stern School of Business since 1978. At NYU Stern he is Academic Director of the Center for Innovation in Teaching and Learning and Academic Director of the Langone MBA Program for Working Professionals, as well as Professor of Economics and Global Business and a Fellow of the Teaching Excellence Program. He received the University's Distinguished Teaching Medal in 1992 and has twice been voted Professor of the Year by Stern's graduate students. He was Co-Coordinator of ITP while it was hosted at the Stern School during 1998–2001. (tpugel@stern.nyu.edu)

Johan Roos is the Bo Rydin and SCA Professor of Strategy at SSE. He was previously Managing Director of Swiss-based Imagination Lab Foundation, Professor of General Management and Strategy at IMD, Associate Professor of Strategy at the Norwegian School of Management and Research Fellow in Multinational Management at the Wharton School. His research and many articles and books concern how to prepare for the unexpected, innovate strategy processes, cultivate intellectual capital and prepare strategic alliances. As Advisor, he has been on the board of several listed and unlisted companies, and continues to work closely with leaders and leadership teams throughout the world. (johan.roos@hhs.se)

Isabelle Sequeira is Professor and Head of Culture and Society at EDHEC Business School, where she teaches courses in the History of Civilisations and Anthropology. Her teaching activities and research revolve around the synergy between the economy and culture. She was given the task of setting up a Department for Culture & Society in 1995 at a time when companies were looking to recruit managers who were both flexible and adaptable. Isabelle Sequeira coordinates approximately 40 adjunct faculty on both EDHEC campuses in Lille and Nice. Moreover, she also directs a Cultural Management and Solidarity Program, where she is in regular contact with numerous NGOs to provide an interface between student projects and the needs of these NGOs. (Isabelle.sequeira@edhec.edu)

J. Janelle (Jan) Shubert is the Acting Director for The Center for Women's Leadership at Babson College. She has more than 30 years' experience as a faculty member and Administrator. Prior to coming to Babson College in 2004, she was at The John F. Kennedy School of Government at Harvard (1992–2004) a visiting faculty member at London Business School (1990–1992), on the faculty at Harvard Business School (1986–1990), a visiting fellow at The Program on Negotiation at Harvard Law School (1985) and both a faculty member and Senior Administrator at The University of Michigan (1975–1985). She earned her Ph.D, at the University of Michigan, holds a Master's degree from Michigan State University and a BA from Southwest Missouri State University. She was the Co-Coordinator for ITP in 1996–1998 while it was hosted at London Business School. (jshubert@babson.edu)

Mel Silberman, Ph.D is Professor Emeritus of Adult and Organizational Development at Temple University, Philadelphia, PA where he was the recipient of The Great Teacher Award. He has an international reputation in the field of active learning and is the author of *Active Learning* and *Teaching Actively*, both published by Allyn & Bacon. Dr Silberman has presented sessions on active learning to numerous colleges and universities internationally, including Manchester (UK) School of Business, Stern College of New York University, Henley Management College and Stockholm School of Economics. He has been part of the ITP faculty since 1999 to the present. (mel1038@comcast.net) – www.activetraining.com

Andrea Sironi is Professor of Financial Markets and Institutions at Bocconi University, where he also holds the position of Dean for International Affairs. He is an honorary member of the Italian Financial Risk Management Assocation (AIFIRM) and a member of the Fitch Academic Advisory Board (FAAB). His research interests include Financial Risk Management & Financial Derivatives, Bank Financial Management & Capital Allocation, and International Banking Supervision & Capital Regulation. He has published articles in journals such as the *Journal of Banking and Finance, the Journal of Business*, the *Journal of Financial Services Research*, the *Journal of Money Credit and Banking*, the *Journal of Financial Intermediation*. He has been a Consultant and independent expert for major Italian and international financial institutions and regulatory authorities. (andrea.sironi@unibocconi.it)

Udo Zander is Professor of International Business at the Stockholm School of Economics (SSE). He has also been Dean of Doctoral Programs at SSE, and a member of the Executive Committee of the European Doctoral Programmes Association. His research interests are international management, including change and learning in the multinational company, and the knowledge-based theory of the firm. He has published in journals like the *Journal of International Business Studies, Organization Science, Management Science, European Management Review*, and *American Sociological Review*. He has taught at the undergraduate, graduate, and executive programs at SSE, the Wharton School, University of Pennsylvania, and has been visiting professor at Stanford University and Victoria University of Wellington, New Zealand. (udo.zander@hhs.se)

Index

If you have found this book useful you may be interested in other titles from Gower

Age Discrimination in Employment
Malcolm Sargeant
978 0 566 08774 5

Commoditization and the Strategic Response
Andrew Holmes
978 0 566 08743 1

Brand Risk:
Adding Risk Literacy to Brand Management
David Abrahams
978 0 566 08724 0

Global Project Management:
Communication, Collaboration and Management Across Borders
Jean Binder
978 0 566 08706 6

The Goal:
A Process of Ongoing Improvement
Third Edition
Eliyahu M. Goldratt and Jeff Cox
Hardback 0 566 08664 6
Paperback 0 566 08665 4

MBA Management Models
Sue Harding and Trevor Long
0 566 08137 7

GOWER

New Business Models for the Knowledge Economy
Wendy Jansen, Wilchard Steenbakkers and Hans Jägers
978 0 566 08788 2

Project Leadership
Second Edition
Wendy Briner, Colin Hastings and Michael Geddes
0 566 07785 X

Project Management
Ninth Edition
Dennis Lock
Hardback: 0 566 08769 3
Paperback: 0 566 08772 3

The Relationship-Driven Supply Chain
Stuart Emmett and Barry Crocker
978 0 566 08684 7

Strategic Negotiation
Gavin Kennedy
978 0 566 08797 4

Tools for Complex Projects
Kaye Remington and Julien Pollack
978 0 566 08741 7

Women in Management Worldwide
Marilyn J. Davidson and Ronald J. Burke
978-0-7546-0837-0

For further information on these and all our titles
visit our website – www.gowerpub.com
All online orders receive a discount

GOWER